HANDBOOK OF ADVANCES I
RESEARCH

Handbook of Advances in Trust Research

Edited by

Reinhard Bachmann

Professor of Strategy, University of Surrey, UK

Akbar Zaheer

Curtis L. Carlson Chair in Strategic Management, Carlson School of Management, University of Minnesota, USA

Edward Elgar
Cheltenham, UK • Northampton, MA, USA

© Reinhard Bachmann and Akbar Zaheer 2013

All rights reserved. No part of this publication may be reproduced, stored in a retrieval system or transmitted in any form or by any means, electronic, mechanical or photocopying, recording, or otherwise without the prior permission of the publisher.

Published by
Edward Elgar Publishing Limited
The Lypiatts
15 Lansdown Road
Cheltenham
Glos GL50 2JA
UK

Edward Elgar Publishing, Inc.
William Pratt House
9 Dewey Court
Northampton
Massachusetts 01060
USA

A catalogue record for this book
is available from the British Library

Library of Congress Control Number: 2013935034

This book is available electronically in the ElgarOnline.com
Business Subject Collection, E-ISBN 978 0 85793 138 2

ISBN 978 0 85793 137 5 (cased)

Typeset by Servis Filmsetting Ltd, Stockport, Cheshire
Printed and bound in Great Britain by T.J. International Ltd, Padstow

Contents

List of figures	vii
List of tables	viii
List of contributors	ix
Introduction *Reinhard Bachmann and Akbar Zaheer*	1

PART I   INTERPERSONAL TRUST

1. HRM and trust, or trust and HRM? An underdeveloped context for trust research ... 9
   Rosalind H. Searle
2. The role of trust in negotiation processes ... 29
   Roy J. Lewicki and Beth Polin

PART II   TRUST AND GOVERNANCE: CONTROL, CONTRACT, INNOVATION

3. Trust and control: the role of intrinsic motivation ... 57
   Antoinette Weibel and Frédérique Six
4. Trust and contracts: together forever, never apart? ... 82
   Paul W.L. Vlaar
5. Trust and innovation ... 106
   Bart Nooteboom

PART III   TRUST ACROSS ORGANIZATIONS

6. Origins of inter-organizational trust: a review and query for further research ... 125
   Laura Poppo
7. Inter-cultural trust and trust-building: the contexts and strategies of adaptive learning in acculturation ... 146
   Peter Ping Li

PART IV SOCIETAL ANALYSIS AND TRUST REPAIR

8 Trust and the global financial crisis — 177
   Nicole Gillespie and Robert Hurley
9 Public trust in the institution of business — 204
   Jared D. Harris, Adrian A.C. Keevil and Andrew C. Wicks

PART V THEORETICAL ADVANCES

10 Trust and the economic theory of the firm — 227
   Jackson Nickerson, Timothy Gubler and Kurt T. Dirks
11 How is trust institutionalized? Understanding collective and long-term trust orientations — 261
   Frens Kroeger
12 Process views of trusting and crises — 285
   Guido Möllering

Index — 307

Figures

1.1	The employment cycle	12
3.1	Framework – trust, hierarchical control and intrinsic motivation as complements	63
4.1	Relative (in)significance of contracting and trust as each other's antecedents	85
4.2	Overstatement of direct effects and underestimation of partially mediating effects	87
4.3	Variation in salience of interrelations between trust and contracting across individuals	91
4.4	Variation in trust-contracting dynamics across functions and dimensions	92
4.5	Different foci of and dynamics amongst trust and contracting over time	95
5.1	Optimal cognitive distance	109
5.2	Upward shift of ability to collaborate	110
7.1	An integrative framework of inter-cultural trust and trust-building	160
11.1	The institutionalization cycle of trust	264
11.2	The structure of institutionalized trust	269
11.3	The symbolic mediation of institutionalized trust	271

Tables

5.1	Sources of reliability	113
7.1	A typology of trust-building contexts for inter-cultural interactions	165
7.2	A typology of trust-building strategies for inter-cultural interactions	168
8.1	An outline of trust failures that contributed to the GFC	182
8.2	Missing elements in trust repair	197
9.1	Results from an open-ended question asking people what they mean by the word 'confidence'	207
10.1	Governance structures of markets, hybrids and hierarchies displaying different capacities for building and maintaining trust	237

Contributors

Reinhard Bachmann is Professor of Strategy and Director of the Centre for Trust Research (CTR) at the University of Surrey. He has published widely on the role of trust in business contexts. His work has appeared in leading journals, including *Organization Studies*, *British Journal of Sociology*, *Cambridge Journal of Economics* and *European Societies*. He is co-editor of various books, among which is the *Handbook of Trust Research* (with Akbar Zaheer, Edward Elgar 2006), and two special issues of *Organization Studies* on trust (2001 and 2014). Also, he serves as deputy editor-in-chief of the *Journal of Trust Research*.

Kurt T. Dirks is the Bank of America Professor of Managerial Leadership and the Senior Associate Dean of Programs at the Olin Business School at Washington University in St. Louis. He holds a PhD from the University of Minnesota and a BS and MS from Iowa State University. His research is in the field of organizational behaviour, and focuses on issues related to leadership and teams, involving a wide range of contexts including the military, financial institutions, technology companies, sports teams, health care teams and laboratory settings. He has served on the editorial review board of premier journals in organizational behaviour, including the *Academy of Management Journal*, the *Journal of Applied Psychology*, *Organizational Behavior and Human Decision Processes*, and *Organizational Science*, and was guest editor of a special issue of the *Academy of Management Review* on relationship repair.

Nicole Gillespie is Senior Lecturer in Management at the University of Queensland. Her research focuses on trust development and repair in organizational contexts, the design of trustworthy organizations, and managing stakeholder trust in organizations. She also researches in the areas of leadership, teams and employee engagement. Her work appears in leading international journals including the *Academy of Management Review*, the *Journal of Management* and *Sloan Management Review* and has been featured in *The Economist* and *The Guardian*. She is co-author of *Building and Restoring Organisational Trust* (Institute of Business Ethics, 2011), co-editor of *Organizational Trust: A Cultural Perspective* (Cambridge University Press, 2010) and serves on the editorial board of the *Journal of Trust Research*.

Timothy Gubler is a PhD candidate in strategy at the Olin Business School, Washington University in St. Louis. His research interests lie in organizational strategy and in the micro-foundations of strategy. He is currently studying the interplay between individual and firm-level drivers of performance.

Jared D. Harris is Associate Professor of Business Administration at the University of Virginia's Darden School of Business and a Senior Fellow at Darden's Olsson Center for Applied Ethics. He earned his PhD at the University of Minnesota, Carlson School of Management. His research centres on the interplay between ethics and strategy, with a particular focus on the topics of corporate governance, business ethics and organizational trust. His work has been published in *Academy of Management Review*, *Organization Science*, *Journal of Business Venturing*, *Business Ethics Quarterly* and *Journal of Business Ethics*, and he is the co-editor of *Kantian Business Ethics: Critical Perspectives* (Edward Elgar, 2012). Jared serves on a number of journal editorial boards, and his work has been highlighted in *The New York Times*, *The Washington Post*, and *The New Yorker*, as well as other media outlets in the United States, Canada, Germany, India, Portugal and the UK.

Robert Hurley, PhD, is Professor at Fordham University and the Director of the Consortium for Trustworthy Organizations. The consortium's mission is to help increase the number of authentically trustworthy companies on a global basis through research, educating leaders, developing tools and creating a dialogue among organizations about what works to create high trust firms. His 2006 *Harvard Business Review* article is one of the magazine's most frequently ordered articles on trust and his book, *The Decision to Trust* (Jossey-Bass), was named one of the best leadership books of 2011 by *The Washington Post*. He has an MBA from the Wharton School, University of Pennsylvania and received his doctorate from Columbia University.

Adrian A.C. Keevil is a PhD candidate at the Darden Graduate School of Business at the University of Virginia. His research is focused on the psychological and economic factors that influence stakeholder behaviours. He is a member of the Behavioral Research group at Darden (BRAD), and the Implicit Social Cognition laboratories at the University of Virginia. His research has appeared in *Business and Professional Ethics Journal* and at various international conferences. He has twice received the Founders' Award from the Society for Business Ethics.

Frens Kroeger is Lecturer in Organization Studies at Surrey Business School, and Deputy Director of the Centre for Trust Research (CTR).

Frens received his PhD from Cambridge University in 2011, and his first paper in a highly ranked journal was published in the same year. His research interests revolve around the issue of trust on and across multiple levels of analysis, a topic that he approaches from a strongly conceptual, sociologically informed and broadly neo-institutionalist perspective.

Roy J. Lewicki is the Irving Abramowitz Professor of Business Ethics and Professor of Management and Human Resources Emeritus at the Max M. Fisher College of Business, The Ohio State University. He has a BA degree from Dartmouth College and a PhD in Social Psychology from Columbia University. He maintains research and teaching interests in the fields of negotiation, conflict management and dispute resolution, trust development, managerial leadership, organizational justice and ethical decision-making, and has published many research articles and book chapters on these topics. He is the author/editor of 35 books, including *Negotiation* (Lewicki, Barry and Saunders, McGraw-Hill/Irwin, 2005) and *Essentials of Negotiation* (Lewicki, Saunders and Barry, McGraw-Hill/Irwin, 2010), the leading academic textbooks on negotiation.

Peter Ping Li (PhD, 1991, George Washington University) is Professor of Chinese Business Studies at Copenhagen Business School. Before joining CBS, he was Professor of Management at California State University. His primary research focus is on re-examining the extant Western theories from the cultural and historical frames of China and East Asia, especially applying the Chinese philosophy of wisdom to the development of holistic, dynamic and duality theories. He has published over 30 articles in various academic journals and serves on the editorial boards of the *Academy of Management Discovery Journal of Management Studies, Journal of International Management, Global Strategy Journal, Management and Organizational Review* and *Asia Pacific Journal of Management*. He is also the founding editor-in-chief of *Journal of Trust Research*.

Guido Möllering is Associate Professor of Organization and Management and holds the EWE Chair of Economic Organization and Trust at the School of Humanities & Social Sciences, Jacobs University Bremen. He earned his PhD in Management Studies at the University of Cambridge and his Habilitation (postdoctoral degree, *venia legendi*) in Business Administration at the Freie Universität Berlin. His main areas of research are inter-organizational relationships, organizational fields, and trust. He has published several books and many articles in leading journals such as *Organization Science, Organization Studies* and *Journal of International Business Studies*. He serves as a senior editor of *Organization Studies* and associate editor of the *Journal of Trust Research*.

Jackson Nickerson is the Frahm Family Professor of Organization and Strategy, Associate Dean and Director of Brookings Executive Education, and a senior non-resident scholar in Governance Studies at the Brookings Institution. He received a BSME from Worcester Polytechnic Institute and a MSME from the University of California. He also earned an MBA and a PhD at the University of California at Berkeley. His research spans organizational choice and design, leadership, inter-organizational exchanges and strategic problem formulation. His research can be found in leading journals including *Administrative Science Quarterly, Journal of Political Economy, Management Science, Organization Science, Strategic Management Journal* and *Strategic Organization*.

Bart Nooteboom is Emeritus Professor of Innovation Policy at Tilburg University. He is author of 11 books and some 300 articles on small business, entrepreneurship, innovation and diffusion, innovation policy, transaction cost theory, inter-firm relations, trust, networks and organizational learning. He is a member of the Royal Netherlands Academy of Arts and Sciences. He was awarded the Kapp prize for his work on organizational learning, the Gunnar Myrdal prize for his book on trust and the Schumpeter prize for his book on a cognitive theory of the firm. His most recent book (*Beyond Humanism: The Flourishing of Life, Self and Other*, Palgrave Macmillan, 2012) is a philosophy book on humanism. In 1988–90 he was member of a government committee on technology policy. In 2006–07 he was a member of the (Dutch) Scientific Council for Government Policy (WRR) where he supervised the production of an advisory report to the Dutch government on innovation policy.

Beth Polin is a graduating PhD candidate in the Management and Human Resources Department at the Max M. Fisher College of Business, The Ohio State University. She will continue her career with the School of Business at Eastern Kentucky University. Her research and teaching interests include conflict management, interpersonal trust development and repair, empowerment, socialization and leadership.

Laura Poppo is the Edmund P. Learned Professor in Business at the University of Kansas. She received her PhD from the Wharton School, University of Pennsylvania and has held academic posts at Washington University and Virginia Tech. Her academic interests include empirical tests of transaction cost economics, knowledge-based perspectives and social processes. She has published primarily in management journals including *Strategic Management Journal, Organization Science, Journal of International Business Studies* and *Administrative Science Quarterly*. She is currently on the editorial boards of *Strategic*

Management Journal, Organization Science and *Journal of Trust Research* and is a former associate editor of the *Journal of Management*.

Rosalind H. Searle is Professor of Organisational Behaviour and Psychology at the University of Coventry's Business School in the UK. She is co-founder and co-director for the Centre for Trust and Ethical Behaviour. Her research interests focus on organizational trust, and trust and HRM. Her interest in organizational level trust considers this as a distinct phenomenon and examines its antecedents and consequences, especially for employees. She has also pioneered attention on trust and HRM, looking at distinct types of processes and their enactment and is particularly interested in recruitment and selection processes, those involved in managing performance and most recently the role of HRM in trust repair. Her work has appeared in journals such as the *British Journal of Social Work*, *International Review of Industrial and Organizational Psychology* and *International Journal of Human Resource Management*.

Frédérique Six is Assistant Professor of Governance and Organization at the VU University Amsterdam. Her research focuses on (public) governance puzzles in general and more particularly the relation between trust and control. She has published in journals such as *Journal of Management Studies*, *Public Management Review*, *International Journal of Human Resource Management*, *Journal of Management and Governance* and *European Management Journal*, and co-edited *The Trust Process* (with Bart Nooteboom, Edward Elgar, 2003) and *Local Integrity Systems* (with Leo Huberts and Frank Anechiarico, Boom Juridische Uitgevers, 2008). She is also associate editor of the *Journal of Trust Research*.

Paul W.L. Vlaar obtained his PhD at RSM Erasmus University and is currently an Associate Professor at the VU University Amsterdam. His research interests include inter-organizational cooperation and cross-disciplinary initiatives, focusing on strategic and organizational change. His research has been published in journals such as *MIS Quarterly*, *Organization Studies* and *Group & Organization Management*. In 2008, Edward Elgar published his book on *Contracts and Trust in Alliances: Creating, Appropriating and Discovering Value*. More recently, his book *Strategy at Every Corner! Inspiration for a New Breed of Strategists* was published by Synspire Publishing, challenging readers to explore what managers may learn from things such as animal behaviour, sports clubs, military operations, bottom of the pyramid markets, the creative sector, as well as drama, games and fights.

Antoinette Weibel is Professor of Management and Public Administration at the University of Konstanz. Her PhD was awarded by the University of Zurich. Her research focuses on motivation, happiness and trust, and appeared in leading journals including *Public Administration Research and Theory*, *Group & Organization Management*, *Organization* and *International Journal of Human Resource Management*. She is President of FINT, the First International Network of Trust Research, a founding member of a Standing Working Group on Organizational Trust at the European Group for Organizational Studies, and she serves on the editorial board of the *Journal of Trust Research*.

Andrew C. Wicks is the Ruffin Professor of Business Administration at Darden School of Business, University of Virginia. He is director of the Olsson Center for Applied Ethics, director of Darden's doctoral programme, academic advisor for the Business Roundtable Institute for Corporate Ethics and an adjunct professor in the Religious Studies department at the University of Virginia. He has co-authored three books including *Managing for Stakeholders: Survival, Reputation and Success* (2007, Yale University Press) and his journal articles appeared in a wide variety of journals in business ethics, management and the humanities. He is actively working with Ethics-LX, an entrepreneurial venture, to create a series of web-based simulations that incorporate ethics into the functional areas of business.

Akbar Zaheer is Curtis L. Carlson Chair in Strategic Management at the Carlson School of Management at the University of Minnesota. He earned his PhD at the MIT and has been researching issues around trust for a number of years. Also, he studies networks, alliances and M&As. He has published numerous articles in top journals, including *Academy of Management Journal*, *Academy of Management Review*, *Organization Science* and *Administrative Science Quarterly*, and serves on the editorial boards of *Strategic Management Journal*, *Strategic Organization* and the *Journal of Trust Research*.

Introduction
Reinhard Bachmann and Akbar Zaheer

Trust is – as a major financial institution, Deutsche Bank, put it in one of their advertising slogans in the late 1990s – *'der Anfang von allem'* ('the beginning of everything'). Only a decade later, the role of trust in economic life was massively challenged by the global financial crisis, which resulted in an ongoing devastating trust crisis. Confidence in the promises of financial institutions to honour their commitments has declined dramatically since 2008, when Lehmann Brothers collapsed overnight. The consequences of this crisis are hard to over-estimate as the ability to create, maintain and repair trust can profoundly affect the future of business, and even the fortunes of nation-states, as Francis Fukuyama (1995) notes in his classic work, *Trust: Social Virtues and the Creation of Prosperity*. In the mid-1990s many other scholars also discovered the importance of trust in business relationships and the interest in this topic suddenly exceeded all limits. A neutral observer might well have concluded that trust was just another research fad that would long be forgotten in the second decade of the 21st century. The reality could not be more different. Trust has meanwhile been very widely accepted as one – if not the – key sources of success in business relationships, and one that influences the efficiency and scale of all economic activity.

Reflecting its great importance in the world of practice, research in the field of trust is complex, evolving and highly dynamic. In the wake of the global financial crisis resurgence and renewed recognition of the role of trust in society has spurred trust research in new directions and along new dimensions. Empirical assessments have been conducted using a multitude of methods, and both theoretically and managerially relevant insights have been developed further. At the time the field began 20 or so years ago, as is appropriate in the early stages of the emergence of a field, research was more concerned with grappling with the poorly understood trust phenomenon and many different approaches to studying trust were presented. Empirical research began developing along divergent lines and numerous alternative definitions as well as operationalizations of trust were deployed in the field. But concurrently, through this initial period, certain seminal ideas and key understandings also began to get established. Some classifications and directions were taken as reference points while others tended to wane in influence. In particular, solid advances – many based on empirically tested ideas – were made in such areas as trust definitions

(Rousseau et al., 1998), trust dimensions (e.g., Sako, 1992; Mayer et al., 1995; McKnight et al., 1998), stages of trust development (Lewicki and Bunker, 1996), trust at multiple levels of analysis (Zaheer et al., 1998), and trust violations (Dirks and Ferrin, 2001), among others. In addition, distinct streams of organizational research on trust developed at the individual, or micro-level of analysis (e.g., Six, 2005) and at the organizational, or macro-level of analysis (e.g., Bachmann, 2001). To take stock of what we had collectively learned then as a research community we, the editors of the present volume, presented the *Handbook of Trust Research* in 2006. Our effort at the time enabled trust researchers to take a step back to review and consolidate the many contours of the then field of trust research. The *Handbook* was a well-received volume.

The current phase differs from the early stages of organizational trust research. Nearly two decades after the field of trust research first formed, research in the field has overall reached a state of greater consolidation and a certain convergence, although this convergence is not nearly as marked as it perhaps could be (McEvily and Tortoriello, 2011). At the same time, business practices are in constant flux, as are the research questions that they generate. Scholars have discovered new approaches and developed new questions and some answers in a field, which, despite its seemingly narrow scope, leads to a plethora of issues once they are pursued. A number of distinct themes have emerged in the world of trust research, such as a clear and well-tested distinction between trust and trustworthiness (Colquitt et al., 2007), the role of institutions in trust development processes (Bachmann and Inkpen, 2011) and the nature of trust repair (Dirks et al., 2009). The field has given rise to its own journal, the *Journal of Trust Research* in 2011, another mark of its maturity.

This evolution of the field is the reason why we, as editors of the 2006 *Handbook of Trust Research* (Bachmann and Zaheer, 2006), thought it appropriate to follow up on the developments in trust research and bring together this fresh collection of chapters. The present *Handbook of Advances in Trust Research* includes 12 chapters, each of which represents important developments in trust research, particularly those undertaken since our last effort. Thus, in some ways this collection of chapters can be taken as an updating supplement to our original *Handbook*. However, the current work can also be seen and read as a stand-alone publication, one that provides a contemporary overview of the most critical issues in current trust research, including themes, such as trust in public institutions, that have gained in prominence since the earlier volume.

In terms of the process of putting together this collection of work, we asked prominent scholars in the field to contribute chapters that reflected how some of their own work on trust had progressed in the last five years or so. We requested that the scholars first send in abstracts, which we as editors scrutinized for any possible overlaps. Once these were identified, we asked the authors to proceed with writing their chapters. Initial drafts of the chapters were sent out for a single-blind developmental review. The authors then used the feedback from the review process to refine and revise their work to produce a final draft.

As in the 2006 *Handbook*, we adopted an unusual process to enhance the quality of the reviews and the subsequent versions of the chapters. Specifically, we sent the drafts written by US-based authors to European-based reviewers, and those by European-based authors to US-based reviewers. The results were enlightening, as the different epistemological approaches of European- and US-based scholars were prominently highlighted. In particular, as before, European-based reviewers typically found the US contributions to be limited in scope, with few connections to trust research conducted by European-based scholars. US-based scholars in contrast typically found the European contributions to be too broad and less focused than they would have liked. In the end, our hope is that the exercise improved both sets of contributions, but from the perspective of the field as a whole, it appears that bridging the transatlantic research divide will continue to be an ongoing challenge, with consequences for the development of an integrated field.

We have organized the chapters by sub-theme beginning with the individual, or micro, level of analysis and progressively moving up levels of analysis. Thus, our first sub-theme deals with interpersonal trust in the organizational context, continuing with the sub-theme of trust as a governance mechanism, and trust across organizations. The broadest level of analysis follows and addresses societal trust and trust repair. The volume concludes with the sub-theme of theoretical advances in trust research. Below, we briefly provide a hint of the rich material contained in each chapter, designed to lead the reader to the full version.

Trust at the inter-personal level was a core theme in early trust research but continues to attract much attention. For the present volume, we asked Rosalind Searle as well as Roy Lewicki and Beth Polin to cover new developments in this area in Part I. While Searle's chapter focuses on the inter-relationship of trust and human resource management, and specifically suggests considering HRM agents' role in trust development within organizations, Lewicki and Polin's contribution provides deep insights into the relationships between trust and negotiation. The latter, among other things, involves balancing the dilemma of trust (how much to trust the other party in negotiations) with the dilemma of honesty (how much to reveal). Marrying the fields of negotiation and trust research, which clearly have a lot in common yet have seen little joint conceptual or empirical work, Lewicki and Polin systematically conjoin trust frameworks with research in negotiations. The result is a solid step forward in the scholarly understanding of the different roles that trust plays in the negotiation process, how different trust components interact with different negotiation stages and types, and how future research should include the tracking of trust through these stages. A noteworthy take-away is that rather than building strong trust in a negotiation process, the goal should be building verifiable trust and periodically testing it.

In recent times, a strong stream of research has debated trust as a governance mechanism. In these debates, it is specifically the themes of 'trust and control' and 'trust and contracts' that have brought forth elaborate discussions, which reach far beyond the simple question of whether or not trust can be fruitfully combined with control or with contracts, and are reflected in our second sub-theme. The role that trust can play in the context of stimulating and facilitating innovation processes is intrinsically connected to these issues. The latter issue focuses on the question of how to control innovation processes, in which trust is clearly indispensable. In this volume in Part II, Antoinette Weibel and Frédérique Six as well as Paul Vlaar represent the state of the art in the 'trust and control' as well as the 'trust and contracts' debates, while Bart Nooteboom's chapter examines trust and innovation. Nooteboom argues that the highly uncertain nature of innovation makes the prospect of control ineffective and the need for trust greater but also harder to bring about. In particular, he raises the issue of 'cognitive distance', which, while enhancing the possibilities of innovation from fruitful recombination, also creates greater barriers to effective governance through trust.

In Part III, Laura Poppo's chapter investigates the parallel sub-theme of inter-organizational trust, and makes a strong case for focusing on trust dynamics, particularly calling for a specification and measurement of how different dimensions of trust evolve. The need to factor in structural bases of trust, including trust signals, their observability and transparency, and their value in creating trust is among the important themes highlighted in the chapter. Another dimension of the sub-theme of inter-organizational trust is tackled in Peter Li's chapter, which presents new insights into the types and functions of trust in international collaborations. The problems around building trust in inter-organizational and inter-cultural collaboration was relatively neglected in the early stages of research on trust in business relationships, but it is now recognized as a highly dynamic area with significant potential to stimulate future research. Li in particular focuses on the distinction between intra-cultural trust and inter-cultural trust, going beyond the well-established notion of cultural distance to highlight adaptive learning.

Our next sub-theme focuses on issues of public trust and trust repair.

These are fields that were almost non-existent when we put our *Handbook of Trust Research* together in 2006. Now, they are – in the face of global financial crisis – some of the fastest-growing domains in trust research. In Part IV, Nicole Gillespie and Robert Hurley's chapter explains the details of the financial meltdown and its consequences for trust as well as the possibilities of repairing public trust after the disillusionment following the crisis. Jared Harris, Adrian Keevil and Andrew Wick's chapter takes a related perspective to examine various aspects of trust in institutions from a research standpoint. Arguing that the measurement of public trust is both important and complex, they parse out trust definitions to argue that measures of trust must include a combination of generalized trust and relational trust in public institutions. They also make the case for avoiding self-reports and moving to behavioural trust measures, including the use of experiments, to measure public trust.

Finally, trust research has reached out to deepen its theoretical basis, reflected in our concluding sub-theme in Part V. The chapter by Jackson Nickerson, Timothy Gubler and Kurt Dirks explores how trust can be analysed as a key issue in the economic theory of the firm. These scholars argue that while the role of trust in economic exchange has been studied, the connection between the theory of the firm and the building, maintenance and repair of trust has yet to be made. They go about systematically establishing the links between formal governance structures – markets, hybrids and hierarchies – and trust, arguing that trust underpinnings strengthen as governance moves from market to hybrid to hierarchy. The authors conclude provocatively by suggesting that the theorized relationships are hardly a foregone conclusion and that adept managers must play appropriate roles for the links between governance structures and trust to materialize. Rounding out the theoretical advances sub-theme, the final two chapters provide the theoretical foundations for two important and complementary facets of trust – trust as a process and an institution. Frens Kroeger explores the oft-cited notion that trust can be institutionalized, detailing how trust can be transformed into a collective and long-term orientation, and giving substance to notions of multi-level trust. Guido Möllering offers an in-depth examination of the process qualities of trust and outlines different ways in which, rather than studying the outcome of 'trust', deeper insights may be generated by studying processes of 'trusting'.

In conclusion, we recognize that no collection of ideas can fully represent the state of a field. Any effort necessarily reflects the perspectives of the editors and the authors and by emphasizing certain themes, omits or underemphasizes certain others. Nevertheless, by including many of the field's leading-edge thinkers from both sides of the Atlantic in this collection, we believe we have made a credible attempt at reflecting the current state of the art in organizational trust research. As always, we are grateful to our authors, and our reviewers, without whom this collection would not have been possible. We are also always appreciative of the efforts of our publishers, particularly the encouragement from Francine O'Sullivan of Edward Elgar.*

NOTE

* For comments on an earlier draft of this introduction we are grateful to Richard Montgomery.

REFERENCES

Bachmann, R. (2001), 'Trust, power and control in trans-organizational relations', *Organization Studies*, **22**(2), 337–65.
Bachmann, R. and A.C. Inkpen (2011), 'Understanding institutional-based trust building processes in inter-organizational relationships', *Organization Studies*, **32**(2), 281–301.
Bachmann, R. and A. Zaheer (2006), 'Introduction', in R. Bachmann and A. Zaheer, *Handbook of Trust Research*, Cheltenham, UK and Northampton, USA: Edward Elgar, pp. 1–12.
Colquitt, J.A., B.A. Scott and J.A. LePine (2007), 'Trust, trustworthiness, and trust propensity: a meta-analytic test of their unique relationships with risk taking and job performance', *Journal of Applied Psychology*, **92**(4), 909–27.
Dirks, K.T. and D.L. Ferrin (2001), 'The role of trust in organizational settings', *Organization Science*, **12**(4), 450–67.
Dirks, K.T., R.J. Lewicki and A. Zaheer (2009), 'Repairing relationships within and between organizations: building a conceptual foundation', *Academy of Management Review*, **34**(1), 68–84.
Fukuyama, F. (1995), *Trust: Social Virtues and the Creation of Prosperity*, New York: Free Press.
Lewicki, R.J. and B.B. Bunker (1996), 'Developing and maintaining trust in work relationships', in R.M. Kramer and T.R. Tyler (eds), *Trust in Organizations: Frontiers of Theory and Research*, Thousand Oaks, CA: Sage.
Mayer, R.C., J.H. Davis and F.D. Schoorman (1995), 'An integrative model of organizational trust', *Academy of Management Review*, **20**(3), 709–34.
McEvily, B. and M. Tortoriello (2011), 'Measuring trust in organisational research: review and recommendations', *Journal of Trust Research*, **1**(1), 23–63.
McKnight, D.H., L.L. Cummings and N.L. Chervany (1998), 'Initial trust formation in new organizational relationships', *Academy of Management Review*, **23**(3), 473–90.
Rousseau, D.M., S.B. Sitkin, R.S. Burt and C. Camerer (1998), 'Not so different after all: a cross-discipline view of trust', *Academy of Management Review*, **23**(3), 292–404.
Sako, M. (1992), *Prices, Quality and Trust. Inter-firm Relations in Britain and Japan*, Cambridge: Cambridge University Press.
Six, F. (2005), *The Trouble with Trust: The Dynamics of Interpersonal Trust Building*, Cheltenham, UK and Northampton, MA, USA: Edward Elgar.
Zaheer, A., B. McEvily and V. Perrone (1998), 'Does trust matter? Exploring the effects of interorganizational and interpersonal trust on performance', *Organization Science*, **9**(2), 141–59.

PART I

INTERPERSONAL TRUST

1. HRM and trust, or trust and HRM? An underdeveloped context for trust research
Rosalind H. Searle

INTRODUCTION

Until recently there has been little systematic consideration of the relationship between Human Resource Management (HRM) and trust. This dearth of attention is a significant omission as it is a topic that is an important context from which to study trust, and with significant implications and benefits for organizations. Prior to joining organizations, recruitment and selection processes provide clues and signals of their trustworthiness. Existing workers, and the wider community through family and friends or via the internet, may become all too aware of their reputation as a fair and trustworthy employer. Indeed, the internet is often a repository of poor examples of HRM practices fuelled by disgruntled employees, as Goldman Sachs and others have discovered to their cost. Incidences of workplace violence can often be traced back to HRM processes, often performance management, in which the expectations and experiences of an employee and those of the designated representative of the organization have gone badly awry. Similarly, examples of unfair treatment of employees around lay-offs and downsizing often make the national news, yet HRM remains an area that is underutilized. HRM policies and practices involve the articulation and direct exposure to the values and integrity of an organization, not once but over time and from a variety of distinct sources. Thus, they can be seen as a domain that offers distillations and germane experience of trust within that distinct context. It is a domain in which the competence, or otherwise, of the organization and those tasked with delivering these systems are exposed. It is an area where comparison can directly be made by individuals reflecting on their own distinct experiences, but also through comparison with the treatment and experiences of their peers, superiors and subordinates. As Colquitt et al. (2012) showed, these experiences can help deepen their commitment to the firm, or enhance their feelings of vulnerability and uncertainty.

Research has considered the relationship between trust and HRM in various ways, for example, in terms of the consequences of HRM on trust (e.g., Mayer and Davis, 1999; Searle et al., 2011b), or as a mediator providing an underlying mechanism or process influencing other variables (e.g., Tsui et al., 1997; Whitener, 2001), or more commonly as a moderator influencing the direction and/or strength of relationships, such as a trusting climate in work, enhancing or diminishing the impact of HRM on performance (e.g., Dirks and Ferrin, 2001; Innocenti et al., 2010; Alfes et al., 2012). However, there has been less emphasis on HRM as an antecedent, an active agent in the development and maintenance of employees' trust in their managers and in the firm (Whitener, 1997; Tzafrir, 2005; Searle and Skinner, 2011b). The latter perspective is a far more compelling for researchers to explore and for organizations to exploit. Similarly, little attention has been paid to whether good systems might sustain organizational trust and act as a buffer to protect against poor managers (Skinner and Searle, 2011). It therefore has a potential role in repairing trust (Gillespie and Dietz, 2009).

This chapter begins by defining trust and HRM and outlines four compelling reasons for their study. Then I summarize why trust is a salient concern in an HRM context and identify distinct dimensions that are often neglected by researchers, including individual difference factors. I then review the dominant research paradigm – in particular, extant work on the influence of HRM policy assemblages and then distinct policy areas regarding trust. I highlight two emergent facets of current work: first, those concerning more frequently studied HRM practices, but from a novel Human Resource (HR) perspective; second, those offering a novel trust perspective on HRM areas, such as bullying and harassment. Next, this relationship between HRM and trust is inverted, challenging researchers to consider whether and how far trust affects HR, summarizing research on the impact of delivery on trust and consider the influence of the HR function on trust. In each section I raise key insights and indicate directions and agendas for future research.

DEFINING TRUST AND HRM

Trust concerns the perceptions, decisions and actions that arise from positive expectations, but also perceived vulnerability derived from the perceived intentions, or behaviours of another party acting as an agent of the organization; in this context the other party is clearly a collective – the organization. At this level of analysis the trust foci involve concerns about the competence, fairness, consistency and benign intent of an institution (Carnevale, 1995), or of an abstract principle (Giddens, 1990). As a result it requires the assessment, evaluation and assimilation of information from multiple sources, often from differing levels, about the organization

(Rousseau et al., 1998; Zaheer et al., 1998; Searle et al., 2011b). While this can be derived from direct experiences, third parties are a rarely considered source, such as insights obtained from witnessing how the organization deals with colleagues and other significant stakeholders. Importantly, there are certain organizational role holders whose actions and behaviours will carry more influence, such as those occupying pivotal leadership roles (see Searle and Ball, 2004; Hope-Hailey et al., 2012). Critically, an assessment of this set of collective characteristics can endure beyond the transition of any one agent (Whitley, 1987; Giddens, 1990), making issues of substitution salient concerns for trust scholars. In addition, there can be an often overlooked symbolic impact from the HR function itself, often regarded as the guardian of important aspects of trustworthiness. (These dimensions will be discussed later.)

Trust in organizations is an area where comparatively little research has been focused, especially between employees' trust in their employing organizations (for overviews see Searle et al., 2011a). Extant research confirms that while organizational trust is related to interpersonal trust, for example the relationship between managers and employees, it is a distinct form of trust, informed by a number of factors. These include perceived organizational support (Tan and Tan, 2000), distributive and procedural justice (Cohen-Charash and Spector, 2001) as well as types of systems (e.g., high commitment HR practices) (Whitener, 1997, 2001; Searle et al., 2011b). Although most previous attention has emphasized trust as a perception (Mayer et al., 1995; Rousseau et al., 1998), in line with Dietz and Den Hartog (2006) I have deliberately widened the scope of considerations beyond that of mere beliefs.

HRM is defined as a set of policies and practices concerned with structuring the interaction of human beings within an organizational context in order to maximize performance (Searle and Skinner, 2011a). The employee is emphasized as a valuable asset to the organization and source of competitive advantage, with HRM focusing on the alignment of a subset of organizational policies to support the overall strategy (Legge, 1995).

Scholars have argued that HRM is amongst the most influential practices on trust (Robinson and Rousseau, 1994), but there is limited research considering either distinct, or combined, policy areas. Although there may be some variation in precisely which policies and practices comprise HRM across different organizations, these areas are common to individuals' experience of employment, if at times due to their omission. HRM touches the lives of all employees throughout their employment cycle within an organization (Searle and Skinner, 2011a) (see Figure 1.1). Even prior to joining an organization the (potential) employee gains some awareness and experience of the organization derived through these policies and their

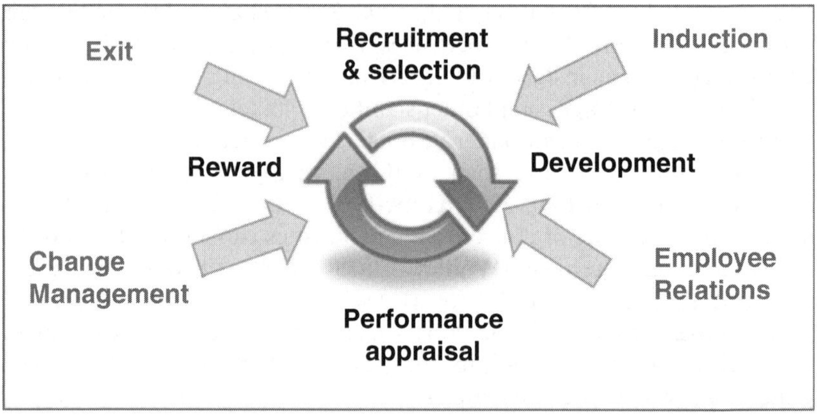

Source: Taken from Searle and Skinner (2011a, p. 6).

Figure 1.1 The employment cycle

delivery, resulting in a set of clues and signals that provide insight into potential vulnerability and expectations within that particular organizational context.

WHY TRUST AND HRM MATTER

There are four persuasive reasons why trust and HRM are important topics from both an academic and organizational perspective. First, trust has teleological merit, as trust offers significant practical benefits to organizations. Extant research shows that organizations with higher trust have enhanced effectiveness, efficiency and performance (e.g., Whitney, 1994; Kramer and Tyler, 1996; Davis and Landa, 1999; Mayer and Davis, 1999; Dirks and Ferrin, 2002; Tzafrir, 2005). Studies demonstrate that employees with high organizational trust put greater effort into their roles and engage more cooperatively with others (Podsakoff et al., 1990; Konovsky and Pugh, 1994; Pillai et al., 1999), while those who do not trust their employing organizations work less effectively (Dirks and Ferrin, 2001), engage in counterproductive behaviours (Bies and Tripp, 1996), or simply leave (Robinson, 1996).

HRM practices that facilitate the fair treatment of employees not only engender trust in the organization, but also directly influence employees' attitudes to their work (Aryee et al., 2002). From an HRM perspective, these findings offer further confirmation for Barney and Hansen's (1994) contention that trustworthy firms have a competitive advantage over their rivals. Significantly, evidence shows that both the content of HRM policies, and the perceived fairness with which they are delivered are central to employees' perceptions of organizational trustworthiness (e.g., Mayer and Davis, 1999; Aryee et al., 2002; Searle et al., 2011b; Colquitt et al., 2012). However, despite assertions that HRM are amongst the most influential areas for trust development, to date it remains an under-recognized topic.

Second, from a deontological perspective, trust has been linked to sound moral and ethical principles (Mayer et al., 1995; Schoorman et al., 1996; Becker, 1998). Perceptions of trust are driven strongly by the perceived trustworthiness of the trusted party (Barber, 1983; Kramer, 1999; Schoorman et al., 2007; Searle et al., 2011b). While trust is derived from assessment of attributes including the trusted party's competence and predictability (Dietz and Den Hartog, 2006), it also focuses attention on two more ethical dimensions: the integrity of the organization and its agents in terms of perceived adherence to moral standards; and benevolence, which emphasizes the benign, if not positive, intentions and behaviours towards those who are trusting and their welfare. Research both conceptually and empirically argues that employees prefer to trust organizations that uphold moral and ethical standards (Gillespie and Dietz, 2009; Searle et al., 2011b).

Third, this context offers researchers insight into the critical interface between the organization's process and systems, and what Blunsdon and Reed (2003) refer to as the 'social system of work'; the more relational aspects in which the vulnerabilities and expectations of key stakeholders, including employees, managers, trade unions and HRM professionals, become salient. This makes it a fertile arena to explore the potential synergies and discrepancies in the trust levels of different stakeholders. It is also a dynamic context in which employees' progress can be chartered through a cycle of HR activities. This gives potential to examine transitions through different types of trust (e.g., cognitive versus affective [McAllister, 1995], or stages of trust [e.g., Lewicki and Bunker, 1995]). Sadly, all too often HRM is a central context in which trust is breached, thus it is also a key context in which to explore the repair of trust (see Gillespie and Dietz, 2009; Hope-Hailey et al., 2012, or Gillespie and Hurley, Chapter 8 this volume for a more detailed discussion). HRM presents a crucible in which the salience of trust, or its violation, becomes germane, crystallized for both the organization and the employee.

Finally, there is considerable academic division between trust and justice researchers. Although some attempts have been made to create more dialogue between these two fields (e.g., Lewicki et al., 2005), there has been limited consensus between the two. In reviewing studies on trust and HRM, many have been undertaken by justice researchers with trust as an important facet, while others are conducted by trust researchers with justice as a critical dimension. Recently, Colquitt and colleagues (Colquitt and Mueller, 2008; Colquitt and Rodell, 2011; Colquitt et al., 2012) have made important strides in disentangling these two domains and show their interrelationships. These recent developments indicate the value of improved conceptualization and operationalization of these two distinct dimensions, particularly the greater precision of items within scales, and in longitudinal studies. Overall, HRM presents a significant context in which the relationships between trust and justice can be explored, and more critically, one in which our understanding of how trust can be both damaged and restored can be enhanced. In summary, there are significant and under-examined benefits to be derived from studying trust in the HR context.

TRUST AND HR POLICIES

In thinking specifically about why trust is salient for HRM, vulnerability and expectations are key issues. It is argued that risk is necessary for trust to be a concern (Luhmann, 1988). Although risks can vary between employees due to different levels of dependence upon, and vulnerability towards, the organization, HR policies and practices touch all employees. Paradoxically, potential risk might be at its highest prior to employment. Here would-be employees have far less insight into whether their trust is well placed, yet scant attention has been paid to trust in this situation (see for an exception Searle and Billsberry, 2011).

The impact of distinct HR policies for trust varies considerably due to their different relative importance, and also the different frequency with which they occur during the employment cycle (Searle and Skinner, 2011a). For example, individual experiences such as recruitment and selection might have a relatively large impact when contrasted with the more frequent annual performance reviews, but this could all change following a negative appraisal with a new line manager. Trust in the manager may decline further if this same manager is witnessed bullying another employee, but turns into the erosion of organizational trust if this harassment is reported to HR but nothing is done.

In many senses trust is at the heart of the employment relationship. Although expectations and vulnerability may vary from employee to employee, there is an obvious imbalance of power between the employee and their employer. While there is a variety of laws designed to protect employees and provide some level of institutional trust (Shapiro, 1987), they nevertheless remain vulnerable to any organization that provides the means for them and their families to thrive, and in some cases literally survive, for example in a US context through provision of health care benefits. It is worth considering further the influence of the employment contract in trust perceptions (see Weibel and Six, Chapter 3 and Vlaar, Chapter 4 in this volume for further discussion).

A DISPOSITION TO TRUST?

Individual difference is an under-researched factor underlying trust perceptions. Extant research and practical observations identifies that some individuals trust more readily than others (see Searle et al., 2011a for a discussion). Rotter (1967) outlined individuals' readiness or propensity to trust as a personality attribute, which is a relatively stable generalized expectancy about the perceived trustworthiness of others. It has a strong connection with individuals' awareness and tolerance of vulnerability. It has been referred to variously as generalized trust (Stack, 1978), trust propensity (Mayer et al., 1995) or disposition to trust (Kramer, 1999) and a sub-facet of the big five personality factors' agreeableness factor (Costa and McCrae, 1992). Importantly, the inclusion of a trust-related personality dimension adds another layer to our understanding, suggesting that disposition, rather than direct experience, informs our levels of trust (Blunsdon and Reed, 2003).

The influence of dispositional trust extends beyond first-hand trusting experience. This is of particular relevance in ambiguous situations (Gill et al., 2005) or those with unfamiliar actors (Bigley and Pearce, 1998). Here situational cues will tend to be weaker, leaving greater scope for individual discretion. Studies of recruitment and selection or of periods of change should not overlook this important dimension.

The inclusion of personality can offer further insight. First, research suggests that the impact of disposition goes beyond the information available about others' trustworthiness. For example, even where previous experience is available about the trusted party, those with higher trust dispositions still show greater levels of trust (Kee and Knox, 1970). Similarly, meta-analysis reveals its underlying impact (Colquitt et al., 2007), and as a significant predictor of organizational-level trust (Searle et al., 2011b). Second, studies suggest that propensity to trust influences the type of information that individuals attend to. For example, those with a higher disposition to trust are more positive and less suspicious in their views of others (Rotter, 1967, 1980). Thus, it may act as a filter mechanism, altering the focus and interpretations of others' actions. Govier (1994) suggests those with high predisposition to trust are less sensitive to information

16 *Handbook of advances in trust research*

about adverse situations. Similarly, dilemma game studies reveal that participants with high propensity to trust attend more to signs of trustworthiness, while those with low trust propensity are more sensitive to signs of betrayal (Parks et al., 1996). Thus, repeated evidence of untrustworthiness is required to alter initial trust levels amongst high trust propensity employees, while their low trust counterparts need far more evidence of trustworthiness to start trusting. Recent work found that high trusting individuals attend more to others' benevolence and integrity (Yakovleva et al., 2010). Therefore propensity can alter levels of sensitivity towards events, particularly important for issues of justice (Colquitt et al., 2007) and so is a significant dimension to include in studies of trust breakdown and repair.

HRM IMPACT ON TRUST

Researchers' attention has focused on the relationship between HRM and trust, examining either distinct combinations of practices, or distinct policy areas. Within each organization, choices are made by HR professionals and senior managers about which HR strategies and policies are deployed. While legal requirements create some constraint, nevertheless the final array of organizational policies will involve active decisions, with policies providing statements of intent towards employees (Skinner et al., 2004). Their mere presence will have some impact (Guest and Conway, 2011), but so too might their omission. Employees interpret these policies together with their perceptions of managers' behaviour as being indicative of 'the personified organization's commitment to them' (Whitener, 2001, p. 530). These signals of and clues to organization trustworthiness clarify and make more predictable what is expected and required for reward and progression (Tzafrir, 2005). For example, high job security signals benevolence and care towards employees (Iles et al., 1990); similarly the inclusion of more family-friendly policies suggests concern about employees' well-being (Grover and Crooker, 1995).

In addition to policy content, how it is implemented provides employees with tangible evidence of the extent to which management's intentions are genuine and can be trusted (Skinner et al., 2004). Recent longitudinal research reveals how informational justice shapes employees' subsequent perceptions of managers' benevolence and integrity (Colquitt and Rodell, 2011). Employees are more trusting of employers who adhere to their own policies and punish those who deviate from their required norms and standards (Weibel et al., 2009). In this way features of the workplace and the interventions of managers shape perceptions of trust (Blunsdon and Reed,

2003). Taken together, HRM policies and their implementation graphically demonstrate the organization's competence, care and concern, integrity and respect for their employees and their interests; consequently they impact significantly on the development and maintenance of organizational trust.

Bundles

One area that has received greater attention is distinct bundles of policies and practices termed high involvement work systems (HIWS). These are a set of practices designed to improve communication flow, promote empowerment and participation, and encourage employees to invest both tangibly, as well as emotionally, in their employer (Vandenberg et al., 1999). HIWS typically include those concerned with information sharing and employee participation, job security, performance management, and training and development (see e.g., Huselid, 1995; Delery, 1998; Boselie et al., 2005). For example, manufacturing employees' experiences of HIWS were found to positively influence their trust in the organization but also commitment and satisfaction, while reducing stress (Appelbaum et al., 2001). Similarly, in a public sector study these practices predict employee trust in colleagues, managers and their department (Gould-Williams, 2003). A large-scale multi-organizational European study showed how perceptions of competence, but also the benevolent intent of the firm, enhanced the overall trust in the employer (Searle et al., 2011b). Importantly, this study showed it was the procedural justice derived from the delivery of these policies that was a key factor. Content and implementation are significant and distinct issues.

Distinct Policies

Earlier research in this field tended to study trust in line managers, rather than the organization per se and concentrated on performance appraisal (e.g., Earley, 1986; Folger and Konovsky, 1989; Dobbins et al., 1993; Mayer and Davis, 1999), or reward and compensation (Pearce et al., 2000). A seminal quasi-experimental study showed how improving performance management processes so that they addressed employees' concerns, created a more acceptable process that increased trust in top management (Mayer and Davis, 1999). (Trust in top teams is often a surrogate for organizational trust.) Similarly, Korsgaard et al.'s work on performance management (1998) identified how subordinates' communication style could influence managers' fairness and, consequently, affects subordinates' attitudes toward their appraisal decision, the manager and the organization.

Another topic of interest to both trust and justice scholars is organizational exit (Brockner et al., 1987, 1997; Brockner, 1988; Mishra and Mishra, 1994; Spreitzer and Mishra, 1997, 2002; Mishra and Spreitzer, 1998). For example, a considerable amount is known about the perceived fairness of lay-offs (e.g., Shah, 2000), the type and level of support required (e.g., Armstrong-Stassen, 1994, 2002), and survivor well-being and productivity (e.g., Allen et al., 2001; Brockner et al., 2004). Until recently little empirical research had considered the impact on those directly involved with the lay-off process – HR managers. Buckley (2011) has looked specifically at the emotional effect and the impact on organizational trust for the group who deliver organizations' downsizing strategies.

Over the last two years the topics of interest for trust researchers have expanded into previously under-researched HRM policies covering the employment cycle (Searle and Skinner, 2011b). These included recruitment and selection (Searle and Billsberry, 2011), career management (Crawshaw, 2011), promotion (Brodt and Dionisi, 2011), change (Saunders, 2011), training (Ashleigh and Prichard, 2011) and bullying and harassment (Harrington and Rayner, 2011). In addition, consideration has been given to wider issues, such as person–organization fit (Boon and Den Hartog, 2011), values (Tzafrir and Enosh, 2011) and the psychological contract (Guest and Clinton, 2011) (to which I shall return shortly). These illustrate further how germane trust can be within an HRM context.

One mechanism that has been used extensively to examine the relationship between HRM and trust is the psychological contract (Robinson and Rousseau, 1994; Guest and Conway, 2002). The psychological contract describes employees' beliefs about the exchange relationship with the organization (Rousseau, 1995). These beliefs refer to their interpretations of implicit and explicit promises made, which often focus on HRM policies (Conway and Briner, 2009). For example, where a greater numbers of practices are included, employees can perceive that more promises have been made between the parties, while lack of provision is more likely to be linked to contract breach (Guest and Conway, 2002). Psychological contract research is often focused on employees' unmet expectations, which ultimately leads to a perceived contract breach and a resultant loss of trust (Rousseau, 1989). This intertwined contract/trust relationship was aptly demonstrated in Robinson's (1996) seminal study. She showed that high initial trust in an employment relationship reduced the likelihood of employees' perceiving psychological contract breach, therefore while unmet expectations did erode their trust in the organization, the decline was less pronounced for those with higher initial trust. More recently, contract breach and performance has been examined and differentiations made between proximal impacts, such as violation and distrust, from more distal influence on work attitudes, including organizational commitment, job satisfaction, intention to quit and work behaviours, such as performance and turnover (Zhao et al., 2007). Psychological contract research opens up possibilities for further longitudinal study of the dynamics of trust from the high point of the start of an employment relationship. Contract breaches have been shown to impact most significantly on affect and attitudes (Conway et al., 2011) and again affect is an under-researched domain for trust scholars. However, perhaps more attention needs to be paid to preventing breach in the first place, with empirical studies of how trust breach may be averted and so reduce the need for its repair (Hope-Hailey et al., 2012).

TRUST – HRM

Relatively little empirical research has looked at how trust itself might actually influence HRM policy and practices. A seminal industrial relations study contended that trust does not simply arise from existing social institutions and processes, but is also embedded within the principles that underlie these institutions (Fox, 1974). Reductions in mutual trust can be a catalyst for an intensification of control, particularly supervision. In contrast, HR managers' high trust in employees can influence employers' training and promotion decisions (Tzafrir, 2005). Mather (2011) contends that negotiations between managers and trade unions to secure more work for less reward undermine trust (see Lewicki and Polin, Chapter 2 in this book for more related debate).

Trust perceptions are not simply one way. Deutsch-Salamon and Robinson's (2008) retail-based study showed how feeling trusted (termed collective-felt trust) could alter employees' attention and behaviours to bring them more in line with achieving the goals of the organization. These changes in responsibility have two suggested components (Cummings and Anton, 1990): enhancing employees' sense of obligation towards the firm and their part in helping to achieve organizational goals, but greater acceptance by employees of their accountability to the firm. Thus, extra-role (Pearce and Gregersen, 1991) and 'taking charge' behaviours (Morrison and Phelps, 1999) are further aspects of a trust dividend for organizations. Critically, organizations in which employees feel more trusted, and return such trust through taking more responsibility, should have less necessity for externally imposed controls (see Part II of this book for related discussion of controls). This raises intriguing questions about whether high trust organizations might have further competitive advantage over their rivals through having lower costs associated with monitoring and regulating employees, but may also have distinct HRM policies.

In these final sections the two central considerations are outlined: the delivery of HRM and the HR function. Although HR may be involved in some aspects of the delivery of HRM, this chapter has identified the prominence of the line manager as the conduit for local HRM. In this last section the distinct symbolic role of the HR function is considered. Taken together, the individual and collective behaviours and decisions of these two groups are aggregated by employees to inform their general overview of the trustworthiness of the organization.

DELIVERING HR PRACTICE

The delivery of HR policy is now often the responsibility of line managers. Critically, the intent of HR practices as conceived by the HR function may deviate from that implemented by line managers. In addition, the intentions of those implementing policies may also be different from how individual employees perceive these in practice (Wright and Nishii, forthcoming). At each stage, distortion is possible, causing a disjunction between the policy as conceived by the HR function and employees' post-delivery perceptions (see Guest and Conway, 2011). Researchers, therefore, must be cognizant when collecting information about HR policies of these possibly different views. Concerns about the manner of implementation of HRM policies and practices are important for trust (e.g., Shapiro, 1987; Perrone et al., 2003) and show the significance of justice, identified as an antecedent of trust (Begley et al., 2002; Ambrose and Schminke, 2003; Colquitt et al., 2012). Concern about the perceived fairness of decisions, procedures and actions are important considerations when determining the level and extent of trust (Leventhal, 1976; Lind and Tyler, 1988; Colquitt and Rodell, 2011).

THE HR FUNCTION

In many organizations HR professionals are responsible for tactical HRM activities (Whitener, 1997). The HR function operationalizes the organization's strategy regarding its human resources, and has three distinct roles: creator, enforcer and maintainer. The first role is pivotal in the inception and development of HR policies to meet strategic goals, deciding which tools and procedures an organization will utilize in particular aspects of the employment cycle. Although senior managers do play a role (Guest and Conway, 2011), this function is central to employees' experiences in building and sustaining, or diminishing their trust in the organization (Whitener, 1997). For example, decisions to include psychometric tests may be treated by some applicants as a sign of an organization's untrustworthiness (Searle and Billsberry, 2011).

Though normatively committed to trust-building models of employment relations, HR professionals might often paradoxically be involved in designing and implementing trust-reducing practices, such as redundancy (e.g., Spreitzer and Mishra, 1997; Allen et al., 2001). The growing emphasis on shareholder value metrics, ongoing organizational restructuring and downsizing, and the extended use of outsourcing has increasingly moved the burden of risk onto employees and away from organizations (Thompson, 2003). The current economic downturn has brought into all organizations the necessity for every employee to work longer for reduced benefits, thus trust may be challenged through an externally created psychological contract breach as retirement ages rise, or over-supply of graduates causes them to be under-employed. All of the aforementioned changes position this professional group to the fore in performing a complex role in the development, implementation and management of policies that may significantly erode trust in the organization.

Second, the HR function plays a significant part as the enforcer in organizations, ensuring policies are implemented correctly. Crucially, HRM is likely to be more prominent during conflict situations between the employee and the organization, such as a formal grievance or warning. As a result the HR profession often sits uneasily between managers and employees (Caldwell, 2003), charged by the organization with finding satisfactory solutions to meet the demands of both parties, while also protecting its interests. Harrington et al. (2012) show these tensions in the context of bullying and harassment policy, and reveal how actions designed to protect the organization, may reduce both employees' and line managers' trust in this function.

Finally, HR may be central to ensuring policies are delivered and managed in line with communicated objectives. Thus, HR has a pivotal role in maintaining policies and processes within organizations. An important antecedent here is perceived organizational support (DeConinck, 2011). This refers to employees' generic beliefs about the extent to which their organization's values contribute to their reward and well-being: HRM provides mechanisms designed to assist in the evaluation and rewarding of employees' efforts, plus policies designed to promote well-being and reduce uncertainty. Beliefs about support have been found to positively affect employees' trust in the organization (Eisenberger et al., 1986, 2001).

The practice of HRM reflects the decisions and attitudes of individuals who represent the organizations in a variety of different functional capacities, with employees abstracting from these agents' actions, signals and signs to provide clues about the organization itself. Importantly, employees respond with attitudes, beliefs and actions that focus on the organization, rather than on these distinct agents (Whitener, 1997). Recent work shows the potential value of differentiating between distinct agents (e.g., Harrington and Rayner, 2011), however, we need to look in more detail at the precise immediate and long-term impact of different functions on employees' trust.

CONCLUSIONS

In this chapter the HR function and the policies and practices are shown to play an often overlooked role in organizational trust. They offer employees signals and clues that inform trust beliefs, decisions and actions. Far more attention needs to be given to the distinct influences of these groups to gain further insight into trust and HRM. Some key dimensions have been outlined, such as personality, which may significantly enhance our understanding and the ongoing value of more systematically disaggregating trust from justice. Through these steps a more nuanced study of organizational trust is emerging, widening our insight into its impact on employees' commitment and retention. While much has been gained from large-scale survey approaches, there is a need for more person-centric perspectives (Weiss and Rupp, 2011), enabling subjective experiences of employees to emerge and so revealing how and why and *to whom* trust matters. The employment cycle presents rich opportunities to examine the dynamics of trust, to consider the triggers for change and through mechanisms, such as the psychological contract and employee self-regulation. Further attention to trust dynamics is vital if we are to gain real insight into how and when trust develops, but also becomes damaged. Finally, little attention has been paid to groups other than managers and their role within organizations in the development and sustaining of trust. The impact of the HR profession as enforcer is interesting and introduces the topics of conflict and sanctions, which are only just emerging in studies of trust. Trust and HRM is an exciting and underdeveloped arena for study, and a key context in which important lessons can be passed on to organizations.

REFERENCES

Alfes, K., A. Shantz and C. Truss (2012), 'The link between perceived HRM practices, performance and wellbeing: the moderating effect of organisational trust', *Human Resources Management Journal*, **22**(4), 409–27.

Allen, T.D., D.M. Freeman, J.E.A. Russell, R.C. Reizenstein and J.O. Rentz (2001), 'Survivor reactions to organizational downsizing: does time ease the pain?', *Journal of Occupational and Organizational Psychology*, **74**(2), 145–64.

Ambrose, M.L. and M. Schminke (2003), 'Organization structure as a moderator of the relationship between procedural justice, interactional justice, perceived organizational support, and supervisory trust', *Journal of Applied Psychology*, **88**(2), 295–305.

Appelbaum, E., T. Bailey, P. Berg and A. Kalleberg (2001), 'Do high performance work systems pay off?', *Research in Sociology of Work* series, vol. 10, pp. 85–107.

Armstrong-Stassen, M. (1994), 'Coping with transition: a study of layoff survivors', *Journal of Organizational Behavior*, **15**(7), 597–621.

Armstrong-Stassen, M. (2002), 'Designated redundant but escaping lay-off: a special group of lay-off survivors', *Journal of Occupational and Organizational Psychology*, **75**(1), 1–13.

Aryee, S., P.S. Budhwar and Z.X. Chen (2002), 'Trust as a mediator of the relationship between organizational justice and work outcomes: test of a social exchange model', *Journal of Organizational Behavior*, **23**(3), 267–85.

Ashleigh, M. and J. Prichard (2011), 'Enhancing trust through training', in R. Searle and D. Skinner (eds), *Trust and HRM*, Cheltenham, UK and Northampton, MA, USA: Edward Elgar.

Barber, B. (1983), *The Logic and Limits of Trust*, New Brunswick, NJ: Rutgers University Press.

Barney, J.B. and M.H. Hansen (1994), 'Trustworthiness as a source of competitive advantage', *Strategic Management Journal*, **15**(S1), 175–90.

Becker, T.E. (1998), 'Integrity in organizations: beyond honesty and conscientiousness', *Academy of Management Review*, **23**(1), 154–61.

Begley, T.M., C. Lee, Y. Fang and J. Li (2002), 'Power distance as a moderator of the relationship between justice and employee outcomes in a sample of Chinese employees', *Journal of Managerial Psychology*, **17**(8), 692–711.

Bies, R. and T. Tripp (1996), 'Beyond distrust: "getting even" and the need for revenge', in R. Kramer and T. Tyler (eds), *Trust in Organizations: Frontiers of Theory and Research*, Thousand Oaks, CA: Sage.

Bigley, G.A. and J.L. Pearce (1998), 'Straining for shared meaning in organisational science: problems of trust and distrust', *Academy of Management Review*, **23**(3), 405–22.

Blunsdon, B. and K. Reed (2003), 'The effects of technical and social conditions on workplace trust', *International Journal of Human Resource Management*, **14**(1), 12–27.

Boon, C. and D.N. Den Hartog (2011), 'Human resource management, person–environment fit and trust', in R. Searle and D. Skinner (eds), *Trust and HRM*, Cheltenham, UK and Northampton, MA, USA: Edward Elgar.

Boselie, P., G. Dietz and C. Boon (2005), 'Commonalities and contradictions in HRM and performance research', *Human Resource Management Journal*, **15**(3), 67–94.

Brockner, J. (1988), 'The effects of work layoffs on survivors: research, theory, and practice', in B.M. Star and L.L. Cummings (eds), *Research in Organizational Behavior*, vol. 10, pp. 213–56.

Brockner, J., S. Grover, T. Reed, R. Dewitt and M. O'Malley (1987), 'Survivors' reactions to layoffs: we get by with a little help from our friends', *Administrative Science Quarterly*, **32**(4), 526–41.

Brockner, J., P.A. Siegel, J.P. Daly, T. Tyler and C. Martin (1997), 'When trust matters: the moderating effect of outcome favorability', *Administrative Science Quarterly*, **42**(3), 558–83.

Brockner, J., G. Spreitzer, A. Mishra, W. Hochwarter, L. Pepper and J. Weinberg (2004),

'Perceived control as an antidote to the negative effects of layoffs on survivors' organizational commitment and job performance', *Administrative Science Quarterly*, **49**(1), 76–100.

Brodt, S.E. and A. Dionisi (2011), 'When peers become leaders: the effects of internal promotion on workgroup dynamics', in R. Searle and D. Skinner (eds), *Trust and HRM*, Cheltenham, UK and Northampton, MA, USA: Edward Elgar.

Buckley, F. (2011), 'Trust and engagement in a downsizing context: the impact on human resource managers', in R. Searle and D. Skinner (eds), *Trust and HRM*, Cheltenham, UK and Northampton, MA, USA: Edward Elgar.

Caldwell, R. (2003), 'The changing roles of personnel managers: old ambiguities, new uncertainties', *Journal of Management Studies*, **40**(4), 983–1004.

Carnevale, D.G. (1995), *Trustworthy Government: Leadership and Management Strategies for Building Trust and High Performance*, San Francisco: Jossey-Bass.

Cohen-Charash, Y. and P.E. Spector (2001), 'The role of justice in organizations: a meta-analysis', *Organizational Behavior and Human Decision Processes*, **86**(2), 278–321.

Colquitt, J.A. and J.B. Mueller (2008), 'Justice, trustworthiness, and trust', in S. Gilliland, D. Skarlicki and D.D. Steiner (eds), *Justice, Morality, and Social Responsibility*, Charlotte, NC: Information Age Publishing.

Colquitt, J.A. and J.B. Rodell (2011), 'Justice, trust, and trustworthiness: a longitudinal analysis integrating three theoretical perspectives', *The Academy of Management Journal*, **54**(6), 1183–1206.

Colquitt, J., B. Scott and J. Lepine (2007), 'Trust, trustworthiness, and trust propensity: a meta-analytic test of their unique relationships with risk taking and job performance', *Journal of Applied Psychology*, **92**(4), 909–1027.

Colquitt, J.A., J.A. Lepine, R.F. Piccolo, A.C.P. Zapata and B.L. Rich (2012) 'Explaining the justice–performance relationship: trust as exchange deepener or trust as uncertainty reducer?', *Journal of Applied Psychology*, **97**(1), 1–15.

Conway, N. and R.B. Briner (2009), 'Fifty years of psychological contract research: what do we know and what are the main challenges?', in G.P. Hodgkinson and J.K. Ford (eds), *International Review of Industrial and Organizational Psychology*, New York: Wiley.

Conway, N., D. Guest and L. Trenberth (2011), 'Testing the differential effects of changes in psychological contract breach and fulfillment', *Journal of Vocational Behavior*, **79**(1), 267–76.

Costa, P.T. and R.R. McCrae (1992), *Revised NEO Personality Inventory (NEO-PI-R) and NEO Five-factor Inventory (NEO-FFI) Professional Manual*, Odessa, FL: Psychological Assessment.

Crawshaw, J.R. (2011), 'Career development, progression and trust', in R. Searle and D. Skinner (eds), *Trust and HRM*, Cheltenham, UK and Northampton, MA, USA: Edward Elgar.

Cummings, L.L. and R.J. Anton (1990), *The Logical and Appreciative Dimensions of Accountability*, San Francisco, CA: Jossey-Bass.

Davis, T. and M. Landa (1999), 'The trust deficit', *The Canadian Manager*, **24**(1), 10–11.

DeConinck, J.B. (2011), 'The effect of organizational justice, perceived organizational support, and perceived supervisor support on marketing employees' level of trust', *Journal of Business Research*, **63**(12), 1349–55.

Delery, J.E. (1998), 'Issues of fit in strategic human resource management: implications for research', *Human Resource Management Review*, **8**(3), 289–309.

Deutsch-Salamon, S. and S.L. Robinson (2008), 'Trust that binds: the impact of collective-felt trust on organizational performance', *Journal of Applied Psychology*, **93**(3), 593–601.

Dietz, G. and D. Den Hartog (2006), 'Measuring trust inside organisations', *Personnel Review*, **35**(5), 557–88.

Dirks, K.T. and D.L. Ferrin (2001), 'The role of trust in organizational settings', *Organization Science*, **12**(4), 450–67.

Dirks, K.T. and D.L. Ferrin (2002), 'Trust in leadership: meta-analytic findings and implications for research and practice', *Journal of Applied Psychology*, **87**(4), 611–28.

Dobbins, G., S. Platz and J. Houston (1993), 'Relationship between trust in appraisal and appraisal effectiveness: a field study', *Journal of Business and Psychology*, **7**(3), 309–22.
Earley, P.C. (1986), 'Trust, perceived importance of praise and criticism, and work performance: an examination of feedback in the United States and England', *Journal of Management*, **12**(4), 457–74.
Eisenberger, R., R. Huntington, S. Hutchison and D. Sowa (1986), 'Perceived organizational support', *Journal of Applied Psychology*, **71**(3), 500–507.
Eisenberger, R., S. Armeli, B. Rexwinkel, P.D. Lynch and L. Rhoades (2001), 'Reciprocation of perceived organizational support', *Journal of Applied Psychology*, **86**(1), 42–51.
Folger, R. and M.A. Konovsky (1989), 'Effects of procedural and distributive justice on reactions to pay raise decisions', *The Academy of Management Journal*, **32**(1), 115–30.
Fox, A. (1974), *Beyond Contract: Work, Power and Trust Relations*, London: Faber and Faber.
Giddens, A. (1990), *The Consequences of Modernity*, Oxford: Blackwell Publishing Ltd.
Gill, H., K. Boies, J.E. Finegan and J. McNally (2005), 'Antecedents of trust: establishing a boundary condition for the relation between propensity to trust and intention to trust', *Journal of Business and Psychology*, **19**(3), 287–302.
Gillespie, N. and G. Dietz (2009), 'Trust repair after an organization-level failure', *Academy of Management Review*, **34**(1), 127–45.
Gould-Williams, J. (2003), 'The importance of HR practices and workplace trust in achieving superior performance: a study of public-sector organizations', *International Journal of Human Resource Management*, **14**(1), 28–54.
Govier, T. (1994), 'Is it a jungle out there – trust, distrust and the construction of social-reality', *Dialogue –Canadian Philosophical Review*, **33**(2), 237–53.
Grover, S.L. and K.J. Crooker (1995), 'Who appreciates family-responsive human-resource policies – the impact of family-friendly policies on the organizational attachment of parents and non-parents', *Personnel Psychology*, **48**(2), 271–88.
Guest, D. and M. Clinton (2011), 'Human resource management, the psychological contract and trust', in R. Searle and D. Skinner (eds), *Trust and HRM*, Cheltenham, UK and Northampton, MA, USA: Edward Elgar.
Guest, D. and N. Conway (2002), 'Communicating the psychological contract: an employer perspective', *Human Resource Management Journal*, **12**(2), 22–38.
Guest, D. and N. Conway (2011), 'The impact of HR practices, HR effectiveness and a "strong HR system" on organisational outcomes: a stakeholder perspective', *International Journal of Human Resource Management*, **22**(8), 1686–702.
Harrington, S. and C. Rayner (2011), 'Whose side are you on? Trust and HR in workplace bullying', in R. Searle and D. Skinner (eds), *Trust and HRM*, Cheltenham, UK and Northampton, MA, USA: Edward Elgar.
Harrington, S., C. Rayner and S. Warren (2012), 'Too hot to handle? Trust and human resource practitioners' implementation of anti-bullying policy', *Human Resource Management Journal*, **22**, 392–408.
Hope-Hailey, V., R.H. Searle and G. Deitz (2012), *Where Has All the Trust Gone?*, Research Report, CIPD.
Huselid, M.A. (1995), 'The impact of human-resource management-practices on turnover, productivity, and corporate financial performance', *Academy of Management Journal*, **38**(3), 635–72.
Iles, P., C. Mabey and I. Robertson (1990), 'HRM practices and employee commitment: possibilities, pitfalls and paradoxes', *British Journal of Management*, **1**(3), 147–57.
Innocenti, L., M. Pilati and A.M. Peluso (2011), 'Trust as moderator in the relationship between HRM practices and employee attitudes', *Human Resource Management Journal*, **21**(3), 303–17.
Kee, H.W. and R.E. Knox (1970), 'Conceptual and methodological considerations in the study of trust and suspicion', *Journal of Conflict Resolution*, **14**(3), 357–66.
Konovsky, M.A. and D.S. Pugh (1994), 'Citizenship behavior and social exchange', *Academy of Management Journal*, **37**(3), 656–69.

Korsgaard, M.A., L. Roberson and R.D. Rymph (1998), 'What motivates fairness? The role of subordinate assertive behavior on managers' interactional fairness', *Journal of Applied Psychology*, **83**(5), 731–44.

Kramer, R.M. (1999), 'Trust and distrust in organizations: emerging perspectives, enduring questions', *Annual Review of Psychology*, **50**(1), 569–98.

Kramer, R.M. and T.R. Tyler (1996), *Trust in Organizations. Frontiers of Theory and Research*, London: Sage.

Legge, K. (1995), 'HRM: rhetoric, reality and hidden agendas', in J. Storey (eds), *Human Resource Management: A Critical Text*, London: Routledge.

Leventhal, G.S. (1976), 'The distribution of rewards and resources in groups and organizations', in L. Berkowitz and E. Walster (eds), *Advances in Experimental Social Psychology*, New York: Academic Press.

Lewicki, R.J. and B.B. Bunker (1995), 'Trust in relationships: a model of trust development and decline', in B.B. Bunker and J.Z. Rubin (eds), *Conflict, Cooperation, and Justice*, San Francisco: Jossey-Bass.

Lewicki, R., C. Wiethoff and E.C. Tomlinson (2005), 'What is the role of trust in organisational justice?', in J. Greenberg and J.A. Colquitt (eds), *Handbook of Organizational Justice*, Mahwah, NJ: Lawrence Erlbaum Associates.

Luhmann, N. (1988), 'Familiarity, confidence, trust: problems and alternatives', in D. Gambetta (ed.), *Trust: Making and Breaking Cooperative Relations*, New York: Basil Blackwell.

Mather, K. (2011), 'Employee relations and the illusiveness of trust', in R. Searle and D. Skinner (eds), *Trust and HRM*, Cheltenham, UK and Northampton, MA, USA: Edward Elgar.

Mayer, R.C. and J.H. Davis (1999), 'The effect of the performance appraisal system on trust for management: a field quasi-experiment', *Journal of Applied Psychology*, **84**(1), 123–36.

Mayer, R.C., J. Davis and F.D. Schoorman (1995), 'An integrative model of organizational trust', *Academy of Management Review*, **20**(3), 709–34.

McAllister, D.J. (1995), 'Affect- and cognition-based trust as foundations for interpersonal cooperation in organizations', *Academy of Management Journal*, **38**(1), 24–59.

Mishra, A. and K. Mishra (1994), 'The role of mutual trust in effective downsizing strategies', *Human Resource Management*, **33**(2), 261–79.

Mishra, A. and G.M. Spreitzer (1998), 'Explaining how survivors respond to downsizing: the roles of trust, empowerment, justice, and work redesign', *Academy of Management Review*, **23**(3), 567–88.

Morrison, E.W. and C.C. Phelps (1999), 'Taking charge at work: extrarole efforts to initiate workplace change', *The Academy of Management Journal*, **42**(4), 403–19.

Parks, C., R. Henager and S. Scamahorn (1996), 'Trust and reactions to messages of intent in social dilemmas', *The Journal of Conflict Resolution*, **40**(1), 134–51.

Pearce, J.L. and H.B. Gregersen (1991), 'Task interdependence and extrarole behavior: a test of the mediating effects of felt responsibility', *Journal of Applied Psychology*, **76**(6), 838–44.

Pearce, J.L., I. Branyiczki and G.A. Bigley (2000), 'Insufficient bureaucracy: trust and commitment in particularistic organizations', *Organization Science*, **11**(2), 148–62.

Perrone, V., A. Zaheer and B. McEvily (2003), 'Free to be trusted? Organizational constraints on trust in boundary spanners', *Organization Science*, **14**(4), 422–39.

Pillai, R., C. Schriesheim and E. Williams (1999), 'Fairness perceptions and trust as mediators for transformational and transactional leadership: a two-sample study', *Journal of Management*, **25**(6), 897–934.

Podsakoff, P.M., S.B. Mackenzie, R.H. Moorman and R. Fetter (1990), 'Transformational leader behaviors and their effects on followers' trust in leader, satisfaction, and organizational citizenship behaviors', *The Leadership Quarterly*, **1**(2), 107–42.

Robinson, S. (1996), 'Trust and breach of the psychological contract', *Administrative Science Quarterly*, **41**(4) 574–99.

Robinson, S. and D. Rousseau (1994), 'Violating the psychological contract – not the exception but the norm', *Journal of Organizational Behavior*, **15**(3), 245–59.

Rotter, J.B. (1967), 'A new scale for the measurement of interpersonal trust', *Journal of Personality*, **35**(4), 651–65.
Rotter, J.B. (1980), 'Interpersonal trust, trustworthiness, and gullibility', *American Psychologist*, **35**(1), 1–7.
Rousseau, D.M. (1989), 'Psychological and implied contracts in organizations', *Employee Responsibilities and Rights Journal*, **2**(2), 121–39.
Rousseau, D.M. (1995), *Psychological Contracts in Organizations: Understanding Written and Unwritten Agreements*, Thousand Oaks, CA: Sage Publications.
Rousseau, D.M., S.B. Sitkin, R.S. Burt and C.F. Camerer (1998), 'Not so different after all: a cross-discipline view of trust', *Academy of Management Review*, **23**(3), 393–404.
Saunders, M.N. (2011), 'Trust and strategic change: an organizational justice perspective', in R. Searle and D. Skinner (eds), *Trust and HRM*, Cheltenham, UK and Northampton, MA, USA: Edward Elgar.
Schoorman, F.D., R.C. Mayer and J.H. Davis (1996), 'Organizational trust: philosophical perspectives and conceptual definitions', *Academy of Management Review*, **21**(2), 337–40.
Schoorman, F.D., R.C. Mayer and J.H. Davis (2007), 'An integrative model of organizational trust: past, present, and future', *Academy of Management Review*, **32**(2), 344–54.
Searle, R. and K.S. Ball (2004), 'The development of trust and distrust in a merger', *Journal of Managerial Psychology*, **19**(7), 708–21.
Searle, R. and J. Billsberry (2011), 'The development and destruction of organizational trust during recruitment and selection', in R. Searle and D. Skinner (eds), *Trust and HRM*, Cheltenham, UK and Northampton, MA, USA: Edward Elgar.
Searle, R. and D. Skinner (2011a) 'Introduction', in R. Searle and D. Skinner (eds), *Trust and HRM*, Cheltenham, UK and Northampton, MA, USA: Edward Elgar.
Searle, R. and D. Skinner (2011b), 'New agendas and perspectives', in R. Searle and D. Skinner (eds), *Trust and HRM*, Cheltenham, UK and Northampton, MA, USA: Edward Elgar.
Searle, R., A. Weibel and D.N. Den Hartog (2011a), 'Employee trust in organizational contexts', in G.P. Hodgkinson and J.K. Ford (eds), *International Review of Industrial and Organizational Psychology*, Chichester: Wiley–Blackwell.
Searle, R., D.N. Den Hartog, A. Weibel, N. Gillespie, F. Six, T. Hatzakis and D. Skinner (2011b), 'Trust in the employer: the role of high involvement work practices and procedural justice in European organizations', *International Journal of Human Resource Management*, **22**(5), 1068–92.
Shah, P.P. (2000), 'Network destruction: the structural implications of downsizing', *The Academy of Management Journal*, **43**(1), 101–12.
Shapiro, S.P. (1987), 'The social control of impersonal trust', *American Journal of Sociology*, **93**(3), 623–58.
Skinner, D. and R.H. Searle (2011), 'Trust in the context of performance appraisal', in R. Searle and D. Skinner (eds), *Trust and HRM*, Cheltenham, UK and Northampton, MA, USA: Edward Elgar, Ch. 10.
Skinner, D., M.N.K. Saunders and H. Duckett (2004), 'Policies, promises and trust: improving working lives in the National Health Service', *International Journal of Public Sector Management*, **17**(7), 558–70.
Spreitzer, G. and A. Mishra (1997), *Survivor Responses to Downsizing: The Mitigating Effects of Trust and Empowerment*, Southern California Studies Center, University of Southern California.
Spreitzer, G. and A. Mishra (2002), 'To stay or to go: voluntary survivor turnover following an organizational downsizing', *Journal of Organizational Behavior*, **23**(6), 707–29.
Stack, L. (1978), 'Trust', in H. London and J. Exner (eds), *Dimensions of Personality*, New York: John Wiley and Sons Inc.
Tan, H.H. and C.S.F. Tan (2000), 'Toward the differentiation of trust in supervisor and trust in organization', *Genetic Social and General Psychology Monographs*, **126**(2), 241–60.
Thompson, P. (2003), 'Disconnected capitalism: or why employers can't keep their side of the bargain', *Work, Employment and Society*, **17**(2), 359–78.

Tsui, A.S., J.L. Pearce, L.W. Porter and A.M. Tripoli (1997), 'Alternative approaches to the employee–organization relationship: does investment in employees pay off?', *Academy of Management Journal*, **40**(5), 1089–121.

Tzafrir, S.S. (2005), 'The relationship between trust, HRM practices and firm performance', *International Journal of Human Resource Management*, **16**(9), 1600–622.

Tzafrir, S. and G. Enosh (2011), 'Beyond attitudes and norms: trust commitment and HR values as triggers of intention to leave', in R. Searle and D. Skinner (eds), *Trust and HRM*, Cheltenham, UK and Northampton, MA, USA: Edward Elgar.

Vandenberg, R.J., H.A. Richardson and L.J. Eastman (1999), 'The impact of high involvement work processes on organizational effectiveness – a second-order latent variable approach', *Group and Organization Management*, **24**(3), 300–339.

Weibel, A., R. Searle, D. Den Hartog, N. Gillespie, F. Six, T. Hatzakis and D. Skinner (2010), 'Control as a driver of trust in the organization', *Social Sciences Research Network*, accessed 3 October 2011 at http://www.researchgate.net/publication/228197932_Control_as_a_Driver_of_Trust_in_the_Organization.

Weiss, H.M. and D.E. Rupp (2011), 'Experiencing work: an essay on a person-centric work psychology', *Industrial and Organizational Psychology*, **4**(1), 83–97.

Whitener, E.M. (1997), 'The impact of human resources activities on employees' trust', *Human Resource Management Review*, **7**(4), 389–404.

Whitener, E.M. (2001), 'Do "high commitment" human resource practices affect employee commitment? A cross-level analysis using hierarchical linear modeling', *Journal of Management*, **27**(5), 515–35.

Whitley, R. (1987), 'Taking firms seriously as economic actors: towards a sociology of firm behaviour, *Organization Studies*, **8**(2), 125–47.

Whitney, J.O. (1994), *The Trust Factor: Liberating Profits and Restoring Corporate Vitality*, New York: McGraw-Hill.

Wright, P.M. and L.H. Nishii (2006), *Strategic HRM and Organizational Behavior: Integrating Multiple Levels of Analysis*, Ithaca, NY: Center for Advanced Human Resource Studies (CAHRS).

Wright, P.M. and L.H. Nishii (forthcoming), 'Strategic HRM and organizational behavior: integrating multiple levels of analysis', in D.E. Guest, J. Paauwe and P.M. Wright (eds), *Human Resource Management and Performance: Progress and Prospects*, Oxford: Blackwell Publishing.

Yakovleva, M., R.R. Reilly and R. Werko (2010), 'Why do we trust? Moving beyond individual to dyadic perceptions', *Journal of Applied Psychology*, **95**(1), 79–91.

Zaheer, A., B. McEvily and V. Perrone (1998), 'Does trust matter? Exploring the effects of interorganizational and interpersonal trust on performance', *Organization Science*, **9**(2), 141–59.

Zhao, H., S.J. Wayne, B.C. Glibkowski and J. Bravo (2007), 'The impact of psychological contract breach on work-related outcomes: a meta-analysis', *Personnel Psychology*, **60**(3), 647–80.

2. The role of trust in negotiation processes
Roy J. Lewicki and Beth Polin

INTRODUCTION

The purpose of this chapter is to examine the role of trust in the negotiation process. While there have been thousands of studies on the nature of negotiation and factors that contribute to its effectiveness or ineffectiveness, only a remarkably small handful of studies have actually examined the role of trust. This chapter will attempt to serve three objectives. First, we will develop the case for the importance of trust in negotiation – the rationale for what trust contributes to an effective negotiation or how distrust detracts from an effective negotiation. Second, we will examine what the research literature has shown about the importance of trust – taken both as an independent and dependent variable – in the negotiation process. That is, we will show how trust contributes to an effective negotiation, and how types of negotiation can contribute to, or detract from, trust. In doing so, we will identify several gaps and challenges in the research literature on the trust–negotiation relationship, and also offer insight on ways that damaged trust can be repaired. Finally, we will highlight some of the research that remains to be done in order to underscore the critical role that trust plays in the negotiation give-and-take.

WHY IS TRUST IMPORTANT TO EFFECTIVE NEGOTIATION?

As we will note several times, trust is a critical element throughout a negotiation, as both the lubricant that enhances and facilitates the negotiation process, and the binding element that often holds deals together. Prior to a negotiation or in the early stages of deliberation, the presence of strong trust can considerably simplify the negotiation process. At the beginning, parties assess how much they can trust one another, and they develop a negotiation strategy based on that assessment. This assessment can be done through initial contact with the other, or by checking out the other's reputation and credentials through friends and associates. But even if one judges the other as trustworthy at the outset, as the negotiation evolves, negotiators should continue to reassess the other's trust through the interpretation of a number of cues and signals. Is the other telling me the truth? Is the other attempting to take advantage of me? After the negotiation, will the other follow through and keep the commitments they are making? If I suspect that they may not follow through, should I ask for some kind of formal agreement? These are important questions, and ones that a negotiator must not only decide (implicitly or explicitly) before a negotiation but also monitor throughout the negotiation process.

To elaborate, there are several ways that trust can simplify negotiation. First, one of the primary purposes of negotiation is the exchange of information between parties in order to persuade the other to 'see it your way'. Trust is integral to this exchange of information. Each party has to be able to believe what the other is saying, since they often cannot verify or confirm all statements, claims and charges. Thus, ultimately, trust between negotiators can minimize transaction costs in closing a deal. Deals can be completed and verified 'on a handshake' because the established trust between the parties creates the expectation that all parties will follow through and keep their promises and commitments. Second, in the exchange of information, the other's trustworthiness becomes as important as trust. To be trustworthy, a negotiator must work to establish and maintain credibility. One's credibility is grounded in the perception that the information being conveyed is accurate and verifiable. We discuss trustworthiness in more detail later in this chapter. Finally, once credibility is established a negotiator can develop a reputation for honesty, a reputation that is conveyed to others in the marketplace. A reputation for credibility and honesty is integral for a negotiator to maintain positive working relationships in all strategic affiliations; deals can be struck efficiently and without investing major time and effort in verification. Hence, maintaining a reputation for trustworthiness is critical to negotiators, and negotiators should frequently monitor whether their reputation is as good as they would like it to be.

If the logic for the importance of trust in establishing and sustaining effective negotiation is not clear, consider the alternative: the ways that low or nonexistent trust can make a negotiation more difficult. As we stated, information is still the primary currency of exchange. However, the negotiator does not believe that they can trust the accuracy of the other party's statements. This doubt in the other's veracity may result from what the negotiator has learned about the other's reputation, or may come about through verbal and nonverbal cues transmitted by the negotiator that suggest exaggeration, bluffing, or outright deception. As a result, much of what the other says must be independently confirmed and verified. Such verification may or may not be possible, and if it is possible may entail significant delays in establishing the accuracy of the information on which the agreement is based. Moreover, even if the information can be verified, low trust between negotiators often necessitates the creation of formalized, complex, written contracts and other documents. While these documents remind people of what they have agreed and are often useful in minimizing some of the miscommunication that may occur if a deal is based only on verbalization and a handshake, creating them can also add significant time delay and cost to the deal itself.

Finally, creation of such agreements usually requires elaborate consequences and penalties for violating the terms of the agreement. Complex penalties for violation, mechanisms for enforcing those penalties, the employment of 'monitors' and police officers to conduct the enforcement, and appeal systems and grievance procedures for wrongful accusations or penalization all become part of this system of enforcement. When we begin to understand that entire professions are built and sustained around managing anticipated or actual distrust – such as attorneys, inspectors, judges, referees, police officers, auditors, monitors and regulators – one can appreciate the power that effective trust can create in minimizing these costs.

We are not so naive as to believe that distrust in negotiation can be eliminated, nor that all deals could be consummated (and/or revised) with a simple handshake and without backup documentation and specification of consequences for noncompliance. We recognize, in fact, that a certain amount of distrust can be very healthy in a negotiation. Checking on the reputation of a new or unfamiliar opponent can clearly be a valuable action. Beyond this, written 'memoranda of understanding', formalized agreements and ways of monitoring the other's compliance can play an extremely important role in cementing a negotiated agreement. But we draw these extremes in order to reinforce how integral strong trust is to effective negotiation, and to reiterate that negotiators must pay attention to ways they can create and manage solid trust in the negotiations themselves.

TRUST AND NEGOTIATION DEFINED

There are many different definitions of trust. Some have defined it as 'confident positive expectations regarding another's conduct' (Lewicki et al., 1998, p. 439), focusing largely on a person's intentions and motives. Others have focused more on the other's behavior, using a definition of 'the willingness of a party to be vulnerable to the actions of another party based on the expectation that the other party will perform a particular action important to the trustor, irrespective of the ability to monitor or control that other party' (Mayer et al., 1995, p. 712). For our purposes in this chapter, we will define trust as 'a psychological state comprising the intention to accept vulnerability based upon positive expectations of the intentions or behavior of another' (Rousseau et al., 1998, p. 395). Given that the trust and negotiation literature has been plagued by both omission of a common definition of trust and inconsistencies in the definition of the construct, we embrace this definition because it is one of the most commonly accepted in the evolving trust literature.[1] Negotiation is a process by which 'two or more parties attempt to resolve their opposing interests' (Lewicki et al., 2010, p. 6). As we noted earlier, the need for trust in negotiation arises because of each party's *interdependence* with the other in attempting to resolve these opposing interests. Negotiators depend on each other to help them achieve their goals and objectives. They depend on the information presented by the other party, on the outcomes to which the parties commit throughout that process, and on the other party delivering on those commitments.

In reflecting on this interdependence and its relationship to managing information, Kelley (1966) suggested that negotiators must grapple with two fundamental dilemmas. The first is the 'dilemma of trust'. How much should negotiators believe what the other party is telling them? If a negotiator believes everything the other party is telling them, then the other is in a position to exploit that trust and take advantage through deception. Conversely, if a negotiator believes nothing that the other party tells them, then it becomes difficult for the parties to reach any viable agreement. The second dilemma, paralleling the first, is the 'dilemma of honesty'. How much should a negotiator tell the truth to the other? If a negotiator is completely honest – disclosing all of their personal preferences, including their walkaway point or least preferred acceptable alternative – then they give away their bargaining position and lose all bargaining power. Conversely, if the party discloses nothing about their personal preferences and interests, then it is difficult for the opponent to know what the negotiator wants or how to structure their offers and proposals in a way that allows the parties to achieve a mutually acceptable agreement (if an integrative solution is indeed desired). Thus, in order for negotiators to be able to reach a viable agreement, they must find a way to navigate through these two dilemmas in a manner focused on attempting to resolve at least two goals: maximizing their own personal outcome in the negotiation, and achieving an agreement that is acceptable to the other side. Moreover, if the parties had some kind of established relationship prior to the negotiation – for example, husband and wife, roommates, business partners, or members of a governing body such as a legislature or city council – then a third goal is to maintain and even strengthen that relationship so that they can continue to successfully negotiate in the future.

With respect to the trust dilemma, negotiators must decide how much to believe what the other party is telling them. Can the information being provided be independently verified for accuracy and completeness, and if so, how much is verification going to cost in time and labor? Have we learned what we need to know to make the agreement workable for us? Is the information about what the other wants sufficient for us to believe that the deal is viable for them? Do we need the deal badly enough to accept it and be willing to live with it, even if we find out later that they were not being fully honest? Can we believe they will follow through on their promises and commitments, or do we need to invest in written and formalized agreements to bind them to their deal?

With respect to the honesty dilemma, negotiators must decide how much and what kind of information to share. What information does the other party need in order to achieve a viable agreement? What information, if revealed, would give away bargaining power and expose our vulnerability, allowing the other to take advantage of us? Can we selectively omit certain information, or bluff, or even be blatantly deceptive and not be discovered? What are the consequences if these bluffs or deceptions fail? Finally, if the negotiator makes promises and commitments, is the negotiator obligated to 'live up to' those promises or commitments?

Clearly, then, while the advantages of high trust and honesty can significantly promote sound negotiations, the consequences of dishonesty and low trust can be severe. Since trust is one important ingredient of the glue that holds relationships together, the consequences of significant dishonesty and high distrust not only endanger the negotiation but also threaten the very existence of the relationship. We will have more to say about this later in the chapter.

Distinguishing Between Different Types of Trust, and Implications for Negotiation

Just as the negotiation experience is an evolving process of dynamic exchange in which the parties hope to end in a better state than they began, trust, too, is evolutionary in nature. Most negotiations require at least some basic level of trust. Shapiro et al. (1992) propose that this basic, 'minimal condition' level of trust is called deterrence-based trust. At the very least, one party must be able to trust that the other will keep their word, follow through with promises made, and act in a consistent manner; this type of trust is 'deterrence based' because this basic trust is enforced through punishments for not keeping one's word. Developing this logic further, Lewicki and Bunker (1995, 1996) suggested that this basic form of trust be called 'calculus-based trust' (CBT), arguing that at this basic level, trust is grounded in both deterrence (the negative consequences for violating trust) as well as inducements and rewards for adhering to the trust agreement and keeping one's word. Trusting someone – even at the most basic level – should be a rational, calculative choice (Rousseau et al., 1998). Behaviors such as meeting the other's expectations, keeping promises, and maintaining a trustworthy reputation and high credibility all build calculus-based trust (Lewicki and Bunker, 1996; Lewicki and Stevenson, 1998). Calculus-based trust is likely to be maintained: (1) if the trustee knows they will engage in future transactions with the trustor; (2) if the trustee has multiple transactions occurring at the same time with the trustor; or (3) if the trustor has some control over the reputation of the trustee (Shapiro et al., 1992).

A second, more advanced level of trust is called 'knowledge-based trust' (KBT) (Lewicki and Bunker, 1995; Shapiro et al., 1992). This type of trust comes from the belief that one party can predict, with a relatively confident degree of accuracy, the behaviors of another party, developed by gaining knowledge about the other's motives, intentions, behavioral tendencies, and interests or preferences. For example, a negotiator may favor a more cooperative, interest-based approach to negotiation if he believes that he fully understands the other's interests. Ways of encouraging knowledge-based trust include maintaining consistent, frequent communication with the other party and learning more about the other party's perspective, interests, needs, and motives so as to better predict their actions (Lewicki and Stevenson, 1998; Shapiro et al., 1992). Knowledge-based trust can be 'monitored' by regularly affirming and verifying the information that one is gaining about the other party.

Third and finally, if negotiating parties develop a strong positive relationship with each other the parties are said to have 'identification-based trust' (IBT), the strongest form of trust (Lewicki and Bunker, 1995; Shapiro et al., 1992). This level of trust is characterized by the parties developing positive emotions and attraction to the other, a deep understanding and identification with the other, and the capacity to actually 'speak for the other in their absence' (Deutsch, 1949). Trust at this level is so strong that the parties often assume there is little need for traditional control or surveillance mechanisms (Lewicki and Stevenson, 1998). However, violations of identification-based trust do occur, and when they happen, they are likely to produce strong feelings of betrayal and even self-doubt in the trustor. As a result, while identification-based trust tends to produce the highest level of trust, it is also most likely to create a certain 'blindness' to the possibility of betrayal. The degree to which a certain amount of 'distrust' is essential to a negotiator, even with a long-standing opponent who one knows well, will always be a source of debate among experienced negotiators.

This evolutionary approach to different types of trust emphasizes that trust develops and changes character over time and is phenomenologically different in different types of negotiation relationships. Most trust development begins at the calculus-based level, where parties engage in 'simple market transactions'. When successful, these transactions reinforce previous transactions, eventually leading a party to know the other well enough to predict the other's behavior or in other words, to move to the knowledge-based trust level. As more and more information is collected about a party, one may begin to identify with the other party's interests and needs, leading to the identification-based level of trust. Note that not all negotiating relationships have a need to progress past the calculus-based level; in fact, few relationships may actually achieve the identification-based level except when the parties have developed long-term, complex, and frequently repeated interactions.

WHAT MAKES A NEGOTIATOR TRUSTWORTHY?

Thus far, our discussion has focused on the initiator's side of the relationship, that is, on the decision to trust another and the decision to be honest toward another. Keeping in line with this discussion, we will now examine those qualities that others use to make trust judgments about the initiator. In other words, how does one party judge the trustworthiness of the other party? Early research by Mayer et al. (1995) and subsequent studies (Ferrin et al., 2007; Gunia et al., 2011; Malhotra and Murnighan, 2002) have suggested that negotiators judge another's trustworthiness on three different and somewhat independent foundations: perceived ability, perceived benevolence and perceived integrity.

Perceived Ability

This first foundation can be demonstrated through three different aspects of competence or ability: being competent by knowing about the core issues under consideration in the negotiation; having broader knowledge of the context in which the negotiation is occurring; and possessing the skills to negotiate effectively. With regard to the first aspect, negotiators need to be well prepared, know what they want, and be able to command the supporting facts, arguments, logic, data and so on to support their case. This knowledge is gained through preparation before the negotiation begins so that the negotiator has mastered the essential facts and figures and developed the compelling arguments that will support their case. For example, those who have learned formal debating practices know that debaters build an elaborate database of information and construct arguments to be used to either support their basic proposition, or to effectively argue against and defuse the other's arguments. With regard to the second aspect, negotiators must also demonstrate knowledge of the context in which they negotiate. For example, an attorney who might be hired by an automobile labor union to negotiate on its behalf needs to demonstrate a complex understanding of the salary issues for which they are attempting to argue, but they must also understand the prevailing salary and benefits issues, packages and precedents within the automotive industry. Finally, a negotiator's trustworthiness is grounded in their demonstrated knowledge about 'how to negotiate'. This knowledge might be demonstrated in a variety of skills: how to structure an argument, present critical information, ask appropriate questions of the other side, make appropriate concessions, and create a viable agreement that can be implemented and that will benefit both parties. Perhaps surprisingly, if negotiators have a choice, they should choose to negotiate with an experienced negotiator as opposed to an inexperienced one. Inexperienced negotiators often behave erratically, do not understand the issues well, and either make concessions too quickly or irrationally hold out for unachievable goals, both of which may contribute to further declines in trust. Experienced negotiators, in contrast, are much more likely to be more efficient in the negotiating process, arrive at a mutually beneficial agreement quicker, and understand the importance of being able to implement that agreement more effectively (Ferrin et al., 2011; Shell, 2006; see also the review of negotiating experience and its impact on the parties in Lewicki et al., 2010). Trust is created in the other by exhibiting rational, transparent and predictable behavior – both in understanding the issues to be addressed, the context in which they occur and the broad dynamics of the negotiation process.

Perceived Benevolence

Demonstrating benevolence in negotiation relates to treating the other well in the process of negotiation. Benevolence relates more directly to actions that maintain or enhance the relationship dimension of trust between the parties. Treating the other with courtesy, respecting the other as a person and respecting the legitimacy of the others' views, actively listening to the other and refraining from using tactics that anger, upset or trick the other would be consistent with benevolent behavior. Finally, benevolence would be most clearly demonstrated by showing that one cares about the other negotiator's interests and is willing to help the other party meet those interests. While we expect a negotiator to primarily worry about achieving their own interests, a benevolent negotiator who recognizes the opportunity to create value and achieve a mutually beneficial agreement will understand how treating the other well benefits both the nature of the agreement as well as their own reputation and the parties' ability to work together in the future (c.f., Carnevale and Isen, 1986, for one example of the benefit of positive affect on negotiations).

Perceived Integrity

Relative to the dilemmas of trust and honesty we discussed at the beginning of this chapter, integrity may be the most important element of trustworthiness. Integrity refers to behaviors such as telling the truth, keeping promises and following through with commitments, and embracing a set of professional or ethical principles that leave little doubt of the negotiator's honest motivations and intentions. Again, these may be signaled to the other side by modeling integrity behaviors and by creating and cultivating a reputation for being committed to standards of professionalism (see Fulmer et al., 2009; McCornack and Levine, 1990; and Strudler, 1995, for related studies on deception and integrity in negotiation).

It should be noted that in attempting to communicate trustworthiness along all of these dimensions, whether the other *actually perceives* the focal negotiator as demonstrating ability, benevolence and/or integrity is key. Receiving feedback from the other or from observers as to whether one is actually conveying these intended messages in these behaviors is critical. People are often ignorant to the subtle verbal and nonverbal messages they may be communicating to the other, particularly when words and actions are inconsistent. A skilled negotiator asks for feedback and learns how they are being perceived, and as a result, can be much more successful in signaling and communicating the trust messages they want to send. Moreover, while there has been extensive research on these dimensions of trustworthiness, the more precise linkages between judgments of trust in the trustor, and specific dimensions of trustworthiness in the other, have yet to be empirically examined.

RESEARCH ON THE ROLE OF TRUST IN NEGOTIATION

Our search for current literature empirically examining trust and its relation to negotiation was broad, but, surprisingly, there is not as much empirical research as we expected. We have organized our review of this work by addressing the role trust plays in the experimental research design: trust as an independent, as a dependent, or as an intervening moderator/mediator variable.

Trust as an Independent Variable

As an independent variable, trust primarily affects three distinct components of negotiation: information sharing, turning points and reciprocity. First, as we noted earlier, the essence of negotiation is the use of information to persuade the other to 'see it our way'. The more information shared, the less time it takes for parties to arrive at an integrative solution (Butler, 1999). Trust enhances this information sharing – both as a way to help the other understand our negotiation position and interests, and to learn more about the other party's position and interests – and hence facilitates cooperation with the other (Irmer and Druckman, 2009).

Olekalns et al. (2007) examined the role of trust more carefully by breaking trust down into several sub-components – reliability, predictability, and empathy – and then examining the effects of these components on negotiator outcomes. The authors distinguish between absolute trust, which they operationally defined as the 'average calculus-based, knowledge-based, and identity-based trust for each party', and relative trust, which they find by dividing the absolute level of trust in one specific negotiator by the average absolute trust in all opponent parties (p. 533). The amount of power each of the parties had in the study was also manipulated. Relative trust proved to be a better predictor of negotiating party outcomes since it predicted the outcomes of all parties, whereas absolute trust only predicted the outcomes of the low-power party. Specifically turning to the components of trust, reliability was found to help the low-power parties, predictability affected the low- and moderate-power parties, and empathy helped the low- and high-power parties.

A turning point refers to 'events or activities that change the direction of negotiation' (Druckman and Olekalns, 2011, p. 1). Turning points can be positive or negative, procedurally-based or outcome-based, and studied in the context of measuring both cognitive and affective-based trust. Olekalns and Smith (2005), recognizing the importance of turning points as value-creation moments, find that high cognitive trust increases when parties experience positive procedural turning points. Those parties with high initial affective trust toward each other are able to recognize more positive characterization turning points; moreover, when a party recognizes positive characterization turning points, they report higher post-negotiation affective trust. When parties identify interests during turning points, they report high post-negotiation cognitive trust.

Reciprocity is an important component to study in negotiations. Pillutla et al. (2003) were interested in how parties in a negotiation calculate reciprocity. Using the Trust Game, they find that the less money the first player sends to the second player – that is, the less the first player trusts the second – the less the second sends back to the first. If, however, the first player sends a high amount of money to the second player – as a gesture of trust – the second player reciprocates with a high amount. But one needs to be wary of whether reciprocity really signals trust. Zhang and Han (2007) were able to manipulate reciprocation wariness in experimental subjects prior to a negotiation. Negotiators with high wariness are found to be more likely to try to maximize their own outcomes, but those with low wariness share more information during the negotiation and seek to maximize joint gains. Furthermore, when dyads negotiate, higher joint gains are realized by low-low wary dyads. The results confirm the importance of high trust leading to information sharing, but perhaps underestimate the vulnerability that this high trust may create without appropriate monitoring and a certain amount of wariness.

Trust as a Dependent Variable

We found a number of studies exploring trust as the dependent variable. The first study sheds more light on the characteristics of information sharing. If a negotiating dyad shares information with its opponent when an integrative solution is possible, the opponent trusts them more (Butler, 1995). Second, a number of studies examined how the medium (negotiation channel) of negotiation affected trust. Negotiators who only interacted through online engagement report both lower pre- and post-negotiation trust (Naquin and Paulson, 2003). Furthermore, the disclaimer (or lack thereof) at the end of an email when exchanged in an online negotiation makes a difference in recipient perceptions of trust (Kurtzberg and Naquin, 2010). Recipients of emails in online-only negotiations that included a disclaimer signature are less trusting of their opponent compared to recipients of emails with a non-disclaimer signature or no signature at all. Finally, untrustworthy behavior will, of course, decrease trust between negotiating parties, but adding deception to that untrustworthy behavior makes restoring trust impossible (Schweitzer et al., 2006). When trying to repair trust, a promise to change behavior after a trust violation is actually no more effective than just initiating a series of trustworthy behaviors. The authors hypothesize that this is because a promise is only words, and actions speak louder than words (see our discussion of 'cheap talk' later in this chapter).

Trust as an Intervening Moderator/Mediator Variable

Again, a number of studies were found in which trust moderated or mediated other relationships. For example, Liu and Wang (2010) studied the mediating potential of trust. They find that anger leads to distrust, which in turn leads a negotiator to have competitive (vs cooperative) goals including wanting 'to get a better deal' and 'to gain power over the other party'. Trust, on the other hand, leads a negotiator to have cooperative goals.

Finally, a few articles provide insight into how negotiators seek to understand others' trust. Gunia et al. (2011) argue that trust produces 'insight' – defined as 'discovering tradeoffs that give negotiators favorable terms on their highest priority issue(s) and incorporating those insights into agreements' (p. 777) – a dynamic similar to our description of knowledge-based trust. These authors combined the study of trust, insight and the impact of culture (Indian and American) with the ways parties engage each other in the negotiation process. Both cultures define trust similarly, but Americans are more willing to trust the negotiation process than Indians. Parties reporting low trust in their opponent tend to use substantiation and offers (S&O) as the primary communication tactics, arguing for a position and making offers to the other side, while parties reporting high trust were more likely to use question and answer (Q&A) tactics, gathering information from the other and sharing information in response to the others' questions. Indians were seen to use S&O more and Americans Q&A more. This negotiation strategy did account for cultural differences in joint gains, too.

Turning away from cultural differences, we see that being the trustor or trustee in a negotiation changes one's perspective of a negotiation (Malhotra, 2004). Trustors tend to focus on the risks they face and view the downside risk of loss as being more important, whereas trustees focus on the benefits they have been given and view the benefits as being more important. Despite the differing viewpoints, trustees are able to put themselves in the shoes of the trustor: trustees accurately predict the importance trustors place on risk. Trustors, however, underestimate the importance trustees place on benefits, or how those benefits will impact the trustee. Malhotra suggests that when viewing the 'trust question', the two parties may be asking different types of questions. Since the study was done in a sequential interaction game, trustors, who make the first move, might be asking, 'how might the other be making their decision' (in other words, a speculative decision based on what the trustee might do). Trustees who make the second move have concrete evidence on what the trustor has actually done. Thus, the trustor has the more difficult decision, since for him to understand the trustee's perspective, he has to anticipate how his initial move will be viewed in the eyes of the other. Such perspective-taking ability has been shown to be an individual difference (Batson et al., 1997), and the actual capacity to do so may be minimized if the parties have a more competitive orientation to each other.

HOW IS TRUST BROKEN IN NEGOTIATION?

Earlier, we described negotiation as the process of managing information in order to resolve conflicts of interest. One of the most common ways for trust to be broken is through one or both parties' use of deception, or in other words, an 'inappropriate' resolution of the dilemma of honesty. As summarized by Lewicki and Hanke (2012), negotiators use deception in order to enhance their power – that is, to gain some advantage by manipulating information to persuade the other party that something is true when in reality it is not. There are a number of ways that this can happen, and these 'tactics' vary in the degree to which they are viewed as appropriate based on ethical standards (does the tactic meet some standard of appropriate moral conduct), legal standards (what the law permits), or standards of 'prudence' (what might be smart to do based on their impact on the negotiation outcome and/or the relationship between the parties) (Missner, 1980). Lewicki and Hanke (2012) point out that most of the ethics issues in negotiation occur when parties disagree about what is the appropriate standard for truth telling in a negotiation. In other words, because negotiators differently confront the dilemma of honesty, many negotiators believe that it is necessary or appropriate to be less than fully honest and self-disclosing. Thus, they are more likely to use tactics that hide, distort or manipulate the truth and are perceived as viable within the normative expectations of negotiating give and take. Several authors (for example, Barry et al., 2000; Robinson et al., 2000) have attempted to classify these tactics, and most agree that there are at least six types of negotiation tactics that are less than completely honest:

- traditionally competitive bargaining (not disclosing your walkaway, making an inflated opening offer);
- emotional manipulation (faking anger, fear, disappointment, elation, satisfaction);
- misrepresentation (distorting information or negotiation events in describing them to others);

42   *Handbook of advances in trust research*

- misrepresentation to others' networks (corrupting your opponent's reputation);
- inappropriate information gathering (bribery, infiltration, spying and so on); and
- bluffing (insincere threats or promises).

As noted by these researchers, because manipulation of information can be an effective negotiating tactic, many negotiators see some of these tactics as ethically and prudently appropriate – particularly the first two categories (traditional competitive bargaining and emotional manipulation) – even though they are less than fully honest. In contrast, the other four tactics are generally seen as ethically (but perhaps not prudently) inappropriate. Thus, there is informal consensus among many negotiators that it is acceptable to 'draw a line' between appropriate dishonest tactics and inappropriate dishonest tactics. And, not unsurprisingly, the willingness to use those tactics varies considerably based on personality and situational variables. The type of lies told (Carson et al., 1982), the negotiator's need for power (Shapiro and Bies, 1994), the expectations of the other party's trustworthiness (Graebner, 2009), the type of the negotiation problems (for example, distributive vs integrative), the situational norms governing the negotiation context (in other words, a negotiation with a used car dealer vs negotiation with a long-term business partner) (O'Connor and Carnevale, 1997) and the magnitude of incentives at stake (Tenbrunsel, 1998) can all affect the willingness and likelihood of using deceptive tactics in a negotiation (see also Lewicki et al., 2010; Lewicki and Hanke, 2012, for more complete reviews).

The net effects of using deceptive tactics in negotiation can have short-term and long-term consequences. In the short term, the research appears to show that if negotiators use deception carefully and work to avoid detection, significant short-term rewards can be gained. A number of studies have shown that negotiators who use deception achieve better outcomes than their opponents: these tactics include lies by omitting information or by making explicitly false statements (Schweitzer and Croson, 1999) and using emotional manipulation tactics (Fulmer et al., 2009). Better outcomes could also be achieved through deception when there were high stakes to be achieved and the negotiator knew that the other party had a weak alterative if a deal was not met (Boles et al., 2000). Not unsurprisingly, however, if this deception is not done carefully or is detected, the long-term consequences are far less positive to the negotiators' future. Research demonstrated that when one party discovers that the other has been deceptive, the deceived negotiator is far more likely to act retributively in an attempt to punish the other. Both negotiators tended to use deception in the future, and the consequences were mutually destructive in terms of joint payoff (Boles et al., 2000; Shapiro and Bies, 1994). In addition, discovering that a party is using deceptive tactics also has consequences for a negotiator's reputation. Negotiators who used deception were rated by their opponents as less trustworthy and less trustful, and the opponents were much less willing to work with that other party in the future (Boles et al., 2000; Tinsley et al., 2002). Thus, the short- and long-term consequences of using deception are much like those predicted by studies of simple games like Prisoner's Dilemma; while short-term defection can lead to enhanced payoffs, the long-term consequences are a significant decline in trust and poor individual and joint gain in the future.

REPAIRING TRUST IN NEGOTIATION

There are only a few research studies on actual trust repair in a negotiation context, which we review below, but it should be noted that there is a growing research literature on broader strategies of trust repair. Several preconditions are important to consider if trust repair is to occur. First, trust repair is not just the responsibility of the trust violator; it is a mutual, multistage process! Knowing this, the person committing the violation must become aware that trust has been violated. This may occur by virtue of detecting changes in the other's disposition, or through direct feedback from the other or from third parties. Then, the violator will have to actively engage in actions to address the violation. Finally, the 'victim' – the person whose trust has been violated – must be willing to accept the repair initiatives in a way that allows the parties to constructively complete the deal. Also, if the parties intend or expect to negotiate with each other in the future then the repair efforts must also create the groundwork for productive future, deliberations. As Lewicki and Polin (2012) note:

> For full repair to occur, both parties must be willing to invest time and energy in the repair process, perceive that the short and long term benefits of repair outweigh the costs, and recognize that the benefits to be derived from repair are preferable to terminating the relationship and attempting to have one's needs met elsewhere. (Lewicki and Polin, 2012, p. 129)[2]

Moreover, efforts to repair trust should focus on the substantive nature of the trust violation and what was damaged by that violation. That is, when we understand the function that trust serves in a particular negotiation context, we can better understand the nature of the damage done by a trust violation, and hence understand what kind of actions might be necessary to repair that trust. One way to categorize violations is to distinguish between those violations that undermine the positive (trustworthy) *intent* of the negotiator from others that undermine the positive (trustworthy) *impact* of the violation. In the former case, in the victim's mind, the trust violation calls into question whether the negotiator is honest, is telling the truth, and intends to keep promises or commitments made during the negotiation. Thus, trust repair efforts may need to focus on restoring the victim's perception of the actor as an honest and credible person. In the latter case, the victim focuses more on the impact of the trust violation, in terms of tangible, economic losses that may have been suffered as a result of the violation. In this case, trust repair efforts may need to focus on restoring the tangible or economic damage caused by the trust violation, that is, acts of restitution for direct losses suffered as a result of the violation (Tomlinson et al., 2012). For example, in negotiation, lies, deceptions, and false promises are often effective because the victim believes these statements to be true, and thus is led astray as the negotiator gains a short-term power advantage by communicating misleading information. In contrast, failures to keep agreements and honor commitments often lead to a direct loss of tangible resources or steer the victim to pursue alternatives that are less beneficial. Admittedly, many trust breaches may be seen as violations of both intent and impact, and as we will suggest, the required 'remedy' may involve addressing both concerns.

Consistent with this view, the emerging trust repair literature has grouped trust repair strategies into three major approaches. First, there are verbal accounts, in which words and emotional expression are employed to attempt to mitigate the consequences of the violation. These approaches largely address efforts to manage perceptions of intent. Second, a violator may engage in the payment of reparations – that is, specific, tangible resources such as money or other forms of compensation to 'repay' or benefit the victim for tangible losses that may have occurred as a result of the violation. These approaches largely address efforts to manage the consequences of impact. Finally, the parties may engage in 'structural solutions', or ways to change the structure of the interaction between the parties so as to minimize the likelihood that future trust violations can occur. Rules, contracts, referees and monitoring systems are all formalized mechanisms for either regulating the process by which parties negotiate, limiting undesirable behaviors and/or specifying consequences and punishments for those undesirable behaviors. Dirks et al. (2011) identify these approaches as 'situational' strategies of trust repair, providing assurance of future trustworthy behavior, as compared to 'dispositional' strategies (accounts and reparations), which seek to repair the effects and consequences of the trust violation. Most of this research has not been conducted in specific negotiating contexts, but has been studied more broadly in a variety of interpersonal exchanges that would readily apply to negotiation dynamics.

Verbal Accounts

In its most general form, a verbal account occurs when a trust violator attempts to account for, or explain, some event that the victim has identified as a violation of trust. In the negotiation context, this might be a mis-statement, a lie, an unkept promise, or some form of injustice. If a violator fails to see the evidence that any mis-statement or injustice has occurred, there is no perceived rationale for a verbal account. It may seem apparent that a verbal account is a natural reaction when a party becomes aware of the negative effect that their actions have on another party. Thus, Tomlinson et al. (2004) found that a simple offer of apology was more effective than offering no apology. Moreover, a victim was more likely to accept an apology that made an internal attribution as opposed to one claiming external causes, that is, 'It was my fault' vs 'I couldn't help it'. Thomas and Millar (2008) note that a failure to apologize leads to more anger when expectations in a relationship are not met, an effect that increases when the recipient of the violation is low in need-for-cognition.

As Kramer and Lewicki (2010) explain, verbal accounts made in response to trust breaches are called by many names in literature: accounts, recounts, explanations, justifications, apologies, to name a few. Upon reviewing the similarities among these different types of verbal accounts, these authors suggest two main categories: explanations and apologies. More recently, Lewicki and Polin (2012) proposed that an explanation is not different from an apology, but is one integral *component* of an effective apology. In this work, they analyze a number of contemporary, high-profile apologies, and build from both academic and non-academic work on apologies to suggest six components necessary for an effective apology: an expression of regret for the offense, an explanation of why the violation occurred, an acknowledgement of responsibility for causing the action, a declaration of repentance, an offer of repair and a request of forgiveness. Future research is directed at determining which of these components, singly or in combination, is more critical to judging an apology as fully effective.

Effectiveness of an apology is more than just its verbal components. Frantz and Bennigson (2005) argue that timing matters: an earlier apology may reflect a lack of thought and reflection on the trust violation and reduce its impact. In their study, they find that recipients of trust violations feel more satisfaction when they receive an apology some time after the violation, once the violator has had time to hear and understand the victim's feelings. In contrast, Tomlinson et al. (2004) find that the more immediately an apology occurs after a violation is recognized, the more effective it is in the victim's willingness to repair trust. Clearly more research is needed here to differentiate when an immediate action vs a delayed action is needed. For negotiation specifically, the characteristic time constraints found in most negotiations may require apologies to occur sooner rather than later, as there may not be a 'later' in short negotiations.

Research has also shown that an apology may not always be the most effective verbal account after a supposed trust violation has occurred. Earlier in this chapter we discussed the differences among the ability, benevolence and integrity dimensions of trustworthiness. Depending on the dimension of trustworthiness on which a party fails to meet expectations, different types of responses may be needed. Kim et al. (2004) examined the impact of apologies on restoring trust after ability (competency)-based trust violations and integrity-based violations. It was found that when an ability-based violation occurred, an apology was more effective – specifically a response that admitted responsibility, expressed regret and affirmed that the violation would not occur again in the future. In contrast, when an integrity-based violation occurred, the researchers found that a denial of culpability was more effective in repairing trust, as long as there was not irrefutable proof that the party was indeed responsible for the violation. The authors explained this result by suggesting that failures due to perceived 'incompetence' (breakdowns in ability) could be rectified by apologies and explanations that implied that conditions leading up to the breakdown were temporary and easily fixable. In contrast, failures due to perceived breakdowns in integrity were not judged by victims to be easily fixable because weak character is not something that can be quickly 'repaired'. As a result, after an integrity violation, the violator was actually better off denying the violation – if it could be done credibly – than by acknowledging a failure in character that was less easily repaired.

Turning to negotiations in particular, the timing of an apology, coupled with the type of breach, could dictate whether the victim continues to negotiate or walks away from the table altogether. For example, consider the various forms of lying that might occur in a negotiation. A negotiator lies and the victim quickly identifies the statement as a lie and challenges the negotiator on the accuracy of the statement. If the negotiator quickly apologizes and attempts to explain the lie as 'an erroneous statement' or a 'miscommunication' or a 'brief mental lapse', the victim may be willing to forgive the event and continue negotiations. If the lie remains unchallenged for some period of time, 'calling' the lie at some future point may be much more difficult for the violator to explain or justify, and the apology may be seen as less credible even if the explanation is sincere. In contrast, if the lie is challenged and it is denied, then the victim must decide whether, in fact, a 'lie' has really occurred. Such proof may be difficult to obtain. When proof is difficult to obtain and the liar knows it, denial may indeed be the best approach; when proof is easier to obtain or the victim is persistent in efforts at verification, denials become less credible and alternative explanations or actions must occur for any trust to be sustained.

Of course, a party who has violated trust may choose to give no verbal account whatsoever, consciously choosing silence instead. They may believe that the trust will not be discovered if they do not break silence, or they may think that they have no obligation to make a statement (Ferrin et al., 2007). When it comes to negotiations, therefore, the pros and cons of making an apology or staying silent must be weighed. Did the other negotiator detect the deception? Was the type of deception one that is more likely to be seen as 'acceptable' or 'unacceptable'? Can the deception be explained as a breakdown in 'competence' and not a breakdown in 'integrity'? Effective deception, and repairing its detection, is not an easy business, and more research needs to be done in this area. And as we noted, while there is a growing literature on the impact and effectiveness of various kinds of verbal statements in repairing trust, little has actually been done in negotiation contexts, and much remains to be done to understand the nature of the violation, the structure of the verbal account and its impact on short- and long-term trust in the negotiation.

Reparations

While apologies are largely focused on correcting the victim's perception of the intent of the violation, some authors have argued that explanations, apologies and other verbal accounts are no more than 'cheap talk' (Farrell and Rabin, 1996). Those who espouse this view dominantly believe that verbal accounts are no more than easy (and often insincere) words, and that only full compensation for tangible losses suffered as a result of the trust violation is likely to be effective. Several studies (for example, Bottom et. al. 2002; Gibson et al., 1999) have examined the role of reparative compensation, combined with or compared against verbal apologies, in repairing trust. While 'cheap talk' (apologies) often enhanced the value of reparations/penance, a financial offer (penance) was clearly necessary for effective trust repair. These authors also demonstrated that the magnitude of the offered penance is less critical than the offer itself; offers of small amounts of compensation were often as important as large amounts, and allowing the victim to specify the amount and way that the compensation will be repaid also enhanced the effect. Further studies on the effects of reparations have recently emerged. Desmet et al. (2011a) examined how reparative compensation interacted with the perceived intent of the violator. They found that reparative compensation can be effective, and often most effective when the amount of compensation is slightly larger than the compensation lost through the violation. This result was completely erased, however, if the victim discovered that the violation came about as a result of the violator's deceptive behavior. Thus, in this study, intent 'trumped' impact in undermining that repair, at least when compensation was designed to restore the damage of impact. Other studies by these authors revealed that larger compensations are only a step in repairing trust when offered voluntarily (Desmet et al., 2010), taking into consideration a victim's individual difference of tendency to forgive (Desmet et al., 2011b).

Structural Arrangements

A third way that trust can be repaired is through the creation of 'structural arrangements' that re-engineer the situation in order to minimize the likelihood that future trust violations can occur. Thus, rather than focus attention on 'rebuilding' trust after a violation has occurred (through some combination of verbal accounts and reparations), new structural arrangements can minimize the likelihood that future violations can occur. Moreover, if the parties expect that a trust violation is possible or likely, these structural arrangements can be set up in anticipation of these possible violations. For example, Sitkin and Roth (1993) proposed that a variety of 'legalistic remedies' (policies, procedures, contracts, rules, monitoring systems) can be introduced to regulate dishonest, deceptive and 'trust violating' behaviors. Moreover, these new structural guidelines can be strengthened through enforcement mechanisms such as fines, penalties, or loss of privileges to assure that they are respected and adhered to. A similar form of enforcement mechanism is proposed by Nakayachi and Watabe (2005) in the form of 'hostage posting', such as a security deposit, which is lost to the negotiator if a violation is detected. Recent research by Dirks et al. (2011) has shown that both reparations and regulation can be effective in repairing trust, assuming that the victim interpreted these actions as signaling intended penance by the violator. Similarly, negotiators frequently invite third parties into a dispute in order to create and enforce rules, facilitate 'honest' dialogue, and monitor agreements in order to stabilize trust. Nevertheless, more work remains to be done in understanding the effect of various types of structural arrangements in minimizing trust, particularly at the organizational level, and Gillespie and Dietz

(2009) have proposed a useful theoretical framework for initiating these studies.

SUMMARY AND IMPLICATIONS

In this chapter we have discussed the important role that trust plays in a negotiation process. We first argued that negotiation is fundamentally about the transmission of information in order to influence the other party toward some preferred outcome, and that trust is central to this information transmission process. Without trust, parties would have to consistently engage in processes of certifying the truthfulness of the information they are sending, and verifying the truthfulness of the information being transmitted by the other. While such certification and verification may indeed be important to do before deals are formally ratified, the efficiency of information transmission and affirmation is considerably aided by strong mutual trust. Second, we reviewed the basic body of research that has been performed on trust in the negotiation context. There appears to be only a small amount of research that has actually been done on the role of trust in negotiation – perhaps because its importance is almost self-evident, and because the work that has been done has affirmed its critical role. We also examined qualities of trustworthiness (as viewed by the trustor), and ways that one's image of trustworthiness can be enhanced for negotiation purposes. Finally, we discussed how trust can be broken during negotiation, and the key role of trust repair processes. Trust is broken either because the truth is manipulated through lies, exaggerations and other distortions of the truth, and/or because negotiators do not follow through by keeping the promises and commitments they make. Trust repair strategies, therefore, can focus on either 'intent' or 'impact'. An intent strategy is an effort by the violator to convince the victim that the violator did not 'intend' to break the trust, and to convince the victim that the violator is still a good, honest person. Explanations, accounts and apologies are tools that the violator often uses to repair trust grounded in intent. In contrast, an impact strategy is used by the violator to compensate the victim for actual losses that may have been incurred as a result of the broken trust. Reparations and financial remuneration are the tactics often used to repair violations of impact. We also examined the role of 'structural arrangements' to repair trust, in which laws, rules, regulations, contracts and monitoring/enforcement systems are put into place to both minimize trust violations and to penalize the violator if and when such violations occur.

A modest agenda for future work remains. Here are some of the areas in which we believe future theory and research could be done. In defining this work, we will discuss two broad approaches: ways that negotiation dynamics could be more thoroughly explored to understand the role of trust, and ways that trust research could be enhanced to understand how it can be applied to negotiation practice.

First, with regard to the negotiation process, future work could explore the role that trust plays in distributive as opposed to integrative processes. If negotiators anticipate a distributive negotiation process, they clearly expect less trust and are likely to express less trust than if negotiators anticipate an integrative process. Moreover, trust violations may be likely to be experienced as greater when dishonest behavior violates the trust in an integrative process, and hence may be far more difficult to repair than when the trust violation occurred in a distributive process. In addition, a variety of other contextual variables may impact trust maintenance and violation: power differences between the parties, the power of strong vs weak BATNAs (best alternatives to negotiated agreements) for the negotiating parties, the amount and kind of regulatory structure in which the negotiation takes place, whether negotiation takes place between agents or directly between the principals, and cultural differences between the parties (c.f., Saunders et al., 2010 for emerging research on the impact of culture on trust across a variety of contexts).

Second, with regard to the study of trust, the stream of work is newer, trust is more difficult to measure and calibrate over time, and hence the accumulated body of knowledge is broader but more piecemeal. We suggest three future avenues of work here. There are numerous issues with regard to the measurement of trust and its calibration over time. Much of the research cited here has measured trust after a negotiation has been completed, or, more rarely, before and after a key event in a negotiation process. Yet as we have noted elsewhere (Dirks et al., 2009; Lewicki and Brinsfield, 2011), a complete understanding of trust and its role in negotiation would require researchers to be able to reliably measure trust at the outset of a negotiation process (in other words, 'presumptive trust', c.f., Kramer and Lewicki, 2010), trust changes as various moves and turns in the negotiation, and the resultant level of trust after a negotiation has been completed. Such measures become more critical in determining the immediate effects of trust violations and trust repair efforts. This measurement work will require the ability to more reliably calibrate trust at various points without being concerned about difficulties of repeated methods and common method variance in grounding these calibrations.

In addition, several authors (for example, Lewicki et al., 1998) have proposed that a full understanding of trust dynamics requires effectively conceptualizing and measuring trust and distrust as independent phenomena. Thus, for example, structural solutions to the repair of trust may limit and minimize the amount of distrust, but may not significantly enhance trust. Future work may also consider distrust as an equally viable and parallel construct and explore the interchange of trust and distrust as negotiation dynamics ebb and flow. Thus, the message to negotiators may not be 'build strong trust', but instead, 'build verifiable trust, and periodically implement the verification process'.

Finally, continued work should occur on trust repair in negotiation. Are there situations where trust cannot be repaired and yet productive negotiations can occur? Is there a critical time frame during which trust violations can be repaired, and after which trust repair is no longer possible? How effectively does trust repair work when the parties have differential power? Finally, as we noted earlier, trust dynamics (and repair) may be different within the context of distributive vs integrative negotiation processes. If trust violations are more 'expected' in a distributive process by virtue of the anticipation of some dishonesty, does this affect the impact and magnitude of various repair processes?

These are but a few of the many research questions that can still be asked about the role of trust in negotiation. Considerable work has been done, but much work remains to shed greater light on this important application of trust.

NOTES

1. We will also explore the nature of trustworthiness. See Colquitt et al. (2007) for an elaboration of the complex relationship between trust and trustworthiness.
2. See also Lewicki and Bunker (1996) for an elaboration of steps in a trust repair process, and Kim et al. (2009) for an elaboration of a dynamic bilateral conceptualization of the trust repair process.

REFERENCES

Barry, B., I.S. Fulmer and A. Long (2000), 'Ethically marginal bargaining tactics: sanction, efficacy, and performance', presented at a meeting of the Academy of Management, Toronto.
Batson, D., S. Early and G. Salvarani (1997), 'Perspective taking: imagining how another feels versus imagining how you would feel', *Personality and Social Psychology Bulletin*, **23**(7), 751–8.
Boles, T.L., R.T.A. Croson and J.K. Murnighan (2000), 'Deception and retribution in repeated ultimatum bargaining', *Organizational Behavior and Human Decision Processes*, **83**, 235–59.
Bottom, W., K. Gibson, S. Daniels and J.K. Murnighan (2002), 'When talk is not cheap:

substantive penance and expressions of intent in the reestablishment of cooperation', *Organizational Science*, **13**(5), 497–513.

Butler, J.K. (1995), 'Behaviors, trust, and goal achievement in a win-win negotiating role play', *Group and Organization Management*, **20**(4), 486–501.

Butler, J.K. (1999), 'Trust expectations, information sharing, climate of trust, and negotiation effectiveness and efficiency', *Group and Organization Management*, **24**(2), 217–38.

Carnevale, P.J.D. and A.M. Isen (1986), 'The influence of positive affect and visual access on the discovery of integrative solutions in bilateral negotiation', *Organizational Behavior and Human Decision Processes*, **37**(1), 1–13.

Carson, T.L., R.E. Wokutch and K.F. Murrmann (1982), 'Bluffing in labor negotiations: legal and ethical issues', *Journal of Business Ethics*, **1**(1), 13–22.

Colquitt, J.A., B.A. Scott and J.A. LePine (2007), 'Trust, trustworthiness and trust propensity: a meta-analytic test of their unique relationships with risk taking and job performance', *Journal of Applied Psychology*, **92**(4), 909–1027.

Desmet, P.T.M., D. De Cremer and E. van Dijk (2010), 'On the psychology of financial compensations to restore fairness transgressions: when intentions determine value', *Journal of Business Ethics*, **95**(1), 105–15.

Desmet, P.T.M., D. De Cremer and E. van Dijk (2011a), 'In money we trust? The use of financial compensations to repair trust in the aftermath of distributive harm', *Organizational Behavior and Human Decision Processes*, **114**(2), 75–86.

Desmet, P.T.M., D. De Cremer and E. van Dijk (2011b), 'Trust recovery following voluntary or forced financial compensations in the trust game: The role of forgiveness', *Personality and Individual Differences*, **51**(3), 267–73.

Deutsch, M. (1949), 'Trust and suspicion', *Journal of Conflict Resolution*, **2**(4), 265–79.

Dirks, K., R.J. Lewicki and A. Zaheer (2009), 'Repairing relationships within and between organizations: building a conceptual foundation', *Academy of Management Review*, **34**(1), 68–84.

Dirks, K.T., P.H. Kim, D.L. Ferrin and C. Cooper (2011), 'Understanding the effects of substantive responses on trust following a transgression', *Organizational Behavior and Human Decision Processes*, **114**(2), 87–103.

Druckman, D. and M. Olekalns (2011), 'Turning points in negotiation', *Negotiation and Conflict Management*, **4**(1), 1–7.

Farrell, J. and M. Rabin (1996), 'Cheap talk', *Journal of Economical Perspectives*, **10**(3), 103–18.

Ferrin, D.L., M.C. Bligh and J.C. Kohles (2007), 'Can I trust you to trust me? A theory of trust, monitoring, and cooperation in interpersonal and intergroup relationships', *Group and Organization Management*, **32**(4), 465–99.

Ferrin, D.L., D.T. Kong and K.T. Dirks (2011), 'Trust building, diagnosis and repair in the context of negotiation', in M. Benoliel (ed.), *Negotiation Excellence: Successful Deal Making*, Singapore: World Scientific Publishers.

Ferrin, D.L., P.H. Kim, C.D. Cooper and K.T. Dirks (2007), 'Silence speaks volumes: the effectiveness of reticence in comparison to apology and denial for responding to integrity- and competence-based trust violations', *Journal of Applied Psychology*, **92**(4), 893–908.

Frantz, C.M. and C. Bennigson (2005), 'Better late than early: the influence of timing on apology effectiveness', *Journal of Experimental Social Psychology*, **41**(2), 201–7.

Fulmer, I.S., B. Barry and D.A. Long (2009), 'Lying and smiling: informational and emotional deception in negotiation', *Journal of Business Ethics*, **88**(4), 691–709.

Gibson, K., W.P. Bottom and J.K. Murnighan (1999), 'Once bitten: defection and reconciliation in a cooperative enterprise', *Business Ethics Quarterly*, **9**(1), 69–86.

Gillespie, N. and G. Dietz (2009), 'Trust repair after an organization-level failure', *Academy of Management Review*, **34**(1), 127–45.

Graebner, M.E. (2009), 'Caveat venditor: trust asymmetries in acquisitions of entrepreneurial firms', *Academy of Management Journal*, **52**(3), 435–72.

Gunia, B.C., J.M. Brett, A.K. Nandkeolyar and D. Kamdar (2011), 'Paying a price: culture, trust, and negotiation consequences', *Journal of Applied Psychology*, **96**(4), 774–89.

Irmer, C. and D. Druckman (2009), 'Explaining negotiation outcomes: process or context?', *Negotiation and Conflict Management Research*, **2**(3), 209–35.
Kelley, H.H. (1966), 'A classroom study of the dilemmas in interpersonal negotiation', in K. Archibald (ed.), *Strategic Interaction and Conflict: Original Papers and Discussion*, Berkeley, CA: Institute of International Studies, pp. 49–73.
Kim, P.H., K.T. Dirks and C.D. Cooper (2009), 'The repair of trust: a dynamic bilateral perspective and multilevel conceptualization', *Academy of Management Review*, **34**(3), 401–22.
Kim, P.H., D.L. Ferrin, C.D. Cooper and K.T. Dirks (2004), 'Removing the shadow of suspicion: the effects of apology versus denial for repairing competence- versus integrity-based trust violations', *Journal of Applied Psychology*, **89**(1), 104–18.
Kramer, R.M. and R.J. Lewicki (2010), 'Repairing and enhancing trust: approaches to reducing organizational trust deficits', *Academy of Management Annals*, **4**(1), 245–77.
Kurtzberg, T.R. and C.E. Naquin (2010), 'Electronic signatures and interpersonal trustworthiness in online negotiations', *Negotiation and Conflict Management Research*, **3**(1), 49–63.
Lewicki, R. and C. Brinsfield (2011), 'Trust research: measures of trusting beliefs and behaviors', in F. Lyon, G. Möllering, M. Saunders and T. Hatzakis (eds), *Handbook of Research Methods on Trust*, Cambridge, UK: Cambridge University Press.
Lewicki, R.J. and B.B. Bunker (1995), 'Trust in relationships: a model of trust development and decline', in B.B. Bunker and J.Z. Rubin (eds), *Conflict, Cooperation and Justice: A Tribute Volume to Morton Deutsch*, San Francisco: Jossey-Bass, pp. 133–73.
Lewicki, R.J. and Bunker, B.B. (1996), 'Trust in relationships: a model of trust development and decline', in R. Kramer and T. Tyler (eds), *Trust in Organizations*, Newbury Park, CA: Sage Publications, pp. 114–39.
Lewicki, R.J. and R. Hanke (2012), 'Once fooled, shame on you! Twice fooled, shame on me! What deception does to deceivers and victims: implications for negotiators in situations where ethicality is unclear', in B. Goldman and D. Shapiro (eds), *The Psychology of Negotiations for the 21st Century*, Oxford: Routledge Press.
Lewicki, R.J. and B. Polin (2012), 'The art of the apology: the structure and effectiveness of apologies in trust repair', in R. Kramer and T. Pittinsky (eds), *Restoring Trust: Challenges and Prospects*, Oxford: Oxford University Press.
Lewicki, R.J. and M. Stevenson (1998), 'Trust development in negotiation: proposed actions and a research agenda', *Journal of Business and Professional Ethics*, **16**(1–3), 99–132.
Lewicki, R.J., B. Barry and D. Saunders (2010), *Negotiation*, 6th edition, Burr Ridge, IL: McGraw-Hill Irwin.
Lewicki, R.J., D.J. McAllister and R.J. Bies (1998), 'Trust and distrust: new relationships and realities', *Academy of Management Review*, **23**(3), 438–58.
Liu, M. and C. Wang (2010), 'Explaining the influence of anger and compassion on negotiators' interaction goals: an assessment of trust and distrust as two distinct mediators', *Communication Research*, **37**(4), 443–72.
Malhotra, D. (2004), 'Trust and reciprocity decisions: the differing perspectives of trustors and trusted parties', *Organizational Behavior and Human Decision Processes*, **94**(2), 61–73.
Malhotra, D. and J.K. Murnighan (2002), 'The effects of contracts on interpersonal trust', *Administrative Science Quarterly*, **47**(3), 534–59.
Mayer, R.C., J.H. Davis and F.D. Schoorman (1995), 'An integrative model of organizational trust', *Academy of Management Review*, **20**(3), 709–34.
McCornack, S.A. and T.R. Levine (1990), 'When lies are uncovered: emotional and relational outcomes of discovered deception', *Communication Monographs*, **57**(2), 119–38.
Missner, M. (1980), *Ethics of the Business System*, Sherman Oaks, CA: Alfred Publishing Company.
Nakayachi, K. and M. Watabe (2005), 'Repairing trustworthiness after adverse events: the signaling effects of voluntary "hostage posting" on trust', *Organizational Behavior and Human Decision Processes*, **97**(1), 1–17.

Naquin, C.E. and G.D. Paulson (2003), 'Online bargaining and interpersonal trust', *Journal of Applied Psychology*, **88**(1), 113–20.

O'Connor, K.M. and P.J. Carnevale (1997), 'A nasty but effective negotiation strategy: misrepresentation of a common-value issue', *Personality and Social Psychology Bulletin*, **23**(5), 504–15.

Olekalns, M. and P.L. Smith (2005), 'Moments in time: metacognition, trust, and outcomes in dyadic negotiations', *Journal of Personality and Social Psychology*, **31**(12), 1696–707.

Olekalns, M., F. Lau and P.L. Smith (2007), 'Resolving the empty core: trust as a determinant of outcomes in three-party negotiations', *Group Decision and Negotiation*, **16**(6), 527–38.

Pillutla, M.M., D. Malhotra and J.K. Murnighan (2003), 'Attributions of trust and the calculus of reciprocity', *Journal of Experimental Social Psychology*, **39**(5), 448–55.

Robinson, R., R.J. Lewicki and E. Donahue (2000), 'Extending and testing a five factor model of ethical and unethical bargaining tactics: the SINS scale', *Journal of Organizational Behavior*, **21**(6), 649–64.

Rousseau, D.M., S.B. Sitkin, R.S. Burt and C. Camerer (1998), 'Not so different after all: a cross-discipline view of trust', *Academy of Management Review*, **23**(3), 393–404.

Saunders, M.N.K., D. Skinner, G. Dietz, N. Gillespie and R.J. Lewicki (eds) (2010), *Organizational Trust: A Cultural Perspective*, Cambridge, UK: Cambridge University Press.

Schweitzer, M.E. and R. Croson (1999), 'Curtailing deception: the impact of direct questions on lies and omissions', *International Journal of Conflict Management*, **10**(3), 225–48.

Schweitzer, M.E., J.C. Hershey and E.T. Bradlow (2006), 'Promises and lies: restoring violated trust', *Organizational Behavioral and Human Decision Processes*, **101**(1), 1–19.

Shapiro, D.L. and R. Bies (1994), 'Threats, bluffs and disclaimers in negotiations', *Organizational Behavior and Human Decision Processes*, **60**(1), 14–35.

Shapiro, D.L., B.H. Sheppard and L. Cheraskin (1992), 'Business on a handshake', *Negotiation Journal*, **8**(4), 365–77.

Shell, R. (2006), *Bargaining for Advantage*, revised edition, New York: Penguin Books.

Sitkin, S. and A. Roth (1993), 'Explaining the limited effectiveness of legalistic "remedies" for trust/distrust', *Organization Science*, **4**(3), 367–92.

Strudler, A. (1995), 'On the ethics of deception in negotiation', *Business Ethics Quarterly*, **5**(4), 805–22.

Tenbrunsel, A.E. (1998), 'Misrepresentation and expectations of misrepresentation in an ethical dilemma: the role of incentives and temptation', *Academy of Management Journal*, **41**(3), 330–39.

Thomas, R.L. and M.G. Millar (2008), 'The impact of failing to give an apology and the need-for-cognition on anger', *Current Psychology*, **27**(2), 126–34.

Tinsley, C.H., K.M. O'Connor and B.A. Sullivan (2002), 'Tough guys finish last: the perils of a distributive reputation', *Organizational Behavior and Human Decision Processes*, **88**(2), 621–42.

Tomlinson, E.C., B.R. Dineen and R.J. Lewicki (2004), 'The road to reconciliation: antecedents of victim willingness to reconcile following a broken promise', *Journal of Management*, **30**(2), 165–87.

Tomlinson, E.C., R.J. Lewicki and S. Wang (2012), 'Trust therapy: the effects of impact and intent strategies on trust repair', in L.L. Neider and C. Schreisheim, *Research in Management*, Charlotte, NC: Information Age Publishers.

Zhang, Z. and Y. Han (2007), 'The effects of reciprocation wariness on negotiation behavior and outcomes', *Group Decision and Negotiation*, **16**(6), 507–25.

PART II

TRUST AND GOVERNANCE: CONTROL, CONTRACT, INNOVATION

3. Trust and control: the role of intrinsic motivation
Antoinette Weibel and Frédérique Six

INTRODUCTION

Simon (1991) argued that the quality and success of an organization depends to a high degree on how the problem of the organizational commons is handled. The problem of the commons depicts a situation where benefits are jointly gained and shared but costs are borne individually. As no employee can be excluded from the commons some amount of free-riding is likely to occur (Hardin, 1968). Miller (1992) called this cooperation problem the core of the managerial task. The cooperation problem stems from organizational members having different and often conflicting goals, and these individual goals often conflict with the goals of the organization. This situation has been analysed in more general terms in the literature on social dilemmas (for an overview see Dawes, 1980; Brewer and Kramer, 1986; Kollock, 1998). A social dilemma situation arises if the actions of self-interested individuals do not lead to socially desirable outcomes. Because self-interested actions have been proposed to be a fundamental aspect of motivation and behaviour, social dilemmas present a serious problem to the organization of collective action in groups and organizations (Tyler and Degoey, 1996).

On a very general level there are two ways to handle a social dilemma: a centralized 'control' solution and a decentralized 'motivation and trust' solution. The first solution is to establish an overarching hierarchy, a Leviathan (Hobbes, 1909) or a central agent (Alchian and Demsetz, 1972) who is entitled to measure, monitor and reward subordinates for their collective action. Thus, cooperation in this first solution is essentially secured by establishing a central authority with far-reaching control rights (Van Vugt, 2002). Hierarchical control is thought to secure cooperative efforts by means of extrinsic motivation: common goals are defined, goal attainment is monitored and employees' compliance is rewarded or sanctioned depending on their compliance. There are, however, drawbacks to this solution. Hierarchical control needs some form of compliance. Laboratory experiments on social dilemmas clearly show that participants are not easily convinced to relinquish their own autonomy in the situation to a third party (Van Vugt, 2002). Furthermore, field evidence demonstrates that compliance is more likely to take place if hierarchical control is perceived to be legitimate (Tyler, 2006; Bijlsma-Frankema and Costa, 2010). In addition, controlling – especially if all aspects of the cooperation need to be controlled – is costly. Costs might be low for simple tasks, but more complex tasks and interdependent team production create high costs (Frost et al., 2010). Even worse some cooperative efforts might not be controllable at all (Eisenhardt, 1985).

Second, social dilemma research has focused on developing an understanding of the conditions under which individuals will voluntarily cooperate because they are self-motivated to do so (for example, De Cremer and Van Vugt, 1999). Simon (1991) argued that many workers go voluntarily beyond commands, because doing the job well 'is not mainly a matter of responding to commands, but is much more a matter of taking initiative to advance organizational objectives' (Simon, 1991, p. 32). Thus, many employees seem to be motivated by something other than narrow material self-interest. These employees are intrinsically motivated to contribute to the corporate commons through their organizational identification or through their intrinsic involvement with their task. Intrinsically motivated employees view cooperation as a benefit rather than as a cost (Frey and Osterloh, 2002). Such intrinsically motivated cooperation, however, tends to be fragile. Laboratory studies demonstrate that a few free-riders in a team can suffice to destroy the self-motivation of the willing cooperators quickly (Fehr and Fischbacher, 2004). Orbell and Dawes (1981) were first to point out the so-called 'sucker-effect', a motivational loss that occurs because 'no one wants to play the sucker' if other team-members free-ride on the contributors' cooperative effort. Therefore, intrinsic motivation can only prevail if contributors expect that their cooperative efforts will be matched in the long run. Thus, as Kramer and co-authors (Kramer et al., 1996; Frey and Torgler, 2007) propose individuals' willingness to cooperate is partially conditioned on the belief that other individuals in the organization will do the same, that is, trust in colleagues and potentially also trust in supervisors and the organization are a necessary complement to intrinsic motivation for overcoming social dilemmas. Employees need to be able to trust that colleagues, supervisor and firm somehow match the employees' cooperative efforts. And supervisor and firm need to be able to trust employees to act in the organization's interest.

In addition, beliefs that other individuals will contribute are influenced positively by hierarchical control. For example, tax morale, the intrinsic motivation to pay taxes, is positively influenced by generalized trust in other taxpayers as well as by the ability of tax authorities to exert hierarchical control, that is, to collect sufficient taxes (Frey and Torgler, 2007).

Thus, a harmonious interplay of centralized control on the one hand and intrinsic motivation/trust on the other hand may strengthen cooperative solutions. Yet our understanding of this interplay is still very limited. More precisely a heated and hitherto unresolved debate has unfolded, particularly on how trust and hierarchical control relate.

The interplay of hierarchical control, intrinsic motivation and trust, however, is not well understood as research often pitches trust and motivation against hierarchical control (for an overview see Bachmann et al., 2001). Either of these solutions are seen as substitutes and as a consequence analysed separately or it is argued that hierarchical control interacts with trust and intrinsic motivation, but the direction of this interaction remains contested. Many researchers argue that hierarchical control drives out trust and undermines intrinsic motivation (Falk and Kosfeld, 2006; Grund and Harbring, 2009) and thus, would argue that control is one of the main drivers of the loss of intrinsic motivation and trust in the workplace. Yet there are also some authors who argue that hierarchical control, trust and intrinsic motivation may interact positively and strengthen each other (Weibel, 2007).

The aim of this chapter is to specify under which conditions hierarchical control, intrinsic motivation and trust may act in positive interaction for cooperation. To analyse the positive interaction we will progress as follows. The first section reviews current takes on the interplay of hierarchical control and trust and intrinsic motivation. In the second section we develop a framework based on self-determination and trust theory that delineates under which conditions and in which way control, trust and intrinsic motivation enhance cooperation in a complementary way. In the last section the framework is brought into a broader context and suggestions for further research are presented.

A FRESH VIEW ON THE DEBATE ABOUT TRUST AND CONTROL

Conceptually the relationship of trust, control and cooperation has been debated intensively, particularly in the last two decades. Yet a second look at the current debate shows that by far the most prominent discourse was to provide a rationale why control rather than trust or vice versa, trust rather than control, should be analysed as the main contributor to cooperation. Möllering (2005, p. 285), for example, in his overview on the debate argues that 'most studies focus on either control or trust'. Only a very small fraction of research is dedicated to the interrelationship of control and trust, that is, on the question of how trust and control in combination affect cooperation.

Analysing Control or Trust

Arguably, a lot of recent work on hierarchical control has been motivated by organizational economics. Organizational economics considers hierarchical control to be an effective solution for cooperation if market solutions fail. To Williamson (1980, p. 11), for instance, 'hierarchy serves to economize on transaction costs', costs that are a direct consequence of market failures, while Eisenhardt (1985, p. 137) argues from an agency point of view that 'the role of control is to provide measures and rewards such that individuals pursuing their own self-interest will also pursue the collective interest'. The role of trust in these scenarios is absent – in full purpose – however. In a famous article Williamson (1993a, p. 484) brands trust as a superfluous if not even a downright dangerous concept: 'trust, if it obtains at all, is reserved for very special relations between family, friends and lovers'. For business relations the more careful assumption of opportunism, to expect that individuals may be 'self-interest-seeking with guile' is seen to be the cautious route to take (Williamson, 1993b). Although such a clear assumption about the role of trust is missing in principal agent theory, the behavioural assumptions of both theories are comparable – agents too are seen as self-interested 'homo oeconomicus' and thus ultimately not trustworthy (Eisenhardt, 1989). This tradition, to picture hierarchical control as an optimal solution to issues originating from individual-level self-interest is of course not limited to organizational economics. A lot of earlier conceptualizations of control essentially relied on very similar behavioural assumptions – hierarchical control was often seen as a device to incite workers to cooperate in the presumed absence of intrinsic motivation (for an overview see Sitkin et al., 2010).

Trust research, too, has often pictured a somewhat one-dimensional picture of human beings in organization. At the heart of many contemporary conceptual trust papers lies the definition of trust as the 'willingness to be vulnerable to . . . the actions of another party . . . irrespective of the ability to monitor or control that other party' (Mayer et al., 1995, p. 712) and thus perhaps unsurprisingly the absence of control is often portrayed as an important signal of trust. Supervisors that share or delegate control are proposed to initiate trust relationships (Whitener et al., 1998) and affectively trusting managers should refrain from control-based monitoring (McAllister, 1995). More generally, control is often seen to be a signal of distrust and thus as an antidote of trust, presumably because many trust researchers consider trust and control to be at opposite ends of the same spectrum (Hardin, 1992; Mishra et al., 2011). More speculatively it could be argued that a lot of trust research draws on a more humanistic perspective – intrinsic motivation and willingness to cooperate in social dilemma situations are seen as very real conditions in organizations. Moreover, as it is often said, trust-begets-trust, individuals who initiate trusting relationships can count with some probability on reciprocity. At the very least trust research assumes that trustworthy individuals can often be differentiated from untrustworthy individuals and that the default assumption 'self-interest' is effectively forestalling trust relationships to develop, whereas the assumption 'willing to cooperate' will spark trusting relations (for example, Hardin, 1992).

Analysing Control *and* Trust

Far less research has addressed control and trust at the same time. Thus, it is fair to say that the pledge by Adler (2001) to investigate the interplay of hierarchical control and trust is still not met sufficiently. If, however, control and trust are seen as two independent variables two combinations can be differentiated: hierarchical control under specified conditions impacts trust positively, for example, an 'enabling' bureaucracy strengthens trust relations or control impacts trust negatively, for example, a 'coercive' bureaucracy destabilizes trust (Adler and Borys, 1996).

Authors have often argued that hierarchical control fuels distrust (Argyris, 1952; Strickland, 1958; Ghoshal and Moran, 1996), raise relational detachment (Thompson and Warhurst, 1998) and strengthen an 'us versus them' perspective between general management and employees (Bijlsma-Frankema et al., 2009). Employees react to this type of control by reducing their positive evaluation and their trust in the controlling party, as well as their voluntary engagement (Kruglanski, 1970). Some empirical evidence from field studies (for example, Barkema, 1995; Ramaswami, 1996; Frey, 1997), as well as experimental data (Falk and Kosfeld, 2006), seem to support the existence of a negative relation between control, trust and voluntary engagement. In addition control might also affect expectations relating to the level of trustworthiness of generalized others. Sitkin and Roth (1993) suggest hierarchical control mechanisms in the guise of legalistic remedies might emphasize perceived social distance between organizational actors and thus raise distrust. Similarly, Sliwka (2007) demonstrates in a formal model that a strong control system could signal to organizational actors that their co-workers in general are not to be trusted and thereby strengthen a norm of untrustworthy behaviour in the organization.

In contrast with the aforementioned negative stance, other authors argue that hierarchical control system has the potential to increase trust. On the one hand control is argued to strengthen fairness perceptions. As Weber already (1921) suggested, control, that is, the universalistic application of general rules, protects individuals from any arbitrariness of the system. Thus, hierarchical control simultaneously creates reliability, with recurring problems dealt with in a consistent manner (Tsui et al., 1997), promotes fairness as rules are applied consistently across all organizational actors (Sitkin and George, 2005) and signals legitimacy of decisions due to the transparency of the standard criteria underlying each decisions (Meyer et al., 1988; Suchman, 1995). Reliability, fairness and legitimacy in turn are proposed to strengthen trust and voluntary compliance (Tyler, 2003). Second, control systems can also create trust among 'generalized others' through their positive impact on employees' willingness to cooperate (Barney and Hansen, 1994; Pearce, 2008). For example, Six and Sorge (2008) suggest that organizations can promote willingness to cooperate amongst employees by instilling and promoting norms at the organizational level and monitoring their practices down to the level of dyadic relations. In addition, Sitkin (1995) suggests that hierarchical control mechanisms may increase trust in other organizational actors by providing objective rules and clear measures on which to base assessments and evaluations of others.

To summarize, research on the interactive effect of hierarchical control and trust on cooperation has been discordant, or as Bachmann et al. (2001, p.v) stated 'there are numerous examples in the literature where control chases out trust and situations in which trust seems to remove the necessity for control, there are equally as many examples of trust and control being complementary, or going hand in hand'. We suggest that this interplay can be analysed more sharply if the third variable conducive to cooperation, namely intrinsic motivation, is entered into the equation.

HIERARCHICAL CONTROL, INTRINSIC MOTIVATION, TRUST AND COOPERATION

In this section we will examine how hierarchical control and intrinsic motivation to cooperate relate and we will do this by drawing on self-determination theory. Subsequently trust will be reintroduced into the equation. For an overview of the whole framework see Figure 3.1.

Self-determination Theory and Intrinsic Motivation

The main question self-determination theory seeks to answer is under which contextual conditions do individuals motivate themselves (Deci and Flaste, 1995; Ryan and Deci, 2000; Gagne and Deci, 2005)? The line of argumentation, in a nutshell, goes as follows: those organizational and

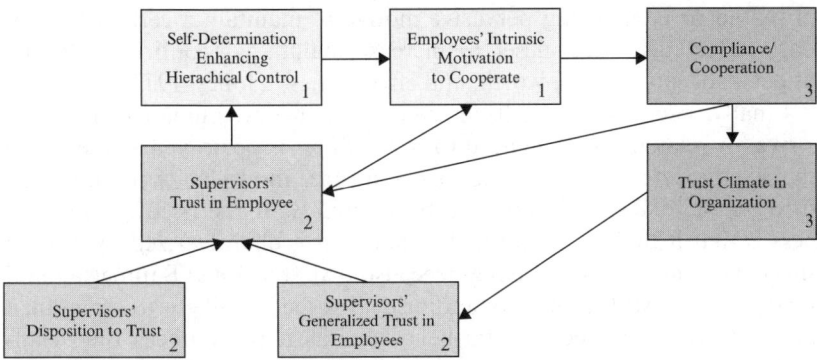

Figure 3.1   Framework – trust, hierarchical control and intrinsic motivation as complements

social contexts that enable individual self-determination have a positive effect on intrinsic motivation. Self-determination is enabled if three innate psychological needs of individuals are satisfied: the need for autonomy, competence and relatedness (Ryan, 1995). A context that forestalls need satisfaction, however, undermines intrinsic motivation.

The need for autonomy plays a central role in self-determination theory. Individuals feel autonomous to the degree that they perceive their behaviour to be truly self-chosen rather than imposed on them by others (Ryan et al., 1996). The need for autonomy as a prerequisite for intrinsic motivation was first introduced by De Charms (1968). De Charms suggests that the fundamental requirement for internal motivation is perceiving oneself as the locus of causality for one's own behaviour. Spreitzer et al. (2005) assume that autonomy enables employees to act agentic: they are more likely to stay focused on a task over a prolonged period of time and to explore new ways of handling tasks.

Intrinsically motivated task engagement is also dependent on how competent individuals feel in acting agentic. In self-determination theory the need for competence rests on two components: (1) the need to develop new skills and new mental frames; and (2) the need to feel a boost in self-esteem. The first aspect of competence – skill and frame development – can be traced back to earlier concepts such as White's concept of mastery (White, 1959) or Bandura's concept of self-efficacy (Bandura, 1977). This need is more likely to be satisfied if individuals see a relationship between their behaviour and desired outcomes (Locke and Latham, 1990) and if they face optimal challenges (Deci, 1985). The second aspect of competence – self-esteem – has been suggested by writers of many theoretical traditions (for example, Bijlsma-Frankema and Costa, 2009). It has been proposed to be a strong pervasive motive to maintain a certain level of positive feelings about oneself to 'increase, maintain or confirm . . . feeling of personal satisfaction, worth, and effectiveness' (Jones, 1973, p. 186).

Finally, according to self-determination theory, human beings also strive for relatedness. The need for relatedness is portrayed as the desire to feel connected to others – to love and care, and to be loved and cared for (Deci and Ryan, 2000). The basic quality of the need for relatedness is that it builds on mutuality, that is, it is characterized by mutual sharing of thoughts and feelings (see also Alderfer, 1969; Baumeister and Leary, 1995). Mutual understanding and respect is likely to strengthen intrinsically motivated agentic behaviour as it pronounces the meaningfulness of certain tasks (Hackman and Lawler, 1971; Conger and Kanungo, 1988).

Hierarchical Control and Intrinsic Motivation

This general framework from self-determination theory may be linked to empirical research on the impact of hierarchical control mechanisms on intrinsic motivation. We will draw heavily on a book chapter by Weibel (2010) on formal managerial control and intrinsic motivation in doing so. In that chapter hierarchical forms of control that undermine intrinsic motivation are distinguished from forms of control that strengthen intrinsic motivation. In contrast here we only focus on forms that strengthen intrinsic motivation, since we are interested in how and under what conditions controls and supervisor trust may complement each other in their effect on intrinsic motivation. Also we will focus on supervisor–employee relationships in firms.

According to self-determination theory, hierarchical control mechanisms and their enactment that support the needs of individuals for autonomy, competence and relatedness will strengthen intrinsic motivation. In research on hierarchical control three areas have been observed to have such a positive effect: autonomy-enhancing control enactment, relatedness-enhancing control enactment and constructive feedback as a competence-enhancing control mechanism.

Autonomy
Quite evidently hierarchical control is bound to reduce employees' autonomy to some degree, yet to what degree employees perceive hierarchical control to be an outside pressure that limits their agentic behaviour depends on the way hierarchical control is enacted by managers. For example, Tannenbaum (1968) distinguished a number of control styles along a continuum of highly autocratic, managerial-directed to highly

participative, employee-co-directed formal control. The expectation is that employees are more likely to feel empowered and self-motivated in a participative control system (Conger and Kanungo, 1988; Spreitzer and Mishra, 1999). Through participation, employees are given some control over the decision process (if not always over the resulting decision) and a possibility to express their concerns (for a related discussion see Lind and Tyler, 1988).

Empirical research on participation shows some fairly stable results in linking participation with perceived autonomy. Studies have shown that employees' participation in general is a strong predictor of internal motivation (Rhodes and Steers, 1981; Leana et al., 1992; Mayer and Schoorman, 1998). There is, however, only limited evidence linking employees' participation in the formal managerial control process to intrinsic motivation.

Conceptually, literature on participation in the development of a set of formal control mechanisms, that is, of the control system, must be distinguished from literature on participation in the execution of singular formal control mechanisms. Participation in the development of a formal control system and its effects are discussed by Adler and Borys (1996) who differentiate 'coercive bureaucracies' from 'enabling bureaucracies'. Enabling bureaucracies are characterized by a high degree of participation by the employees in the constant redesign of organizational control systems. Workers in an enabling bureaucracy typically show higher internalized commitment to their work and their organization. Sitkin and co-authors (1994) differentiate total quality control systems from total quality learning systems. As opposed to total quality control systems, total quality learning systems offer opportunities for a continuous and participatory redesign of quality control principles and mechanisms. These opportunities for employees to have a say in the redesign of the control system are discussed to raise the incentives for innovative, self-driven behaviour.

Participative execution of generic formal control mechanisms is also shown to strengthen intrinsic motivation. Pearson (1991), for example, finds positive links between internal motivation and participation in traditional performance monitoring processes. Frey (1997) looks at participative standard setting. He compares the amount of civic virtue as displayed in the tax morale of different Swiss states and demonstrates that the more extensive the political participation possibilities, the higher the internalized tax morale (for a recent overview see Feld and Frey, 2007). Thus:

Proposition 1a: Participative development of the hierarchical control system will strengthen intrinsic motivation.

Proposition 1b: Participative execution of hierarchical control mechanisms will strengthen intrinsic motivation.

Relatedness
Hierarchical control under certain conditions enhances feeling of relatedness and thus strengthens intrinsic motivation. We suggest that: (1) hierarchical control focused on intrinsic job engagement; and (2) supervisor's trust in the employee will strengthen intrinsic motivation. The latter aspect will be discussed when trust is reintroduced into the model.

Research in self-determination theory suggests that employees feel socially connected if their intrinsic engagement for the job is valued (Frey and Osterloh, 2002). This implies that employees may value those control practices that put a spotlight on their overall, that is, their work-related and their contextual, assumingly voluntary performance. Furthermore, employees should react more positively if they are informed about their performance evaluation in a way that is fair and signals respect for their overall contribution (Bies and Moag, 1986). For example, Mayer and Davis (1999) demonstrate in a field experiment that a performance appraisal system that more adequately reflects 'true', that is, overall performance of employees raises employees' positive perceptions of managers' care and benevolence. Pettijohn and colleagues (2001) identify fairness in the evaluation process as integral for employees' internal motivation. Thus:

Proposition 2: Hierarchical control focused on intrinsic work engagement will strengthen intrinsic motivation.

Competence
Competence-enhancing control mechanisms strengthen intrinsic motivation. Employees feel competent with respect to an activity if they understand reliable ways to achieve desired outcomes. Feedback as part of the control system can play an important role in initializing self-efficacy-enhancing feelings. In a meta-analysis, Kluger and DeNisi (1996) conclude that feedback has on average a moderately positive effect on job outcomes. However, more than 38 per cent of the effects found in the literature were negative. From a self-determination perspective there are two reasons why feedback does not always seem to affect self-motivation as hoped for: (1) it does not support individuals sufficiently in their self-development and learning; and/or (2) it does not boost self-esteem.

First, Sitkin et al. (1994) distinguish two different feedback systems: a controlling feedback system, which is geared towards increasing reliability and small-scale learning, and a learning feedback system, which is geared towards exploration and large-scale learning. Of these two types of feedback systems the latter system appears to be better equipped to assist individuals in their self-development and learning. It should thus affect intrinsic motivation positively. This relationship between learning feedback systems and intrinsic motivation has also been extensively researched in didactics. For example, Higgins et al. (2002) show that formative feedback in teaching deepens students' learning and students' intrinsic motivation to learn. Hattie and Timperley (2007) conclude in a recent overview on this literature that this learning-oriented feedback is enhancing a deeper learning process, and it enables intrinsically motivated behaviour to a much higher degree than controlling feedback.

Second, Kluger and DeNisi (1996) believe that only constructive feedback can have positive effects because constructive feedback boosts self-esteem. Baron (1993) characterizes constructive feedback as feedback that is specific in content, timely, delivered in an appropriate setting and does not contain threats and attributions concerning causes of poor performance. Empirical findings on the effects of constructive feedback on internalization are, however, not entirely conclusive. Oldham and Cummings (1996) find that manufacturing employees produced the most creative outcomes when they worked on complex, challenging jobs and were given positive and mainly informational feedback. Such feedback, according to Oldham and Cummings, encourages employees' feelings of self-determination. Also, in a theoretical article referring to earlier studies, London and Smither (1999) state that organizations can encourage self-development and internalization processes by providing non-threatening performance feedback. In their own empirical study however, they were not able to show that constructive feedback had a positive effect on intrinsic motivation (London et al., 1999). Thus:

Proposition 3a: Learning-oriented feedback will strengthen intrinsic motivation.

Proposition 3b: Constructive feedback will strengthen intrinsic motivation.

The Effect of Supervisor's Trust on Hierarchical Control and Intrinsic Motivation

Self-determination theory enables a clearer understanding of the effect of control on intrinsic motivation. Trust theory has the potential to complement self-determination theory in important ways. More precisely we suggest that 'supervisor's trust' in the employee is an important variable in the framework. Supervisor's trust is the supervisor's willingness to be vulnerable towards the employee as the latter is expected to have a willingness to cooperate even in social dilemma situations. Such trust will influence the employee's intrinsic motivation to cooperate in two ways: trust reduces the distrust-signalling capacity of control and thus leads to self-determination-enhancing hierarchical control and it strengthens intrinsic motivation directly. We will discuss the possible antecedents of supervisor's trust and then examine the consequences.

Antecedents of supervisor's trust

Supervisor's trust in the employee will be influenced by two relatively stable variables: the supervisor's disposition to trust and the supervisor's generalized trust towards employees of the same organization. In addition, supervisor's trust is influenced by a positive interaction history with the employee, which will be discussed later in the section on the feedback loop.

Some individuals trust more readily than others. Rotter (1980) was the first to identify distinct personality attributes that affected individuals' readiness, or propensity, to trust. He defined trust propensity as a relatively stable generalized expectancy about the trustworthiness of others, leading towards the formation of trusting relationships with others and an acceptance of vulnerability. This personality factor is referred to as a disposition to trust or trust propensity and has been conceptualized as a sub-factor of the agreeableness dimension of the big five personality model (Costa and McCrae, 1992). One of the most important influences of the disposition to trust is on the development and maintenance of trust (Searle et al., 2011). Kee and Knox (1970) argue that trust beliefs of the trustor are shaped by dispositional trust even where previous experience with a trustee is available. A recent meta-analysis found trust propensity was still significantly related to interpersonal trust once dimensions of trustworthiness were controlled for (Colquitt et al., 2007). Thus, a supervisor with a strong disposition to trust is more likely to initiate and maintain trusting relationships with the employee irrespective of the specific situation and the specific employee:

Proposition 4: High supervisor disposition to trust is positively related to supervisor trust in the employee.

Generalized trust too, is trust given in the absence of specific information about the employee. However, different from the disposition to trust it is not modelled as a personality variable, which is slow to change and observable across situations, but rather as a socially learned condition, which is malleable and observable within a defined context (Eberl, 2004; Eberl et al., 2011). Generalized trust is a learned and relatively stable expectation of cooperative behaviour within a specific social unit, for example within an organization or within a profession (Blomqvist, 1997; Stolle, 1998). Barber (1983, pp. 164f), for instance, talks about a set of 'socially learned and socially confirmed expectations that people have of each other, of organizations and institutions in which they live' and Fukuyama (1995, p. 26), points out that 'trust is the expectation that arises within a community of regular, honest, and cooperative behaviour, based on commonly shared norms, on the part of other members of that community'. Again a supervisor with high generalized trust towards one social unit is likely to initiate and maintain trusting relationships with an employee who belongs to the same social unit:

Proposition 5: High supervisor generalized trust in employees is positively related to supervisor trust in an employee.

Consequences of supervisor's trust

Hierarchical control is often said to bear negative consequences on intrinsic motivation under the condition that the supervisor holds a 'controlling', that is, suspicious intention (Argyris, 1952; Strickland, 1958; Ghoshal and Moran, 1996). Current empirical work supports McGregor's (1960) conceptual model of the negative effect of monitoring on working relations and intrinsic work engagement under the condition that the supervisor initiates control with a 'theory X' in mind, that is, a suspicious and negative view about employees' work morale. For example, Falk and Kosfeld (2006) test the negative effect of managerial monitoring in a two-stage principal agent game and demonstrate that participants only react negatively if monitoring is evidently done with a suspicious/controlling intention of the principal (see also the studies of Strickland, 1958). A supervisor with a high trust, however, is less likely to control with a suspicious intention. In particular, research on trust as a disposition demonstrates that individuals with a high disposition to trust show a more positive and less suspicious view of others. One suggested mechanism for this is a filter altering the interpretations of others' actions (Govier, 1994). Experimental research has shown that those with high propensity to trust are more sensitive to signs of trustworthiness, while those with a low-trust propensity are more sensitive to signs of betrayal (Komorita and Parks, 1995). In addition, Rotter (1980) suggested further distinctions, which recent field studies confirmed: those high on trust propensity have more favourable perceptions of others' trustworthiness, particularly of their benevolence and integrity (Yakovleva et al., 2010). Therefore, a strongly trusting supervisor is more likely to see the cooperative efforts of the employee than a supervisor with low trust and is more likely to control without a suspicious intention. Thus:

Proposition 6: High supervisor trust in an employee bears positively on self-determination-enhancing control.

In addition, trusting individuals are proposed to inspire intrinsic motivation to cooperate directly for two reasons. First, the tendency to trust appears to affect individuals' cooperation, with those high on tendency to trust demonstrating more frequent cooperative behaviours. High-trust tendency individuals show behaviours that promote the building and maintenance of better exchange relationships with others. They show more honest and compliant behaviour, which includes less cheating than others (Rotter, 1971; Stack, 1978; Rotter, 1980) and are more sensitive to the norms of reciprocity (Gouldner, 1960). These genuine cooperative efforts are likely to be 'contagious'. For example, in gift-exchange experiments individuals are more inclined to intrinsically cooperate if they assume the other player to have an intrinsic tendency to cooperate (for an overview see Fehr et al., 2003). Also, De Cremer and van Knippenberg (2002) demonstrate that people are more willing to contribute to a public good if a leader makes personal sacrifices to achieve the collective vision rather than personally benefiting from his action. Second, trust has been shown to satisfy the need for relatedness and to thus bear positively on intrinsic motivation. Deci and Ryan (2000, p. 235) suggest that intrinsic motivation is more likely to flourish in a context 'characterized by a sense of secure relatedness', a sense of security that is arguably more likely to evolve in a trusting atmosphere. Tyler and colleagues (Tyler and Blader, 2005; De Cremer and Tyler, 2007) have demonstrated both in experimental and field studies that individuals show more voluntary compliance towards trusting authorities (supervisors) as this trust strengthened group identity, the we-feeling between employees and supervisors. Thus, we suggest:

Proposition 7: High supervisor's trust in an employee bears positively on employee intrinsic motivation to cooperate.

Feedback Loop: Cooperation and Trust

In this section we explore the consequences of employees' intrinsic motivation to cooperate. We will first shortly review evidence that intrinsically motivated individuals indeed cooperate in social dilemma situations. Such a cooperative effort, which is visible to other individuals is likely to affect trust. More precisely, higher cooperation should strengthen the general climate of trust in an organization, the supervisor's generalized trust in employees and the supervisor's specific trust in the cooperating individual.

Intrinsic motivation and cooperation
Dawes (1980) argues that individuals cooperate in social dilemma situations if they perceive cooperation as a utility rather than as a cost; for example, because they have an intrinsic desire to help others or because they feel internally obliged to cooperate. Kollock (1998, p. 192) describes these sources to cooperation as 'motivational solutions to social dilemmas' and Frost et al. (2010) argue that employees with intrinsic motivation are more likely to see cooperation as a utility in comparison to employees who are extrinsically motivated. Empirically the effect of intrinsic motivation on cooperation in social dilemma situations has been studied from a number of different theoretical traditions. For example, Brewer and colleagues have shown that cooperation rates in dilemma situations are raised by promoting group (social) identity (Brewer, 1979; Messick and Brewer, 1983). Members who strongly identify with their group are more willing to invest in public goods and to exercise restraint in resource dilemmas than low identifiers (Kramer and Brewer, 1984; Brewer and Kramer, 1986). De Cremer and Van Vugt (1999) have demonstrated that such a positive effect on cooperation can be attributed because a salient group identity transforms motives: individuals become intrinsically motivated to help the group. In addition, there is evidence that intrinsic involvement with a task reduces free-riding behaviour. For example, Harkins and Petty (1982) showed that individuals working on a challenging task did not free-ride. Robbins (1995) showed that free-riding was absent when tasks were thought-provoking and personally involving, provided that the participants thought that other participants would also contribute. Finally, Smith and co-authors (Smith et al., 2001) also demonstrated that high task interest or involvement tends to attenuate free-riding. Thus, we suggest:

Proposition 8: Intrinsic motivation to cooperate leads to higher cooperation in social dilemma situations.

Cooperation and trust
Mayer et al. (1995, p. 728) suggests that the 'trustor's perceptions of the trustee are enhanced' if the latter cooperates and thereby trust between the parties is likely to grow. Other researchers propose a more direct connection. For instance Nahapiet and Ghoshal explain that 'trust lubricates cooperation, and cooperation itself breeds trust' (Nahapiet and Ghoshal, 1998, p. 255) and quite clearly saw trust as an outcome of cooperation. Finally, Ferrin et al. (2008) talk about a complex trust–cooperation spiral.

Extrapolating from these different positions we explore three ways how cooperation of the employee can impact trust: cooperation is speculated to have a positive effect on the supervisor's specific trust in the employee, on the trust climate in the organization and on the supervisor's generalized trust.

Ferrin and co-authors (2008) argue that the trust–cooperation spiral is driven 'by own present cooperation on other's future trust', more specifically, that cooperation should lead to higher specific trust of the supervisor in the employee. This is paralleled by what has been termed 'shadow of the past' in the economic literature, which means that 'a party's trust of the other is developed over time by accumulating through the relationship exchange experiences that indicate the kind of behaviour to expect from the other party' (Poppo et al., 2008, p. 39) and what Lewicki and Bunker (1995) have called knowledge-based trust, which is a function of parties having a history of interaction. The effect of cooperation on specific trust is speculated to function via a variety of mechanisms. Poppo and co-authors (2008), for instance, demonstrate that a history of interaction generates a long-term perspective and expectations of continuity, thereby promoting specific trust. Gulati (1995) on the other hand suggests a more direct link between cooperation and trust: a history of successful collaboration strengthens trust. Either way, cooperation seems to have a positive effect on specific trust and thus we suggest:

Proposition 9: Employees' cooperation leads to higher specific trust of supervisor in employee.

Furthermore, cooperation should also affect the trust climate in an organization. Here we define the trust climate of an organization as the attitude of organizational members concerning trustworthiness of the generalized 'other', that is, of all members of the organization. Thus, trust climate is similar to the ethical work climate of the organization as it also entails 'aggregated perceptions of the existence of organizational norms supporting values such as providing warmth and support to peers and subordinates' (Victor and Cullen, 1988, p. 102). However, it also differs from the ethical work climate in two important ways. First, the trust climate is narrower than the ethical work climate at it centres on benevolence and group interest only; the interest and well-being of the reference group becomes paramount. Second, an organizational trust climate needs not extend beyond the organization's border, that is, individuals can show high benevolence towards their organization but at the same time react very instrumentally towards non-organizational members. Indeed, it is a longstanding discussion in the trust literature that trust can produce highly unethical side-effects, for instance, because it may evoke out-group 'hate' (Brewer, 1999) or because high-trust groups like the Mafia can protect their members much more efficiently than low-trust groups (Gambetta, 1988).

In a high-trust climate, employees have strong generalized trust towards all members of the organization. A high-trust climate may spring from a strong identification with the organization and in that case resemble identification-based trust, which is based on a salient group identity (Lewicki and Bunker, 1995). Such a high identification is partially caused by success of collective action – attractive groups are more likely to entice strong identification (Haslam et al., 2000). Alternatively, such collectively high generalized trust might also be an outcome of a history of successful interactions. Social dilemma research, for example, has shown that a small number of free-riders can undermine cooperation and collectively high generalized trust quite quickly (Fehr and Fischbacher, 2004). Conversely, a few adamant cooperators, who are even willing to incur costs to protect cooperation by punishing defectors informally, are demonstrated to lead to very high levels of cooperation and to positive expectation of future cooperation (Fehr and Gachter, 2000). Thus:

Proposition 10: Employees' cooperation leads to a high-trust climate in the organization.

Finally, to close the feedback loop we propose that a high-trust climate in the organization should augment supervisor's trust. This effect is caused by the socializing effect of a high-trust climate: a high-trust climate strengthens supervisors' generalized trust in organizational members. Thus, we suggest:

Proposition 11: A high-trust climate has a positive effect on supervisors' generalized trust in organizational members.

CONCLUSIONS AND FURTHER RESEARCH

The framework developed in this chapter depicts a reinforcing cycle in which hierarchical controls that enhance self-determination lead to higher employee intrinsic motivation to cooperate and to higher cooperation; this in turn leads to higher trust in three ways, which positively affect self-determination-enhancing controls. This is, however, not the whole story. As already mentioned, not all hierarchical controls enhance self-determination. Self-determination-thwarting hierarchical controls will drive out employee intrinsic motivation and thus dampen the cycle of positive trust–control–intrinsic motivation interaction. See Weibel (2010) for an exposé of controls that thwart self-determination and thus undermine intrinsic motivation. A full appreciation of the interaction of trust, hierarchical control and intrinsic motivation on cooperation therefore can only be developed once both positive and negative effects are accounted for.

Furthermore, our framework also highlights the need for another important differentiation, namely the one between trust and distrust. We mentioned that trust and control are often seen as two ends of one continuum. The same appears to hold true for trust and distrust, despite Lewicki et al.'s (1998) convincing argument that trust and distrust should be conceived as two separate constructs. Lack of trust does not imply high distrust. High trust and high distrust may coexist. There is a relationship between the assumptions often made regarding trust–control and trust–distrust. When trust and distrust are seen as two ends on one continuum, control and trust are usually seen as substitutes (Van de Walle and Six, forthcoming). Lindenberg (2000) argued that you first need to take away distrust before you can begin to build trust. He introduced the notion of legitimate distrust situations, situations where 'any explicit or implicit promise . . . is blatantly against the self-interest of the promising party' (p. 12). Because the distrust is seen as legitimate, that is, 'reasonable observers would say that any other reasonable person put into this situation' would judge similarly, remedies can be relationally neutral, meaning that the distrusting individual can 'claim the necessity of remedies, pinpoint to a menu of solutions and show good faith at the same time' (ibid.). In other words, the introduction of certain controls may be considered legitimate and not a sign of distrust if the temptations are considered too great.

The framework also allows delineating fields in the circumplex of trust, control and motivation, which begs for further research. First, there are a number of studies on a trustor's general propensity to trust other human beings: supervisor disposition to trust in our model. There is much less research, however, on the concept of generalized trust in collectives of trustees, such as employees within an organization, in particular with a supervisor or other hierarchically higher-placed actor as trustor and the collectivity of employees, as trustee.

Second, the framework developed in this chapter is focused on hierarchical relations within organizations. We propose that the mechanisms at work are also applicable to other hierarchical relations, such as between mother company and subsidiaries, between regulator and regulated organizations and possibly also between government and citizens

(Six, 2013). Research to adapt and test our framework to these contexts is needed. Finally, we believe that the framework would profit from a multi-level perspective. In a large-scale empirical survey Weibel and co-authors (Weibel et al., 2009) found that hierarchical control is positively related to trust in the organization. Thus, the effect of any kind of hierarchical control at the organizational level might look quite different from the effect on interpersonal trust and individual motivation.

Thus, our framework is a first step to disentangling the combined effects of hierarchical control and trust on cooperation. Yet a full understanding of these complex relationships needs the united efforts of the whole field – it is time to answer the call for research that Bradach and Eccles (1989) issued more than 20 years ago.

REFERENCES

Adler, P.S. (2001), 'Market, hierarchy, and trust. The knowledge economy and the future of capitalism', *Organization Science*, **12**(2), 215–34.
Adler, P.S. and B. Borys (1996), 'Two types of bureaucracy: enabling and coercive', *Administrative Science Quarterly*, **41**(1) 61–89.
Alchian, A.A. and H. Demsetz (1972), 'Production, information costs and economic organization, *American Economic Review*, **62**(5), 777–95.
Alderfer, C.P. (1969), 'Empirical test of a new theory of human needs', *Organizational Behavior and Human Performance*, **4**(2), 142–75.
Argyris, C. (1952), *The Impact of Budgets on People*, New York: Controllership Foundation.
Bachmann, R., D. Knights and J. Sydow (2001), 'Trust and control in organizational relations', *Organization Studies*, **22**(2), V–VIII.
Bandura, A. (1977), 'Self-efficacy – toward a unifying theory of behavioral change', *Psychological Review*, **84**(2), 191–215.
Barber, B. (1983), *The Logic and Limits of Trust*, New Brunswick, NJ: Rutgers University Press.
Barkema, H.G. (1995), 'Do job executives work harder when they are monitored?' *Kyklos*, **48**(1), 19–42.
Barney, J.B. and M.H. Hansen (1994), 'Trustworthiness as a source of competitve advantage', *Strategic Management Journal*, **15**(Special Issue), 175–90.
Baron, J.N. (1993), 'Criticism (informal negative feedback) as a source of perceived unfairness in organizations: effects, mechanisms, and countermeasures', in R. Cropanzano (ed.), *Justice in the Workplace*, Hillsdale, NJ: L. Erlbaum Associates.
Baumeister, R.F. and M.R. Leary (1995), 'The need to belong: desire for interpersonal attachments as a fundamental human motivation', *Psychological Bulletin*, **117**(3), 497–529.
Bies, R.J. and J.S. Moag (1986), 'Interactional justice: communication criteria of fairness', in R.J. Lewicki, B.H. Sheppard and B.H. Bazerman (eds), *Research on Negotiations in Organizations*, Vol. 1, Greenwich CT: JAI Press, pp. 43–55.
Bijlsma-Frankema, K. and A.C. Costa (2009), 'Juggling multiple meanings of organizational control: a natural system approach', in S.B. Sitkin and L.B. Cardinal and K. Bijlsma-Frankema (eds), *Control in Organizations: New Directions in Theory and Research*, Cambridge, UK: Cambridge University Press.
Bijlsma-Frankema, K. and A. Costa (2010), 'Consequences and antecedents of managerial and employee legitimacy interpretations of control: a natural open system approach I',

in S.B. Sitkin, L.B. Cardinal and K. Bijlsma-Frankema (eds), *Control in Organizations: New Directions in Theory and Research*, Cambridge, UK: Cambridge University Press, pp. 396–433.

Bijlsma-Frankema, K., S.B. Sitkin and A. Weibel (2009), 'Breaking out of inter-group distrust: judges and administrators in a court of law', mimeo, Hochschule Liechtenstein.

Blomqvist, K. (1997), 'The many faces of trust', *Scandinavian Journal of Management*, **13**(3), 271–86.

Bradach, J.L. and R.G. Eccles (1989), 'Price, authority, and trust: from ideal types to plural forms', *Annual Sociological Review*, **15**(1), 97–118.

Brewer, M.B. (1979), 'In-group bias in the minimal intergroup situation – cognitive-motivational analysis', *Psychological Bulletin*, **86**(2), 307–24.

Brewer, M.B. (1999), 'The psychology of prejudice: ingroup love or outgroup hate?' *Journal of Social Issues*, **55**(3), 429–44.

Brewer, M.B. and R.M. Kramer (1986), 'Choice behavior in social dilemmas – effects of social identity, group-size, and decision framing', *Journal of Personality and Social Psychology*, **50**(3), 543–9.

Colquitt, J.A., B.A. Scott and J.A. LePine (2007), 'Trust, trustworthiness, and trust propensity: a meta-analytic test of their unique relationships with risk taking and job performance', *Journal of Applied Psychology*, **92**(4), 909–27.

Conger, J.A. and R.N. Kanungo (1988), 'The empowerment process – integrating theory and practice', *Academy of Management Review*, **13**(3), 471–82.

Costa, P.T. and R.R. McCrae (1992), *NEO PI-R (Professional Manual)*, Florida: Psychological Assessment Resources.

Dawes, R.M. (1980), 'Social dilemmas', *Annual Review of Psychology*, **31**(1), 169–93.

De Charms, R. (1968), *Personal Causation: The Internal Affective Determinants of Behavior*, New York: Academic Press.

Deci, E.L. (1985), *Intrinsic Motivation and Self-determination in Human Behavior*, New York: Plenum Press.

Deci, E.L. and R. Flaste (1995), *Why We Do, What We Do. Understanding Self-motivation*, Rochester: Penguin Books.

Deci, E.L. and R.M. Ryan (2000), 'The "what" and "why" of goal pursuits: human needs and the self-determination of behavior' *Psychological Inquiry*, **11**(4), 227–68.

De Cremer, D. and T.R. Tyler (2007), 'The effects of trust in authority and procedural fairness on cooperation', *Journal of Applied Psychology*, **92**(3), 639–49.

De Cremer, D. and D. van Knippenberg (2002), 'How do leaders promote cooperation? The effects of charisma and procedural fairness', *Journal of Applied Psychology*, **87**(5), 858–66.

De Cremer, D. and M. Van Vugt (1999), 'Social identification effects in social dilemmas: a transformation of motives', *European Journal of Social Psychology*, **29**(7), 871–93.

Eberl, P. (2004), 'The development of trust and implications for organizational design: a game- and attribution-theoretical framework', *Schmalenbach Business Review*, **56**(3), 258–73.

Eberl, P., U. Clement and H. Moeller (2011), 'Socializing employees' trust in the organization: an exploration of apprentices' socialization in two high-trusted companies', *EGOS*, Gothenburg.

Eisenhardt, K.M. (1985), 'Control: organizational and economic approaches', *Management Science*, **31**(2), 134–49.

Eisenhardt, K.M. (1989), 'Agency theory: an assessment and review', *Academy of Management Review*, **14**(1), 57–74.

Falk, A. and M. Kosfeld (2006), 'The hidden costs of control', *American Economic Review*, **96**(5), 1611–30.

Fehr, E. and U. Fischbacher (2004), 'Social norms and human cooperation', *Trends in Cognitive Sciences*, **8**(4), 185–90.

Fehr, E. and S. Gachter (2000), 'Cooperation and punishment in public goods experiments', *The American Economic Review*, **90**(4), 980–94.

Fehr, E., A. Falk and U. Fischbacher (2003), 'On the nature of fair behavior', *Economic Inquiry*, **41**(1), 20–26.
Feld, L.P. and B.S. Frey (2007), 'Tax compliance as the result of a psychological tax contract: the role of incentives and responsive regulation', *Law and Policy*, **29**(1), 102–20.
Ferrin, D.L., M.C. Bligh and J.C. Kohles (2008), 'It takes two to tango: an interdependence analysis of the spiraling of perceived trustworthiness and cooperation in interpersonal and intergroup relationships', *Organizational Behavior and Human Decision Processes*, **107**(2), 161–78.
Frey, B.S. (1997), 'A constitution for knaves crowds out civic virtues', *Economic Journal*, **107**(443), 1043–53.
Frey, B.S. and M. Osterloh (2002), *Successful Management by Motivation. Balancing Intrinsic and Extrinsic Incentives*, Berlin/Heidelberg/New York: Springer.
Frey, B.S. and B. Torgler (2007), 'Tax morale and conditional cooperation', *Journal of Comparative Economics*, **35**(1), 136–59.
Frost, J., M. Osterloh and A. Weibel (2010), 'Governing knowledge work: transactional and transformational solutions', *Organizational Dynamics*, **39**(2), 126–36.
Fukuyama, F. (1995), *Trust: The Social Virtues and the Creation of Prosperity*, New York: Free Press.
Gagne, M. and E.L. Deci (2005), 'Self-determination theory and work motivation', *Journal of Organizational Behavior*, **26**(4), 331–62.
Gambetta, D. (1988), *Trust: Making and Breaking Cooperative Relations*, New York: Basil Blackwell.
Ghoshal, S. and P. Moran (1996), 'Bad practice: a critique of the transaction cost theory', *Academy of Management Review*, **21**(1), 13–47.
Gouldner, A.W. (1960), 'The norm of reciprocity: a preliminary statement', *American Sociological Review*, **25**(2), 161–78.
Govier, T. (1994), 'Is it a jungle out there – trust, distrust and the construction of social-reality', *Dialogue – Canadian Philosophical Review*, **33**(2), 237–53.
Grund, C. and C. Harbring (2009), 'Trust and control at the workplace: evidence from representative samples of employees in Europe', Discussion Paper No. 4297, IZA, Bonn.
Gulati, R. (1995), 'Does familiarity breed trust? The implications of repeated ties for contractual choice in alliances', *Academy of Management Journal*, **38**(1), 85–112.
Hackman, J.R. and E.E. Lawler (1971), 'Employee reactions to job characteristics', *Journal of Applied Psychology*, **55**(3), 259–86.
Hardin, G. (1968), 'The tragedy of the commons', *Science*, **162**(3859), 1243–8.
Hardin, R. (1992), 'The street-level epistemology of trust', *Analyse and Kritik*, **14**(2), 152–76.
Harkins, S.G. and R.E. Petty (1982), 'Effects of task-difficulty and task uniqueness on social loafing', *Journal of Personality and Social Psychology*, **43**(6), 1214–29.
Haslam, S.A., C. Powell and J.C. Turner (2000), 'Social identity, self-categorization, and work motivation: rethinking the contribution of the group to positive and sustainable organisational outcomes', *Applied Psychology – An International Review*, **49**(3), 319–39.
Hattie, J. and H. Timperley (2007), 'The power of feedback', *Review of Educational Research*, **77**(1), 81–112.
Higgins, R., P. Hartley and A. Skelton (2002), 'The conscientious consumer: reconsidering the role of assessment feedback in student learning', *Studies in Higher Education*, **27**(1), 53–64.
Hobbes, T. (1909), 'Leviathan', in W.G. Pogson (ed.), *Leviathan*, Oxford: The Clarendon Press.
Jones, S.C. (1973), 'Self-and interpersonal evaluations – esteem theories versus consistency theories', *Psychological Bulletin*, **79**(3), 185–99.
Kee, H.W. and R.E. Knox (1970), 'Conceptual and methodological considerations in the study of trust and suspicion', *Journal of Conflict Resolution*, **14**(3), 357–66.
Kluger, A.N. and A. DeNisi (1996), 'The effects of feedback interventions on performance: a historical review, a meta-analysis, and a preliminary feedback intervention theory', *Psychological Bulletin*, **119**(2), 254–84.

Kollock, P. (1998), 'Social dilemmas: the anatomy of cooperation', *Annual Review of Sociology*, **22**(1), 183–205.
Komorita, S.S. and C.D. Parks (1995), 'Interpersonal relations: mixed-motive interaction', *Annual Review of Psychology*, **46**, 183–207.
Kramer, R.M. and M.B. Brewer (1984), 'Effects of group identity on resource use in a simulated commons dilemma', *Journal of Personality and Social Psychology*, **46**(5), 1044–57.
Kramer, R.M., M.B. Brewer and B.A. Hanna (1996), 'Collective trust and collective action', in R. Kramer and K. Cook (eds), *Trust in Organizations: Frontiers of Theory and Research*, New York: Russell Sage Foundation, pp. 357–89.
Kruglanski, A.W. (1970), 'Attributing trustworthiness in supervisor–worker relations', *Journal of Experimental Social Psychology*, **6**(2), 214–32.
Leana, C.R., R.S. Ahlbrandt and A.J. Murrell (1992), 'The effects of employee involvement programs on unionized workers' attitudes, perceptions, and preferences in decision making', *Academy of Management Journal*, **35**(4), 861–73.
Lewicki, R.J. and B.B. Bunker (1995), 'Trust in relationships: a model of trust development and decline', in B.B. Bunker and J.Z. Rubin (eds), *Conflict, Cooperation, and Justice*, San Francisco: Jossey-Bass.
Lewicki, R.J., D.J. McAllister and R.J. Bies (1998), 'Trust and distrust: new relationships and realities', *Academy of Management Review*, **23**(3), 438–58.
Lind, E.A. and T.R. Tyler (1988), *The Social Psychology of Procedural Justice*, New York: Plenum.
Lindenberg, S. (2000), 'It takes both trust and lack of mistrust: the workings of cooperation and relational signaling in contractual relationships', *Journal of Management and Governance*, **4**(1/2), 11–33.
Locke, E.A. and G.P. Latham (1990), *A Theory of Goal Setting and Task Performance*, Englewood Cliffs, NJ: Prentice-Hall.
London, M. and J.W. Smither (1999), 'Empowered self-development and continuous learning', *Human Resource Management*, **38**(1), 3–15.
London, M., H.H. Larsen and L.N. Thisted (1999), 'Relationships between feedback and self-development', *Group and Organization Management*, **24**(1), 5–27.
Mayer, R.C. and J.H. Davis (1999), 'The effect of the performance appraisal system on trust for management: a field quasi experiment', *Journal of Applied Psychology*, **84**(1), 123–36.
Mayer, R.C. and F.D. Schoorman (1998), 'Differentiating antecedents of organizational commitment: a test of March and Simon's model', *Journal of Organizational Behavior*, **19**(1), 15–28.
Mayer, R.C., J.H. Davis and F.D. Schoorman (1995), 'An integrative model of organizational trust', *Academy of Management Review*, **20**(3), 709–34.
McAllister, D.J. (1995), Affect- and cognition-based trust as foundations for interpersonal cooperation in organizations', *Academy of Management Journal*, **38**(1), 24–59.
McGregor, D. (1960), *The Human Side of Enterprise*, New York: McGraw Hill.
Messick, D.M. and M.B. Brewer (1983), 'Solving social dilemmas: a review', in L. Wheeler (ed.), *Review of Personality and Social Psychology*, Vol. 4, Beverly Hills: Sage, pp. 11–44.
Meyer, J.W., W.R. Scott, D. Strang and A.L. Creighton (1988), 'Bureaucratization without centralization: changes in the organizational system of US public education, 1940–80', in L.G. Zucker (ed.), *Institutional Patterns and Organizations: Culture and Environment*, Cambridge, MA: Ballinger, pp. 139–68.
Miller, G. (1992), *Managerial Dilemmas. The Political Economy of Hierarchy*, Cambridge, UK: Cambridge University Press.
Mishra, K., G. Schwarz and A. Mishra (2011), 'The evolution of trust and control as seen through an organization's human resource practices', in R. Searle and D. Skinner (eds), *Trust and Human Resource Management*, Cheltenham, UK and Northampton, MA, USA: Edward Elgar Publishing.
Möllering, G. (2005), 'The trust/control duality', *International Sociology*, **20**(3), 283–305.

Nahapiet, J. and S. Ghoshal (1998), 'Social capital, intellectual capital and the organizational advantage', *Academy of Management Review*, **23**(2), 242–66.
Oldham, G.R. and A. Cummings (1996), 'Employee creativity: personal and contextual factors at work', *Academy of Management Journal*, **39**(3), 607–34.
Orbell, J.M. and R.M. Dawes (1981), 'Social dilemmas', in G. Stephenson and J.H. Davis (eds), *Progress in Applied Social Psychology*, Vol. 1, Chichester: Wiley, pp. 37–65.
Pearce, J.L. (2008), 'Bureaucracy and trust: a review of recent volumes in the Russell Sage Foundation series on trust', *International Public Management Journal*, **11**(4), 481–5.
Pearson, C.A.L. (1991), 'An assessment of extrinsic feedback on participation, role perceptions, motivation, and job-satisfaction in a self-managed system for monitoring group achievement', *Human Relations*, **44**(5), 517–37.
Pettijohn, C., L.S. Pettijohn, A.J. Taylor and B.D. Keillor (2001), 'Are performance appraisals a bureaucratic exercise or can they be used to enhance sales-force satisfaction and commitment?', *Psychology and Marketing*, **18**(4), 337–64.
Poppo, L., K.Z. Zhou and S. Ryu (2008), 'Alternative origins to interorganizational trust: an interdependence perspective on the shadow of the past and the shadow of the future', *Organization Science*, **19**(1), 39–55.
Ramaswami, S.N. (1996), 'Marketing controls and dysfunctional employee behaviors: a test of traditional and contingency theory postulates', *Journal of Marketing*, **60**(2), 105–20.
Rhodes, S.R. and R.M. Steers (1981), 'Conventional vs worker-owned organizations', *Human Relations*, **34**(12), 1013–35.
Robbins, T.L. (1995), 'Social loafing on cognitive tasks: an examination of the "sucker effect"', *Journal of Business and Psychology*, **9**(3), 337–42.
Rotter, J.B. (1971), 'A new scale for the measurement of interpersonal trust', *Journal of Personality*, **35**(4), 651–65.
Rotter, J.B. (1980), 'Interpersonal trust, trustworthiness, and gullibility', *American Psychologist*, **35**(1), 1–7.
Ryan, R.M. (1995), 'Psychological needs and the facilitation of integrative processes', *Journal of Personality*, **63**(3), 397–427.
Ryan, R.M. and E.L. Deci (2000), 'Self-determination theory and the facilitating of intrinsic motivation', *American Psychologist*, **55**(1), 68–78.
Ryan, R.M., K.M. Sheldon, T. Kasser and E.L. Deci (1996), 'All goals are not created equal: an organismic perspective in the nature of goals and their regulation', in P.M. Gollwitzer and J.A. Bargh (eds), *The Psychology of Action. Linking Cognition and Motivation to Behavior*, pp. 7–26, New York: Guilford Press.
Searle, R., A.Weibel and D.N. Den Hartog (2011), 'Employee trust in organizational contexts', *International Review of Industrial and Organizational Psychology*, **26**, 143–91.
Simon, H.A. (1991), 'Organization and markets', *Journal of Economic Perspectives*, **5**(2), 25–44.
Sitkin, S.B. (1995), 'On the positive effect of legalization on trust', *Research on Negotiation in Organizations*, **5**(30), 185–217.
Sitkin, S.B. and E. George (2005), 'Managerial trust-building through the use of legitimating formal and informal control mechanisms', *International Sociology*, **20**(3), 307–38.
Sitkin, S.B. and N.L. Roth (1993), 'Explaining the limited effectiveness of legalistic 'remedies' for trust/distrust', *Organization Science*, **4**(3), 367–92.
Sitkin, S.B., L.B. Cardinal and K. Bijlsma-Frankema (2010), *Control in Organizations: New Directions in Theory and Research*, Cambridge, UK: Cambridge University Press.
Sitkin, S.B., K.M. Sutcliffe and R.G. Schroeder (1994), 'Distinguishing control from learning in total quality management – a contingency perspective', *Academy of Management Review*, **19**(3), 537–64.
Six, F.E. (2013), 'Trust in regulatory relations: how new insights from trust research improve regulation theory', *Public Management Review*, **15**(2), 163–85.
Six, F.E. and A. Sorge (2008), 'Creating a high-trust organization: an exploration into

organizational policies that stimulate interpersonal trust building', *The Journal of Management Studies*, **45**(5), 857–84.

Sliwka, D. (2007), 'Trust as a signal of a social norm and the hidden costs of incentive schemes', *American Economic Review*, **97**(3), 999–1012.

Smith, B., N. Kerr, M. Markus and M. Stasson (2001), 'Individual differences in social loafing: need for cognition as a motivator in collective performance', *Group Dynamics, Theory, Research, and Practice*, **5**(2), 150–58.

Spreitzer, G.M. and A.K. Mishra (1999), 'Giving up control without losing control – trust and its substitutes', effects on managers' involving employees in decision making', *Group and Organization Management*, **24**(2), 155–87.

Spreitzer, G., K. Sutcliffe, J. Dutton, S. Sonenshein and A. Grant (2005), 'A socially embedded model of thriving at work', *Organization Science*, **16**(5), 537–49.

Stack, L. (1978), 'Trust', in H. London and J. Exner (eds), *Dimensions of Personality*, New York, NY: John Wiley and Sons Inc.

Stolle, D. (1998), 'Bowling together, bowling alone: the development of generalized trust in voluntary associations', *Political Psychology*, **19**(3), 497–525.

Strickland, L.H. (1958), 'Surveillance and trust', *Journal of Personality*, **26**(2), 200–215.

Suchman, M.C. (1995), 'Managing legitimacy – strategic and institutional approaches', *Academy of Management Review*, **20**(3), 571–610.

Tannenbaum, A.S. (1968), *Control in Organizations*, New York: McGraw Hill.

Thompson, P.J. and C. Warhurst (1998), *Workplaces of the Future*, Basingstoke: Macmillan Business.

Tsui, A.S., J.L. Pearce, L.W. Porter and A.M. Tripoli (1997), 'Alternative approaches to the employee–organization relationship: does investment in employees pay off?', *The Academy of Management Journal*, **40**(5), 1089–121.

Tyler, T.R. (2003), 'Trust within organisations', *Personnel Review*, **32**(5), 556–68.

Tyler, T. (2006), 'Psychological perspectives on legitimacy and legitimation', *Annual Review of Psychology*, **57**, 375–400.

Tyler, T. and S.L. Blader (2005), 'Can businesses effectively regulate employee conduct? The antecedents of rule following in work settings', *Academy of Management Journal*, **48**(6), 1143–58.

Tyler, T.R. and P. Degoey (1996), 'Collective restraint in social dilemmas: procedural justice and social identification effects on support for authorities', *Journal Personality and Social Psychology*, **69**(3), 482–97.

Van de Walle, S. and F.E. Six (forthcoming), 'Trust and distrust as distinct concepts: why studying distrust in institutions is important', *Journal of Comparative Policy Analysis*.

Van Vugt, M. (2002), 'Central, individual, or collective control?' *American Behavioral Scientist*, **45**(5), 783–800.

Victor, B. and J.B. Cullen (1988), 'The organizational bases of ethical work climates', *Administrative Science Quarterly*, **33**(1), 101–25.

Weber, M. (1921), *Wirtschaft und Gesellschaft*, Köln/Berlin: Kiepenheuer & Witsch.

Weibel, A. (2007), 'Formal control and trustworthiness – never the twain shall meet?', *Group and Organization Management*, **32**(4), 500–517.

Weibel, A. (2010), 'Managerial objectives of formal control: high motivation control mechanisms', in S.B. Sitkin, L.B. Cardinal and K. Bijlsma-Frankema (eds), *Control in Organizations: New Directions in Theory and Research*, Cambridge UK: Cambridge University Press, pp. 434–62.

Weibel, A., R. Searle, D. Den Hartog, D. Skinner, F. Six and N. Gillespie (2009), 'Formal control as a driver of organizational trustworthiness', University of Liechtenstein.

White, R.W. (1959), 'Motivation reconsidered: the concept of competence', *Psychological Review*, **66**(5) 297–333.

Whitener, E.M., S.E. Brodt, M.A. Korsgaard and J.M. Werner (1998), 'Managers as initiators of trust: an exchange relationship framework for understanding managerial trustworthy behavior', *Academy of Management Review*, **23**(3), 513–30.

Williamson, O.E. (1980), 'The organization of work a comparative institutional assessment', *Journal of Economic Behavior and Organization*, **1**(1), 5–38.
Williamson, O.E. (1993a), 'Calculativeness, trust and economic organization', *Journal of Law and Economics*, **36**(1), 453–86.
Williamson, O.E. (1993b), 'Opportunism and its critics', *Managerial and Decision Economics*, **14**(2), 97–107.
Yakovleva, M., R.R. Reilly and R. Werko (2010), 'Why do we trust? Moving beyond individual to dyadic perceptions', *Journal of Applied Psychology*, **95**(1), 79–91.

4. Trust and contracts: together forever, never apart?
Paul W.L. Vlaar

INTRODUCTION

Potential ties between the construct of 'trust' and the concept of 'contracting' find resonance in popular sayings and statements on collaborative relationships, such as 'contracts destroy trust', 'no contract without trust', 'contracting as a deed of trust', and 'trust has to emerge from the contract'. Correspondingly, scholars studying interorganizational relations have established various interrelationships between both constructs. Some, for instance, have suggested that both phenomena substitute (Gulati, 1995; Kvaløy and Olsen, 2009), and/or complement each other (Arrighetti et al., 1997; Poppo and Zenger, 2002; Weibel et al., 2007; Li et al., 2010). Others have explored their dynamic interactions, suggesting that changes in trust and contracting may trigger reactions and responses from exchange partners (Vlaar et al., 2007; Ferrin et al., 2008).

The implicit assumption underlying most work in this area is that contracting and trust are intimately related. For various reasons though, I suggest that we are overly sensitive to observable associations between both constructs, possibly overstating their salience and significance. This partly derives from pragmatic causes, such as the inclination of academic scholars and journals to favour significant relationships above insignificant effects. Yet, in this chapter I suggest several more fundamental arguments supporting the notion that trust and contracting are less tightly related than we are sometimes led to believe.

To substantiate the line of thought set out in this chapter, I present a number of arguments, which at their core hold the following:

- Compared to other variables, contracting may be a relatively insignificant antecedent of trust, while trust may be a relatively insignificant antecedent of contracting.
- Trust and contracting tend to be conflated with their own antecedents, resulting in the overstatement of direct effects and the underestimation of partially mediating effects.
- Organizational members exhibit strong variation in terms of their

involvement in contracting processes, limiting the validity of the relationship between both constructs.
- Research has largely ignored the multi-functional nature of trust and contracting, focusing on and overstating their joint role in coping with uncertainty and risk.
- Trust and contracting can take different forms, something that is largely dependent on the institutional and cultural context.
- The dynamics amongst trust and contracting vary across different stages of collaboration, limiting the significance of their interrelationships at particular times.
- Existing research often inaccurately refers to the concept of trust in situations for which distrust and understanding would be more appropriate.

Yet, to establish my arguments, I first present basic definitions of trust and contracting, as well as a brief overview of some of the most common perspectives held on the interaction between both constructs.

PREVAILING PERSPECTIVES

Following Mayer et al. (1995, p. 712), I define trust as: 'the willingness of a party to be vulnerable to the actions of another party based on the expectation that the other will perform a particular action important to the trustor, irrespective of the ability to monitor or control that other party'. Moreover, I recognize that it is individual managers and not organizations as a whole that trust others (Dodgson, 1993; Zaheer et al., 1998; Ferrin et al., 2007), which is why I refer to trust as a 'focal person's belief' in a counterpart's ability to accomplish a task, their goodwill, positive intentions and adherence to acceptable values (Mayer et al., 1995; Serva et al., 2005).

Contracting, in turn, consists of the codification and enforcement of inputs, outcomes and interorganizational activities (Kvaløy and Olsen, 2009), as well as the processes involved with 'projecting exchanges into the future' (McNeil, 1980, p. 4; Vlaar, 2008). Contracts and the processes from which they arise are not only aimed at curbing opportunistic behaviour, establishing control and aligning interests with others (Williamson, 1985; Oxley, 1997), but also at coordinating activities amongst collaborating parties (Klein Woolthuis et al., 2005) and making sense of one's partner, the relationship developing amongst both organizations and the environment in which it is embedded (Vlaar et al., 2006).

Prior work on the interrelationships between both constructs principally emphasizes the idea that trust and contracting may act as substitutes and/or complements. The argument for a substitution effect, for instance, holds that the presence of trust reduces the need to contract, and vice versa (for example, Gulati, 1995; Zaheer and Venkatraman, 1995; Dyer and Singh, 1998; Das and Teng, 2001; Inkpen and Currall, 2004). From this point of view, trust and contracting provide 'functionally equivalent strategies for absorbing uncertainty and dealing with the freedom and indeterminacy of other agents' (Knights et al., 2001, p. 329).

Alternatively, both concepts have been proposed to behave as complements (for example, Arrighetti et al., 1997). Trust may, for example, stimulate communication and information exchange, and thereby enable parties to negotiate and write contracts, even including 'thorny sensitive clauses like relationship termination' (Klein Woolthuis et al., 2005, p. 831). Moreover, contracting may help to create congruent expectations amongst representatives of different firms, making it easier for them to interpret the behaviour of their counterparts (Malhotra and Murnighan, 2002; Carson et al., 2006; Vlaar and Klijn, 2011; Weber and Mayer, 2011), thereby possibly stimulating trust. Likewise, as Li et al.'s (2010) study on collaborative relationships between Chinese foreign subsidiaries and their suppliers shows, formal contracts may strengthen the effects of trust on the acquisition of tacit and explicit knowledge.

Interactions amongst trust and contracting have further been proposed to develop along self-reinforcing cycles (for example, Macaulay, 1963; Zand, 1972; Ghoshal and Moran, 1996; Inkpen and Currall, 2004). For instance, when actors initially experience high levels of trust in a partner organization, attempts at contracting by their counterparts may be regarded as a symbol of commitment, shared values and communal norms and customs (Zucker, 1986; Serva et al., 2005; Klein Woolthuis et al., 2005), which in turn allow them to capture other aspects of the relationship in formal documents (Poppo and Zenger, 2002; Mayer and Argyres, 2004).

In contrast, in the absence of trust, focal actors may hesitate to reveal information, reject influence and evade control (Zand, 1972; Arrighetti et al., 1997; Anderson and Jap, 2005). In such cases, acts of contracting may in fact undermine the development of trust (for example, Sitkin and Roth, 1993; Lewicki et al., 1998), since they can be regarded as evidence that one's goodwill or competence is thrown into doubt (Sitkin and Roth, 1993; Ghoshal and Moran, 1996; Das and Teng, 2001; Poppo and Zenger, 2002). This can ignite 'inflationary spirals' of increasingly formalized relationships (Sitkin and Roth, 1993, p. 367) or relationships that become 'locked up' in formalities (Parkhe, 1993; Nooteboom, 1999).

Summarizing, we can conclude that existing work on trust and contracting has established positive as well as negative associations between both constructs, both from a static as well as a dynamic perspective. Current views may suffer from strong biases though, inaccurately representing both constructs as intimately related. In the remainder of this chapter, I will outline a number of arguments that challenge conventional wisdom on this matter.

OTHER ANTECEDENTS OF TRUST AND CONTRACTING

My first argument supporting the claim that trust and contracting may be less tightly related than we are sometimes led to believe, involves the notion that, compared to other variables, contracting may be a relatively insignificant antecedent of trust, while trust may be a relatively insignificant antecedent of contracting (see Figure 4.1). The idea behind this argument is fairly straightforward, and holds for both concepts; trust and contracting are each influenced by a great number of other variables, reducing the significance of their interrelationship.

Taking the literature on trust as the point of departure, it becomes clear that antecedents of trust can be divided, amongst others, in terms of personal characteristics, transaction variables, organizational factors and environmental characteristics. Examples of personal characteristics

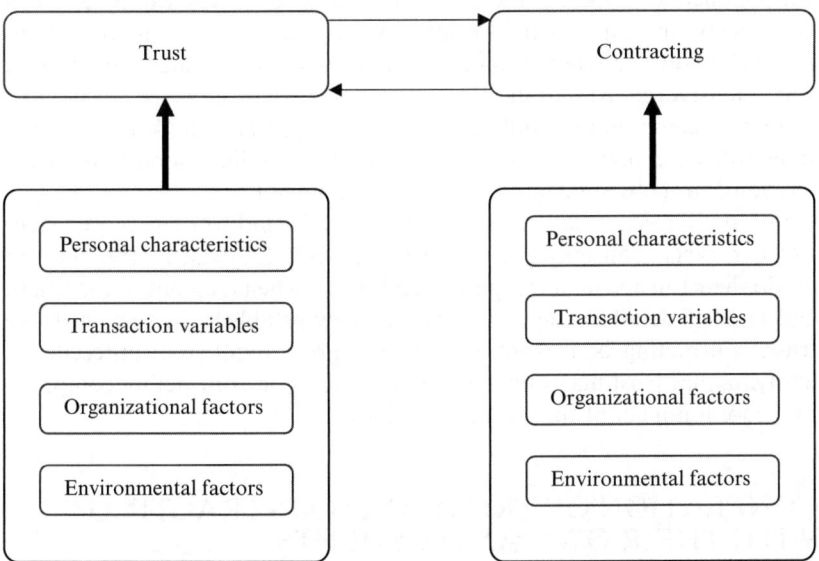

Figure 4.1 Relative (in)significance of contracting and trust as each other's antecedents

influencing trust, for example, include professional credentials and citizenship behaviour (McAllister, 1995). Transaction, exchange or relational variables affecting trust include, amongst others, partners' history of previous cooperation and their 'shadow of the future' (Zhou et al., 2008).

In a similar vein, organizational factors influencing trust involve aspects such as firm age, firm reputation and the type of leadership prevailing in an organization. Finally, environmental characteristics influencing trust consist of, for example, national culture, market dynamism and the presence (or absence) of various institutions. As becomes clear from this brief – and far from comprehensive – discussion, trust has a great number of antecedents. Extrapolating from this insight, it becomes clear that contracting may only have minor effects on trust compared to the joint impact of all these other variables.

The same is supposed to hold for the influence that trust is likely to have on contracting. Antecedents of contracting can also be divided across personal characteristics, transaction variables, organizational factors and environmental characteristics. Individuals with a risk-averse personality and extensive experience with contracting, for instance, are likely to deploy different negotiation and contracting styles from people that are more uncertain and less experienced with the law and legal procedures.

Likewise, negotiations and contracts tend to become more complete and detailed the higher risks become. This occurs, for example, when investments in relation-specific investments may give rise to opportunistic behaviour or when complex exchanges require mutual adaptation and intensive coordination (Williamson, 1985). In contrast, exchanges involving commodities and mass-produced goods are likely to entail standardized contracts (Vlaar, 2008), reducing the likelihood that strong relationships between contracting and trust prevail.

In a similar vein, mature organizations are bound to write more extensive contracts than entrepreneurial ones, while US-based firms tend to outdo their European and Japanese colleagues when it comes to the length and level of detail in the contracts that they establish. In sum, just like trust, contracting is also influenced by a great number of antecedents, implying that trust may only have minor effects on contracting compared to the joint impact of these other variables.

CONFLATION OF TRUST AND CONTRACTING WITH THEIR OWN ANTECEDENTS

My second argument as to why trust and contracting may be less tightly related than we are sometimes led to believe, concerns the idea that it is not

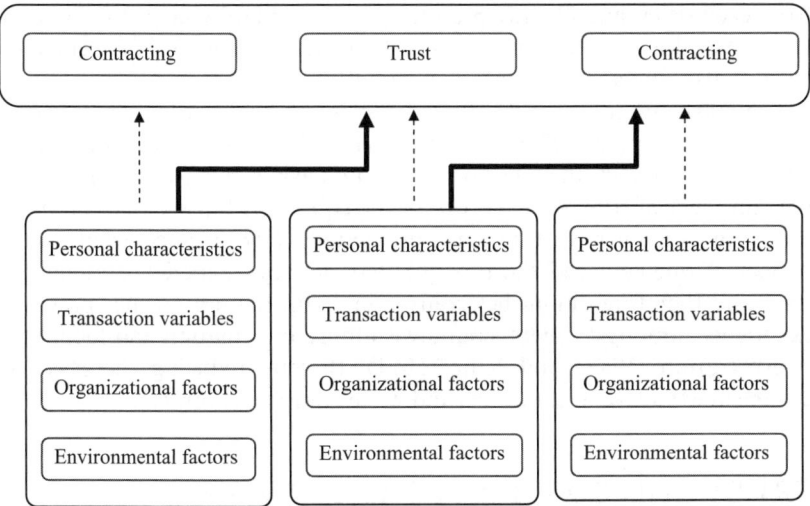

Figure 4.2   Overstatement of direct effects and underestimation of partially mediating effects

the constructs themselves that have a strong interrelationship, but rather their antecedents. Conflation of these variables results in an overstatement of the direct effects of trust and contracting and an underestimation of partially mediating effects (see also Figure 4.2).

Let me offer a few examples to clarify this matter. Take the personal characteristic 'risk averseness'. This variable undoubtedly influences contracting and thereby indirectly trust, but it may simultaneously influence trust directly. More specifically, risk-averse people not only write more complete contracts, but they may simultaneously exhibit lower levels of trust in their counterparts. In turn, this may lead them to write more detailed and complex contracts. The question then becomes, what part of the presupposed interrelationship between trust and contracting in fact emerges from the antecedent 'risk averseness'? In other words, to what extent can one attribute associations between both constructs to the notions of trust and contracting themselves?

Another example constitutes situations in which parties have previously cooperated with each other as compared to situations in which partners collaborate for the first time. In the first instance, parties may have developed mutual trust, which diminishes their perceived need to establish complex contracts. On the other hand, one could argue that previous cooperation has a direct negative influence on contracting, because partners have developed collaborative routines, know better what to expect from each other and already preside over a 'standard contract form' that they have adopted during previous exchanges. Although this may enhance trust, it also directly influences contracting.

Summarizing, the issue put up for discussion here is whether it is trust and contracting themselves that influence each other, or their underlying antecedents. In fact, the question one should ask is, what would happen if the construct of trust were left out of the equation? I argue that, in many cases, we would arrive at the same predictions. For instance, what would happen if one replaced the thought that previous experience augments trust and therefore diminishes contracting with the notion that previous experience, amongst others, comes with more information and facilitates interpretation (Vlaar and Klijn, 2011), thereby reducing the need to engage in extensive negotiations and write complex contracts?

TRUST AND CONTRACTING ACROSS INSTITUTIONAL AND CULTURAL CONTEXTS

Existing research on trust and contracting, as well as their interrelationships, tends to pertain to stable contexts such as Western Europe and the USA in which institutions and culture promote trust-based collaboration (Child and Möllering, 2003; Ferrin 2007; Tillmar and Lindkvist, 2007). Yet, interactions between trust and contracting are likely to vary considerably amongst cultural and institutional settings (Bachmann and Inkpen, 2011).

Reliable institutional frameworks, for example, have been found to play an important role in establishing trust (McKnight et al., 1998; Cook et al., 2005), and in the enforcement of contracts (Vlaar, 2008). In the absence of strong institutions, exchange partners find it hard to establish trust in others, and they attribute less value to contracts, since it is more difficult to make them comply with earlier made agreements. Consequently, in environments characterized by weak institutional regimes, trust and contracting exhibit little interaction.

In a similar vein, actors' propensity to trust has been shown to differ across cultures (Kim, 2008), influencing actors' inclination to initiate and maintain collaborative relations (Cook et al., 2005), and affecting the payoffs they receive from behaving trustworthily (Slemrod and Katuščásk, 2005), as well as the chances that trust is restored after the occurrence of incidents or crises (Ren and Gray, 2009). The same holds for contracting, which strongly differs in nature across, for example, Asian, European, African and Anglo-Saxon cultures.

As an example, contracts in the USA tend to be much more detailed than in many other countries. At the same time, Northern Americans exhibit a relatively high inclination to trust. The opposite holds for many African countries, in which most exchanges are accompanied by basic contracts and trust is often limited to the family and exchange partners in nearby areas. Obviously, the interactions between trust and contracting vary considerably across these settings, remaining especially limited when one or both constructs prevail at low levels.

DIFFERENCES IN INVOLVEMENT AND PERCEPTIONS AMONGST INDIVIDUALS

A third factor diminishing the potential for interactions between contacting and trust concerns differences in involvement and perception amongst individuals in trust and contracting processes. In constructing the argument underlying this claim, I follow Argyres and Mayer (2007), who argue that managers and engineers will be the primary repositories of a firm's contract design capabilities when it comes to the allocation and description of roles and responsibilities, as well as the structuring of communication between parties. Lawyers and legal experts, instead, are more likely to be involved in discussions and negotiations on the allocation of decision and control rights, dispute resolution and contingency planning.

In pursuing this argument further, I argue that both groups of individuals are likely to respond differently to negotiation and contracting in terms of the level of trust they install in partner organizations. Negotiating and drafting legal documents by the first group of persons, for instance, is much more likely to enhance trust, as persons in this cluster primarily focus on how parties can create value through collaboration and as these processes entail the possibility for them to exhibit their competencies and their knowledge of the relationship's subject matter. Alternatively, I propose that the second group of persons tends to focus much more on topics related to value appropriation, potential conflicts and risks, that is, the downsides of relationships. Activities associated with negotiation and contracting by this group therefore tend to involve different trust dynamics (see Figure 4.3).

In a similar vein, one could argue that it is often just the higher-level managers and executives that take part in negotiation and contracting processes, whereas employees lower in the organization only become involved after contracts have been signed. This means that these persons may only be vaguely aware of the considerations standing at the basis of particular contract terms. In fact, in many cases contract details are kept secret on purpose and not even communicated to lower-level employees. Consequently, contracting may play only a minor role in building, maintaining and repairing trust these employees hold in a partner firm. In that regard, it is not surprising that practitioners often contend that it is not so much contracts or other legal artefacts influencing their trust in another company, but rather the persons in front of them, on whom they are dependent and with whom they deal directly.

Relatedly, those employees that have been involved in negotiating and writing contracts are often, and for numerous reasons, not the ones supposed to apply these during the course of collaborative relationships. An important cause resides in the fact that persons responsible for operational matters are not always skilled in and accountable for the benefits that a firm reaps from its contracts with other parties. Especially in larger firms, this means that potential conflicts or disputes are relegated to in-house lawyers and legal experts. Lower-level employees tend to be primarily concerned with coordinating activities and creating value, while higher-level managers and executives often focus more on value-claiming activities as well, referring to contract terms when necessary. Consequently, interactions between trust and contracting may for the large part be circumscribed to high-level employees, as well as in-house lawyers and legal experts.

Individuals may further vary in the extent to which they are able to identify and verify whether partners conform to contracts and therefore confirm or disconfirm one's expectations. This may depend, amongst others, on their history with a partner firm, their knowledge of the subject matter of a relationship and their alertness and proactivity when it comes to monitoring the partner firm and evaluating intermediate outcomes and interaction processes. In line with work by Faems et al. (2008), I further suggest that the application of contracts may vary across individuals, since legal documents are often read by a limited number of stakeholders in collaborative relationships, something that especially holds for standard contracts (Vlaar, 2008).

Likewise, contract application may be delimited by personnel turnover, causing fewer people in a focal organization to be aware of the information contained in contract terms. In a similar vein, firms and their employees may have little experience in writing contracts (Mayer and Argyres, 2004), possibly causing them to be unsure as to whether and when to refer to contracts and making them reluctant to enforce particular clauses or specific terms in practice. The aforementioned factors suggest that interactions between trust and contracting are much less salient, for example, when one zooms in on individuals having a technical background at lower levels of an organization, when there is a clear separation between legal departments and functional and operational staff in an organization, and when appellation to contracts and assessments of contract breach are not straightforward.

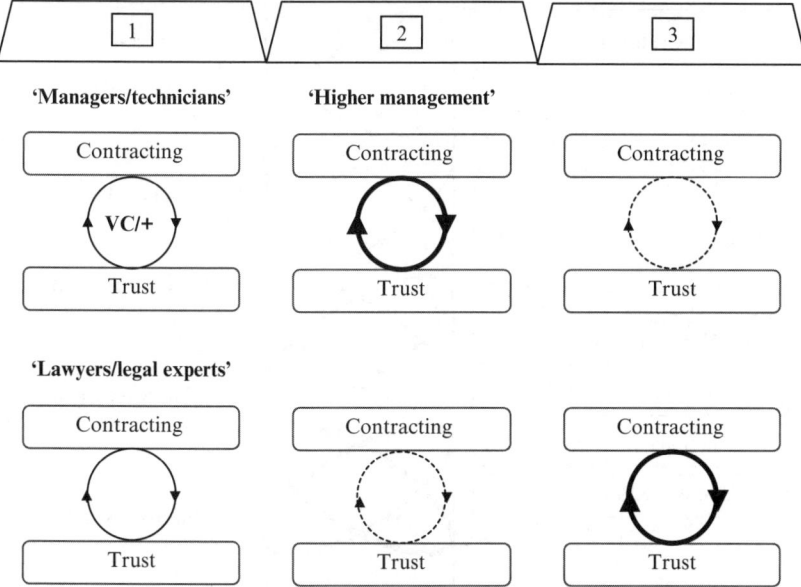

Figure 4.3 Variation in salience of interrelations between trust and contracting across individuals

This is visualized in Figure 4.3. By using two identical circles in block 1, I suggest that relationships between trust and contracting per se are unlikely to differ between managers/technicians and lawyers/legal experts. Yet, the emphasis on value creation (VC) in the upper circle will lead to more positive trust dynamics as compared to the lower circle, in which the emphasis shifts more towards value appropriation. In block 2, the bold line of the upper circle suggests that the interplay between trust and contracting can be expected to be much more intense at higher management levels than at the level of operational employees, reflected by the dashed line of the lower circle. Likewise, the circles in block 3 suggest similar differences in trust-contracting dynamics between 'ignorant' and 'informed' employees.

IGNORANCE OF THE MULTI-DIMENSIONAL AND MULTI-FUNCTIONAL NATURE OF BOTH CONSTRUCTS

Next to issues of involvement and perception, research on the interaction between trust and contracting has to date almost neglected the

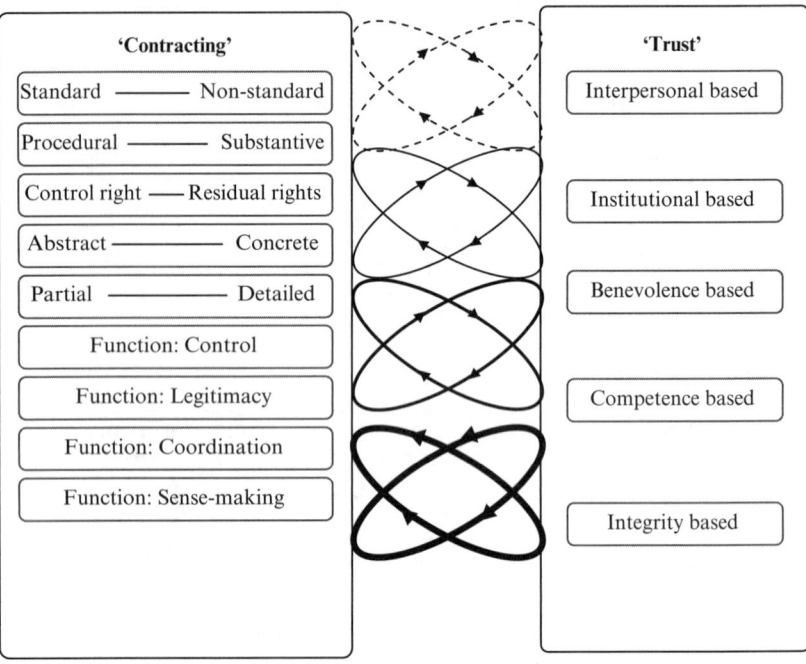

Figure 4.4   Variation in trust-contracting dynamics across functions and dimensions

multi-dimensional and multi-functional nature of both constructs. Starting with trust, researchers have distinguished multiple dimensions of trust, such as interpersonal trust and institutional-based trust (Bachmann and Inkpen, 2011). As another example, Mayer et al. (1995) suggest that trust may alternatively be grounded in benevolence (in other words, disposition to do good), competence (in other words, possessing the required resources and capabilities) and integrity (in other words, adherence to moral values).

The question then becomes whether certain dimensions of trust are more likely to interact with contracting than others (see also Figure 4.4). In this regard, one could speculate that expectations regarding a partner firm's benevolence, for example, are not necessarily grounded in contracts or the processes associated with their creation and application. Instead, these expectations may, for example, derive from previous experiences, a firm's reputation, small talk by (former) employees, and so on. Similarly, a partner firm's integrity may not so much be assessed by how others deal with contracts and contracting processes, but possibly much more by the squareness and consistency with which people behave, irrespective of contracts. Likewise, in terms of competence, one may ask whether one trusts a partner because promises have been made in contracts, or because one is aware of the actual competencies underlying these promises.

More generally speaking, I suggest that interactions between trust and contracting are less important than we are led to believe, because benevolence-based trust, integrity-based trust, and competence-based trust largely derive from sources other than the contract and contracting processes (in other words, the creation, modification and application of contracts). We may falsely attribute correlations between contracting and trust to changes in these constructs, although they may in fact derive from their underlying factors or dimensions.

For example, when a partner does not hold its contractual promise to produce good A at time $t = 1$ due to a failure by one of its employees, authors might suggest that contract breach reduces competence-based trust. Yet, one could also state that one's expectations about the partner firm's competence were not appropriate, irrespective of what was written in the contract. Similarly, although one's expectations regarding a partner's competence may have been reinforced by a contractual promise, they would undoubtedly not be completely reversed when there was no contract to confirm them.

When we turn to contracts and contracting processes, numerous dimensions may be distinguished as well. One can think of differences between standard contracts and tailor-made contracts (Vlaar, 2008), procedural and substantive contract clauses (Furlotti, 2007), promotion- versus prevention-framed contracts (Weber and Mayer, 2011) and contracts primarily featuring control rights as compared to contracts principally containing residual rights (Foss, 2005). Regarding the first, standardized contracts are less likely to provoke changes in trust than tailor-made contracts, while changes in trust are unlikely to provoke large changes in standardized contracts. Concerning procedural and substantive contract clauses, the first are much more likely to provoke changes in trust, since violations are relatively easy to observe and as they may occur more frequently than violations of substantive clauses, which are often concerned with the input and outcomes of a relationship (in other words, centred towards the beginning and the end of a relationship).

Looking at the distinction between residual and control rights, it becomes clear that the latter leave far less room for discussion after the contract has been signed, reducing the significance of possible interactions between trust and contracting per se. Finally, I wish to note that contracts that are short and abstract probably entail different trust dynamics than ones that are long and detailed. In contrast to concrete and detailed contracts, for instance, abstract contracts leave a lot to interpretation, and they provide little leeway for hold-up situations in which parties abuse contract terms for unintended purposes. Alternatively, the latter type of contracts diminish creativity and flexibility, reducing opportunities for parties to perform beyond expectations.

Next to distinguishing different dimensions, interactions between trust and contracts may vary with the functions that partners aim to achieve through the contracting process and the contracts resulting from these processes (Vlaar, 2008). Almost all discussions on the interrelationships between trust and contracting focus on the role of contracts as mechanisms to align incentives and control partners. Yet, contracting may also facilitate knowledge sharing (Arrighetti et al., 1997; Li et al., 2010), and it may function as a firm's memory (Osadchiy, 2011). Alternatively, it can serve as a means to gain legitimacy, achieve coordination and give and make sense of one's partner, the collaborative relationship in which one is engaged and the environment in which it is embedded (Vlaar et al., 2006). This raises the question as to whether and how trust and contracting interact when the latter is not primarily aimed at aligning incentives and controlling one's partner.

VARIATION IN TRUST-CONTRACTING DYNAMICS ACROSS STAGES OF COLLABORATION

Variation in trust-contracting dynamics may also arise across distinct stages of collaboration. Following prior work, one could subdivide the collaboration process in interorganizational relationships, for example, in a formation, management and renegotiation or dissolution stage (see Figure 4.5). In the *formation stage*, contracting processes primarily facilitate sense-making, sense-giving, sense-demanding and sense-breaking (Vlaar et al., 2008). Moreover, parties both consider opportunities for value creation as well as prospects for appropriating reasonable parts of this value during the contact development process. This stage in the contracting processes is further characterized by an emphasis on the discovery of possibilities and opportunities and the presence and persistence of uncertainties and open-ends.

In the same stage, trust tends to be grounded amongst others in prior experience and observable facts about the partner firm, such as publications, recommendations, endorsements and ratings or rankings by third parties. Yet, in cases in which partners are not very familiar with each other and have little joint history, interorganizational cooperation demands that they embrace residual risks and uncertainty, compelling

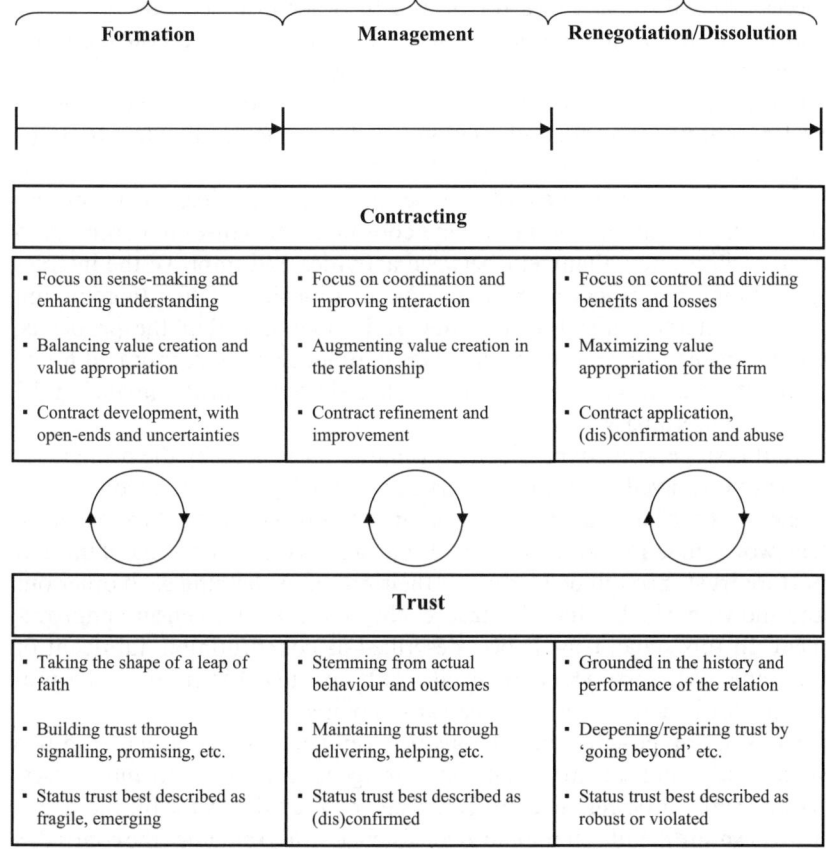

Figure 4.5   Different foci of and dynamics amongst trust and contracting over time

them to take a leap of faith (see also Möllering, 2006; Latusek and Vlaar, 2011). Partners further conduct considerable investments in building trust. They make promises, show evidence of their trustworthiness, provide positive signals about their behaviour, and so on. Although the status of trust in this stage is best described as fragile and emerging, a minimum level of trust tends to be necessary for prospective partners to engage in interorganizational relationships.

When we start exploring possible interactions between trust and contracting in the formation stage, the only possible conclusion then is that these are likely to vary a lot across distinct interorganizational relationships. In certain cases, the contracting process may be considered as a 'necessary evil' or a 'cause for delay'. In other instances, parties really aim to 'get to know each other', 'test the water', and 'see how the other responds and how far they can go'. In the first situation, interactions amongst trust and contracting tend to be weak and infrequent, whereas under the latter condition interactions can be strong, leading to a boost or a quick crumbling of initial levels of trust.

In the *management stage* of collaborative relationships, parties primarily work on refining and improving coordination clauses in contracts so as to facilitate the alignment between activities and improve the interaction amongst partners in collaborative relationships. They thereby aim to augment the realization of value and make sure that the problems, contingencies and conditions they face in practice are incorporated in the contract. In a sense, the emphasis has thus shifted towards enhancing the 'practical usefulness' of contracts.

In this stage, trust dynamics are primarily influenced by the behaviours actually displayed by firm representatives and by the intermediary outcomes that are being achieved. These may confirm or disconfirm partners' trustworthiness (Vlaar et al., 2007). Parties further try to maintain and nurture trust through delivering on their promises, helping each other out and showing which internal measures they have taken to ensure improvement. In this stage, trust is best described as constituting a 'lubricant of economic exchange' (Knights et al., 2001, p.312) that needs to be preserved, cultivated, and when necessary, repaired.

Considering possible interactions between trust and contracting in this stage, one could advance that these are generally weak. In most cases, parties make little reference to contracts, or they do so to 'fill the gaps', 'provide more detail', 'eliminate inconsistencies', and enhance the contract's practicality and conformity to reality (see also Mayer and Argyres, 2004). Although these actions could signal partners' competence, benevolence and integrity, one may wonder whether these signals are exclusively tied to the contracting process and would not be given off otherwise. Furthermore, changes in trust are unlikely to cause major amendments in contract clauses in this stage, especially when these terms sketch the broad outlines and major conditions under which both parties have agreed to cooperate, as this would involve renegotiations, and possibly termination of the relationship.

Partners would then find themselves in the *renegotiation or dissolution* stage of their relationship. In that phase, contracts are frequently being applied to control the partner, divide benefits and losses and maximize value appropriation for the own organization. It is in this stage that parties are most likely to explicitly juxtapose the relationship against stipulations in the contract so as to assess whether promises have been kept and agreements have been abided. Moreover, at that point in time, they may 'abuse' the contract to create hold-up situations (Klein et al., 1978), and refer to specific contract terms to obtain private benefits (Dyer et al., 2008), even though these were originally intended for other purposes. In the end, contracting processes in this stage are often aimed at coping with conflicts and weighing one's options concerning the continuation or termination of joint initiatives.

Trust in this stage is grounded in the history of the collaborative process and the intermediate outcomes attained in the relationship up until that point. It may be reinforced or repaired, for example, when parties 'go beyond what they have previously agreed upon', 'stretch the scope and depth of the relationship' and 'occasionally let collective interests, responsibilities, and ambitions prevail above individual ones'. In this stage, trust may best be characterized by the term 'robust' or 'violated', dependent on how the relationship has evolved. In the first case, trust may act as a kind of 'glue', making sure that parties stick together, and even identify themselves with each other. In the second case, trust has to be re-established, either by taking contractual or extra-contractual measures.

Concerning the interaction between contracting and trust in this stage of cooperation, it has been observed that contract structures may shape interfirm dispute resolution (Lumineau and Malhotra, 2010) and that control and coordination provisions in contracts may have different effects on competence-based and goodwill-based trust in the aftermath of a conflict, influencing the likelihood of continued collaboration (Malhotra and Lumineau, 2011). Furthermore, interactions between both constructs tend to be strong when conflicts prevail, but they may be rather weak, for instance, when relationships are 'silently extended', or when exploratory relationships have become successful, gradually turning into exploitation relationships, characterized by less uncertainty and more routine activities.

Summarizing, the interaction between trust and contracting is probably most pronounced during the formation and the renegotiation/dissolution stage of collaboration. In the management stage of collaborative relationships instead, interactions between contracting and trust tend to remain modest; contracts stay in drawers or safes, and parties are focused on 'getting the job done', 'handling open issues' and 'solving ad hoc and operational problems'.

CONFLATION AMONGST THE CONCEPTS OF TRUST, DISTRUST AND UNDERSTANDING

Finally, I wish to put up for discussion a rather fundamental question here, namely, does existing research aimed at investigating interactions between trust and contracting actually focus on those two constructs? I argue, instead, that trust is often conflated with the construct of 'distrust' and the concept of 'understanding'. To further elucidate this point, I will first clarify the major differences between each construct, starting with distrust.

Although trust and distrust are sometimes viewed as two ends of a continuum, several scholars acknowledge that they are separate concepts (Sitkin and Roth, 1993; Lewicki et al., 1998; Hardin, 2004). Following Lewicki et al. (1998, p. 439), I define distrust as 'confident negative expectations regarding another's conduct' that may manifest themselves in fear, vigilance or suspicion (Sitkin and Roth, 1993). Distrust then derives from the negative hypothetical possibility regarding a partner's behaviour and actions (Bachmann, 2001) and it is most likely to prevail when partners have an interest in behaving opportunistically (Williamson, 1985).

Although trust and distrust are clearly different constructs, they may coexist within a single relationship. Partners may, for example, trust each other in one respect and distrust each other regarding other issues (Lewicki et al., 1998), but they may also cultivate trust and distrust at the same time so as to reap the benefits from both and compensate for the weaknesses associated with each individually (Vlaar et al., 2007). Furthermore, distrust may arise from sources other than incompetence, and a lack of benevolence and integrity. It may also originate, for instance, from inconsistencies in a partner's behaviour or utterances, its connections with other organizations having questionable reputations, and counterparts making awkward moves or withholding information.

Correspondingly, contracting not only interacts with trust, but also with distrust. In fact, the argument can even be stretched a little bit further, since in many cases it is not only expectations – that is, trust and distrust – that matter, but also the clearness of the mental accounts that we have of a partner's competencies, the conditions under which it has to perform, and the environment on which it is dependent. In other words, I argue that next to *expectations* – positive or negative – partners value having rich and accurate *understandings* of the collaborative reality in which they and their partners find themselves (see also Kumar and Andersen, 2000; Huber and Lewis, 2010; Vlaar and Klijn, 2011).

This is supported by several empirical accounts of interorganizational relationships, in which the construct of trust is accompanied by, but considered apart from the notion of understanding (for example, Doz, 1996; Akkermans et al., 2004; Huemer, 2004; Mayer and Argyres, 2004). In discussing a case on collaborative supply chain planning in high-tech electronics, for instance, Akkermans et al. (2004, p. 453, italics added) observed the following: 'Only after spending a number of workshops, focused on explaining businesses, processes, and systems, did a mutual *understanding* for each other's perceived volatility (or rigidity) materialise. ... Creating this level of transparency significantly contributed to creating *trust*'. Similarly, in describing the relationship between a large software firm and one of its clients, Mayer and Argyres (2004, p. 401, italics added) noted that managers and engineers found: 'that it was easier to build *trust* when the SOWs [Statements of Work] were more detailed because *misunderstandings* were avoided and agreement on expectations, roles, and responsibilities of the parties was facilitated'. As these examples indicate, trust and understanding often go hand in hand, but should nevertheless be regarded as separate constructs. Basically 'understandings' comprise accounts or representations of specific phenomena. They constitute meaningful thought structures that allow us to make sense of new cues and stimuli, and that enable us to interpret novel information and act upon it (Harrison and Boyle, 2006; Vlaar et al., 2008). When developing understandings, individuals focus their attention on a particular topic or domain of interest and they invest mental efforts to reduce the doubts and ambiguity they experience (Bakhtin, 1986; Spender, 1989, 1996; Weick et al., 2005).

Regarding interorganizational relationships, for instance, actors may try to better understand the primary functions, activities, resources, capabilities, structures, cultures, interests and intentions of partner organizations. In doing so, they develop pragmatic, moral and cognitive meaning, implying that they comprehend better why the relationship functions as it does, and how the behaviour of partners should be interpreted (Kumar and Andersen, 2000).[1]

Whereas trust necessarily involves a three-part relation grounded in the trustor's assessment of the intentions of the trustee with respect to a particular action – that is, actor A trusting actor B in relation to event X (Hardin, 2002) – understandings pertain not only to the accounts and representations that individuals develop of their partners, but also the representations they develop of themselves, the interorganizational relationship and the broader environment in which it is embedded (Spender, 1989, 1996). In fact, understandings may even develop separately from the interactions that we have with other people, and vary, for example, with the experience, knowledge, and expertise that individuals have accumulated, and the ways in which we represent things, reflect on issues and apply our imagination (for example, see Vlaar et al., 2008).

Moreover, whereas it 'may be possible to trust and distrust others' at the same time, just as 'it is possible to experience attraction and aversion, to like and dislike and to love and hate' (Lewicki et al., 1998, p. 449), actors' understandings tend to be more holistic in scope, as they should be consistent with the accounts they hold of other phenomena. More specifically, when understandings become fragmented and incompatible, most individuals will engage in cognitive processes to ensure alignment and reduce experiences of internal conflicts and discomfort with the accounts or representations they have developed of themselves and their environments (Weick, 1995). They try to fit incoming information into existing understandings, or they may disregard this information when a fit is difficult to achieve (Sandberg and Targama, 2007).[2]

Taking the discussion thus far back to the central question that I attempt to address in this chapter, I contend that it is often not so much trust but understanding that interacts with contracting. For example, extensive negotiation and contracting processes may increase partners' understandings of each other's competencies, intentions, limitations, and so on. This may or may not, in turn, fuel trust or distrust in the partner. Likewise, partners may engage in all kinds of activities that increase their understandings of each other and the relationship, but which do not necessarily affect trust or distrust. For instance, discussions about new technologies may enhance partners' understandings and thereby facilitate the drafting of contracts, but they may leave trust and distrust relatively unaffected, especially when the discussions remain factual and informative.

CONCLUSION

In this chapter, I have scrutinized the implicit assumption underlying most work on trust and contracting, suggesting that both constructs are intimately related. I have challenged this view by proposing the following:

- Both constructs are affected by a wide range of other variables.
- Each concept tends to be conflated with its own antecedents.
- Interactions may vary across subjects and levels in an organization.
- Interactions primarily pertain to the control function of trust and contracting.
- Trust and contracting vary across institutional and cultural contexts.
- Interactions vary across distinct stages of collaboration.
- Authors refer to trust, when observations in fact concern distrust and understanding.

Correspondingly, I conclude that both constructs need not necessarily be considered 'together forever, never apart', but I also wish to emphasize that this should not be regarded as criticism on existing research, but much more as an implicit recommendation for scholars and practitioners to more clearly demarcate the nature of possible interactions between trust and contracting, as well as the boundaries within which these are most likely to occur.

In fact, the chapter was intended to offer fertile ground for new questions and lines of thinking on trust and contracting, such as, who are involved in trust-contracting dynamics? Where and when are these dynamics most intensive? And, what prevents the development of inter-relationships between trust and contracting?

NOTES

1. Next to trust, having better understandings may augment the ability of actors to co-create value in at least three ways. First, it allows actors to ascertain promising opportunities for joint value creation, since clear understandings help partners to jointly create new images, conceptions or accounts of what to do, how to do it and under what constraints to do it (Witt, 2000). Having better understandings helps them to conceptualize what has to be developed together and how this has to be done (Foss and Klein, 2008). Second, understandings serve as the basis for coordinated and collective action (Witt, 1998, 2000; Vlaar et al., 2006, 2008; Cronin and Weingart, 2007), helping actors to translate 'otherwise meaningless or ambiguous information into significant agendas and action plans' (Witt, 1998, p.162), appreciate the risks involved in exchanges or foresee potential opportunistic behaviours by partners (Foss, 1999; Ariño and Ring, 2010) and design more appropriate governance structures (Ring and van de Ven, 1994). Third, having better understandings reduces partners' reliance on explicit forms of coordination and control (for example, contracting), since it allows them to better predict and anticipate the actions, needs and reactions of others, and because it enables them to provide task-relevant information, knowledge and feedback without prior request, and adapt their behaviour to the actions expected of others (for example, Rico et al., 2008). Understandings may thus concert individual motivations and dispersed knowledge, thereby substituting for more costly forms of governance (Puranam and Gulati, 2008).
2. Trust and understanding differ with respect to their centrifugal and centripetal forces. Trust tends to decrease when partners behave opportunistically and when focal actors' expectations are disconfirmed. It is likely to increase when the interests of different parties become more aligned and when actors' expectations are confirmed or exceeded. Understanding, instead, diminishes when partners become more specialized, when they are situated in different areas and industries, and when they have different characteristics, such as resources, cultures, structures, dominant logics, customers and strategies. Understandings are promoted, amongst others, by the efforts that partners invest in discovering common ground, and by processes such as negotiation and contracting, which allow partners to give, make, demand and break sense (Vlaar et al., 2006, 2008).

REFERENCES

Akkermans, H., P. Bogerd and J. Van Doremalen (2004), 'Travail, transparency and trust: a case study of computer-supported collaborative supply chain planning in high-tech electronics', *European Journal of Operational Research*, **153**(2), 445–56.

Anderson, E. and S.D. Jap (2005), 'The dark side of close relationships', *MIT Sloan Management Review*, **46**(3), 75–82.

Argyres, N. and K.J. Mayer (2007), 'Contract design as a firm capability: an integration of learning and transaction cost perspectives', *Academy of Management Review*, **32**(4), 1060–77.
Ariño A. and P.S. Ring (2010), 'The role of fairness in alliance formation', *Strategic Management Journal*, **31**(10), 1054–87.
Arrighetti, A., R. Bachmann and S. Deakin (1997), 'Contract law, social norms and inter-firm cooperation', *Cambridge Journal of Economics*, **21**(2), 171–95.
Bachmann, R. (2001), 'Trust, power and control in trans-organizational relations', *Organization Studies*, **22**(2), 337–65.
Bachmann, R. and A. Inkpen (2011), 'Understanding institutional-based trust building processes in inter-organizational relationships', *Organization Studies*, **32**(2), 281–301.
Bakhtin, M. (1986), *Speech Genres and Other Essays*, Austin, TX: University of Texas Press.
Carson, S.J., A. Madhok and T. Wu (2006), 'Uncertainty, opportunism and governance: the effects of volatility and ambiguity on formal and relational contracting', *Academy of Management Journal*, **49**(5), 1058–77.
Child, J. and G. Möllering (2003), 'Contextual confidence and active trust development in strategic alliances', *Organization Science*, **14**(1), 69–80.
Cook, K., R. Hardin and M. Levi (2005), *Cooperation Without Trust?*, New York: Russell Sage Foundation.
Cronin, M.A. and L.R. Weingart (2007), 'Representational gaps, information processing, and conflict in functionally diverse teams', *Academy of Management Review*, **32**(3), 761–73.
Das, T.K. and B.S. Teng (2001), 'Trust, control, and risk in strategic alliances: an integrated framework', *Organization Studies*, **22**(2), 251–83.
Dodgson, M. (1993), 'Learning, trust, and technological collaboration', *Human Relations*, **46**(1), 77–95.
Doz, Y.L. (1996), 'The evolution of cooperation in strategic alliances: initial conditions or learning processes?', *Strategic Management Journal*, **17**(S1), 55–83.
Dyer, J.H. and H. Singh (1998), 'The relational view: cooperative strategies and sources of interorganizational competitive advantages', *Academy of Management Review*, **23**(4), 660–79.
Dyer, J.H., H. Singh and P. Kale (2008), 'Splitting the pie: rent distribution in alliances and networks', *Managerial & Decision Economics*, **29**(2/3), 137–48.
Faems, D., M. Janssens, A. Madhok and B. Van Looy (2008), 'Toward an integrative perspective on alliance governance: connecting contract design, contract application, and trust dynamics', *Academy of Management Journal*, **51**(11), 1053–78.
Ferrin, D. (2007), 'Understanding the effect of national/societal culture on interpersonal trust', Keynote speech at the 4th Workshop on Trust Within and Between Organizations, Amsterdam.
Ferrin, D.L., M.C. Bligh and J.C. Kohles (2007), 'Can I trust you to trust me? A theory of trust, monitoring, and cooperation in interpersonal and intergroup relationships', *Group & Organization Management*, **32**(4), 465–99.
Ferrin, D., M.C. Bligh and J.C. Kohles (2008), 'It takes two to tango: an interdependence analysis of the spiraling of perceived trustworthiness and cooperation in interpersonal and intergroup relationships', *Organizational Behavior and Human Decision Processes*, **107**(2), 161–78.
Foss, N.J. (1999), 'Capabilities, confusion, and the costs of coordination: on some problems in recent research on inter-firm relations', Keynote speech for the Conference 'Cooperation Industrielle: Diversité and Synthèse', Paris.
Foss, N.J. (2005), *Strategy, Economic Organization, and the Knowledge Economy*, Oxford: Oxford University Press.
Foss, N.J. and P.G. Klein (2008), 'Entrepreneurship: from opportunity discovery to judgment', SMG Working Paper No. 5/2008.
Furlotti, M. (2007), 'There is more to contracts than incompleteness: a review and assessment of empirical research on inter-firm contract design', *Journal of Management and Governance*, **11**(1), 61–99.

Ghoshal, S. and P. Moran (1996), 'Bad for practice: a critique of the transaction cost theory', *Academy of Management Review*, **21**(1), 13–47.
Gulati, R. (1995), 'Social structure and alliance formation: a longitudinal analysis', *Administrative Science Quarterly*, **40**(4), 619–52.
Hardin, R. (2002), *Trust and Trustworthiness*, New York: Russell Sage Foundation.
Hardin, R. (2004), *Distrust*, New York: Russell Sage Foundation.
Harrison, J. and E. Boyle (2006), 'Falling into capability learning traps: the role of the firm's predominant managerial mental models', *Management Decision*, **44**(1), 31–42.
Huber, G.P. and K. Lewis (2010), 'Cross-understanding: implications for group cognition and performance', *Academy of Management Review*, **35**(1), 6–26.
Huemer, L. (2004), 'Activating trust: the redefinition of roles and relationships in an international construction project', *International Marketing Review*, **21**(2), 187–201.
Inkpen, A.C. and S. Currall (2004), 'The coevolution of trust, control, and learning in joint ventures', *Organization Science*, **15**(5), 586–99.
Kim, D.J. (2008), 'Self-perception-based versus transference-based trust determinants in computer-mediated transactions: a cross-cultural comparison study', *Journal of Management Information Systems*, **24**(4), 13–45.
Klein, B., R. Crawford and A. Alchian (1978), 'Vertical integration, appropriable rents, and the competitive contracting process', *Journal of Law and Economics*, **21**(2), 297–326.
Klein Woolthuis, R., B. Hillebrand and B. Nooteboom (2005), 'Trust, contract and relationship development', *Organization Studies*, **26**(6), 813–40.
Knights, D., F. Noble, T. Vurdubakis and H. Willmott (2001), 'Chasing shadows: control, virtuality and the production of trust', *Organization Studies*, **22**(2), 311–36.
Kumar, R. and P.H. Andersen (2000), 'Inter firm diversity and the management of meaning in international strategic alliances', *International Business Review*, **9**(2), 237–52.
Kvaløy, O. and T.E. Olsen (2009), 'Endogenous verifiability and relational contracting', *American Economic Review*, **99**(5), 2193–208.
Latusek, D. and P.W.L. Vlaar (2011), 'Trust in practice: "encapsulated interest" and the "leap of faith" in collaborative relations', Working Paper VU University Amsterdam.
Lewicki, R., D. McAllister and R. Bies (1998), 'Trust and distrust: new relationships and realities', *Academy of Management Review*, **23**(3), 438–512.
Li, J.J., L. Poppo and K.Z. Zhou (2010), 'Relational mechanisms, formal contracts, and local knowledge acquisition by international subsidiaries', *Strategic Management Journal*, **31**(4), 349–70.
Lumineau, F. and D. Malhotra (2010), 'Shadow of the contract: how contract structure shapes interfirm dispute resolution', *Strategic Management Journal*, **32**(5), 532–55.
Macaulay, S. (1963), 'Non-contractual relations in business: a preliminary study', *American Sociological Review*, **28**(1), 55–67.
McNeil, I.R. (1980), *The New Social Contract: An Inquiry into Modern Contractual Relations*, London: Yale University Press.
Malhotra, D. and F. Lumineau (2011), 'Trust and collaboration in the aftermath of conflict: the effects of contract structure', *Academy of Management Journal*, **54**(5), 981–98.
Malhotra, D. and J. Murnighan (2002), 'The effects of contracts on interpersonal trust', *Administrative Science Quarterly*, **47**(3), 534–59.
Mayer, K.J. and N. Argyres (2004), 'Learning to contract: evidence from the personal computer industry', *Organization Science*, **15**(4), 394–410.
Mayer, R., J. Davis and F. Schoorman (1995), 'An integrative model of organizational trust', *Academy of Management Review*, **20**(3), 709–34.
McAllister, D.J. (1995), 'Affect- and cognition-based trust as foundations for interpersonal cooperation in organizations', *Academy of Management Journal*, **38**(1), 24–59.
McKnight, D.H., L.L. Cummings and N.L. Chervany (1998), 'Initial trust formation in new organizational relationships', *Academy of Management Review*, **23**(3), 473–90.
Möllering, G. (2006), *Trust: Reason, Routine, Reflexivity*, Oxford: Elsevier.
Nooteboom, B. (1999), *Inter-firm Alliances: Analysis and Design*, London: Routledge.

Osadchiy, S. (2011), *The Dynamics of Formal Organization: Essays on Bureaucracy and Formal Rules*, published PhD dissertation, RSM Erasmus University.

Oxley, J.E. (1997), 'Appropriability hazards and governance in strategic alliances: a transaction cost approach', *Journal of Law, Economics and Organization*, **13**(2), 387–409.

Parkhe, A. (1993), 'The structuring of strategic alliances: a game theoretic and transaction cost examination of interfirm cooperation', *Academy of Management Journal*, **36**(4), 794–829.

Poppo, L. and T. Zenger (2002), 'Do formal contracts and relational governance function as substitutes or complements?', *Strategic Management Journal*, **23**(8), 707–25.

Puranam, P. and R. Gulati (2008), 'Coordination in vertical relationships: the (un)importance of information flows', Working Paper, London Business School.

Ren, H. and B. Gray (2009), 'Repairing relationship conflict: how violation types and culture influence the effectiveness of restoration rituals', *Academy of Management Review*, **34**(1), 105–26.

Rico, R., M. Sánchez-Manzanares, F. Gil and C. Gibson (2008), 'Team implicit coordination processes: a team knowledge-based approach', *Academy of Management Review*, **33**(1), 163–85.

Ring, P.S. and A.H. Van de Ven (1994), 'Developmental processes of cooperative interorganizational relationships', *Academy of Management Review*, **19**(1), 90–118.

Sandberg, J. and A. Targama (2007), *Managing Understanding in Organizations*, London: Sage Publications.

Serva, M.A., M.A. Fuller and R.C. Mayer (2005), 'The reciprocal nature of trust: a longitudinal study of interacting teams', *Journal of Organizational Behavior*, **26**(6), 625–48.

Sitkin, S.B. and N. Roth (1993), 'Explaining the limited effectiveness of legalistic "remedies" for trust/distrust', *Organization Science*, **4**(3), 367–92.

Slemrod, J.B. and P. Katuščásk (2005), 'Do trust and trustworthiness pay off?', *Journal of Human Research*, **40**(3), 621–46.

Spender, J.C. (1989), *Industry Recipes: An Inquiry into the Nature and Sources of Management Judgement*, London: Basil Blackwell.

Spender, J.C. (1996), 'Making knowledge the basis of a dynamic theory of the firm', *Strategic Management Journal*, **17**(Winter Special Issue), 45–62.

Tillmar, M. and L. Lindkvist (2007), 'Cooperation against all odds: finding reasons for trust where formal institutions fail', *International Sociology*, **22**(3), 343–66.

Vlaar, P.W.L. (2008), *Contracts and Trust in Alliances: Creating, Appropriating and Discovering Value*, Cheltenham, UK and Northampton, MA, USA: Edward Elgar.

Vlaar, P.W.L. and E. Klijn (2011), 'Positive expectations or clear accounts? Trust and understanding as interrelated determinants of alliance performance', Working Paper, VU University Amsterdam.

Vlaar, P.W.L., F.A.J. Van den Bosch and H.W. Volberda (2006), 'Coping with problems of understanding in interorganizational relationships: using formalization as a means to make sense', *Organization Studies*, **27**(11), 1617–38.

Vlaar, P.W.L., F.A.J Van den Bosch and H.W. Volberda (2007), 'On the evolution of trust, distrust, and formal coordination and control in interorganizational relationships: towards an integrative framework', *Group & Organization Management*, **32**(4), 407–28.

Vlaar, P.W.L., P.C. Van Fenema and V. Tiwari (2008), 'Cocreating understanding and value in distributed work: how members of onsite and offshore vendor teams give, make, demand and break sense', *MIS Quarterly*, **32**(2), 227–55.

Weber, L. and K.J. Mayer (2011), 'Designing effective contracts: exploring the influence of framing and expectations', *Academy of Management Review*, **36**(1), 53–75.

Weibel, A., A. Madhok and T. Mellewigt (2007), 'Trust and formal contracts in interorganizational relationships – substitutes and complements', *Managerial and Decision Economics*, **28**(8), 833–47.

Weick, K.E. (1995), *Sensemaking in Organizations*, Thousand Oaks, CA: Sage Publications.

Weick, K.E., K.M. Sutcliffe and D. Obstfeld (2005), 'Organizing and the process of sensemaking', *Organization Science*, **16**(4), 409–421.

Williamson, O.E. (1985), *The Economic Institutions of Capitalism: Firms, Markets, Relational Contracting*, New York: Macmillan Publishers.
Witt, U. (1998), 'Imagination and leadership – the neglected dimension of an evolutionary theory of the firm', *Journal of Economic Behavior & Organization*, **35**(2), 161–77.
Witt, U. (2000), 'Changing cognitive frames – changing organizational forms: an entrepreneurial theory of organizational development', *Industrial and Corporate Change*, **9**(4), 733–55.
Zaheer, A. and N. Venkatraman (1995), 'Relational governance as an interorganizational strategy: an empirical test of the role of trust in economic exchange', *Strategic Management Journal*, **16**(5), 373–92.
Zaheer, A., B. McEvily and V. Perrone (1998), 'Does trust matter? Exploring the effects of interorganizational and interpersonal trust on performance', *Organization Science*, **9**(2), 141–59.
Zand, D.E. (1972), 'Trust and managerial problem solving', *Administrative Science Quarterly*, **17**(2), 229–39.
Zhou, K.Z., L. Poppo and Z. Yang (2008), 'Relational ties or customized contracts? An examination of alternative governance choices in China', *Journal of International Business Studies*, **39**(3), 526–34.
Zucker, L.G. (1986), 'Production of trust: institutional sources of economic structure', in B.M. Staw and L.L. Cummings (eds), *Research in Organizational Behavior*, Vol. 8, Greenwich, CT: JAI, pp. 53–111.

5. Trust and innovation
Bart Nooteboom

TRUST, UNCERTAINTY, CONTROL AND INNOVATION

In innovation, trust is especially needed as well as especially problematic. One needs trust under uncertainty and in innovation uncertainty is high. If one were certain about conditions, conduct and outcomes one would no longer talk about trust. This is related to a paradox of information concerning trust (Pagden, 1988). On the one hand, trust entails lack of information, since that entails risk of vulnerability to actions of others, and if one were certain about such actions, there would no longer be risk. On the other hand, trust is seldom completely uninformed, and is to some extent based on information, in attributions of trustworthiness or lack of it based on observed or reported behaviour.

Trust entails uncertainty of conditions, conduct or outcomes that may be calculable (usually referred to as 'risk' in this technical sense) or incalculable (radical uncertainty). The uncertainty of trust entails a possibility of loss due to mishap or misconduct. It is useful to distinguish between the probability and the size of possible loss (Nooteboom et al., 1997). The problem with radical uncertainty is that the probability of loss is not known, so that trust and trustworthiness become difficult to calculate. Under radical uncertainty one does not know what eventualities, options for conduct and outcomes could arise. If one did and had no further information, the theory of decision-making under risk advises assigning equal probabilities to all possible eventualities, and calculating from there, adjusting probabilities as information becomes available (in the so-called Bayesian procedure).

In innovation it is useful to distinguish between radical innovation (or exploration) and incremental innovation (or exploitation) (March, 1991). Exploitation entails change within the compass of basic design logic, principles, or architecture. This entails the maintenance of meanings, roles, tasks and goals. Exploration entails a breaking through these limits, which requires room for ambiguity of meanings and roles, and a loosening of principles and architecture. The challenge of innovation is to engage in both exploitation, for short-term survival, and exploration, for longer-term viability. It is difficult to combine the two in one organization, since they entail different mentalities and cultures. In sum, there are two mutually reinforcing reasons for a connection between trust and innovation: a high degree of uncertainty and need for collaboration. Uncertainty is radical especially in exploration, so that especially there trust is incalculable. Not knowing what contingencies may arise, one may not even know what actions one may undertake oneself. One cannot be sure even of one's own trustworthiness.

Trust and control are complements as well as substitutes (c.f., Klein Woolthuis et al., 2005). Complete, that is, unconditional or blind trust, is ill advised, and where trust ends one needs control. Vice versa, complete control is impossible, and trust is needed where control ends. At the same time, more trust allows for less control. It is useful to distinguish between opportunity control (constraining action space) and incentive control (affecting the choice between options for action) (Nooteboom, 2002). Opportunity control may be exerted by contract between independent partners or by direct supervision in a hierarchical relationship. Incentive control may also be contractual or hierarchical, but can also be more informal. Implicit or explicit threat of retaliation in case of opportunistic behaviour and loss of reputation are important examples. The formal or informal use of 'hostages' is also an instrument of control, where the hostage may take the form of sensitive information that may be divulged, or a stake in share ownership. Beyond control there may be trust based on morality, ethics, friendship or routinization. To prevent terminological misunderstanding, I proposed earlier (Nooteboom, 2002) using 'reliance' as an overarching term that includes on the one hand 'control' and on the other hand 'trust', beyond control.

Due to relatively high uncertainty under innovation, concerning future conditions (technology, markets), actions (options and choices, for both self and other) and outcomes, control is relatively difficult and therefore trust is more needed. For contracts it is more difficult to specify conditions, actions, outcomes, responsibilities, ownership and rewards, particularly in exploration. If, nevertheless, one imposes contracts, those will constrain the scope for improvisation and changes of direction that innovation requires. For both contracts and hierarchical control, monitoring is relatively difficult under innovation. If outcomes or actions are less specified, deviance is less defined. And how can one judge novelty, in the absence of benchmarks? Particularly in innovation one often engages in partnerships because the partner can offer competencies that one does not have oneself, and how then does one judge those competencies?

COGNITIVE DISTANCE

Trust is more needed as well as more difficult to the extent that the people concerned differ in their thought. Different people develop different cognitive structures along different life paths in different environments. This yields 'cognitive distance', and to collaborate one must cross that distance. Cognitive distance entails difference in cognition in the narrow sense of knowledge but also difference in perceptions and views of values, ethics and morality. This combination of the intellectual and the moral has the implication for the study of the firm that we should combine perspectives of competence and governance (Nooteboom, 2004a), while in the literature on the firm these perspectives run in largely separate streams, in on the one hand studies of competence, learning, innovation and the like, and on the other hand studies of collaboration and its governance, as in transaction cost economics and the literature on trust.

On the level of firms (rather than individuals) cognitive distance is defined as the difference in 'cognitive focus' of the firms (Nooteboom, 2009), which in empirical work has been operationalized as the difference in the firms' technological profiles composed from patent data (Nooteboom et al., 2007). Cognitive distance yields both a problem and an opportunity. The problem is that to the extent that cognitive distance is larger, people understand each other less, have different normative views and inclinations, and have less empathy, less ability to imagine themselves in the position of the other, which all limit ability to collaborate. The positive side of cognitive distance is that it provides an opportunity for learning and innovation. The relevance to the present chapter is that to the extent that collaboration is more aimed at innovation, cognitive distance needs to be larger, while this also makes collaboration more difficult. Cognitive distance can be too small to generate novelty or too large to utilize its opportunities. A higher level of trust and, more widely, an increased ability to collaborate, enables one to operate at a larger cognitive distance and thereby generate more innovative potential. That, I think, is the crux of the relation between trust and innovation.

This may be modelled as follows, illustrated in Figure 5.1 (Nooteboom, 2000). If we model the decline with cognitive distance of ability to collaborate as a downward sloping straight line, the increase of novelty potential as an upward sloping straight line, and performance of innovation by interaction as the mathematical product of the two, the result is an inverted U-shaped parabola (being the result of multiplying a downward sloping line with an upward sloping line). This yields the notion of 'optimal cognitive distance'. With this term I do not wish to suggest that

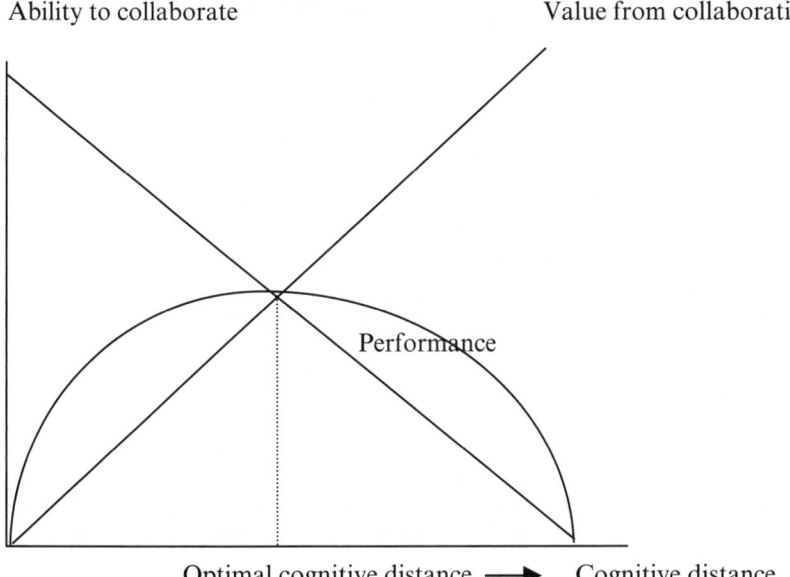

Figure 5.1 Optimal cognitive distance

the optimum can be calculated prior to choice of partners, but rather that it is approximated by trial and error.

The optimum depends on how radical the innovation involved in the interaction is. If we employ the distinction between exploitation, defined as improvements within a basic design, set of principles or architecture, and exploration as the breaking of such frames, then in exploitation the marginal disutility of lack of understanding and agreement (slope of the downward sloping line) is relatively high, and the marginal utility of novelty (slope of the upward sloping line) is lower than in exploration, resulting in a lower optimal distance. This accords with intuition: the more the focus is on efficiency of exploitation rather than the novelty of exploration, the higher the penalty on lack of mutual understanding, and hence the smaller cognitive distance should be.

The optimum is not fixed in time. It depends, in particular, on the ability to collaborate at any level of cognitive distance, in other words the ability to master the art of trust, and this may increase as a function of the accumulation of knowledge and experience in collaboration. The more experience one has in collaborating with others who think differently the better one is able to manage trust. That may be modelled as an upward shift of the downward sloping line that represents ability to collaborate as

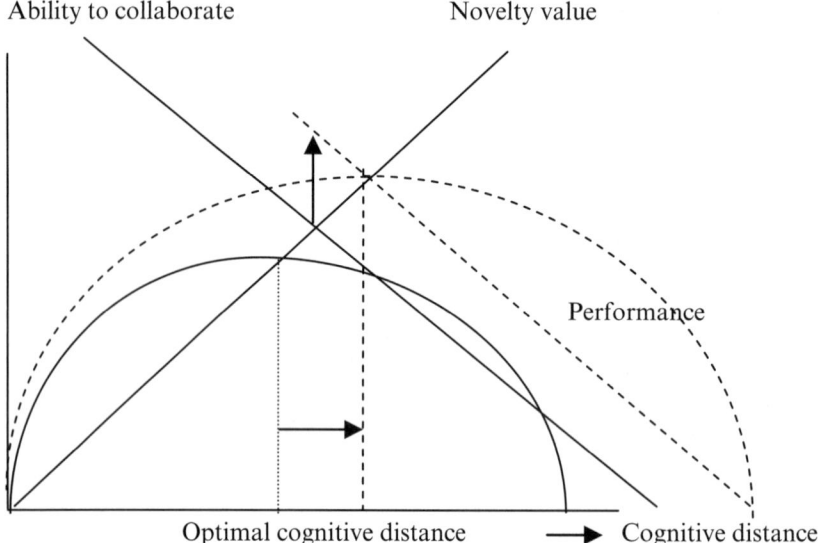

Figure 5.2 Upward shift of ability to collaborate

a function of cognitive distance: at any given level of cognitive distance the ability to deal with it is greater. This causes optimal distance and innovative performance to increase (Nooteboom, 2000). This is illustrated in Figure 5.2.

This shows how the development of ability to collaborate with people who think differently yields economic advantage. The idea of optimal cognitive distance and its shift on the basis of experience is tested empirically (econometrically) in a study of innovation in inter-firm alliances (Nooteboom et al., 2007). There, innovative performance is measured by new patents.

Ability to collaborate is associated with the art of trust. It includes the well-known notion of absorptive capacity, the ability to understand what a partner says and does, but that requires a conceptual widening to encompass the wider notion of cognition: not only the 'competence' side of substantive understanding but also the 'governance' side of insight and empathy with respect to styles of thought and action, motives, survival conditions of a partner firm, and moral views and predilections (Nooteboom, 2004a). Absorptive capacity refers to the receiver side in communication and needs to be complemented by expressive capacity on the sender side, in the ability to be clear, to explain and to give clever examples and metaphors that trigger understanding. Together, wider absorptive capacity in combination with expressive capacity yields a wider notion of collaborative capacity. This is associated with the notion of 'voice' (Hirschman, 1970), recognized as being of central importance in matters of trust, as discussed later. In sum, the ability to cross cognitive distance, by means of collaborative capacity, is important for innovation as well as trust.

GOVERNANCE

So, how, then, does one conduct relational governance, how does one manage risk and trust, under the greater uncertainty of innovation that increases both the need and the difficulty of reliance, and the difficulties of cognitive distance? Above, I argued that relatively more trust is needed, but next to trust control is needed, in a way that takes into account the special features of innovation. Trust is affected by emotions and feelings such as fear, suspicion, friendship, hope, despair, and so on, but there is also rational trust based on an evaluation of reasons why and when other people might or might not be trustworthy. Here I will focus on those reasons. This issue of governance is too large to discuss in full detail here, and I will pick up only a few salient points (using Nooteboom, 2002).

First, let us ask: 'What are the risks of collaboration in innovation; what does one stand to lose?' From transaction cost economics (TCE) we can use the notion of relation-specific investments. Relationships need to have sufficient duration to recoup such specific investments. One-sided specific investments are only one source of one-sided or asymmetrical dependence. Other sources are inequality of knowledge, competence, market position, diversification of risks, and so on. For a more complete analysis of dependence and relational risk we should include considerations of knowledge, from the knowledge-based theory of the firm, including the notion of cognitive distance discussed above. Next to the usual types of specific investment that are known from TCE, and which arise also outside innovation, specific investments are likely to arise especially in innovation in view of the need to cross cognitive distance by establishing adequate understanding and alignment of moral views, and to build trust. Often those are specific to the relationship.

One instrument of governance is to equalize dependence, in particular ownership of specific assets. Another is to balance mutual dependence in other features of the relationship, such as unique quality of services offered, bargaining position on the basis of market position, or the offering of hostages. One-sided dependence may also be mended by building coalitions with others to build countervailing power.

From the knowledge-based theory of the firm, a second risk that arises especially in innovation is that of spillover: unintended transfer of knowledge or competence that is expropriated or imitated and used to compete. This risk can be direct, in the partner becoming a competitor, or indirect, in spillover through the partner to a competitor with whom the partner has a tie. This risk has often been overestimated. The issue is not only whether sensitive information reaches a potential competitor, but also whether he or she then has the absorptive capacity for it, and the resources needed to exploit it, and the incentives to do so. If by the time all those conditions are fulfilled the information has become obsolete, the risk disappears.

One measure of control against this risk is to demand exclusiveness: to forbid application or divulging of the information to third parties, but the monitoring of this may be impossible. It is feasible if, for example, the information is embodied in some product that can be dissembled to check for that feature. Another possible measure is to forbid relationships with one's competitors. For this one pays a price of locking the partner up in a conceptual prison. It is important for oneself that the partner keeps on learning and improving, and it is by engaging in relationships with others, also one's competitors, perhaps especially one's competitors, to tap from more varied sources of knowledge and competence, that the partner learns. In view of these drawbacks it is important not to demand exclusiveness unless it is strictly needed, as discussed in the previous paragraph.

An important measure of more informal incentive control is reputation. For this, it is important that a reliable reputation mechanism is in place. I will return to this in a later discussion of third parties and trust networks.

According to economic logic of markets there is no room for altruism: competition forces agents to take the maximum possible profit since anything less will jeopardize survival in the market. And indeed, the harsher competition is the less room there will be for altruism, and hence the less room there will be for trust. Also, in times of greater external pressure, in economic crisis or crisis of a firm, trustworthiness will decline. However, often there is room for altruism. I will return to this issue later. Also, altruism can be part of the objective, as part of the quality, the intrinsic value next to instrumental value of relationships, as part of the quality of life.

Most important, in the present context, is that under innovation there is not only more need for trust but also more room for it. Trust depends on the need to trust and that depends on the absence of alternatives. People who are 'condemned' to each other, needing each other in the absence of alternatives, will simply have to make the relationship work. They can afford distrust less. That is often the case in innovation, since there is not yet any established standard of competence, and agents tend to be more unique in what they offer, in the struggle for novelty. Often, the basis for

Table 5.1 Sources of reliability

	Macro Universalistic between organizations	Micro Relation-specific, particularistic within organizations
Self-interest Opportunity control Incentive control	Contracts, legal enforcement Reputation, dependence	Hierarchy, managerial 'fiat' Hostages, careers, bonus schemes
Altruism	Values, social norms of proper conduct, moral obligation, sense of duty, bonds of kinship	Empathy, routinization benevolence, identification, affect, friendship, org. culture

Source: Adapted from Nooteboom (2002).

trust here is mutual professional appreciation and a sense 'of being in it together' and sharing a destiny or innovative challenge or adventure. A second, more economic, factor is that in early stages of innovation the focus is not on price or low cost but on technical, organizational and commercial viability. It is only later, when an innovation breaks through and becomes a bandwagon onto which many newcomers jump, that competitive pressures on cost gather force. A survey of the different sources of reliability, as a basis for governance, is given in Table 5.1.

THIRD PARTIES

Innovation and governance are often not just bilateral. One can also employ third parties, or mediators in trust, in a variety of roles (Nooteboom, 2002), some of which are especially important in innovation. The roles can be distinguished analytically but they may be combined, in some package of services offered by the mediator.

The first role is related not only to governance but also to the competence side of relationships, in helping parties to learn from each other, and to achieve the mutual understanding needed for that. On the competence side this concerns substantive or 'technical' understanding; on the governance side it concerns empathy, an ability to understand the position of the other. In other words, the go-between may help partners to 'cross cognitive distance' by contributing to the ability to collaborate. In the transfer of knowledge, there is not only a problem on the part of the sender of 'externalizing' tacit knowledge, or of dislodging knowledge from the tacit basis of underlying cognitive categories, there is also a problem for the receiver of interpreting the information, by embedding it in his or her more or less tacit cognitive categories. To the extent that the knowledge transferred has to replace existing tacit knowledge, there is the problem that existing tacit practice is taken for granted and is difficult to subject to criticism. Then, the tacit knowledge underlying practice may first have to be made explicit (Nooteboom, 2000). The go-between may have an important role to play here. Typically, in a small firm, where a greater proportion of knowledge is tacit, based on practice and stored in procedural memory, an outsider who comes with a proposal to change existing practice will be dismissed as not making sense and being 'impractical'. Only people who are trusted to be familiar with existing practice and the exigencies of that particular small firm may get the attention of the entrepreneur. This may be a colleague, or it might be a go-between who is known to be familiar with the firm and its practice.

A second role is related to the first one. It is to solve the 'revelation problem'. In the selling of information, there is Arrow's (1973) paradox of information: to judge the value of information one must already have it, but then there is nothing left to pay for. One solution is to offer licences with only a small payment up front, and a subsequent payment in proportion to the proceeds the patent yields. However, this may not be easy to observe, for the purpose of control. An alternative is to let the go-between assess the value of the information. For this, the third party has to know both sides well enough to reliably inform them on the competence and intentions of each other, without surrendering much information on content.

A third role, connected to the second, is to control spillover, seeing to it that knowledge does not flow beyond where it is intended. This is relevant when one partner would not allow the other to come into the firm and monitor knowledge flow, because he or she would thereby have access to other sensitive information, creating a risk of reverse spillover, while the third party does not constitute such a risk.

A fourth role was indicated already in TCE. Williamson (1985) indicated the possibility of engaging a third party as a go-between for 'trilateral governance'. That was inspired by considerations of efficiency. It suggests that governance to control transaction costs is needed but the transactions involved are too small or infrequent to justify the often considerable costs of a 'bilateral' governance scheme. Then it is more efficient to make a simpler overall agreement and engage a third party for arbitration. Under innovation an additional consideration is to minimize the constraints that a contract would impose, reducing the scope for improvisation and changes of direction that innovation requires.

A fifth, and perhaps most crucial role, is to act as an intermediary in the building of trust. Trust relations are often entered with partners who are trusted partners of someone you trust (Sydow, 2000). If X has competence as well as intentional trust in Y and Y has intentional trust in Z, then X may rationally give intentional trust in Z a chance. X needs to feel that Y is able to judge well and has no intention to lie about his or her judgement. This can speed up the building of trust between strangers, which might otherwise take too long. To limit risks, new relationships may have to start small, with low stakes that are raised as trust builds up. This may be needed especially when contracts are not feasible or desirable, as in innovation. The disadvantage of such a procedure is its slowness. In a competitive environment where speed to market is of increasing importance it may be too slow. Then, a go-between may provide help for a more speedy development. The intermediary can perform valuable services in protecting trust when it is still fragile: to eliminate misunderstanding and allay suspicions when errors or mishaps are mistaken for opportunism. Intermediation in the first small and ginger steps of cooperation, to ensure that they are successful, can be very important in the building of a trust relation. The third party can also help to adjust collaboration as conditions change, to prevent misunderstandings that trigger distrust and set a vicious circle going where trust unravels and becomes difficult to restore. Things may go wrong in a relation either because of mistakes or because of opportunism, but in practice they are difficult to distinguish because an opportunist will claim mistakes or mishaps as the cause of disappointing results. The intermediary may solve misunderstandings that turn mistakes into perceived indications of opportunism.

A sixth role, related to the fifth, is to help in the timely and least destructive disentanglement of relations. A third party may help to prevent an escalation of conflict that damages reputations on both sides. Ending a relationship with a minimum of conflict is as important as starting a relationship and is often more difficult. It is important especially under the uncertainty of innovation, where one has to guess what partners are needed under volatile conditions of exploring technologies, organization and markets. A dilemma arises in ending a relation. If one wants to end a relation because a more attractive option has emerged, should one announce this intention at an early stage, or should one drop it on the partner at the last moment? In other words should one go for an adversarial or a collaborative mode of divorce (Nooteboom, 1996)? With the first, one offers the partner a way out with least damage: he or she stops making specific investments that would maintain his or her switching cost, one can help to find a new partner to minimize disruption. However, one also gives the partner time to obstruct one's departure. Collaborative divorce is viable if the partner can be expected to cut his or her losses and welcome the help to get out with minimal damage. There is a more subtle point attached to this. One may hesitate to criticize the partner even when it is part of voice, in the mutual honesty that can deepen trust, lest it should be interpreted as a signal of an intention to leave. This kind of sensitivity is most likely to arise in the case of asymmetric dependence. Here also, to eliminate misunderstanding, and to prevent acrimonious and mutually damaging battles of divorce, a go-between can offer valuable services.

A seventh role is to act as a lookout, a sieve, a channel and an amplifier in reputation mechanisms. For a reputation mechanism to work, infringement of agreements must be observable, its report must be credible, and it must reach potential future partners of the culprit. The go-between can help in all respects: to monitor infringement, to sift true reports from gossip, to connect with future potential partners of the culprit and bridge the distances involved.

An eighth role is to act as a guardian of hostages. Without that, there may be a danger that the hostage keeper does not return the hostage even if the partner sticks to the agreement. The third party has an interest in maintaining symmetric trust and acceptance by both protagonists. He or she can be trusted more to sacrifice the hostage without hesitation if the giver does not stick to the agreement, and not to keep the hostage longer than agreed.

The first three roles (aid understanding, judge value and control spillover) are knowledge related. The other five roles (arbitration, trust building, disentanglement, reputation building and guarding hostages) are governance related. As indicated, most of the roles of the go-between are especially important in innovation. Here, exchange of knowledge is crucial, with corresponding risks of spillover, and specific investments are needed to set up mutual understanding and cooperation. There are corresponding risks of hold-up, while especially in innovation the competencies, intentions and performance of strangers are difficult to judge. Especially in innovation, detailed contracts tend to have the adverse effect of a straitjacket, constraining the variety of actions and initiatives that innovation requires. Third party arbitration then yields a less constraining alternative, in trilateral governance and the development of trust instead of using detailed contracts to preclude opportunism.

There are connections between the roles, so that they cannot all be separated as stand-alone. Different roles may need to be combined by a single intermediary. For example, help in mutual understanding is needed to help in the valuation of competence, and in controlling spillover. Those are the knowledge-related roles. The governance-related roles of arbitration, help in the building of trust and help to disentangle and end relationships also appear to go together. Perhaps the contribution to a reputation mechanism, and acting as a guardian of hostages can be more stand-alone.

Note that in all roles it is crucial that the go-between command trust in both his or her competence and his or her intentions. He or she should be competent concerning the technologies involved, and concerning the relational skills required. He or she should be known to be impartial and incorruptible, and should have an interest to act scrupulously, with a view to his or her reputation as a go-between.

There is a range of actors who could possibly play these roles, and not all roles have to be played by a single actor. Possible go-betweens are banks, consultants, interlocking directorates and local government agencies, such as municipalities or development agencies, or subsidized technology transfer centres.

Returning to the more suspicious view of go-betweens identified by Burt (1992), with the notion of the *'tertius gaudens'* ('rejoicing third') derived from Simmel (1950), one should recognize that they may occupy a position of power that can be used opportunistically. When the role is played by government agencies there is a risk of corruption. This yields the question, discussed earlier by Shapiro (1987) of how go-betweens, in turn, can be subjected to control.

NETWORKS

Beyond bilateral and trilateral relations, both innovation and governance, including trust, are a network phenomenon, with multiple agents. In the literature there has been a lively debate on the strengths and weaknesses of dense and strong ties (Granovetter, 1973; Coleman, 1974, 1988; Burt, 1992, 2000). On the competence side, *especially in innovation* there is an argument that dense and strong ties constrain novelty, associated with 'structural holes' between agents that offer opportunities for novel combinations by bridging the hole, and an argument that dense and strong ties tend to lock agents into existing ties, limiting exit and flexibility of ties needed for novel combinations. There is also a cost argument: with many ties, some will be redundant, for example, when there are ties not only between A and B and between B and C but also between A and C. One of them is redundant. If we scrap the tie between A and C, for example, A still has indirect access to C through B.

On the other hand, on the governance side there is an argument in favour of dense and strong ties. A certain density of ties is needed for the use of third parties and for a reputation mechanism to work, which is needed *especially for innovation*, in view of the limits and drawbacks of contracts under the uncertainty of innovation, as discussed earlier. A traditional argument for dense and strong local ties was that they are needed to transfer tacit knowledge, and knowledge tends to be tacit *especially in early and in radical innovation*. However, increasing scepticism has been raised against this: with modern multimedia interaction such transfer has become more possible also over large distances. The transfer of tacit knowledge typically requires demonstrative, ostentative, visual information on the execution of a practice, and inspection and correction of its trial by an apprentice. Multimedia increasingly yield the means for this. Another argument for dense and weak ties comes more from the governance side. Especially for building trust, local ties may be needed for frequent social interaction and participation in clubs and meetings to exchange gossip and to judge trustworthiness.

Ties that are strong in mutual investment, commitment and trust help to govern a relationship with limited contracts. There are also two competence arguments in favour of density, *under innovation*. First, under innovation there is volatility of entry and exit of relevant participants, due to the high incidence of failures and unexpected changes of direction, and redundant ties are needed to hedge one's bets concerning the right partners. Second, having many direct ties one can use them to pool absorptive capacity. A and B can compare their interpretations and understanding of C. This is especially important under the *uncertainty of innovation*. Furthermore, the excess of costs of redundant ties matters less under innovation, because the size of investments in ties is often still limited, and the focus is not so much on costs as on technical, organizational and practical viability. For an empirical paper using this logic, see Gilsing and Nooteboom (2005).

How, then does one trade off the advantages and drawbacks of dense/strong and sparse/weak ties? This issue is particularly salient in the debate on clusters or local/regional networks among geographers (for example, Asheim and Isaksen, 2002; Oinas and Malecki, 2002). How does one make local networks strong in exploitation and trust and at the same time strong in innovation? One solution is to have relatively dense and strong ties for the sake of governance, combined with sufficient turnover of participants, in entry and exit into the local network. Another solution is to combine locally strong and dense ties in local communities with some peripheral agents entertaining weak and sparse ties with peripheral agents of similar communities elsewhere (which yields what is known as a 'small world' structure) (Nooteboom, 2004b).

PROCESSES OF TRUST AND INNOVATION

A key feature of trust is that it is not static but develops. At several places in the above analysis there were indications of the process nature of trust. The process of trust development was studied by, among others, Zand (1972), McAllister (1995), Lewicki and Bunker (1996) and Six (2005).

In the process, people vacillate between two fundamental, instinctive dispositions ingrained in evolution. One is the drive to survive and to 'guard one's resources' (Lindenberg, 2003) for it, the other is a drive to be accepted as a reliable, loyal member of a community. At any moment people are in a mind frame oriented towards self-interest or to loyalty. Trust relations require the latter but when there is a serious threat to survival and critical interests there is likely to be a frame switch to self-interest, and the switch back to altruism is a difficult one. Consciously or not, people interpret actions as indicators of the frame the other is in, and when they sense a frame of self-interest this may trigger a switch of the self to that frame. The question is what actions signal what frame, and how they affect the attribution of a frame to a partner and the stability of one's own frame. Six et al. (2010) investigated how trust-building actions reported in the literature may be interpreted in these terms.

Here, the relation between trust and innovation emerges in shared features of process. What they share becomes clear from the perspective of philosophical pragmatism. Trust and innovation are both a matter of 'muddling through'. The key notion of pragmatism is that ideas and truth are not fixed or absolute but serve as 'useful fictions' that we revise as we run into contradictions and alternative ideas.

Trust is adaptive: one starts with a hunch concerning someone's trustworthiness and adapts expectations according to what one encounters along the way. Trust, not distrust is the default. If one began with distrust, this would withhold one from giving a trusting relationship a chance. If one starts with trust and it is betrayed, one can readjust the relationship towards more control.

Similarly, in innovation one has some prior idea what to aim for, but one needs the flexibility to adapt goals and ideas depending on obstacles and novel opportunities that arise on the way. In both trust and innovation one needs a peculiar combination of tenacity, not to exit too soon, flexibility, to adapt to changing circumstances, and realism, to see when a current path is hopeless, and the ability to disentangle oneself from a hopeless situation.

According to pragmatism goals, means and action interact. We do have goals, preferences and largely subconscious dispositions to action but they are revised as the result of discovery of means and of results of actions, especially when action encounters problems or new opportunities are found. That happens especially in innovation but also in dealing with relationships. The dynamics of cognition and action is not an add-on to statics as the base case, it is the base case. Situations and institutions not only condition goal achievement but also are constitutive of goals.

CONCLUSION

Innovation suffers under distrust. The widespread belief that economic behaviour is inherently and irreparably egotistic and that business is warfare is false and counterproductive. The challenge, especially in innovation, is to carefully seek mutual advantage in novel combinations of competencies from different partners, in relationships that are sufficiently durable to recoup specific investments in mutual understanding, trust and collaboration. Trust requires time to build and maintain. The customary rhetoric is that for innovation one should seek maximum flexibility, with relationships that can be broken instantly, for the sake of innovative novel combinations. And indeed, for innovation relationships should not be rigid and everlasting. However, there should also be sufficient stability to elicit the specific investments needed to build mutual understanding and trust, to let collaboration flourish and to recoup the investments in it. In other words, one should go for optimal, not maximum flexibility. Like innovation, trust is a matter of pragmatics.

REFERENCES

Arrow, K.J. (1973), *Information and Economic Behavior*, Stockholm: Federation of Swedish Industries.
Asheim, B.T. and A. Isaksen (2002), 'Regional innovation systems: the integration of local "sticky" and global "ubiquitous" knowledge', *Journal of Technology Transfer*, **27**(1), 77–86.
Burt, R. (1992), 'Structural holes: the social structure of competition', in N. Nohria and R. Eccles (eds), *Networks and Organizations: Structure, Form and Action*, Boston: Harvard Business School Press, pp. 57–91.
Burt, R.S. (2000), 'The network structure of social capital', in R.I. Sutton and B.M. Staw (eds), *Research in Organizational Behavior*, pp. 345–423.
Coleman, J.S. (1974), *Power and the Structure of Society*, New York: W.W. Norton and Co.
Coleman, J.S. (1988), 'Social capital in the creation of human capital', *American Journal of Sociology*, **94**(Special Supplement), 95–120.
Gilsing, V.A. and B. Nooteboom (2005), 'Density and strength of ties in innovation networks: an analysis of new media and biotechnology', *European Management Review*, **2**(3), 179–97.

Granovetter, M.S. (1973). 'The strength of weak ties', *American Journal of Sociology*, **78**(6), 1360–80.
Hirschman, A.O. (1970), *Exit, Voice and Loyalty: Responses to Decline in Firms, Organizations and States*, Cambridge, MA: Harvard University Press.
Klein Woolthuis, R., B. Hillebrand and B. Nooteboom (2005). 'Trust, contract and relationship development', *Organization Studies*, **26**(6), 813–40.
Lewicki, R.J. and B.B. Bunker (1996), 'Developing and maintaining trust in work relationships', in R.M. Kramer and T.R. Tyler (eds), *Trust in Organizations: Frontiers of Theory and Research*, Thousand Oaks, CA: Sage Publications, pp. 114–39.
Lindenberg, S. (2003), 'Governance seen from a framing point of view: the employment relationship and relational signalling', in B. Nooteboom and F.E. Six (eds), *The Trust Process, Empirical Studies of the Determinants and the Process of Trust Development*, Cheltenham, UK and Northampton, MA, USA: Edward Elgar, pp. 37–57.
March, J. (1991). 'Exploration and exploitation in organizational learning', *Organization Science*, **2**(1), 88–115.
McAllister, D.J. (1995), 'Affect- and cognition-based trust as foundations for interpersonal cooperation in organizations', *Academy of Management Journal*, **38**(1), 24–59.
Nooteboom, B. (1996), 'Trust, opportunism and governance: a process and control model', *Organization Studies*, **17**(6), 985–1010.
Nooteboom, B. (2000), *Learning and Innovation in Organizations and Economies*, Oxford: Oxford University Press.
Nooteboom, B. (2002), *Trust: Forms, Foundations, Functions, Failures and Figures*, Cheltenham, UK and Northampton, MA, USA: Edward Elgar.
Nooteboom, B. (2004a), 'Governance and competence, how can they be combined?', *Cambridge Journal of Economics*, **28**(4), 505–26.
Nooteboom, B. (2004b), *Inter-firm Collaboration, Learning and Networks; An Integrated Approach*, London: Routledge.
Nooteboom, B. (2009), *A Cognitive Theory of the Firm: Learning, Governance and Dynamic Capabilities*, Cheltenham UK and Northampton, MA, USA: Edward Elgar.
Nooteboom, B., J. Berger and N.G. Noorderhaven (1997), 'Effects of trust and governance on relational risk', *Academy of Management Journal*, **40**(2), 308–38.
Nooteboom, B., W.P.M. Van Haverbeke, G.M. Duijsters, V.A. Gilsing and A. V.d. Oord (2007), 'Optimal cognitive distance and absorptive capacity', *Research Policy*, **36**(7), 1016–34.
Oinas, P. and E.J. Malecki (2002), 'Technical trajectories in time and space: from national and regional to spatial innovation systems', *International Regional Science Review*, **25**(1), 102–31.
Pagden, A. (1988), 'The destruction of trust and its economic consequences in the case of eighteenth-century Naples', in D. Gambetta (ed.), *Trust, the Making and Breaking of Cooperative Relations*, Oxford: Blackwell, pp. 127–41.
Shapiro, S.P. (1987), 'The social control of impersonal trust', *American Journal of Sociology*, **93**(3) 623–58.
Simmel, G. (1950), *The Sociology of Georg Simmel*, translation Kurt Wolff, Glencoe IL: The Free Press.
Six, F.E. (2005), *The Trouble with Trust, the Dynamics of Interpersonal Trust Building*, Cheltenham, UK and Northampton, MA, USA: Edward Elgar.
Six, F., B. Nooteboom and A. Hoogendoorn (2010), 'Actions that build interpersonal trust: a relational signalling perspective', *Review of Social Economy*, **68**(3), 285–315.
Sydow, J. (2000), 'Understanding the constitution of interorganizational trust', in C. Lane and R. Bachmann (eds), *Trust In and Between Organizations*, Oxford: Oxford University Press, pp. 31–63.
Williamson, O.E. (1985), *The Economic Institutions of Capitalism; Firms, Markets, Relational Contracting*, New York: The Free Press.
Zand, D.E. (1972), 'Trust and managerial problem solving', *Administrative Science Quarterly*, **17**(2), 229–39.

PART III

TRUST ACROSS ORGANIZATIONS

6. Origins of inter-organizational trust: a review and query for further research
Laura Poppo

INTRODUCTION

While there is much theorizing regarding trust, there is a paucity of empirical work regarding inter-organizational trust. In this chapter, I review this empirical literature and related conceptual frameworks in an effort to: (1) synthesize these empirical approaches and discuss their limitations; (2) redirect empirical measurement of inter-organizational trust to consider multiples 'types' of trust; and (3) re-orient empirical study to understand dynamics, such as its origins. Consider two situations:

Story 1

A director of Hyvee, a Midwestern US grocery chain, describes the differences between how Walmart and Hyvee interact with their suppliers. When Walmart receives an invoice indicating how much it owes Procter & Gamble (P&G), Walmart does not pay it immediately; first, it wants to see if consumers will pay the initial (mutually agreed) retail price for the product. If they won't, Walmart unilaterally lowers the retail price until consumers are satisfied, then discounts the initial invoice price accordingly and pays the discounted amount. Hyvee just pays the invoice price for products received from P&G. To explain the difference, the director notes, 'We have a cooperative relationship with Procter & Gamble, such that when they are interested in testing a new product, they will try it out in our stores. We really like offering new products to our customers – we pride ourselves on giving our customers access to new and different products'. This director also warns that the low prices available at Kroger's, the second-largest grocery chain in the country, can be deceptive, because the chain increases the suggested retail price of products to exaggerate the level of savings when products go on sale.

Story 2

Following the Sprint–Nextel merger, Sprint found itself cash poor but in need of a substantial upgrade to its network capabilities. It therefore formed an equity joint venture with Clearwire, in which Sprint owned 54 percent of Clearwire, and Clearwire took responsibility for building and servicing a 4G network compatible with Sprint's existing network. Unfortunately, the relationship suffered some rough patches, including reports of a failure to make the 4G network compatible with Sprint's existing network. Sprint's president of network operations complained: 'We have no control or governance in the decisions Clearwire made . . . and we have suffered for it accordingly'. But now both companies are trying to patch things up, moving many of their own employees to a third party, Ericsson (also a network provider), which shares a physical campus with Sprint's corporate offices.

As social scientists, our task is to distill business practices into causal models. In our attempts, we translate and label phenomena, realizing such efforts might not be perfect. In the opening stories, I assert that following translation: there are significant, inherent challenges to coordinating business through inter-organizational exchanges – cooperation does not always occur. The structure of the inter-organizational exchange – including independent profit streams and incomplete contracts – often undermines cooperation (for example, positive bilateral actions) and trust (for example, confident, positive expectations). I also infer from the opening stories the phenomena in inter-organizational trust: employees who manage key accounts at P&G would likely report that Hyvee is a more cooperative, trusting partner than Walmart. Employees at Sprint who work with Ericsson and Clearwire are also likely to view Ericsson as more trusting and cooperative than Clearwire. The question for social scientists then is to determine how firms can create positive bilateral relationships across their inter-organizational exchanges. In this chapter, I focus on how and whether inter-organizational trust can remedy the problem of how to achieve cooperation in inter-organizational exchanges.

This chapter asserts that the study of a more aggregate level of trust, between organizations, is both meaningful and productive. Prior reviews (for example, Zaheer and Harris, 2005) focused primarily on construct definition and the outcomes associated with inter-organizational trust, such as lower transaction costs, higher performance satisfaction and greater knowledge transfer (for example, Zaheer et al., 1998; Artz and Brush, 2000; Carson et al., 2003; Dyer and Chu, 2003; Krishnan et al., 2006; Gulati and Nickerson, 2008; Li et al., 2010). Yet, important gaps and criticism exist. The study of inter-organizational trust also needs to include dynamics (see also Möllering, Chapter 12 this volume). Bell et al. (2006, p. 1607) argue that research into the dynamics of cooperation remains 'characterized by fragmentation, lack of coherence and non-comparable research output' and thus not only creates an academic gap but also focuses on research questions irrelevant to managers' needs, causing a managerial relevance gap. They call for research to focus on proper theoretical development: a more refined focus on the processes that underlie cooperative alliances. Yet this approach I should note is not favored by all. Hennart (2006, p. 1623) is somewhat less sanguine: 'we do not need detailed accounts of human interactions and of their consequences to predict what will happen to alliances. Often a good analysis of their initial structure suffices'.

Another viable criticism is the often broad and general operationalization of inter-organizational trust: a collective set of beliefs and/or behaviors that produce confident expectations about another entity and a willingness to be vulnerable (Rousseau et al., 1998; Zaheer et al., 1998). Although valid, this definition does not distinguish among alternative bases or origins of trust. For example, there is a relational basis for trust – a non-calculative belief in the goodwill of others, honesty and good-faith efforts that stems from the internalization of values, principles and standards of behavior (Barney and Hansen, 1994; Ring, 1996; Bromiley and Harris, 2006). In contrast, calculative trust emphasizes structural conditions as a basis of cooperation, including specialized co-investments in tangible and intangible (for example, relational) assets and positive expectations of continuance (Parkhe, 1993; Williamson, 1993; Bercovitz et al., 2006; Srinivasan and Brush, 2006; Poppo et al., 2008a). Empirical work focused on perceptions of trustworthiness cannot comment on which basis of trust determines its effectiveness though (see also Vlaar, Chapter 4 this volume).

The goal of this chapter is to review empirical works pertaining to what we know about inter-organizational trust and direct future research toward current empirical and conceptual gaps. To accomplish these goals, I (1) review two approaches, psychological and behavioral, to defining and measuring inter-organizational trust; (2) briefly discuss the theoretical and empirical shortcomings of these definitions; and (3) review various theoretical perspectives used in empirical research to examine how inter-organizational trust emerges. I conclude by revisiting some broad criticisms and propose that a greater consideration of the various origins of trust can mitigate the managerial relevance problem, as well as help resolve the tension between structural versus relational determinants of inter-organizational trust.

DEFINING INTER-ORGANIZATIONAL TRUST: PSYCHOLOGICAL AND BEHAVIORAL TRADITIONS

For situations characterized by risk and uncertainty, coordination across a market interface is difficult. Bounded rationality results in incomplete contracts; exogenous uncertainty results in ex post adaptation; exchange parties must adapt often without the convenience of mutually agreed upon rules or processes, all of which increases transaction costs. Asymmetries in bargaining power make these negotiations even more difficult as parties haggle over quasi-rents associated with specialized investments. In addition, when a lack of observability exists, parties cannot perfectly monitor each other's performance of processes or effort levels. Transaction costs also result when parties do not perform as expected.

To minimize the transaction costs associated with these settings, a prevailing logic states that managers should select optimal governance means to optimize performance and mitigate losses to due opportunism and/or ex post adaptations (Williamson, 1996; Das and Teng, 1998). Whereas the transaction cost tradition focuses on formal controls – primarily, drafting more complex contracts – social theorists advocate an alternative: inter-organizational trust (for example, confident positive expectations). Early literature along these lines sought to legitimate the role of social relations in business exchanges, in contrast with the under-socialized view that typified most economic treatments of inter-organizational exchanges (for criticisms, see Granovetter, 1985; Bradach and Eccles, 1989).

I should at this time highlight the need to study inter-organizational relationships at multiple levels; consistent with prior studies, I therefore maintain that inter-personal trust differs from inter-organizational trust (for example, Rousseau et al., 1998; Zaheer et al., 1998). With inter-personal trust, the level of analysis is a pair of individual actors; for inter-organizational trust, the level of analysis captures an aggregate entity, such as the company or organization. The precise relationship between inter-personal and inter-organizational trust remains underexplored, with little research into the social psychological and cognitive processes that underlie aggregation processes. I presume they are similar to the processes underlying phenomena such as identification, sense-making, social comparisons and reputation formation, such that people ascribe a characteristic to an organization. In crafting this review, I therefore acknowledge the incompleteness in the study of inter-organizational exchanges and the continuing critiques of studies of inter-organizational trust (for example, Ariño et al., 2005).

Psychological View of Inter-organizational Trust

With that acknowledgement though, the development of the concept of trust consists of two separate traditions: psychological and behavioral. The more widely discussed approach, conceptually, is the psychological one. Scholars from various disciplines define trust as the 'confident expectations and a willingness to be vulnerable' (Rousseau et al., 1998, p. 393), which reflects a psychological tradition that favors perceptions and attributions of others' intentions and capabilities as measures of trust. For example, definitions such as a 'collectively held trust orientation toward a partner firm' (Zaheer et al., 1998, p. 143), 'an expectation that alleviates the fear that one's exchange partner will act opportunistically' (Bradach and Eccles, 1989, p. 104), or 'faithfulness' in social relationships (Simmel, 1978, p. 379) share a focus on trust as an expectation and attribution characterizing another party. Trusting beliefs arise from rational inferences based on observations of another's actual behavior and information relevant to this belief. The psychological tradition also allows for perceptions and attributions to arise from emotional responses to actions, such as goodwill, or negative emotional reactions, such as betrayal, to influence trusting beliefs.

Most empirical works instead measure cognitive components of inter-organizational trust, using managerial perceptions. These studies tend to consider three main components of inter-organizational trust: reliability, predictability and fairness (for example, Zaheer et al., 1998; Dyer and Chu, 2003; Krishnan et al., 2006; Poppo et al., 2008a), using survey items such as 'Supplier X has always been even-handed in its negotiations with us', 'Supplier X may use opportunities that arise at our expense', or 'Based on past experience, we cannot with complete confidence rely on supplier X to keep promises made to us' (Zaheer et al., 1998, p. 148). Thus, the defining feature of trust is positive, confident expectations.

Behavioral View of Inter-organizational Trust

A second approach employs behavioral measures in which the level of observed 'cooperative behavior' proxies for trust (Axelrod, 1984; Lewicki et al., 2006). The logic behind this behavioral tradition is that sequential acts of reciprocal cooperation foster the development of trust. High trust 'is revealed in a high number of cooperative choices, whereas low trust is indicated in a low number of cooperative choices' (Lewicki et al., 2006, pp. 995–6). Thus, a critical distinction in the behavioral tradition is that trust is an evolutionary process, 'better understood as a result rather than a precondition of cooperation' (Gambetta, 1988, p. 225).

McNeil's (1978, 1980) conceptualization of relational governance also greatly influenced the measure of cooperation by describing behavioral norms that produce or are associated with cooperation in inter-organizational exchanges. A fundamental assumption of this conceptualization is that inter-organizational exchanges are rarely discrete transactions; rather they tend to be relational, characterized by norms that support solidarity and continuance. Most empirical works focus on norms such as flexibility, solidarity and information sharing and measure the degree to which exchange partners (1) are flexible with respect to changes; (2) treat problems that arise in a collaborative fashion, as opposed to an individualistic, self-maximizing way; and (3) solicit and exchange private information often (Heide and John, 1992; Jap and Ganesan, 2000; Poppo and Zenger, 2002; Carson et al., 2003, 2006; Bercovitz et al., 2006). These norms govern and encourage exchange partners to behave in mutually beneficial and supportive fashions, even in the presence of exchange hazards (McNeil, 1980).

Alternative behavioral approaches also exist. For example, trust may be inferred from the specification of decision rights (Currall and Inkpen, 2002). In a joint venture, partners should trust each other when they share decision-making rights for resource allocation and operational control or do not monitor one another. A behavioral orientation also lends itself to the specification of structural solutions that favor the evolution of cooperation, such as a long window of future exchanges, so the rewards from acting cooperatively are greater than those from defecting from cooperation. This game-theoretic logic holds that the decision to cooperate can be a stable, reciprocal strategy if the shadow of the future is sufficiently long. This logic is also a simple extension of a tit-for-tat strategy: one player reciprocates whatever the other player did on the prior move (for example, defection as well as cooperation; Axelrod, 1984). When a sufficient shadow of the future exists, the benefits of acting in a cooperative fashion outweigh its costs. If parties no longer expect to transact, the future is discounted, and they defect from cooperative play to maximize their own interests. Thus, as an expectation of continued interaction, the shadow of the future is necessary to promote a stable strategy of reciprocal cooperative moves (Axelrod, 1984; Ring and Van de Ven, 1992; Parkhe, 1993; Poppo et al., 2008a), which depends critically on sufficient value being placed on future returns, as well as on the expected time horizon for future exchanges (Axelrod, 1984).

Limitations to the Behavioral and Cognitive Traditions

Both psychological and behavioral branches are appealing because of their focus on actual behavior or inferences that managers make about another entity using relevant information to develop perceptions of trust. Empirical work from both traditions confirms the simple main effect of inter-organizational trust on performance outcomes, and thus both traditions appear to be valid indicators and interpretations of inter-organizational trust. Yet these empirical approaches are not without limitations, as the following subsections summarize.

Simple vs contingent effects
Many empirical works demonstrate a main effect association of inter-organizational trust and lower transaction costs or positive performance (for example, Zaheer et al., 1998, Artz and Brush, 2000; Poppo and Zenger, 2002; Szulanski et al., 2004; Li et al., 2010). Thus, trust can operate as a governance mechanism: its use minimizes transaction costs and fosters greater exchange performance (though this inference comes from cross-sectional survey designs). More complex model specifications in turn are needed to understand how trust operates in settings fraught with risk and uncertainty. Does the presence of exchange risks weaken the effectiveness of control mechanisms or, alternatively, are some control mechanisms better safeguards for a given exchange risk than others (Zaheer and Harris, 2005)? The scant research available demonstrates the value of examining contingencies: Krishnan et al. (2006) find that the effect of trust on alliance performance is stronger when inter-partner competition is high but weaker when market instability is high. Poppo et al. (2008b) report that trust-based relational governance has a less positive effect on performance for high levels of asset specificity and difficult performance measurement. More research is needed to understand the situational effectiveness of inter-organizational trust. Examining boundary constraints or limits to a reliance on trust is a theoretically rich area but empirically underexamined.

Single vs multiple respondents
When research designs employ one key informant to fill out psychological survey items, their reliability is questionable (Currall and Inkpen, 2002). Research in this area generally relies on a single respondent, so reliability is a valid concern. Ariño et al. (2005, p. 15) 'ascribe to the view that trust is, indeed, an inter-personal phenomenon, and that any effort to define, measure, and empirically investigate trust as a characteristic of inter-organizational exchanges is counterproductive'. They propose an alternative label: relational quality, which they define as 'the extent to which the principals and agents of alliance partners feel confident in dealing with their counterparts' organizations' (pp. 15–16). Two solutions thus emerge: (1) use behavioral measures of inter-organizational trust,

which could extend to decision rights, formal policies, or informal routines (relational norms); or (2) use multiple respondents to measures perceptions of inter-organizational trust.

Effect of monitoring on trust
Yet unresolved is the relationship between monitoring and trust. Some argue that monitoring is a proxy; its use implies distrust (Currall and Inkpen, 2002). The prevailing logic is that monitoring damages performance by lowering task motivation and commitment, or else it encourages opportunistic behavior for tasks that are not easily monitored (Ghoshal and Moran, 1996; Heide et al., 2007). But monitoring also might foster a social pressure to comply with the agreement, which leads to improved outcomes, but only for aspects that are observed (Wathne and Heide, 2000). Its absence also could be destructive, because when alliance partners fear appropriation and leakage and avoid monitoring and information exchange, their expectations of the new project's feasibility diminish (Faems et al., 2008). In this sense, monitoring may encourage the development of norms that govern complex exchanges effectively by requiring the transfer of highly specialized, idiosyncratic knowledge. When uncertainty makes it difficult to clarify and fully specify joint expectations, the distinction between fine-grained coordination and monitoring may become blurred. More work is needed to resolve these divergent ideas, because the relationship between trust and monitoring appears context specific.

Types of trust
Largely absent in inter-organizational literature is any specification of different factors that underlie the construct of trust. For prior research, which generally focuses on the simple association of performance and trust, this lack of specification is not problematic. Yet understanding the varying types of trust becomes essential when trying to address more nuanced questions, such as how inter-organizational trust develops over time. Do some types of trust result in more stable and cooperative inter-organizational exchanges than others? This intersection of trust and its causes remains unclear; though rich in ideas, it demands far more empirical attention, not only to establish empirical facts but also to enrich theory and translate it into practice. Therefore, the next section assimilates prior literature to build a collective view of what we know about trust formation and its various types.

PERSPECTIVES ON THE ORIGINS OF INTER-ORGANIZATIONAL TRUST

Theory regarding the formation of trust is not cohesive but rather has evolved over time. To structure this discussion, I review four logics: selection, time (in other words, shadow of the past versus shadow of the future), the development of different types of trust over time, and credible signals of trustworthiness and cooperation (for related discussion on institutional sources of trust see also Kroeger, Chapter 11 this volume; Nickerson, Gubler and Kirks, Chapter 10 this volume; Harris, Keevil and Wicks, Chapter 9 this volume).

Selection Logic

Because trust safeguards transactions from opportunistic behavior, managers seemingly should select this governance choice in response to exchange hazards, such as asset specificity and uncertainty (Bradach and Eccles, 1989; Heide and John, 1990; Noordewier et al., 1990). This logic extends the transaction cost reasoning underlying formal governance choices: knowing the ex ante governance risks, managers select the most efficient governance choice in a transaction cost-minimizing way. Therefore, firms should invest in the development of trust only when significant hazards are present. Absent these hazards, the cost of developing trust may not be warranted. Such logic is intuitively appealing, because trust by definition is most critical in situations characterized by risk and uncertainty. When present, it alleviates fears about an exchange partner acting opportunistically (Bradach and Eccles, 1989).

There is no empirical support for this line of reasoning though (Heide and John, 1990; Anderson and Weitz, 1992; Ganesan, 1994; Poppo and Zenger, 2002). The inconsistent findings might occur because studies failed to measure key contingencies, such as the power asymmetry in the (distribution) channel (Sheng et al., 2006) or because the emergence of trust is a relatively idiosyncratic process that cannot be controlled systematically through selection (Bercovitz et al., 2006).

Temporal Dynamics

Shadow of the past vs shadow of the future
Perhaps inter-organizational trust just evolves over time, with a dynamic vision, not a static decision governance choice, as implied by the selection logic. Therefore, the decision to trust is a rational choice, built over time on the basis of observations of others' behaviors and other trust-relevant

information (Lewicki et al., 2006). Models of relationship development similarly propose that buyers engage in trials and tests of their suppliers early in the exchange history to assess their cooperation, which enables them to establish initial trust beliefs. The party's trust in the other develops over time by accumulating through relationship exchange experiences that indicate the kind of behavior to expect from the other party (Larson, 1992; Zajac and Olsen, 1993; Ring and Van De Ven, 1994; Ariño and De La Torre, 1998). Central to this logic is the notion that trust building occurs incrementally over time and emerges from prior experience (Blau, 1964; Gulati, 1995).

In the psychological tradition, trusting beliefs likely become more stable over time (in other words, less variance, greater confidence that the other party is trustworthy). In the behavioral tradition, the level of trust increases as a function of the number and degree of serial reciprocity of trustworthy behaviors. Stronger levels of trust are a desirable quality because once they exist they decrease exchange uncertainty through behavioral predictability (Lewicki and Bunker, 1996). This logic then assumes that past experiences – the shadow of the past – transform an undersocialized relationship into one in which the history of prior relations and interactions provide a social institution capable of building trust (for example, Blau, 1964; Granovetter 1985, 1992; Gulati 1995; Poppo et al., 2008a).

Early empirical work that adopted this perspective uses prior experience as a proxy for the level of trust in an inter-organizational exchange (Gulati, 1995). The length of prior interactions, such as prior alliances between two firms, presumes that trust must exist, otherwise, why would one firm choose to repeat the business? The prior interaction creates a level of familiarity and provides a platform for developing mutually trusting relationships; the greater the length of the prior interaction, the more confident the expectations of another's trustworthiness. Empirical work further verifies that prior experience is associated with trust (Poppo and Zenger, 2002; Gulati and Sytch, 2008), though as a surrogate for trust, this measure is limited and appears especially problematic when examining the link between trust and performance: the length of prior engagement cannot distinguish whether performance gains in an inter-organizational exchange arise from trust or from learning (Zollo et al., 2002).

A second perspective also informs the evolution of trust: rather than the shadow of the past, trust might depend on the future rewards associated with behaving in a trustworthy fashion. This alternative path constitutes the shadow of the future. Similar to the process when in the shadow of the past, trust follows from cooperation, and the formation of trust is deliberate. However, the shadow of the future reflects a rational assessment of forward-looking conditions, such that it can be rewarding to behave as if we trusted others, even in vulnerable situations. When the expected payoff from cooperation outweighs the gain from self-interested behavior, cooperation emerges through reciprocity: first you act in a cooperative manner, and then I will. Thus, reciprocal acts of cooperation depend on the value of future returns (Bercovitz et al., 2006; Poppo et al., 2008a). When a party knows that it is in its best financial interest to cooperate fully, and assuming that the other party is also aware of this condition, cooperation can dominate (Hill, 1990; Parkhe, 1993).

Empirical work examining these two rationales, the shadow of the past and the shadow of the future, as determinants of inter-organizational trust, is limited (Poppo et al., 2008a). Contrary to the shadow of the past theory though, prior history does not directly affect trust; instead, expectations of continuity mediate the positive relationship between the prior history and trust. These findings suggest the criticality and centrality of a shadow of the future (in other words, forward-looking calculus) in generating inter-organizational trust. Learning is more probably an outcome of trust from prior interactions between exchange partners. Prior history certainly shapes trust: a longer prior history makes the effect of continuity on trust much stronger than a shorter prior history. Thus, the shadow of the past and the future appear intertwined as optimal determinants to trusting beliefs.

Development of different types of trust over time
Inter-personal models of trust assume that over time the type of trust that one party holds for another may change, because as trust develops over time, salient features that define expectations of others change (Lewicki and Bunker, 1996). At some level, these conceptualizations are relevant to inter-organizational exchanges. For example, early in an exchange parties do not know what to expect of each other; trust is initially developed by employing rewards and sanctions tied to specific outcomes. This calculus-based trust includes rewards associated with the shadow of the future (for example, repeat business due to a positively earned reputation) and contractually specified penalties for noncompliance. Inter-organizational trust is simply created through appropriate levels of rewards and sanctions. This generally impersonal type of trust may invoke an arm's-length transaction (in other words, consistent with transaction cost ideas of how to govern inter-organizational exchanges).

As time passes, a party learns more relevant information. If this information extends to knowledge of the other's abilities and capabilities, trust may be described as knowledge-based. This form of trust is grounded in predictability, reliability and regular, intimate communication, which establishes enough information to judge whether the parties can work well together (Lewicki and Bunker, 1996). Trust in this case should extend readily to the governance of complex exchanges that require high levels of task interdependence and/or coordination.

An alternative formulation is competence-based trust, which refers to the perception that the other party possesses requisite skills and knowledge for a task (Butler and Cantrell, 1984). Yet knowledge-based trust is predicated on frequent, personal interaction, such that exchanges enable parties to understand what each party wants and discuss problem-solving approaches. In addition, according to Lewicki and Bunker (1996, p. 121), knowledge-based trust presumes that some emotional attachment begins to develop, otherwise, the parties 'lose touch'. Whereas knowledge-based trust requires frequent, personal interactions, competence-based trust may well be granted due to a company's reputation or certification of its business processes and capabilities.

The deepest, most enduring form of trust is identification based. Relational trust entails the internalization of another's preferences and mutual understanding; the parties make decisions in each other's interests (Lewicki and Bunker, 1996; Lewicki et al., 2006; Kramer and Lewicki, 2010; Pirson and Malhotra, 2011). Relational trust not only has 'social' and 'reciprocal' aspects but also includes a collective orientation such that 'the parties effectively understand and appreciate the other's wants' because they '"think like" the other, "feel like" the other, and "respond" like the other' (Lewicki and Bunker, 1996, pp. 122–3). This characterization highlights the relational features of deep, internalized principles, values and standards, which foster motivation and commitment to serve the interests of the whole (see also Barney and Hansen, 1994; Ring, 1996).

This characterization of trust may define close, intimate relationships in which boundary spanners develop close ties with the organization, consistent with Uzzi's (1997, p. 42) description of inter-organizational ties in a textile industry: they 'become friends with these people – business friends', or they treat one another as if 'they're . . . part of the company' or 'the family'. Such relationships get reinforced and supported through the 'social-psychological bonds of norms, sentiments and friendships' and faith in the morality and goodwill of others (Ring and Van de Ven, 1994, p. 93; Uzzi, 1997). This type of trust is potentially important (but likely rare) in inter-organizational exchanges because the shadow of the future may not be needed to encourage cooperation. Long-standing exchange partners would continue to act in a cooperative, trusting fashion, even if an end-game existed. High levels of inter-personal or inter-group trust thus should be most operative in this situation.

Other forms of trust have also been conceptualized but do not develop in a sequential fashion. For example, in addition to competence-based trust, integrity-based trust refers to a perception that the trustee is adhering to a set of acceptable principles (Sitkin and Roth, 1993; Mayer et al., 1995; Kim et al., 2004). A violation means that one party has intentionally violated an agreed-on practice or principle (Kim et al., 2006), which implies opportunism or self-interest seeking with guile (Williamson, 1996). Integrity instead implies upholding promises, such as good faith efforts to behave in accordance with implicit or explicit commitments, and being perceived as honest and fair (for example, Cummings and Bromiley, 1996; Zaheer et al., 2002; Husted and Folger, 2004).

Trust also features a strong affective component, involving benevolence or the 'extent to which a trustee is believed to want to do good to the trustor, aside from an egocentric profit motive' (Mayer et al., 1995, p. 718). At an individual level of analysis, this form of trust is inherently personal and relational, characterized by a strong emotional attachment, affective commitment and expressions of genuine care and consideration for the other. Recent work redefines benevolent trust at a collective level: a concern for the well-being of stakeholders (Gillespie and Dietz, 2009). Yet this view does not explore whether positive affect or emotion characterizes the development of deeper levels of trust over time. Perhaps emotion plays a central role in creating long-term attachments (Lawler, 2001). Recent experiments support this inference. Repeated exchanges with the same partners generate positive emotions that promote perceived cohesion and commitment behavior (Lawler and Yoon, 1996, 1998).

Yet more research is needed to understand how emotional components affect inter-organizational trust (Poppo and Lambe, 2006). Betrayal conveys one emotional reaction; similarly, shared achievements generate positive emotions. But how does emotion define or influence inter-organizational trust? Related to this, what are the processes that influence the aggregation and dissemination of observations regarding trustworthiness? That is, how does inter-personal trust expand to inter-group or inter-organizational trust?

Credible (Structural) Signals of Trustworthiness and Cooperation

According to signaling literature, the effectiveness of any firm action to build a perception of trust depends on whether that act credibly signals the party's intent. Signals are observable features, 'intentionally displayed for the purpose of raising the probability the receiver assigns to a certain state of affairs' (Gambetta, 2009, p. 170). The key feature of a signal is that it is too costly for those with untrustworthy quality to display. Yet signals are rarely perfect; they are semi-shorting, and though they convey information, they cannot do so perfectly clearly. As Gambetta (2009,

p. 173) concludes, 'We rarely encounter a fully mimic-proof signal'. The strength of a signal is reflected in its cost, which the firm must pay if it fails to achieve the promised quality. Partial signals cause receivers to 'probe and seek more credible signals' (Gambetta, 2009, p. 174). With my focus on trust building, I view signals as a form of pre-commitment: actions that restrict the extent to which 'others have to worry about our trustworthiness' (Gambetta, 1988, p. 221).

Signals should be influential determinants of inter-organizational trust early in the exchange relationship. When one party lacks specific (personalized) information and knowledge about the other's competences, abilities and intent (honesty or opportunistic), it may be influenced by institutional sources of trust, which refer to 'the phenomenon that individuals or collective actors develop trust *in the face of* specific institutional arrangements in the business environment' (Bachmann and Inkpen, 2011, p. 284; original emphasis). When groups are socially and geographically distant, trust builds through legitimate institutions (Zucker, 1986); formal institutions can serve as administrative or symbolic substitutes for personal or relational trust (Sitkin and Roth, 1993). A lack of close interdependence between two parties implies they cannot develop relational (Kramer, 1999; Zaheer and Harris, 2005) or process-based (Zucker, 1986) sources of trust.

For inter-organizational exchanges, institutional sources of trustworthiness are important: in economies in which legal systems enforce contract law, parties may rely more on contracts to coordinate more complex exchanges, rather than personalized ties (Zhou and Poppo, 2010). Legal institutions coupled with contract law form a credible basis for trust; if one party fails to honor the agreement, the legal system enforces contractual commitments (see also Bachmann and Inkpen, 2011). Although contracts are costly, they represent a weak form of pre-commitment because they 'do not rule out certain actions, they just make them more costly' (Gambetta, 1988, p. 221). That is, for some types of exchanges, weak signals are risky because they do not ensure cooperation. This gap may emerge for reputation and third-party certification of exchange partners too. As Bachmann and Inkpen (2011) argue, these signals are more effective for relatively simple exchanges, such as those characterized by low levels of asset specificity.

But which types of signals encourage greater perceptions of inter-organizational trust in more complex exchanges? The signals might need to satisfy two criteria: (1) 'it is necessary to trust others before acting cooperatively, but also to believe that one is trusted by others'; and (2) 'trust is ... a probability that another agent or group of agents will perform a particular action, both before he can monitor such action (or independently of his capacity ever to be able to monitor it)' (Gambetta,

1988, p. 216). Trust exists in the absence of monitoring – which may not be a realistic assumption for the formation of trust in inter-organizational exchanges.

Impersonal institutional vehicles designed for trust production thus might build trust or simply regulate distrust. Sitkin and Roth (1993) argue that formal controls and procedures effectively regulate task-specific reliability, such as providing assurance in the organizational competencies that underlie manufacturing and service, but they cannot develop personal, relational sources of trust. Gambetta (1988, p. 217) more generally argues that these types of symbols 'limit the extent to which we worry about trust, but [do] not increase trust'. Yet Bachmann and Inkpen (2011) suggest that legal regulation, reputation and certifications are effective trust-building mechanisms for relatively non-specialized exchanges (for example, simple market exchanges). Others argue and empirically confirm that customized contracts and trust can function as complements in the governance of more complex exchanges, emphasizing the coordinating function of contracts and the production of trust (Poppo and Zenger, 2002; Reuer and Ariño, 2007; Mellewigt et al., 2007; c.f., Hoetker and Mellewigt, 2009).

Consistent with a focus on the structural origins of inter-organizational trust, an emerging perspective refers to how self-enforcing agreements produce cooperative behavior, perceptions of trust, or greater exchange performance. In these works, structural constraints underlie the production of cooperation and/or trust. For example, Bercovitz et al. (2006) argue and empirically confirm that joint specialized investments and transparency (for example, observability) underlie the development of cooperation (measured by relational norms). Poppo et al. (2008b) argue and empirically confirm that reciprocal investments in specialized assets function as a pledge for exclusivity and commitment to the exchange relationship, which in turn is associated with greater expectations of continuance and thus greater perceptions of trustworthiness.

Their logics are routed in transaction cost economics language: credible commitments and self-enforcing agreements. For example 'the buyer's commitment to the exchange is more assuredly signaled by his willingness to accept reciprocal exposure to specialized assets' (Williamson, 1996, p. 135). Trust production for more complex exchanges requires a combination of signs and signals, including greater interdependencies, such as reciprocal investments in specialized assets, greater willingness to share private information, actions that signal transparency in situations in which information is tacit and difficult to verify, and elements that encourage relationship stability and expectations of continuance (Bercovitz et al., 2006; Srinivasan and Brush, 2006; Poppo et al., 2008a).

Other types of signals and symbols also may influence perceptions of trustworthiness. Talk and symbols are cheap of course – but not all words or symbols are cheap. Thus, research should examine what kinds of talk or symbols can produce value congruence, which may be a cornerstone for cooperative, productive inter-organizational exchanges (McNeil, 1978; Ring and Van de Ven, 1992; Madhok and Tallman, 1998). Alternatively, what kinds of normative operating procedures can signal transparency and observability? This line of reasoning reorients the study of trust production, to test when or whether the production of inter-organizational trust demands monitoring and transparency.

CONCLUSION

I began this chapter with two stories about inter-organizational exchanges. The Walmart and P&G story as well as the Sprint–Clearwire joint venture illustrate the challenges of achieving bilateral cooperation of inter-organizational exchanges. Yet, alternative courses of action exist, as outlined in this chapter, and the goal of this review was to encourage empirical researchers to think more broadly about different conceptual perspectives but also more narrowly about which routes best inform the study of cooperation and inter-organizational trust. Second, the criticisms reviewed at the beginning of this chapter are valid: our theorizing about trust is conceptually rich, yet underexplored empirically. Future research needs to broaden its focus so that empirical work can inform which aspects of the vast conceptualizations of trust are pertinent to and productive in our understanding of inter-organizational exchanges. While this chapter examines cooperation as a focal exchange outcome, other important related outcomes exist (for example, innovation and intrinsic motivation; see Nooteboom, Chapter 5 this volume and Weibel and Six, Chapter 3 this volume).

One path outlined in this chapter is a more rigorous empirical specification of trust focusing on the behaviors, policies and normative or formal procedures and processes coupled with the core values/types of trust that they signal. The integration of behavioral practices and trusting beliefs would establish a better understanding for how trusting beliefs develop as well as what kinds of trust exists. For example, if new practices were developed, using relational governance as the theoretical anchor, such that Walmart works jointly with P&G in creating products at a certain price point, would this kind of bilateral practice (cooperation) lead to greater perceptions of inter-organizational trust? What dimensions of inter-organizational trust are enhanced, and how widespread are these beliefs (inter-personal; inter-group; inter-organizational)? This direction for future research also has greater managerial relevance – for we have better understanding of which managerial practices establish which kinds of trusting beliefs and how widespread these are. In addition, a focus on managerial practices will help us better understand whether trust formation depends on the level of monitoring and transparency inherent in such managerial practices.

Second, this review suggests that the structural aspects that shape cooperation and trusting beliefs are important and cannot be ignored. Structural aspects refer to formal institutions, such as contracts and legal systems, co-specialized investments (for example, credible commitments), as well as a not-always-specified and expectations of continuance – according to signaling literature, the effectiveness of any firm action to build a perception of trust depends on whether that act credibly signals the party's intent. As illustrated in the Sprint–Clearwire joint venture, a dominant equity position is not sufficient to produce an effective inter-organizational exchange. This is not surprising (for example, Ariño and De La Torre, 1998; Das and Teng, 1998) – but what is less researched in this literature are the cluster of actions, the congruency of their signals, perceptions of trustworthiness, and the effectiveness of the inter-organizational exchange

Third, unknown is how relational and emotional bases of trust can be meaningfully studied and captured at the inter-organizational level of analysis, given that these forms of trust may be idiosyncratic and bound at an inter-personal level of analysis. I am not implying that more relational forms of trust are not worthy of study; instead, I am advocating that future empirical develop these ideas further and examine them closely for their relevance and impact.

REFERENCES

Anderson, E. and B. Weitz (1992), 'The use of pledges to build and sustain commitment in distribution channels', *Journal of Marketing Research*, **29**(1), 18–34.
Ariño, A. and J. De La Torre (1998), 'Learning from failure: towards an evolutionary model of collaborative ventures', *Organization Science*, **9**(3), 306–25.
Ariño, A., J. De La Torre and P.S. Ring (2005), 'Relational quality and inter-personal trust in strategic alliances', *European Management Review*, **2**(1), 15–27.
Artz, K.W. and T.H. Brush (2000), 'Asset specificity, uncertainty and relational norms: an examination of coordination costs in collaborative strategic alliances', *Journal of Economic Behavior and Organization*, **41**(4), 337–62.
Axelrod, R. (1984), *The Evolution of Cooperation*, New York: Basic Books.
Bachmann, R. and A.C. Inkpen (2011), 'Understanding institutional-based trust building processes in inter-organizational relationships', *Organization Studies*, **32**(2), 281–301.
Barney, J.B. and M.H. Hansen (1994), 'Trustworthiness as a source of competitive advantage', *Strategic Management Journal*, **15**(S1), 175–90.

Bell, J., B. Den Ouden and G.W. Ziggers (2006), 'Dynamics of cooperation: at the brink of irrelevance', *Journal of Management Studies*, **43**(7), 1607–19.
Bercovitz, J., S.D. Jap and J.A. Nickerson (2006), 'The antecedents and performance implications of cooperative exchange norms', *Organization Science*, **17**(6), 724–40.
Blau, P.M. (1964), *Exchange and Power in Social Life*, New Jersey: Transaction Publishers.
Bradach, J. and R.G. Eccles (1989), 'Price, authority and trust: from ideal types to plural forms', *Annual Review of Sociology*, **15**(1), 97–118.
Bromiley, P. and J. Harris (2006), 'Trust, transaction cost economics, and mechanisms', in R. Bachmann and A. Zaheer (eds), *Handbook of Trust Research*, Cheltenham, UK and Northampton, MA, USA: Edward Elgar Publishing, pp. 124–43.
Butler, J.K. and R.S. Cantrell (1984), 'A behavioral decision theory approach to modeling dyadic trust in superiors and subordinates', *Psychological Reports*, **55**(1), 19–28.
Carson, S.J., A. Madhok and T. Wu (2006), 'Uncertainty, opportunism, and governance: the effects of volatility and ambiguity on formal and relational contracting', *Academy of Management Journal*, **49**(5), 1058–77.
Carson, S.J., A. Madhok, R. Varman and G. John (2003), 'Information processing moderators of the effectiveness of trust-based governance in interfirm R&D collaboration', *Organization Science*, **14**(1), 45–56.
Cummings, L.L. and P. Bromiley (1996), 'The organizational trust inventory (OTI), development and validation', in Roderick M. Kramer and Tom R. Tyler (eds), *Trust in Organizations: Frontiers of Theory and Research*, Thousand Oaks, CA: Sage Publications, pp. 302–30.
Currall, S.C. and A.C. Inkpen (2002), 'A multilevel approach to trust in joint ventures', *Journal of International Business Studies*, **33**(3), 479–95.
Das, T.K. and B.S. Teng (1998), 'Between trust and control: developing confidence in partner cooperation in alliances', *Academy of Management Review*, **23**(3), 491–512.
Dyer, J.H. and W. Chu (2003), 'The role of trustworthiness in reducing transaction costs and improving performance: empirical evidence from the United States, Japan, and Korea', *Organization Science*, **14**(1), 57–68.
Faems, D., M. Janssens, A. Madhok and B. Van Looy (2008), 'Toward an integrative perspective on alliance governance: connecting contract design, trust dynamics, and contract application', *Academy of Management Journal*, **51**(6), 1053–78.
Gambetta, D. (1988), 'Can we trust trust?', in D. Gambetta (ed.), *Trust: Making and Breaking Co-operative Relations*, Oxford: Basil Blackwell, pp. 213–37.
Gambetta, D. (2009), 'Signaling', in P. Hedström and P. Bearman (eds), *The Oxford Handbook of Analytical Sociology*, Oxford: Oxford University Press.
Ganesan, S. (1994), 'Determinants of long-term orientation in buyer–seller relationships', *Journal of Marketing*, **58**(2), 1–19.
Ghoshal, S. and P. Moran (1996), 'Bad for practice: a critique of the transaction cost theory', *Academy of Management Review*, **21**(1), 13–47.
Gillespie, N. and G. Dietz (2009), 'Trust repair after an organization-level failure', *Academy of Management Review*, **34**(1), 127–45.
Granovetter, M. (1985), 'Economic action and social structure: the problem of embeddedness', in Nicole Woolsey Biggart (ed.), *Readings in Economic Sociology*, pp. 63–8.
Granovetter, M. (1992), *Decision Making: Alternatives to Rational Choice Models Economic Action and Social Structure: The Problem of Embeddedness*, Newbury Park, CA: Sage.
Gulati, R. (1995), 'Does familiarity breed trust? The implications of repeated ties for contractual choice in alliances', *Academy of Management Journal*, **38**(1), 85–112.
Gulati, R. and J.A. Nickerson (2008), 'Inter-organizational trust, governance choice, and exchange performance', *Organization Science*, **19**(5), 688–708.
Gulati, R. and M. Sytch (2008), 'Does familiarity breed trust? Revisiting the antecedents of trust', *Managerial and Decision Economics*, **29**(2/3), 165–90.
Heide, J.B. and G. John (1990), 'Alliances in industrial purchasing: the determinants of joint action in buyer–supplier relationships', *Journal of Marketing Research*, **27**(1), 24–36.

Heide, J.B. and G. John (1992), 'Do norms matter in marketing relationships?', *Journal of Marketing*, **56**(2), 32–44.
Heide, J.B., K.H. Wathne and A.I. Rokkan (2007), 'Interfirm monitoring, social contracts, and relationship outcomes', *Journal of Marketing Research*, **44**(3), 425–33.
Hennart, J.F. (2006), 'Alliance research: less is more', *Journal of Management Studies*, **43**(7), 1621–8.
Hill, C.W.L. (1990), 'Cooperation, opportunism, and the invisible hand: implications for transaction cost theory', *Academy of Management Review*, **15**(3), 500–513.
Hoetker, G. and T. Mellewigt (2009), 'Choice and performance of governance mechanisms: matching alliance governance to asset type', *Strategic Management Journal*, **30**(10), 1025–44.
Husted, B.W. and R. Folger (2004), 'Fairness and transaction costs: the contribution of organizational justice theory to an integrative model of economic organization', *Organization Science*, **15**(6), 719–29.
Jap, S.D. and S. Ganesan, (2000), 'Control mechanisms and the relationship life cycle: implications for safeguarding specific investments and developing commitment', *Journal of Marketing Research*, **37**(2), 227–45.
Kim, P.H., K.T. Dirks, C.D. Cooper and D.L. Ferrin (2006), 'When more blame is better than less: the implications of internal vs. external attributions for the repair of trust after a competence- vs. integrity-based trust violation', *Organizational Behavior and Human Decision Processes*, **99**(1), 49–65.
Kim, Peter H., D.L. Ferrin, C.D. Cooper and K.T. Dirks (2004), 'Removing the shadow of suspicion: the effects of apology versus denial for repairing competence- versus integrity-based trust violations', *Journal of Applied Psychology*, **89**(1), 104–18.
Kramer, R.M. (1999), 'Trust and distrust in organizations: emerging perspectives, enduring questions', *Annual Review of Psychology*, **50**(1), 569–98.
Kramer, R.M. and R.J. Lewicki (2010), 'Repairing and enhancing trust: approaches to reducing organizational trust deficits', *Academy of Management Annals*, **4**(1), 245–77.
Krishnan, R., X. Martin and N.G. Noorderhaven (2006), 'When does trust matter to alliance performance?', *Academy of Management Journal*, **49**(5), 894–917.
Larson, A. (1992), 'Network dyads in entrepreneurial settings: a study of the governance of exchange relationships', *Administrative Science Quarterly*, **37**(1), 76–104.
Lawler, E.J. (2001), 'An affect theory of social exchange', *American Journal of Sociology*, **107**(2), 321–52.
Lawler, E.J. and J. Yoon (1996), 'Commitment in exchange relations: test of a theory of relational cohesion', *American Sociological Review*, **61**(1), 89–108.
Lawler, E.J. and J. Yoon (1998), 'Network structure and emotion in exchange relations', *American Sociological Review*, **63**(6), 871–94.
Lewicki, R. and B. Bunker (1996), 'Developing and maintaining trust in work relationships', in R.M. Kramer and T.R. Tyler (eds), *Trust in Organizations: Frontiers of Theory and Research*, London: Sage, pp. 114–39.
Lewicki, R.J., E.C. Tomlinson and N. Gillespie (2006), 'Models of inter-personal trust development: theoretical approaches, empirical evidence, and future directions', *Journal of Management*, **32**(6), 991–1022.
Li, J.J., L. Poppo and K. Zheng Zhou (2010), 'Relational mechanisms, formal contracts, and local knowledge acquisition by international subsidiaries', *Strategic Management Journal*, **31**(4), 349–70.
McNeil, I.R. (1978), 'Contracts: adjustment of long-term economic relations under classical, neoclassical and relational contract law', *Northwestern University Law Review*, **72**(6), 854–905.
McNeil, I.R. (1980), *The New Social Contract: An Inquiry into Modern Contractual Relations*, New Haven, CT: Yale University Press.
Madhok, A. and S. Tallman (1998), 'Resources, transactions and rents: managing value through interfirm collaborative relationships', *Organization Science*, **9**(3), 326–39.
Mayer, R.C., J.H. Davis and F.D. Schoorman (1995), 'An integrative model of organizational trust', *Academy of Management Review*, **20**(3), 709–34.

Mellewigt, T., A. Madhok and A. Weibel (2007), 'Trust and formal contracts in inter-organizational relationships – substitutes and complements', *Managerial and Decision Economics*, **28**(8), 833–87.
Noordewier, T.G., G. John and J.R. Nevin (1990), 'Performance outcomes of purchasing arrangements in industrial buyer–vendor relationships', *Journal of Marketing*, **54**(4), 80–93.
Parkhe, A. (1993), 'Strategic alliance structuring: a game theoretic and transaction cost examination of interfirm cooperation', *Academy of Management Journal*, **36**(4), 794–829.
Pirson, M. and D. Malhotra (2011), 'Foundations of organizational trust: what matters to different stakeholders', *Organization Science*, **22**(4), 1087–104.
Poppo, L. and J. Lambe (2006), 'A time dependent framework on developing perceptions of relational norms: the role of emotion and uncertainty reduction factors', in A. Ariño and Jeff Reuer (eds), *Strategic Alliances: Governance and Contracts*, New York: Palgrave Macmillan, pp. 135–47.
Poppo, L. and T. Zenger (2002), 'Do formal contracts and relational governance function as substitutes or complements?', *Strategic Management Journal*, **23**(8), 707–25.
Poppo, L., K.Z. Zhou and S. Ryu (2008a), 'Alternative origins to inter-organizational trust: an interdependence perspective on the shadow of the past and the shadow of the future', *Organization Science*, **19**(1), 39–55.
Poppo, L., K.Z. Zhou and T.R. Zenger (2008b), 'Examining the conditional limits of relational governance: specialized assets, performance ambiguity, and long-standing ties', *Journal of Management Studies*, **45**(7), 1195–216.
Reuer, J.J. and A. Ariño (2007), 'Strategic alliance contracts: dimensions and determinants of contractual complexity', *Strategic Management Journal*, **28**(3), 313–30.
Ring, P.S. (1996), 'Fragile and resilient trust and their roles in economic exchange', *Business and Society*, **35**(2), 148–75.
Ring, P.S. and A.H. Van de Ven (1992), 'Structuring cooperative relationships between organizations', *Strategic Management Journal*, **13**(7), 483–98.
Ring, P.S. and A.H. Van de Ven (1994), 'Developmental processes of cooperative inter-organizational relationships', *Academy of Management Review*, **19**(1), 90–118.
Rousseau, D.M., S.B. Sitkin, R.S. Burt and C. Camerer (1998), 'Not so different after all: a cross-discipline view of trust', *Academy of Management Review*, **23**(3), 393–404.
Sheng, Shibin, James R. Brown, Carolyn Y. Nicholson and Laura Poppo (2006), 'Exchange hazards and relational governance: an empirical test of the role of communication', *International Journal of Research in Marketing*, **23**(1), 63–77.
Simmel, G. (1978), *The Philosophy of Money*, London and New York: Routledge.
Sitkin, S.B. and N.L. Roth (1993), 'Explaining the limited effectiveness of legalistic "remedies" for trust/distrust', *Organization Science*, **4**(3) 367–92.
Srinivasan, R. and T.H. Brush (2006), 'Supplier performance in vertical alliances: the effects of calculative trust and enforceable contracts', *Organization Science*, **17**(4), 436–52.
Szulanski, G., R. Cappetta and R.J. Jensen (2004), 'When and how trustworthiness matters: knowledge transfer and the moderating effect of casual ambiguity', *Organization Science*, **15**(5), 600–613.
Uzzi, B. (1997), 'Social structure and competition in interfirm networks: the paradox of embeddedness', *Administrative Science Quarterly*, **43**, 35–67.
Wathne, K.H. and J.B. Heide (2000), 'Opportunism in interfirm relationships: forms, outcomes, and solutions', *Journal of Marketing*, **64**(4), 36–51.
Williamson, O.E. (1993), 'Calculativeness, trust, and economic organization', *Journal of Law & Economy*, **36**, 453–86.
Williamson, O.E. (1996), *The Mechanisms of Governance*, New York: Oxford University Press.
Zaheer, A. and J. Harris (2005), 'Inter-organizational trust for inclusion', in O. Shenkar and J. Reuer (eds), *Handbook of Strategic Alliances*, Thousand Oaks, CA: Sage.
Zaheer, A., S. Lofstrom and V.P. George (2002), 'Inter-personal and inter-organizational trust in alliances', *Cooperative Strategies and Alliances*, **1**, 347–77.

Zaheer, A., B. McEvily and V. Perrone (1998), 'Does trust matter? Exploring the effects of inter-organizational and inter-personal trust on performance', *Organization science*, **9**(2), 141–59.

Zajac, E.J. and C.P. Olsen (1993), 'From transaction cost to transactional value analysis: implications for the study of inter-organizational strategies', *Journal of Management Studies*, **30**(1), 131–45.

Zhou, Kevin Zheng and Laura Poppo (2010), 'Exchange hazards, relational reliability and contracts in China: the contingent role of legal enforceability', *Journal of International Business Studies*, **41**(5), 861–82.

Zollo, M., J. Reuer and H. Singh (2002), 'Inter-organizational routines and performance in strategic alliances', *Organization Science*, **13**(6), 701–13.

Zucker, L.G. (1986), 'Production of trust: institutional sources of economic structure, 1840–1920', *Research in Organizational Behavior*, **8**(1), 53–111.

7. Inter-cultural trust and trust-building: the contexts and strategies of adaptive learning in acculturation
Peter Ping Li

INTRODUCTION

There is a growing recognition that trust plays a critical role in inter-personal and inter-firm relationships not only within a single nation or culture but also between distinctive nations or cultures (Zaheer and Zaheer, 2006; Li, 2008). It is surprising that, despite its importance, the role of trust in inter-cultural interaction has been rarely studied. The extant research on so-called cross-cultural trust has primarily focused on the comparative study of 'intra-cultural trust' for within-cultural behavior and relationship, rather than 'inter-cultural trust' for between-cultural behavior and relationship. In other words, the extant research is on the influence of culture on trust and trust-building within a single culture, rather than between diverse cultures (see Ferrin and Gillespie, 2010 for a recent review; for some notable exceptions, see Sullivan et al., 1981; Johnson et al., 1996; Pornpitakpan, 1998; Kuhlmann, 2005; Burger et al., 2006; Zaheer and Zaheer, 2006). This problem extends beyond the research on trust. For instance, the same problem exists in the research on international negotiation because 'almost all of that research has been conducted in intracultural settings' (Lee et al., 2006, p. 624). This problem also exists across the broad field of cross-cultural organizational behavior, where much of the research focuses on intra-cultural behaviors. Despite the repeated calls to close this gap (for example, Adler, 1983; Smith, 2003; Tjosvold and Leung, 2003), 'far less attention has been paid to the dynamics of culture in inter-cultural encounters, or what we would refer to as the "cross-cultural interface"' (Gelfand et al., 2007, p. 497; also see Taras et al., 2009 for a review).

To fill the gap in the literature, we address four key questions regarding trust and trust-building via 'cultural interface' (highlighting inter-cultural interaction) beyond 'cultural distance' (comparing intra-cultural interaction) due to 'adaptive learning': (1) Does inter-cultural trust differ categorically from intra-cultural trust? (2) Why does inter-cultural trust differ from intra-cultural trust? (3) How is inter-cultural trust built as compared to intra-cultural trust-building? (4) Is the process of inter-cultural trust-building a linear pattern over time? The purpose of this chapter is to answer the above four questions by integrating three salient constructs, that is, trust asymmetry (related to cultural distance), trust integration (related to cultural interface), and adaptive trust-building (related to adaptive learning), as the three primary pillars or building blocks of an integrative framework of inter-cultural trust and trust-building. We refer to 'culture' as a mental program shared by a community (Hofstede, 2001). For the purpose of this study, we focus on the culture at the level of ethnic community within or beyond national boundaries.

By addressing the above four critical questions concerning inter-cultural trust, we seek to make three primary contributions. First, we provide the theoretical rationale for distinguishing between inter-cultural and intra-cultural trust as two distinctive phenomena toward an 'imperative premise' that inter-cultural trust differs categorically from intra-cultural trust due to the effect of cultural distance, but cultural distance is not sufficient for inter-cultural trust in particular and inter-cultural interaction in general; hence, dynamic variables, including cultural interface and adaptive learning, are required to supplement the static variable of cultural distance. Second, extending the imperative premise, we propose a central theme for an integrative framework of inter-cultural trust and trust-building. The central theme posits that different features of trust (for example, level, form, base, mechanism and stage) are evoked by people from different cultures, but the same people are capable of building inter-cultural trust via adaptive learning to bridge cultural distance in an acculturation pattern as a process of cultural interface. Third, we develop two key typologies to specify four trust-building contexts as well as four trust-building strategies.

The rest of the chapter is organized into three key sections. First, we present the imperative premise to differentiate between inter-cultural and intra-cultural interaction in general and trust in particular. Second, we propose the central theme of inter-cultural trust and trust-building toward an integrative framework. Third, we develop two typologies about inter-cultural trust-building as the application of the framework. Fourth, we discuss the research implications of the framework, and conclude at the end. In particular, we highlight the above issues in organizational settings.

THE INTER-CULTURAL AND INTRA-CULTURAL DISTINCTION

The Need to Differentiate Between Inter-cultural and Intra-cultural Interactions

The accumulated evidence shows that inter-cultural interaction in general and inter-cultural trust (and other specific behavioral and psychological elements) in particular differ categorically from intra-cultural interaction or trust (for example, Sullivan et al., 1981; Adler and Graham, 1989; Rao and Hashimoto, 1996; Netzer and Sutter, 2009). 'Inter-cultural interaction (trust)' refers to the interplay (trustworthiness and trustfulness) between people from diverse cultural backgrounds, in contrast to the notion of 'intra-cultural' interplay between people with the same cultural background (Gelfand et al., 2007). Even though both inter-cultural and intra-cultural interactions (trust) are important for us to understand the impact of culture on organizational behavior, the importance of the former is rapidly growing because of the pace and breadth of globalization (Berry, 2008). However, there is a paucity of attention to inter-cultural interaction, with virtually all attention devoted to intra-cultural comparative studies (for example, Lane and Bachmann, 1996; Bachmann, 2001). Adler (1983) found that merely 0.8 percent of the articles in 24 top management journals between 1971 and 1980 were related to inter-cultural interaction, and no comprehensive dynamic models for studying inter-cultural interaction were available. This dire problem remains today as serious as in the past. As Takahashi and colleagues (Takahashi et al., 2008, p. 216) pointed out, the 'current methods of cross-cultural comparison are in some sense autistic because the participants from the two or more societies studied never interact with one another'. This view is echoed by others (for example, Tjosvold and Leung, 2003; Gelfand et al., 2007; Taras et al., 2009). Tjosvold and Leung (2003, p. 5) argued that the 'theorizing and research on cultural differences remain central to cross-cultural management. However, the contribution of this emphasis should not obscure its limitations', so 'much more attention is needed directly on how diverse people interact and work together'. As the result of this neglect, 'little is known about change in one's cultural values as one is exposed to a new cultural environment' (Taras et al., 2009, p. 14). Hence, 'the presumed vulnerability of cross-cultural interactions must be assessed relative to intra-cultural interactions' (Bond, 2003, p. 50), especially in organizational settings (Li, 2008). There are only few empirical studies that compare both intra-cultural and inter-cultural interactions in specific organizational settings (for example, Adler and Graham, 1989; Rao and Hashimoto,

1996), and even fewer focus on trust-building over time (for example, Kuhlmann, 2005; Newell et al., 2007). These studies have found that inter-cultural interaction and trust-building generally differ significantly from intra-cultural counterparts, either positively or negatively in their relative impact, but none have provided any compelling explanations regarding why intra-cultural and inter-cultural trust patterns differ. Hence, there is no theoretical framework of inter-cultural trust and trust-building as distinctive from intra-cultural counterparts.

Given the apparent significance of inter-cultural interaction, it is very surprising to find so little research on such a critical issue. Possible reasons for the paucity of research on inter-cultural interaction may include both theoretical and methodological factors. Theoretically, it is possible that most scholars assume that the comparative intra-cultural research on cultural distance would be sufficient to explain the 'presumed vulnerability' of inter-cultural interaction as directly tied to the magnitude of cultural distance (in other words, the larger distance tends to result in the bigger difficulty in inter-cultural interaction). In other words, they may deem the distinction between inter-cultural and intra-cultural interactions only a matter of degree rather than that of category (Bond, 2003). Methodologically, there are a number of challenges to empirically studying inter-cultural interaction. For instance, it requires dynamic models and longitudinal data rather than static models or cross-sectional data; it also requires well-matched inter-cultural and intra-cultural samples to compare. We argue, however, that inter-cultural interaction (trust) differs categorically from intra-cultural interaction, and this distinction lies at the core of our imperative premise. This imperative premise gives us the anchor or platform to build up a novel theoretical framework of inter-cultural interaction in general and inter-cultural trust (trust-building) in particular.

The Imperative Premise of Inter-cultural Interaction

To remedy the theoretical problem, we propose a holistic and dynamic framework for the study of inter-cultural trust in particular and inter-cultural interaction in general as distinctive from intra-cultural trust and interaction. Our proposed framework is based on the 'imperative premise' that inter-cultural trust differs categorically from intra-cultural trust due to the effect of cultural distance, but cultural distance is not sufficient for inter-cultural interaction, so 'dynamic variables', including cultural interface and adaptive learning, are required to supplement the 'static variable' of cultural distance. In other words, cultural distance is sufficient for comparative intra-cultural study, but cultural interface is required for research on inter-cultural interaction. In particular, the dynamic dimension for interaction is one of the three integral generic natures of any complex phenomena or issues. The other two are the holistic dimension for interdependence as well as the duality dimension for curvilinear balancing. 'Duality' refers to a pair of partially conflicting and partially complementary elements as opposites-in-unity. The above three dimensions constitute the three core tenets of the Eastern frame of *Yin–Yang* balancing in contrast to the prevailing frame of 'either/or' logic as well as the increasingly popular dialectical logic in the West (Li, 1998, 2008, 2011, 2012a, 2012b; c.f., Chen, 2002, 2008; Smith and Lewis, 2011). In particular, the frame of *Yin–Yang* balancing is uniquely capable of reframing paradoxes, dilemmas or dichotomies into dualities as a holistic and dynamic balance in a form of curvilinear pattern (Li, 2012b). Applying the frame of *Yin–Yang* balancing to inter-cultural trust and trust-building, we can treat inter-cultural trust and trust-building as a duality with the critical double-edged features of in-group and out-group favoritisms, cultural distance as both negative and positive, and the curvilinear pattern of inter-cultural adaptation (too little and too much adaptation as negative for trust-building).

Specifically, the imperative premise is embodied in three sub-premises. The first sub-premise claims that inter-cultural interaction is distinctive from, and more difficult than, intra-cultural interaction, due to the *negative* impact of cultural distance on cultural interaction. In this sense, inter-cultural interaction differs fundamentally from intra-cultural interaction because the former involves the interface between two or more different cultures (in other words, cultural interface), while the latter does not deal with the issue of cultural interface. When two or more cultures interact, the magnitude of the differences between them (in other words, cultural distance) tends to make inter-cultural interaction harder than intra-cultural interaction because cultural distance can render cultural interface challenging due to the unfamiliar, uncertain, ambiguous and uncontrollable features of cultural interface, which often results in cultural shock (Ward et al., 2001) and conflicts (Ting-Toomey and Oetzel, 2001). This perspective is consistent with the 'similarity–attraction paradigm' (Bryne, 1971) and 'social identity theory' (Tajfel, 1974), both of which maintain that intra-group interactions tend to differ categorically from inter-group interactions. However, the impact of cultural distance on cultural interface is not always negative. Cultural distance is able to play a unique *positive* role in terms of providing a valuable opportunity to learn across cultures for the cross-fertilization of cultural integration. This is similar to the dual effects of conflict in terms of task and people conflicts (Jehn, 1997). Further, in-group favoritism, as predicted by both the similarity–attraction paradigm and social identity theory, may not apply to all inter-cultural interactions. For instance, it is evident that 'out-group favoritism' can often occur in the process of inter-cultural interaction (for example, Adler and Graham, 1989; Rodriguez and Wilson, 2002; Kuhlmann, 2005; Yamagishi et al., 2005; Kuwabara et al., 2007). In this sense, we can conceive cultural distance as a duality with both positive and negative effects.

The second sub-premise claims that cultural interface via adaptive learning in the pattern of acculturation can mediate between the negative or positive effect of cultural distance on those outcomes of inter-cultural interaction. In other words, cultural distance can affect the outcome of inter-cultural interaction only indirectly through cultural interface. In particular, cultural interface can largely dictate the effect of cultural distance as either positive or negative. Hence, cultural interface, rather than cultural distance, is central to the research on inter-cultural interaction since the former is a dynamic construct related to interactive process while the latter is a static notion. This view is critical in the sense that cultural interface should be conceptualized as dynamic, so it is necessary to combine it with the notion of 'adaptive learning' (Masgoret and Ward, 2006) in an 'acculturation pattern', that is, the one of adapted changes in the cultures involved in the 'continuous first-hand' inter-cultural interactions (Redfield et al., 1936, p. 149). In this sense, cultural interface builds upon and extends beyond cultural distance. We can treat inter-cultural interface as a duality to serve as the primary *mediator* between cultural distance and performance outcome. Evoking the dynamics of adaptive learning in an acculturation pattern, this sub-premise will challenge the static positions of both the similarity–attraction paradigm and social identity theory by highlighting the potentials of bridging and integrating diverse cultures so as to not only reduce the negative inter-cultural conflicts but also enhance the positive inter-cultural conflicts, especially in organizational settings (Francis, 1991; Janssens, 1995; Thomas and Ravlin, 1995; Adair et al., 2001; c.f., Ward and Kennedy, 1999; Ward et al., 2001). For example, the 'cross-cultural code-switching' process proposed by Monlinsky (2007) has specific implications for adaptive learning for trust and trust-building. He defined the construct of 'code-switching' as 'the act of purposely modifying one's behavior, in a specific interaction in a foreign setting, to accommodate different cultural norms' (Monlinsky, 2007, p. 623). The code-switching behaviors represent the effort of adaptive learning in the inter-cultural setting.

The third sub-premise claims that the negative or positive effect of cultural distance on cultural interface and then on the outcomes of interaction can be either *reduced* or *enhanced* by adaptive learning in an acculturation pattern because inter-cultural interface requires either one-way or two-way adaptation through learning. This inter-cultural adaptive learning can serve as the underlying mechanism in an acculturation pattern. In this sense, both the negative and positive types of effect will be contingent upon the dimensions of *time* (in other words, the length of acculturation pattern in terms of multiple stages) and *effort* (in other words, the strength of acculturation content in terms of sensitivity and motive) as two basic 'moderators' on the main effects of cultural distance on cultural interface as well as the outcomes of interaction, especially in organizational settings (Janssens, 1995; c.f., Watson et al., 1993; Ward and Kennedy, 1999). However, the elements of time and effort must be treated as dualities. For example, it is possible that the initial effort may even reduce the perceived trustworthiness (Zolin et al., 2004; Newell et al., 2007). Even though the lack of longitudinal study on trust-building over time makes it impossible to know if and how inter-cultural adaptation may enhance inter-cultural trust, we argue that inter-cultural trust-building is most likely to follow a curvilinear pattern.

In sum, the imperative premise presented is the claim that inter-cultural interaction (with trust being central to such interaction) differs categorically from intra-cultural interaction, and cultural distance as a static construct is insufficient for inter-cultural interaction, so the dynamic variables of cultural interface and adaptive learning are necessary to explain inter-cultural interaction as a dynamic process. In other words, the imperative premise implies that inter-cultural trust is an element of inter- or out-group interaction, in contrast to intra-cultural trust as one of intra- or in-group interaction. In particular, the dynamic dimension will be most effectively treated by the unique frame of *Yin–Yang* balancing, which can seamlessly integrate the dynamic dimension with the holistic and duality dimensions. Applying the unique frame to inter-cultural trust and trust-building, all relevant constructs will be reframed into dualities (both positive and negative for inter-cultural trust and trust-building in contrast to their intra-cultural counterparts).

THE CENTRAL THEME OF AN INTEGRATIVE FRAMEWORK

The Specific Arguments Concerning Inter-cultural Trust

Applying the imperative premise of inter-cultural interaction to inter-cultural trust as well as trust-building, we develop five arguments concerning trust. First, we claim that, while trust as a general notion may be conceptualized as 'etic' (in other words, culture-general or universal), the specific forms and bases of trust as well as the specific mechanisms and stages of trust-building must be conceived as 'emic' (in other words, culture-specific or indigenous), at least at the initial stage of inter-cultural interaction in contrast to the later stage of globalization when the etic notion may be more likely (Berry, 2008). This argument bears critical implications for the research into, and the practice of, international business. We take issue with the unqualified assumption of trust features (for example, level, form, base, mechanism and stage) as etic, thus referring to the same thing or being measured in the same manner across diverse cultures. We share the perspective that this view is premature at the current stage of immature globalization, especially in the cultural sense (Yuki et al., 2005; Wasti et al., 2007; Chua et al., 2008). Consistent with the frame of *Yin–Yang* balancing, we posit that even in the context of mature globalization in the future, etic and emic forces will co-exist and interact with each other to constitute a duality. This is consistent with the emerging consensus delineated by the notion of 'variform universal' (Ferrin and Gillespie, 2010).

Given the existence of many emic features of trust, the etic assumption of trust symmetry between international or inter-cultural partners that have informed the extant literature should be challenged. While the economic bases of asymmetrical inter-personal or inter-firm interactions by diverse alliance partners (for example, the uneven distribution of resources or assets) have been explicitly examined (for example, Hamel et al., 1989; Khanna et al., 1998), the social ones of asymmetrical relationships, including the imbalances in trust, commitment and social capital, especially those deriving from diverse cultural origins, have received little attention (Zaheer and Zaheer, 2006), although some have noted the problem (for example, Johnson et al., 1996; Ariño et al., 2001). Any satisfaction with the extant literature in this aspect must be tempered with the disquieting sense that, because trust features tend to be context dependent, much trust research may be limited in its applicability to specific national contexts, especially when trusting parties are interacting across cultures. Worse still, when many scholars ignore the institutional or cultural embeddedness of trust in national contexts, they tend to reach erroneous conclusions (Li, 2008). To remedy the above problem, we apply the notion of cultural distance to inter-cultural trust in terms of 'trust asymmetry' as the differences in trust features across diverse cultures (Zaheer and Zaheer, 2006), including the differences not only in the level or magnitude of trust but also those in other more critical features of trust (for example, form and base of trust as well as the mechanism and stage of trust-building) evoked by people from different cultures (Sullivan et al., 1981; Rodriguez and Wilson, 2002; Yuki et al., 2005; Chua et al., 2008), either with or without any inter-cultural interactions, especially in organizational settings (Li, 2008). In other words, trust asymmetry is the special application of cultural distance to trust. It is worth noting that trust asymmetry is also directly related to the counter-intuitive finding of out-group favoritism in inter-cultural trust, and it seems to derive largely from the country-level reputation in terms of generic trustworthiness (for example, Kuhlmann, 2005; Yamagishi et al., 2005; Takahashi et al., 2008).

The implication of the first argument is that people from different cultures often evoke different bases of trust (for example, institutional or inter-personal bases) with different preferences for various forms of trust (for example, strong or weak forms) as well as adopt different mechanisms to build trust (for example, formal or informal) in different stages (for example, initial or later). This trust asymmetry derives primarily from the preexisting cultural distance. In other words, cultural distance tends to affect inter-cultural trust and trust-building in a critical way. However, the argument is far from sufficient to explain inter-cultural trust because it fails to explain the dynamics of inter-cultural trust-building as an integral part of the acculturation pattern with adaptive learning as the underlying mechanism for building inter-cultural trust. We explicitly regard adaptive learning as the primary mechanism for inter-cultural trust-building because we conceptualize inter-cultural trust-building as the result of adaptive learning about other cultures. We assume that the more or better anyone is willing and able to learn about the others' cultures (especially the positive features of other cultures), the higher inter-cultural trust he or she is expected to build toward others in the other cultures. There is some initial evidence to support this general argument (for example, Pornpitakpan, 1998, 2005; Kuhlmann, 2005).

Second, related to the first argument, we also claim that, if the basic features of trust are emic, inter-cultural trust cannot be assumed to be similar to intra-cultural trust. In other words, the trust we have in those people from the same culture may not be in the same form and from the same base as the trust we have in those from other cultures, so inter-cultural trust cannot be built with the same mechanism or at the same stage for intra-cultural trust. In fact, inter-cultural trust often differs from intra-cultural trust (Sullivan et al., 1981; Johnson et al., 1996; Netzer and Sutter, 2009). This extends beyond the domain of trust into other domains of inter-cultural behavior and attitude. For instance, Rao and Hashimoto (1996) found that the Japanese managers applied the stronger influence strategies to their Canadian subordinates rather than their Japanese ones. Adler and Graham (1989) also found that the behaviors in inter-cultural negotiation differed in important ways from those in intra-cultural negotiations, especially the out-group favoritism (for example, by the

Japanese toward the Americans). This unexpected out-group, rather than the expected in-group, favoritism in inter-cultural interaction is further evident in a few other experimental studies (for example, Yamagishi et al., 2005; Takahashi et al., 2008; Netzer and Sutter, 2009), and even in a rare study within the real organizational setting regarding inter-cultural alliances (for example, Kuhlmann, 2005).

This puzzle directly challenges both the similarity–attraction paradigm and social identity theory. One possible explanation lies in the stereotypic expectation (Thomas and Ravlin, 1995; Yamagishi et al., 2005). When the adaptive behavior (in other words, the change in behavior to become more typical of the behavioral norm in the other culture) is consistent with the stereotypic expectation held by others or by oneself about others, it may generate higher trust and stronger cooperation. Similarly, Netzer and Sutter (2009) explained their finding in terms of the perceived reputation of the Japanese as highly trustworthy by the Austrians. In this sense, the perception and expectation of cultural distance are more salient than the actual cultural distance, and the latter is often studied in the typical comparative intra-cultural research. In addition to the possible effect of cultural stereotypes, either negative or positive, the concern for fairness could also play an important role (Yamagishi et al., 2005). However, the most interesting study is the one by Kuhlmann (2005) with a focus on the cooperation between German (the case of in-group favoritism) and Mexican (the case of out-group favoritism) firms. The finding is that different partners can reduce inter-cultural asymmetry and build inter-cultural trust by demonstrating those qualities perceived by the other culture as the most relevant for trust. Further research is required to explain why inter-cultural interactions differ from intra-cultural ones, especially the out-group favoritism as a new 'distinction-attraction puzzle'. To remedy the lack of research on inter-cultural trust and trust-building, we evoke the construct of cultural interface and apply it to trust in terms of 'trust integration', which refers to cultural-integrative geocentric trust (Li, 2008). The notion of geocentric trust covers the bridged and aligned levels of trust, and, more importantly, the forms and bases of trust across diverse cultures as the results of adaptive trust-building, especially in organizational settings. In other words, trust integration can be regarded as a special application of cultural interface to inter-cultural trust.

It is clear that trust integration has a stronger connotation of dynamic effort than trust asymmetry. Hence, the key implication of the second argument is that people from different cultures learn to adapt or adjust to the diverse forms and bases of trust (in addition to the different levels of trust) as well as diverse mechanisms and stages of trust-building across all cultures. The resulted trust integration derives primarily from adaptive learning for trust-building in an acculturation pattern. In other words, adaptive learning affects both trust integration and performance outcomes of trust integration. However, this argument is still not sufficient to explain inter-cultural trust because it does not consider the moderating effects of time and effort on adaptive trust-building as a special form of adaptive learning as well as an integral part of acculturation pattern.

Third, we further claim that the uniqueness of inter-cultural trust tends to be more salient at the initial stage of inter-cultural trust-building. In this sense, it is expected that trust asymmetry (cultural distance) can render trust integration (cultural interface) highly problematic at the initial stage of inter-cultural trust-building (adaptive learning). However, the problem tends to ease over time with trust asymmetry shifts toward trust integration primarily because of the accumulative effect of adaptive trust-building in an acculturation pattern (Watson et al., 1993; Janssens, 1995; Ward and Kennedy, 1999; c.f., Zolin et al., 2004; Newell et al., 2007). Hence, trust asymmetry can be bridged by various mechanisms of adaptive learning concerning trust-building, especially those positive strategies of assimilation and integration in contrast to the negative strategies of marginalization and separation (Berry, 1997, 2008). In particular, we highlight the significant effects of cultural interface on cultural distance in terms of mutual assimilation via reciprocal adaptation and joint integration via shared learning. Hence, we conceptualize inter-cultural trust-building toward trust integration as a special form of adaptive learning for cultural interface. Because the process of adaptive trust-building is directly related to the factor of time, we regard it as the *time* dimension of inter-cultural trust-building (adaptive learning) that specifies and explains the temporal aspect of the causal relationships between trust asymmetry (cultural distance), trust integration (cultural interface) and performance outcome in terms of both reciprocal connections and recursive loops, especially in organizational settings (Li, 2008). In other words, adaptive trust-building serves as the special application of adaptive learning to trust.

Fourth, we posit that, counter-intuitively, trust asymmetry (cultural distance) can have a positive impact on trust integration (cultural interface) in the sense that higher trust asymmetry (large cultural distance) can result in higher trust integration (effective cultural interface) as well as better performance outcome (Janssens, 1995). This may be due to the greater effort triggered by the enhanced cultural sensitivity in terms of expected challenges in cultural interface (Johnson et al., 1996) and the enhanced motive in terms of active accommodation and learning. Consistent with the notions of stereotypic expectation (Thomas and Ravlin, 1995; Netzer and Sutter, 2009) and fairness concern (Yamagishi et al., 2005), it is logical to assume that, if trust asymmetry (cultural distance) is perceived by both parties as large enough, they tend to be highly sensitive to cultural differences, thus highly committed to mutual accommodation and learning, as long as they want to trust each other. In contrast, if trust asymmetry (cultural distance) is perceived by one or both parties as too small or insignificant, they would be insufficiently sensitive, thus non-committal to accommodation and learning. Because the content of trust-building is related to the key elements of cultural sensitivity and accommodation motive, we can regard it as the *effort* dimension of inter-cultural adaptive trust-building (adaptive learning) that specifies and explains the 'spatial' aspect of the causal relationships between trust asymmetry (cultural distance), trust integration (cultural interface) and performance outcome in terms of expected challenges and behavioral commitment, especially in organizational settings (Li, 2008). Hence, time and effort can both serve as the moderators of the main effects of trust asymmetry (cultural distance) initially on trust integration (cultural interface), and later on performance outcome. The two constitute two additional core dimensions to influence or moderate the specific process and content of adaptive trust-building, with time primarily for the process of trust-building as well as effort primarily for the content of trust-building.

However, both time and effort are likely to follow different curvilinear patterns. In the case of time, it is plausible that the initial trust at the early stage, as well as the mature trust at the later stage, could be high, while the trust at the middle stage could be low (Zolin et al., 2004; Newell et al., 2007). Hence, the curvilinear pattern of time appears to be a U-shaped curve. In the case of effort, it is plausible that the limited effort as well as the overwhelming effort could be negative for trust-building, while the moderate effort could be highly positive (Thomas and Ravlin, 1995). Hence, the curvilinear pattern of effort appears to be an inverted U-shaped curve. Given the opposite curvilinear effects of time and effort, it is helpful to treat time and effort as a duality in terms of their opposite effects on the possible link between adaptive learning and inter-cultural trust-building. Because of their curvilinear effects, it is reasonable to expect a curvilinear link between adaptive learning and inter-cultural trust.

Finally, we conclusively posit that the above four arguments should be the most salient in organizational settings, either at the intra-firm or inter-firm level due to four major reasons. First, inter-cultural trust not only occurs at the national level, but also at the organizational level. It is generally accepted that nation and organization are the two most salient contextual levels (see Scott, 2003 for a review). Being the context at the organizational level (as a salient part of multi-level overall context), organizational settings are key to trust within and between organizations, which can be defined as 'organizational trust' (Li, 2008). Second, organizational trust differs from personal or societal trust because the former contains both personalized and depersonalized bases (ibid.), especially the three key depersonalized institutional bases of organizational structure, culture and leadership (Li et al., 2012). This unique feature relates to, but extends beyond, the two factors of socio-cultural adaptation (Ward and Kennedy, 1999). This view is also related to the controversy over the appropriate conceptualization and operationalization of inter-firm trust in particular and inter-firm relationship in general (see Currall and Inkpen, 2002 for a review). We take issue with the argument that inter-firm trust is only a collective sum of inter-personal trust (c.f., Zaheer et al., 1998). The micro–macro transformation from inter-personal trust to inter-firm trust requires more than the domain shift from dyad to network via trust transfer (for example, inter-firm socialization); it requires trust conversion from personalized bases to depersonalized ones (for example, a shift from relational bases into institutional ones) in a process of institutionalization (Li et al., 2006).

Third, organizational settings are also salient to globalization because the driving forces behind the trend are the governmental (for example, the state agencies) and business organizations (for example, multinational firms). Hence, inter-cultural trust at the organizational level plays a unique role in international business, including its impact on the choice of market entry mode (for example, Shane, 1994; Li, 2010) and the performance of inter-firm cooperation (for example, Johnson et al., 1996; Katsikeas et al., 2009; Li et al., 2010). The role of organizational trust as a mode of governance to regulate the behaviors both within and between organizations is central to the distinction between trust-as-attitude (in psychological terms) and trust-as-choice (in behavioral terms). To understand the role of trust-as-choice as a unique governance mode (Powell, 1990; Li, 1998, 2008), we need to examine trust in its organizational settings. Fourth, it is worth noting that cultural trust and organizational trust share one common theme, which is the most salient distinction between intra-group interaction and inter-group interaction. Both organizational trust and cultural trust can be categorized into both out-group and in-group types, with intra-firm and intra-cultural trust as the in-group trust, while inter-firm and inter-cultural trust as the out-group type (c.f., Yuki et al., 2005; Katsikeas et al., 2009). The above four reasons provide the rationales for taking organizational settings as an additional salient context for trust besides national culture in the sense that organizational settings render inter-cultural trust a multi-level, multi-base and multi-role phenomenon due to the shared theme between inter-cultural trust and organizational trust. In sum, the five trust-related arguments jointly embody the central theme of an integrative framework of inter-cultural trust with adaptive trust-building as the core mechanism.

The Central Theme of an Integrative Framework

Based on the imperative premise that inter-cultural interaction differs categorically from intra-cultural one, the central theme posits that different features of trust (for example, the level, form, base, mechanism and stage of trust) can be evoked by the people from different cultures, but these people are highly capable of adapting to cultural distance via learning in an acculturation pattern, especially given the facilitators of extended time and enhanced effort. Just as cultural interface builds upon, and extends beyond, cultural distance with the dynamic effect of adaptive learning, trust integration can also build upon, and extends beyond, trust asymmetry with the dynamic effect of adaptive trust-building. In sum, the major constructs of trust asymmetry, trust integration and adaptive trust-building (containing the dimensions of time for its process as well as effort for its content), jointly delineate the central theme of inter-cultural trust. In this sense, they act as three core pillars or building blocks of an integrative framework, while performance outcome can be added as the last building block for this framework.

Based on the imperative premise and central theme, we propose a framework to integrate the four pairs of constructs, that is, cultural distance and trust asymmetry, cultural interface and trust integration, adaptive learning and adaptive trust-building in an acculturation pattern, and finally the performance outcomes of cultural interface and trust integration (for example, effective inter-cultural negotiation and alliance), into specific causal relationships. We regard the first pair (in other words, cultural distance and trust asymmetry) as the initial conditions or antecedents of inter-cultural interaction and trust. Further, we regard the second pair (in other words, cultural interface and trust integration) as the mediator. In addition, we regard the third pair (in other words, adaptive learning and adaptive trust-building with both time and effort dimensions as well as the other dimensions of organizational settings, including organizational structure, culture and leadership) as two sets of moderators. Finally, we regard the fourth pair (in other words, performance effects of trust and interaction) as the intended core outcomes or consequences. In sum, the above five pairs and their causal links (both reciprocal and recursive, with the main effect as well as the mediating and moderating effects) constitute an integrative framework (see Figure 7.1 for details).

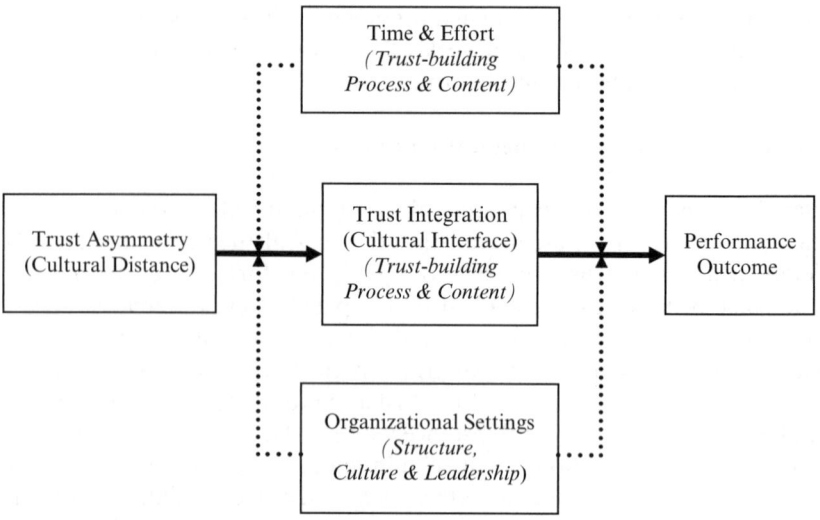

Notes:
Solid lines indicate the main effects (including the mediating effect).
Dotted lines indicate the moderating effects.
All contents and processes are the activities of human agents involved.

Figure 7.1   An integrative framework of inter-cultural trust and trust-building

THE TYPOLOGIES OF INTER-CULTURAL TRUST-BUILDING

The Need to Open the Black Box of Process

As we mentioned earlier, there is little research on why inter-cultural trust will differ from intra-cultural trust. So far only two possible reasons have been suggested: stereotypic expectation (Thomas and Ravlin, 1995; Netzer and Sutter, 2009) and concern for fairness (Yamagishi et al., 2005). In this sense, the expectation of, or concern for, trust asymmetry (cultural distance) is assumed to be more salient than the actual trust asymmetry (cultural distance), which can be easily measured by the typical comparative intra-cultural research. We challenge such explanations as insufficient because it is the very gap between the real and perceived trust asymmetry (cultural distance) that adequately represents the contextual conditions for trust interface (cultural interface). Further, we also maintain that it is the actual behavioral process in terms of adaptive trust-building (adaptive learning) that reduces and/or enhances the negative or positive effect of trust asymmetry (cultural distance), rather than those psychological expectations or concerns. Our perspective is consistent with the distinction between trust as a psychological expectation (trust-as-attitude) and trust as a behavioral decision (trust-as-choice), and also consistent with the centrality of trusting behavior in the trust-building process (see Li, 2007, 2008 for reviews). We posit that trust asymmetry is more related to trust-as-attitude, while trust integration is more directly related to trust-as-choice. Hence, while cultural distance is more related to psychological expectation, cultural interface is more related to behavioral pattern. In other words, the process from trust asymmetry (cultural distance) to trust integration (cultural interface) can be regarded as one from attitude to behavior, while the process from trust integration to performance outcome is entirely behavioral in nature. Our perspective on the distinction and link between psychological and behavioral adaptations is consistent with the ABC model of cultural shock (Ward et al., 2001) as well as those attempts to integrate the similarity–attraction paradigm with the social identity theory (for example, Francis, 1991; Thomas and Ravlin, 1995). More important, our perspective extends such attempts by integrating the two theories further with the theories of cultural distance and acculturation. In particular, our perspective has the potential to explain the distinction–attraction puzzle by taking the distinction–attraction and similarity–attraction as a duality, especially in organizational settings. For instance, trust asymmetry (cultural distance) is not always negative by default; it can be positive in certain aspects at certain times to certain degrees (consistent with the frame of *Yin–Yang* balancing; Li, 1998, 2008); further, the negative aspects can be transformed into positive ones (consistent with the frame of *Yin–Yang* balancing) via adaptive trust-building (adaptive learning) in a pattern of acculturation.

As shown in the integrative framework, trust integration (cultural interface) is theorized to serve as the mediator between trust asymmetry (cultural distance) and performance outcome. The primary reason for this mediating effect lies in the dynamic pattern of trust-building across different cultures by all the parties involved, despite the preexisting condition of trust asymmetry (cultural distance). The key is to conceptualize trust integration (cultural interface) as a dynamic process (with trust-building as the underlying mechanism), rather than a fixed or given state. In other words, if we theorize trust integration (cultural interface) as a change agent, the challenging contexts of trust asymmetry (cultural distance) can be strategically transformed in the domains of trust integration (cultural interface) via adaptive trust-building (adaptive learning). Such strategic options can reduce the negative effect, as well as enhance the positive effect, of trust asymmetry (cultural distance) on performance outcome.

Because trust integration (cultural interface) is central to the integrative framework as the mediator between trust asymmetry (cultural distance) and performance outcome, we will have to specify and explain the contextual conditions and strategic options for trust integration (cultural interface). To open the black box of trust integration (cultural interface) we should specify and explain the dynamic role of trust-building (adaptive learning) as the underlying mechanism for the mediating effect of trust integration (cultural interface) as well as the moderating effects of time and effort on the main effects. Specifically, we focus on two critical questions: (1) How does trust asymmetry evolve into trust integration? (2) How does trust integration lead to good performance outcome? We address the first question by relating both real and perceived contexts to adaptive trust-building as two contextual conditions. Further, we address the second question by relating both strategic goals and patterns to adaptive trust-building as two strategic options. For these two purposes we apply the typological approach to adaptive trust-building by proposing two specific typologies to operationalize the contexts and strategies for adaptive trust-building, especially in organizational settings (Li, 2008).

A Typology of Trust-building Contexts

To address the question regarding how trust asymmetry evolves into trust integration, we identify two primary dimensions of contextual conditions for trust-building: the real context and perceived context. Consistent with the literature on the distinction and link between the real and perceived environment (for example, Bourgeois, 1980; Smircich and Stubbart, 1985), we differentiate the real context from the perceived context, with the former as the actual and objective conditions, and the latter as the expected and subjective conditions. Further, for the purpose of linking the two dimensions to adaptive trust-building, we subcategorize the real context into the initial stage (short-term) as well as later stage (long-term), which are related to the dimension of time as the temporal process; we also subcategorize the perceived context into the unbalanced expectation (negative) and balanced expectation (positive), which are related to the dimension of effort as the 'spatial' content. In particular, consistent with the claim and evidence for an inverted U-shaped link between intercultural similarity and attraction as related to the inverted U-shaped pattern of effort (for example, Francis, 1991; Thomas and Ravlin, 1995; c.f., Janssens, 1995) as well as the U-shaped pattern of time (less concern for trust asymmetry at the initial and later stages, but more concern for trust asymmetry at the middle stage, for example, Zolin et al., 2004; Newell et al., 2007), we expect a similar curvilinear link between trust asymmetry and adaptive learning, with the moderate trust asymmetry being associated with the highest adaptive learning due to the balanced expectations at the middle stage rather than the initial and later stages. In other words, the inverted U-shaped link implies the duality of similarity and distinction (with the modest level of either similarity or distinction being the most conducive to trust and trust-building as compared with both high and low levels), especially with the moderate level of effort as compared to both low and high levels of effort as well as at the middle stage as compared to both initial and later stages.

Together, these dimensions delineate four ideal-typical contextual profiles as a typology. First, the initial stage and unbalanced expectation define the profile of 'neglect' to reflect either the over- or under-confidence for low or high challenge perception. If we perceive the context as very challenging (for example, the expected large trust asymmetry and cultural distance), we tend to be over-sensitive and lack the motive to accommodate and learn; if we perceive the context as not challenging at all (for example, the expected small trust asymmetry and cultural distance), we tend to ignore the significance of such challenge and dismiss it as trivial. In other words, both cases tend to result in a negative attitude toward trust asymmetry (cultural distance). These two scenarios are more likely to occur at the initial stage. Second, the later stage and unbalanced expectation define the profile of 'indifference' to reflect the similar problem with the profile of neglect. If we perceive the challenge continuously as either too high or too low, we will be over-sensitive or not sensitive at all with little motive to accommodate and learn. This scenario is more likely to occur at the later stage. Third, the middle stage and balanced expectation define the profile of 'attention' to reflect the moderate confidence for a moderate challenge perception. If we perceive the context as adequately challenging (for example, moderate trust asymmetry and cultural distance), we tend to be properly sensitive and motivated to accommodate and learn. In other words, a proper challenge results in a positive attitude toward trust asymmetry (cultural distance). This scenario is more likely to occur at the middle stage. Fourth, the middle stage and balanced expectation define the profile of 'commitment' to reflect the potential in the profile of attention. If we perceive the challenge in the middle stage as adequate, we will continue the balanced sensitivity with the strongest motive to accommodate and learn. This scenario is more likely to occur at the middle stage. Taken together, the above four specific and distinctive profiles serve as four ideal types of contextual conditions for adaptive trust-building (see Table 7.1 for details). Finally, all the above links will be more salient in the proper organizational settings, so the three primary elements of organizational settings (in other words, organizational structure, culture and leadership) will positively moderate the above four sets of links. Based upon the above discussion, we can develop five propositions as follows:

Proposition 1: The profile of neglect, characterized by an unbalanced expectation in terms of trust asymmetry (cultural distance) and more likely to occur at the initial stage, is positively associated with low inter-cultural sensitivity and accommodation motive as well as low inter-cultural learning and adaptation potentials.

Proposition 2: The profile of indifference, characterized by an unbalanced expectation in terms of trust asymmetry (cultural distance) and more likely to occur at the later stage, is positively associated with low inter-cultural sensitivity and accommodation motive as well as low inter-cultural learning and adaptation potentials.

Proposition 3: The profile of attention, characterized by a balanced expectation in terms of trust asymmetry (cultural distance) and more likely to occur at the middle stage, is positively associated with moderate inter-cultural sensitivity and accommodation motive as well as moderate inter-cultural learning and adaptation potentials.

Proposition 4: The profile of commitment, characterized by a balanced expectation in terms of trust asymmetry (cultural distance) and more likely to occur at the middle stage, is positively associated with high inter-cultural sensitivity and accommodation motive as well as high inter-cultural learning and adaptation potentials.

Proposition 5: The links between the four profiles and the four attitudes at all stages will be positively moderated by the three central components of organizational settings (in other words, organizational structure, culture and leadership).

A Typology of Trust-building Strategies

Based upon but extending beyond the first typology, we develop the second typology to explore the distinctive strategic options available for trust integration (cultural interface) in the pattern of adaptive trust-building. For this purpose, we adapt the well-established typology of acculturation strategy from the fields of anthropology and psychology (Berry,

Table 7.1 A typology of trust-building contexts for inter-cultural interactions

Real and Perceived Contexts for Inter-cultural Interactions	Perceived Context and Responding Content Negative Expectation with Unbalanced Confidence	Perceived Context and Responding Content Positive Expectation with Balanced Confidence
Real context and responding process *Short term at the initial stage*	*Neglect* → *Contextual conditions:* Low or high real asymmetry Low or high real uncertainty Low or high perceived asymmetry Low or high perceived uncertainty *Responding attitudes:* Low sensitivity Low accommodation motive Low adaptation potential Low learning potential ↓	*Attention* *Contextual conditions:* Moderate real asymmetry Moderate real uncertainty Moderate perceived asymmetry Moderate perceived uncertainty *Responding attitudes:* Moderate sensitivity Moderate accommodation motive Moderate adaptation potential Moderate learning potential ↓
Real context and process *Long term at the later stage*	*Indifference* → *Contextual conditions:* Low real asymmetry Low real uncertainty Low perceived asymmetry Low perceived uncertainty *Responding attitudes:* Low sensitivity Low accommodation motive Low adaptation potential Low learning potential	*Commitment* *Contextual conditions:* Moderate real asymmetry Moderate real uncertainty Moderate perceived asymmetry Moderate perceived uncertainty *Responding attitudes:* High sensitivity High accommodation motive High adaptation potential High learning potential

Notes:
The arrows indicate the positive trends.
All contents and processes are the activities of human agents involved.

1997, 2008) to the issue of inter-cultural trust-building in organizational settings (for example, Nahavandi and Malekzadeh, 1988). According to the existing typology of acculturation, there are four ideal-typical strategies: marginalization, separation, assimilation and integration (Berry, 1997, 2008). These four generic strategies are categorized according to the dimensions of losing or keeping one's own culture and seeking strong or weak inter-cultural relationships (Berry, 1997, 2008): (1) marginalization is the strategy to lose one's own cultural identity, but without acquiring any other cultural identity (for example, the cultural exclusion everywhere in the world); (2) separation is the strategy to isolate different cultures with minimum inter-cultural interaction (for example, the cultural segregation as well as passive multiculturalism); (3) assimilation is the strategy to merge into other cultures without keeping one's own cultural identity (for example, the melting pot); and (4) integration is the strategy to learn from each other while maintaining the original cultural distinctions (for example, geocentrism as well as active multiculturalism). It is obvious that the first two strategies are passive strategies with negative outcomes, while the last two strategies are active with positive outcomes. Applying this typology to the pattern of adaptive trust-building, especially in organizational settings, we can develop a typology of trust-building strategies. In particular, the strategies of assimilation and integration suggest the possible out-group favoritism in order to explain the distinction–attraction puzzle.

Specifically, we categorize four ideal-typical strategies of adaptive trust-building along the dimensions of adapting to other cultures or maintaining one's own culture (in other words, strategic goals and outcomes) as well as weak/rare inter-cultural interaction (in other words, strategic patterns and modes). These two dimensions delineate four key strategies (see Table 7.2): (1) marginalization with both weak intra-cultural and inter-cultural trust; (2) separation with strong intra-cultural trust but weak inter-cultural trust; (3) assimilation with weak intra-cultural trust but strong inter-cultural trust, and (4) integration with both strong intra-cultural and inter-cultural trust; Further, the intensity of trust-building will result in the strengths of trustworthiness (in other words, trust-as-attitude as the perceived trustworthiness of others) and trustfulness (in other words, trust-as-choice as the self-initiated decision to trust others), because the strengths of trust type are due to the strengths of trust forms (in other words, weak or strong trust) and trust bases (in other words, depersonalized or personalized trust) (see Li, 2008 for a review). In particular, the strategies of marginalization and separation are hardly related to the goals and outcomes as well as the modes and patterns of inter-cultural trust-building. In contrast, the strategies of assimilation and integration are closely related to the goals and outcomes as well as the modes and patterns of inter-cultural trust-building. However, the key difference between assimilation and integration lies in one distinctive feature of the two strategies, with assimilation as a unilateral mode for unilateral goal in contrast to integration as a bilateral mode for bilateral goal. It is obvious that we recommend integration as the best strategy to build inter-cultural trust. Taken together, the above four strategic options (with distinctive goals and outcomes as well as different modes and patterns) are four ideal-typical strategies for trust-building. In other words, while the typology of trust-building contexts emphasizes the role of psychological attitude, the typology of trust-building strategies highlights the key role of behavioral choice. Finally, all the above links are expected to be more salient in the effective organizational settings, so the three primary elements of organizational settings (in other words, organizational structure, culture and leadership) will positively moderate the four sets of links. It is worth noting that we do not expect particular moderating effects of effort and time on the set of strategies. Based upon the above discussion, we develop five propositions as follows:

Proposition 6: The strategy of marginalization, characterized by weak intra-cultural trust and weak inter-cultural trust, is positively related to low inter-cultural trustworthiness and trustfulness as well as weak forms and bases of inter-cultural trust.

Proposition 7: The strategy of separation, characterized by strong intra-cultural trust but weak inter-cultural trust, is positively related to low inter-cultural trustworthiness and trustfulness as well as weak forms and bases of inter-cultural trust.

Proposition 8: The strategy of assimilation, characterized by weak intra-cultural trust but strong inter-cultural trust, is positively related to moderate inter-cultural trustworthiness and trustfulness as well as moderate forms and bases of inter-cultural trust.

Proposition 9: The strategy of integration, characterized by strong intra-cultural trust and strong inter-cultural trust, is positively related to high inter-cultural trustworthiness and trustfulness as well as strong forms and bases of inter-cultural trust.

Proposition 10: The links between the four strategies and the four outcomes will be moderated by the three basic components of organizational settings (in other words, organizational structure, culture and leadership).

Table 7.2 A typology of trust-building strategies for inter-cultural interactions

Intra- and Inter-cultural Trust	Weak Intra-cultural Trust Trust-building Goal & Outcome	Strong Intra-cultural Trust Trust-building Goal & Outcome
Weak inter-cultural trust Trust-building mode & pattern	*Marginalization* → *Trust-building patterns:* Little intra-cultural interaction Little inter-cultural interaction Little adaptive learning Little adaptive trust-building *Trust-building outcomes:* Weak trust forms Weak personalized bases Weak depersonalized bases ↓ Weak inter-cultural cooperation	*Separation* *Trust-building patterns:* Much intra-cultural interaction Little inter-cultural interaction Little adaptive learning Little adaptive trust-building *Trust-building outcomes:* Weak trust forms Weak personalized bases Weak depersonalized bases ↓ Weak inter-cultural cooperation
Strong inter-cultural trust Trust-building mode & pattern	*Assimilation* → *Trust-building patterns:* Little intra-cultural interaction Much inter-cultural interaction Unilateral adaptive learning Unilateral adaptive trust-building *Trust-building outcomes:* Moderate trust forms Moderate personalized bases Moderate depersonalized bases Moderate inter-cultural cooperation	*Integration* *Trust-building patterns:* Much intra-cultural interaction Much inter-cultural interaction Bilateral adaptive learning Bilateral adaptive trust-building *Trust-building outcomes:* Strong trust forms Strong personalized bases Strong depersonalized bases Strong inter-cultural cooperation

Notes:
Adapted from Berry (2008) and Li (2008).
The arrows indicate the positive trends.
All contents and processes are the activities of human agents involved.

DISCUSSION AND CONCLUSION

To fill in the gap in the research, we have addressed four questions about trust and trust-building via 'cultural interface' (highlighting inter-cultural interaction) beyond 'cultural distance' (comparing different intra-cultural interactions) due to 'adaptive learning': (1) Does inter-cultural trust differ categorically from intra-cultural trust? (2) Why does inter-cultural trust differ from intra-cultural trust? (3) How is inter-cultural trust built as compared to intra-cultural trust-building? (4) Is the process of inter-cultural trust-building a linear pattern over time? To address such questions we have integrated three salient constructs, that is, trust asymmetry (cultural distance), trust integration (cultural interface tied to the similarity–attraction paradigm and social identity theory), and adaptive trust-building (adaptive learning tied to the acculturation theory), as the three primary pillars or building blocks of an integrative framework of inter-cultural trust and trust-building. Further, we have opened the black box of adaptive trust-building by developing two typologies to specify and explain the content and process of trust-building via adaptive learning, especially in organizational settings. Hence, we have made three key contributions. First, we have provided the strong theoretical rationale for distinguishing between inter-cultural and intra-cultural trust as two different phenomena with an 'imperative premise' that inter-cultural trust differs categorically from intra-cultural trust due to the effect of cultural distance, but cultural distance is insufficient for inter-cultural interaction in general and inter-cultural trust in particular, so dynamic variables are required to supplement any static variables. Second, by extending the imperative premise, we have developed a central theme toward an integrative framework of inter-cultural trust and trust-building. The central theme posits that the core features of trust are emic in nature, but such emic features can be properly bridged via adaptive learning as a result of cultural interface. Third, we have opened the black box of trust-building process with two broad typologies to specify four trust-building contexts as well as four trust-building strategies.

The primary implication of this study for future research is the potential to integrate the similarity–attraction paradigm and social identity theory with the theories of cultural distance and acculturation. While the first three perspectives emphasize the challenges of cultural distance to cultural interface, the last perspective highlights the potential of adaptive learning for cultural integration. In this sense, our integrated framework has the potential to holistically, dynamically and dialectically explain the distinction–attraction puzzle as an integral aspect of the similarity–distinction duality as a whole. Future research should focus on the conceptual refinement as well as the empirical test of the proposed overall framework and specific typologies. In particular, to take full advantage of the valuable frame of *Yin–Yang* balancing, we should further explore the holistic dimension (for example, the complex nature of inter-cultural trust from multi-disciplinary and interdisciplinary perspectives), dynamic dimension (for example, the transitional nature of inter-cultural trust with multiple stages and mechanisms of adaptive trust-building and learning), and duality dimension (for example, the curvilinear nature of balancing between opposites-in-unity by reframing paradoxes, dilemmas or dichotomies into dualities) of trust and trust-building in the inter-cultural and organizational contexts. Hence, complex models and longitudinal data, rather than simple models and cross-sectional data, are very critical to our research on inter-cultural trust. Equally important are the properly matched samples of inter-cultural and intra-cultural interactions for more comparative studies. One interesting possibility is to compare the two distinctive types of cultural interaction even within a single nation with sufficient cultural diversity between the multiple ethnic communities (Tung, 2008). Further, the moderating effects of effort and time should be taken into serious consideration, especially their curvilinear patterns. Finally, the critical organizational settings should be incorporated into future research on inter-cultural trust and trust-building, especially the contexts for the duality of similarity-attraction and distinction-attraction.

REFERENCES

Adair, W.L., T. Okumura and J.M. Brett (2001), 'Negotiation behavior when cultures collide: the United States and Japan', *Journal of Applied Psychology*, **86**(3), 371–85.
Adler, N.J. (1983), 'Cross-cultural management research: the ostrich and the trend', *Academy of Management Review*, **8**(2) 226–32.
Adler, N.J. and J.L. Graham (1989), 'Cross-cultural interaction: the international comparison fallacy?', *Journal of International Business Studies*, **20**(3), 515–37.
Ariño, A., J. De La Torre and P.S. Ring (2001), 'Relational quality: managing trust in corporate alliances', *California Management Review*, **44**(1), 109–31.
Bachmann, R. (2001), 'Trust, power and control in trans-organizational relations', *Organization Studies*, **22**(2), 341–69.
Berry, J.W. (1997), 'Immigration, acculturation and adaptation', *Applied Psychology: An International Review*, **46**(1), 5–68.
Berry, J.W. (2008), 'Globalization and acculturation', *International Journal of Inter-cultural Relations*, **32**(3), 328–36.
Bond, M.H. (2003), 'Cross-cultural social psychology and the real world of culturally diverse teams and dyads', in D. Tjosvold and K. Leung (eds), *Cross-cultural Management: Foundation and Future*, Aldershot: Ashgate Publishing, pp. 43–58.
Bourgeois, L.J. (1980), 'Strategy and environment: a conceptual integration', *Academy of Management Review*, **5**(1), 25–39.
Bryne, D. (1971), *The Attraction Paradigm*, New York: Academic Press.
Burger, J., M. Luke and H. Indelaova (2006), 'Inter-personal trust in German–Czech

work relations: mutual expectations and suggestions for improvement', *Journal of Organizational Transformation and Social Change*, **3**(2), 173–99.

Chen, M-J. (2002), 'Transcending paradox: the Chinese "middle way" perspective', *Asia Pacific Journal of Management*, **19**(2), 179–99.

Chen, M-J. (2008), 'Reconceptualizing the competition–cooperation relationship: a trans-paradox perspective', *Journal of Management Inquiry*, **17**(4), 288–304.

Chua, R.Y.J., P. Ingram and M. Morris (2008), 'From the head and the heart: locating cognition- and affect-based trust in managers' professional networks', *Academy of Management Journal*, **51**(3), 436–52.

Currall, S.C. and A.C. Inkpen (2002), 'A multilevel approach to trust in joint ventures', *Journal of International Business Studies*, **33**(3), 479–95.

Ferrin, D. and N. Gillespie (2010), 'Trust differences across national-societal cultures: much to do, or much ado about nothing?', in M. Saunders, D. Skinner, G. Diez, N. Gillespie and R. Lewicki (eds), *Organizational Trust: A Cultural Perspective*, Cambridge, MA: Cambridge University Press, pp. 42–86.

Francis, J.N.P. (1991), 'When in Rome? The effects of cultural adaptation on inter-cultural business negotiations', *Journal of International Business Studies*, **22**(3), 403–28.

Gelfand, M.J., M. Erez and Z. Aycan (2007), 'Cross-cultural organizational behavior', *Annual Review of Psychology*, **58**, 479–514.

Hamel, G., Y.L. Doz and C.K. Prahalad (1989), 'Collaborate with your competitors – and win', *Harvard Business Review*, **67**(1), 133–8.

Hofstede, G. (2001), *Cultural Consequences: Comparing Values, Behaviors, Institutions, and Organizations Across Nations*, Thousand Oaks, CA: Sage.

Janssens, M. (1995), 'Inter-cultural interaction: a burden on international managers?', *Journal of Organizational Behavior*, **16**(2), 155–67.

Jehn, K.A. (1997), 'A qualitative analysis of conflict types and dimensions in organizational growth', *Administrative Science Quarterly*, **42**(3), 530–57.

Johnson, J.L., J.B. Cullen, T. Sakano and T. Takenouchi (1996), 'Setting the stage for trust and strategic integration in Japanese–U.S. cooperative alliances', *Journal of International Business Studies*, **27**(5), 981–1004.

Katsikeas, C.S., D. Skarmeas and D.C. Bello (2009), 'Developing successful trust-based international exchange relationships', *Journal of International Business Studies*, **40**(1), 132–55.

Khanna, T., R. Gulati and N. Nohria (1998), 'The dynamics of learning alliances: competition, cooperation, and relative scope', *Strategic Management Journal*, **19**(3), 193–210.

Kuhlmann, T.M. (2005), 'Formation of trust in German–Mexican business relationships', in K.M. Bijlsma-Frankema and R. Klein Woolthuis (eds), *Trust Under Pressure: Empirical Investigations of Trust and Trust Building in Uncertain Circumstances*, Cheltenham, UK and Northampton, MA, USA: Edward Elgar, pp. 37–53.

Kuwabara, K., R. Willer, M.W. Macy, R. Mashima, S. Terai and T. Yamagishi (2007), 'Cultural, identity, and structure in social exchange: a web-based trust experiment in the United States and Japan', *Social Psychology Quarterly*, **70**(4), 461–79.

Lane, C. and R. Bachmann (1996), 'The social constitution of trust: supplier relations in Britain and Germany', *Organization Studies*, **17**(3), 365–95.

Lee, K., G. Yang and J.L. Graham (2006), 'Tension and trust in international business negotiations: American executives negotiating with Chinese executives', *Journal of International Business Studies*, **37**(5) 623–41.

Li, P.P. (1998), 'Towards a geocentric framework of organizational form: a holistic, dynamic and paradoxical approach', *Organization Studies*, **19**(5), 829–63.

Li, P.P. (2007), 'Towards an interdisciplinary conceptualization of trust: a typological approach', *Management and Organization Review*, **4**(3), 421–45.

Li, P.P. (2008), 'Toward a geocentric framework of trust: an application to organizational trust', *Management and Organization Review*, **4**(3), 413–39.

Li, P.P. (2010), 'Toward a learning-based view of internationalization: the accelerated trajectories of cross-border learning', *Journal of International Management*, **16**(1), 43–59.

Li, P.P. (2011), 'The rigor–relevance balance for engaged scholarship: new frame and new agenda for trust research and beyond', *Journal of Trust Research*, **1**(1), 1–21.

Li, P.P. (2012a), 'Toward an integrative framework of indigenous research: the geocentric implications of *Yin–Yang* balance', *Asia Pacific Journal of Management*, **29**(4), 849–72.

Li, P.P. (2012b), 'Exploring the unique roles of trust and play in private creativity: from the complexity–ambiguity–metaphor link to the trust–play–creativity link', *Journal of Trust Research*, **2**(1), 71–97.

Li, P.P., X. Yao and Y. Xi (2006), 'To unpack the black-box of micro–macro link: the mediating role of strategy', paper presented at the 2006 Conference of the Academy of International Business, 23–26 June, Beijing, China.

Li, P.P., Y. Bai and Y. Xi (2012), 'The contextual antecedents of organizational trust: a cross-level analysis', *Management and Organizational Review*, **8**(2), 371–96.

Li, Y., P.P. Li, Y. Liu and D. Yang (2010), 'Learning trajectory in offshore OEM cooperation: the transaction value for local suppliers in the emerging economies', *Journal of Operations Management*, **28**(3), 269–82.

Masgoret, A. and C. Ward (2006), 'Cultural learning approach to acculturation', in D.L. Sam and J.W. Berry (eds), *The Cambridge Handbook of Acculturation Psychology*, New York: Cambridge University Press, pp. 58–77.

Monlinsky, A. (2007), 'Cross-cultural code-switching: the psychological challenges of adapting behavior in foreign cultural interactions', *Academy of Management Review*, **32**(2), 622–40.

Nahavandi, A. and A.R. Malekzadeh (1988), 'Acculturation in mergers and acquisitions', *Academy of Management Review*, **13**(1), 79–90.

Netzer, R.J. and M. Sutter (2009), 'Inter-cultural trust: an experiment in Austria and Japan', Working Paper, University of Innsbruck, Austria.

Newell, S., G. David and D. Chand (2007), 'An analysis of trust among globally distributed work teams in an organizational setting', *Knowledge and Process Management*, **14**(3), 158–68.

Pornpitakpan, C. (1998), 'The effect of cultural adaptation on perceived trustworthiness', *Journal of Global Marketing*, **11**(3), 41–64.

Pornpitakpan, C. (2005), 'The effect of cultural adaptation on perceived trustworthiness: Americans adapting to Chinese Indonesians', *Asia Pacific Journal of Marketing and Logistics*, **17**(1), 70–88.

Powell, W.W. (1990), 'Neither market nor hierarchy: network forms of organization', in L.L. Cummings and B.M. Staw (eds), *Research in Organizational Behavior*, Vol. 12, Greenwich, CT: JAI, pp. 295–336.

Rao, A. and K. Hashimoto (1996), 'Inter-cultural influence: a study of Japanese expatriate managers in Canada', *Journal of International Business Studies*, **27**(3), 443–66.

Redfield, R., R. Linton and M. Herskovits (1936), 'Memorandum on the study of acculturation', *American Anthropologist*, **38**(1), 54–60.

Rodriguez, C.M. and D.T. Wilson (2002), 'Relationship bonding and trust as a foundation for commitment in US–Mexican strategic alliances: a structural equation modeling approach', *Journal of International Marketing*, **10**(4), 53–76.

Scott, W.R. (2003), *Organizations: Rational, National, and Open System*, 5th edition, Upper Saddle River, NJ: Prentice-Hall.

Shane, S.A. (1994), 'The effect of national culture on the choice between licensing and direct foreign investment', *Strategic Management Journal*, **15**(8), 627–42.

Smircich, L. and C. Stubbart (1985), 'Strategic management in an enacted world', *Academy of Management Review*, **10**(4), 724–38.

Smith, P.B. (2003), 'Meeting the challenge of cultural difference', in D. Tjosvold and K. Leung (eds), *Cross-cultural Management: Foundation and Future*, Aldershot: Ashgate Publishing, pp. 59–71.

Smith, W.K. and M.W. Lewis (2011), 'Toward a theory of paradox: a dynamic equilibrium model of organizing', *Academy of Management Review*, **36**(2), 381–403.

Sullivan, J., R.B. Peterson, N. Kameda and J. Shimada (1981), 'The relationship between

conflict resolution approaches and trust – a cross-cultural study', *Academy of Management Journal*, **24**(4), 803–15.
Tajfel, H. (1974), 'Social identity and intergroup behavior', *Social Science Information*, **13**(2), 65–93.
Takahashi, C., T. Yamagishi, J.H. Liu, F. Wang, Y. Lin and S. Yu (2008), 'The international trust paradigm: studying joint cultural interaction and social exchange in real time over the Internet', *International Journal of Inter-cultural Relations*, **32**(3), 215–28.
Taras, V., J. Rowney and P. Steel (2009), 'Half a century of measuring culture: review of approaches, challenges, and limitations based on the analysis of 121 instruments for quantifying culture', *Journal of International Management*, **15**(4), 357–73.
Thomas, D.C. and E.C. Ravlin (1995), 'Responses of employees to cultural adaptation by a foreign manager', *Journal of Applied Psychology*, **32**(1), 1–10.
Ting-Toomey, S. and J.G. Oetzel (2001), *Managing Inter-cultural Conflict Effectively*, Thousand Oaks, CA: Sage.
Tjosvold, D. and K. Leung (2003), 'Cross-cultural foundations: traditions for managing in a cross-cultural world', in D. Tjosvold and K. Leung (eds), *Cross-cultural Management: Foundation and Future*, Aldershot: Ashgate Publishing, pp. 1–10.
Tung, R.L. (2008), 'The cross-cultural research imperative: the need to balance cross-national and intra-national diversity', *Journal of International Business Studies*, **39**(1), 41–6.
Ward, C.A. and A. Kennedy (1999), 'The measurement of sociocultural adaptation', *International Journal of Inter-cultural Relations*, **23**(4), 659–77.
Ward, C.A., S. Bochner and A. Furham (2001), *The Psychology of Cultural Shock*, 2nd edition, London: Routledge.
Wasti, S.A., H.H. Tan, H.H. Brower and C. Onder (2007), 'Cross-cultural measurement of supervisor trustworthiness: an assessment of measurement invariance across three cultures', *Leadership Quarterly*, **18**(5), 477–89.
Watson, W.E., K. Kumar and L.K. Michaelsen (1993), 'Cultural diversity's impact on interaction process and performance: comparing homogeneous and diverse task groups', *Academy of Management Journal*, **36**(3), 590–602.
Yamagishi, T., Y. Makimura, M. Foddy, M. Matsuda, T. Kiyonari and M.J. Platow (2005), 'Comparisons of Australians and Japanese on group-based cooperation', *Asian Journal of Social Psychology*, **8**(2), 173–90.
Yuki, M., W.W. Maddux, M.B. Brewer and K. Takemura (2005), 'Cross-cultural differences in relationship- and group-based trust', *Personality and Social Psychology Bulletin*, **31**(1), 48–62.
Zaheer, S. and A. Zaheer (2006), 'Trust across borders', *Journal of International Business Studies*, **37**(1), 21–9.
Zaheer, A., B. McEvily and V. Perrone (1998), 'Does trust matter? Exploring the effects of interorganizational and inter-personal trust and performance', *Organization Science*, **9**(2), 141–59.
Zolin, R., P.J. Hinds, R. Fruchter and R.E. Levitt (2004), 'International trust in cross-functional, geographical distributed work: a longitudinal study', *Information and Organization*, **14**(4), 1–26.

PART IV

SOCIETAL ANALYSIS AND TRUST REPAIR

8. Trust and the global financial crisis
Nicole Gillespie and Robert Hurley

INTRODUCTION

Trust is central to exchange and growth. Nowhere is this more apparent than in the financial arena. Indeed, the term 'credit' is derived from the Latin word *credere*, meaning 'to believe or trust' (*Oxford Dictionary*, 2003). In the latter part of 2008 into 2009, with the collapse of Bear Sterns and Lehman Brothers, trust was eroded and financial institutions stopped lending to one another. The subsequent lack of credit caused a broader economic slowdown and the lack of trust spread from Wall Street to Main Street and across the globe. The result was a rise in unemployment in many countries and, according to the International Monetary Fund, the destruction of $4.1 trillion worth of wealth on a global scale.

The Global Financial Crisis (GFC) presents a unique setting to examine trust, trust violation and trust repair from a multi-level perspective that crosses the individual (for example, investors, retirees, employees), organizational (for example, Lehman Brothers, Citibank, Goldman Sachs), industry (for example, finance and insurance) and societal (for example, global economy and governments) levels. In this chapter, we analyze the breakdown of trust in the global financial system, revealing that there was a trust failure at multiple levels and by multiple agents. We further examine the foundations of repairing trust in the financial sector post-GFC, arguing that the repair process must also be a multi-level and multi-agent phenomenon. In so doing, we draw on sociological theories of impersonal trust. We connect this with an examination of the role of control mechanisms in underpinning and supporting institutional trust and trust repair and the recent debates on the relationship between trust and control.

UNDERSTANDING TRUST AT THE SYSTEMS LEVEL

Trust has been defined as the willingness to be vulnerable to the actions of another party, based upon positive expectations of the intentions or behavior of the other, under conditions of risk and interdependence

(Mayer et al., 1995; Rousseau et al., 1998). It has also been defined as a judgment of confident reliance on another person, group, organization or system when there is uncertainty and risk (Deutsch, 1973; Hurley, 2006, 2012). Both of these definitions underscore the criticality of predictability for trust and identify that trust is only relevant when there is an element of risk. The latter definition makes salient that trust exists in different types of relationships and at various levels, and our focus in this chapter is on trust in the financial system.

We adopt the definition of trust as confident reliance in recognition that trust at the systems level may involve instances where 'willingness' is less relevant because reliance and vulnerability may not be optional due to a lack of practical alternatives. For example, investors must rely on the appointed public accounting firm concerning the accuracy of financial statements – they cannot do their own audit. This is in line with Shapiro's (1987) argument that in modern society, collectivization, specialization and differentiation results in principals having to rely on agents to perform services they are either unable, or for which it is inefficient, to perform for themselves (for example, medical diagnoses; tests of the safety of food, drugs, multi-story buildings, elevators, automobiles and airplanes; banking, investment and insurance services). But even in situations where reliance is not optional, we still exercise judgment in the level of confidence we hold and choice in the extent of counter-measures that we might employ to mitigate against possible harm. While investors are reliant on audits from accounting firms – depending on their confidence or 'positive expectations' – they can do more or less of their own due diligence concerning the financial health of a target firm.

Perceived trustworthiness has been shown to be a strong antecedent to trust (Mayer et al., 1995; Colquitt et al., 2007). People, groups and organizations make judgments about the trustworthiness of another party, which in turn leads to postures of trust or suspicion. They do this to protect themselves in vulnerable situations involving trustees (Hurley, 2006, 2012). Prior conceptual and empirical work suggests that across situations, levels and national cultures there are three basic elements that are considered when evaluating trustworthiness: ability, benevolence and integrity (ABI) (Mayer et al., 1995; Schoorman et al., 2007):[1]

- *ability*: competence to deliver on commitments and fundamental responsibilities;
- *benevolence*: a positive orientation towards stakeholders, including concern for their interests;
- *integrity*: adherence to commonly accepted moral principles, including fulfilling promises and contracts, honesty and fairness.

In applying these three dimensions of trustworthiness to organizations and systems, it is important to recognize that various stakeholders will have access to different cues ranging from more personal (for example, relationships, direct interaction) to impersonal forms (for example, media, websites and documentation) drawn from multiple elements of the system (Gillespie and Dietz, 2009; Dietz and Gillespie, 2011). For example, investors' perceptions may be primarily influenced by a bank's advertising, their exposure to the products, services and individual agents, and third party evaluations of the firm, its leaders and its goods/services. In contrast, bank employees will have an insider view based on interactions with leaders, experience of the organization's culture, systems and processes, and their work on product or service development and delivery. In each case, stakeholders observe multiple signals from a variety of sources and agents that indicate whether the system, or the particular agents and institutions within that system, can be trusted to serve their interests.

It is recognized that the trustworthiness of socio-technical systems involves personal and impersonal relations across multiple boundaries and subsystems (Katz and Kahn, 1966; Luhmann, 1988). This is certainly true of the financial system. It involves a range of interacting and interdependent actors (for example, investors, borrowers, bankers, financial advisors, pension funds, accountants, regulators and ratings agencies), operating within organizations and broader systems and subsystems that govern transactions, standards, licensing and enforcement of laws and regulation.

While certainly there are a myriad of personal trust relations that enable exchange in the financial system, an examination of trust in this large socio-technical system highlights the criticality of impersonal trust. From a sociological perspective, numerous scholars argue that modern socio-economic systems depend on impersonal forms of trust (for example, Luhmann, 1979; Giddens, 1984; Zucker, 1986; Shapiro, 1987). This perspective is based on the insight that interpersonal relationships are often not efficient or even possible where trust is needed – rather, we often need to trust specialized 'experts' with whom we have no opportunity to build a personalized relationship (Giddens, 1984; Zucker, 1986; Shapiro, 1987). For example, when we deposit our savings in a bank, we trust the bankers not as individuals but rather as representatives of complex 'expert systems'. Indeed, we may deal with a different banker every time we interact with the bank, yet keep the same level of trust in the new representatives. As Shapiro (1987, p. 632) states 'long-term relationships with trusted bankers, stockbrokers, insurance agents, and others . . . merely provide a personalized smokescreen for inherently collective forms of actions'.

What makes these 'experts' trustworthy is the systems of education and training they have completed, coupled with the standards of expertise, rules and procedures they adhere to, their membership of regulated professional communities, and the legal system that constrains their behavior (Luhmann, 1988; Giddens, 1990; Bachmann, 2001). As Bachmann (2001) notes, when these institutionalized norms, procedures and rules form the basis of our trust in individuals, rather than one-on-one personalized experiences with them, then the relevant form of trust can be called 'system trust' (in other words, Luhmann) or 'institutional-based' trust (in other words, Zucker).

Niklas Luhmann's work provides a useful theoretical framework to understand trust and the financial system. Luhmann's (1988) theory suggests that systems emerge to cope with and contain complexity so that we can function more effectively (Seidl, 2005; see also Shapiro, 1987). Without a set of integrated and reliable systems and structures to enable the transfer of money from savers to borrowers, exchange would occur only in smaller trust networks rather than in society at large. If the financial system lacked a trustworthy infrastructure, the vast amount of due diligence and decision-making required would paralyze all but the experts, leaving the rest of us overwhelmed and, in all likelihood, poorer. This is the experience in parts of the world where economic and legal systems are less developed (for example, Zimbabwe, Nigeria).

Luhmann (1988) further suggests that trust between agents depends on the establishment of confidence in the system as an antecedent. There are a variety of expert systems in the financial sector designed to generate confidence that exchange can occur safely and efficiently. These confidence-inducing system mechanisms (or 'guardians of trust'; Shapiro, 1987) include defining standards and training requirements for financial advisors prior to registration and licensing, the auditing of financial statements of public companies, the requirement that companies follow accepted accounting standards, and evaluations by 'experts' such as credit rating agencies. We could go on, as there are a myriad of structures, laws, processes and other facilitating mechanisms that underpin the global financial system. Prior to the GFC, these mechanisms produced a high level of confidence in the financial system. But once eroded, the system rapidly ground to a halt – money literally stopped moving.

Luhmann (1988, p.103) states 'structural and operational properties of such a system may erode confidence and thereby undermine one of the essential conditions of trust'. Translating this to the financial sector, it may matter little whether investors' trust the individual broker or advisor, or individual investment firms, such as Lehman Brothers or Goldman Sachs, if they have no confidence in the more macro-system of exchanges that governs trading. Rather, a well-functioning financial system requires confidence in both the system and trust in the particular agents on whom stakeholders directly interact and rely.

THE GFC: UNDERSTANDING THE LOSS OF TRUST

Research reveals a host of common reasons why organizations and systems become untrustworthy. An examination of them may lead us to wonder why there are not more failures and to recognize that system trust requires a threshold of assurance rather than absolute trustworthiness. Economists and sociologists suggest that system failures occur because of poorly aligned or conflicting interests of agents and principals, problematic incentive systems that reward the wrong behaviors, lax monitoring and oversight, constrained monitoring due to asymmetries in information or expertise, and overly complex systems that render bureaucratic controls incomplete and inefficient (Shapiro, 1987; Milgrom and Roberts, 1988). Typically, not all of these sources of system failure operate at the same time and weaknesses can be corrected before system-wide failures occur. What is particularly interesting in the case of the GFC is that we see each of these problematic conditions simultaneously – a perfect storm so powerful that credit markets froze.

Table 8.1 focuses on the US financial system and identifies key players at multiple levels and summarizes their contributions to the loss of trust in the financial system. We provide a more detailed discussion of the failures below, clustered according to three groups: the financial institutions (including their boards, senior executives and employees), the ratings agencies, and the government and regulatory bodies. For each group, we use the three dimensions of trustworthiness – ability, benevolence and integrity – to isolate the behavior that contributed to the loss of trust. Our intention is not to provide a detailed analysis of all contributing causes but rather to articulate a framework to locate and make sense of key contributing factors. To sharpen focus and clarity, our scope is primarily limited to events within the USA.

Financial Institutions

Lack of ability
Two essential responsibilities of banks and financial intermediaries are to manage risk and allocate capital. Joseph Stiglitz, the Nobel award-winning economist, concluded that America's financial system failed in these two crucial responsibilities (Stiglitz, 2008). Over-leveraging and poor underwriting standards were central to the banks' failures in risk management.

Table 8.1 An outline of trust failures that contributed to the GFC

Agent	Failures of Trustworthiness		
	Ability	Benevolence	Integrity
Financial institutions	Failure of risk management and poor lending standards	Benevolence directed at option and short-term stockholders over employees and communities Use of predatory lending techniques	Misleading communication to boards, employees and investors as firms declined
Senior managers	Failure of leadership, stewardship and multi-stakeholder management	Benefited financially when employees and investors suffered	Misled employees and investors as firms declined
Boards	In some cases there was a lack of expertise (e.g., Lehman) and a failure to hold management accountable	Loyalty to CEO who in many cases recruited the board rather than shareholders	Failed to live up to espoused fiduciary role
Ratings agencies	Lack of expertise to evaluate new exotic instruments Inadequate resources to deal with volume of ratings demanded	Served those paying for the rating not those relying on them	Integrity of ratings compromised
Regulators	SEC became a more passive watchdog under Chairman Chris Cox	Misdirected benevolence and unintended consequences as the Federal Reserve under Greenspan kept interest rates artificially low after the dotcom bust to stimulate the economy	Political ideology and considerations adversely affected oversight
US government	Chose not to regulate mortgages, CDOs, CDSs, which were larger than the stock market	Misdirected benevolence and social policy tampered with housing market by increasing home ownership using Fannie Mae and Freddie Mac Wall Street insiders in key government positions advocated for their former industry (e.g., Rubin)	Millions of dollars of campaign contributions to politicians by the financial industry created conflicts

Bank leverage ratios were at historical highs prior to the GFC at nearly $1 of equity supporting $40 of debt. From 2004–07, the top five US investment banks each significantly increased their financial leverage to over $4.1 trillion in debt for fiscal year 2007, about 30 percent of US nominal GDP. Further, the percentage of subprime mortgages originated to total originations increased from below 10 percent in 2001–03 to between 18 and 20 percent from 2004–06. How can we understand this competence failure of financial firms? We identify three underlying factors that contributed: cultural and political shifts towards a high-risk trading culture; a failure of integration and learning across organizational departments; and ineffective board structures.

With the elimination of the Glass-Steagall Act in 1999, for which the financial industry groups heavily lobbied, there was a shift in the culture and power brokers within the banks. This Act removed the long-standing separation between the risk-averse conservative commercial (depository) banks and the high-risk, high-growth investment banks. Cultural forces promoting growth and profit trumped those concerned with risk management (McDonald and Robinson, 2009; Tett, 2009; Lanchester, 2010). This shift in the underlying culture and values of the commercial banks facilitated and legitimized high-risk strategies and the creation of incentive structures to match. Traders – the group that was making the most money – moved into positions of power, leaving more traditional bankers (who were more versed in risk and underwriting) with a weaker voice in strategic decision-making. Traders by their nature are aggressive risk-takers (Turbeville, 2010).

There was also a failure of integration and learning within many of the financial institutions that led to a fatally delayed response to the emerging crisis. As firms like Lehman Brothers and Merrill Lynch created new securities to grow, they failed to upgrade their capability to manage these new profit pools. For example, at Lehman Brothers, the distressed debt department tried to get senior management to reduce its exposure to subprime instruments, while the real estate department was loading Lehman's books with these instruments. There was no clear process for sorting through the data and taking a reasoned firm-wide approach to managing risk (McDonald and Robinson, 2009).

Another key contributor was the failure of boards to fulfill their essential responsibilities – to hold management accountable and manage institutional risks prudently (Zingales, 2009). A well-functioning, competent and committed board is an essential foundation to the trustworthiness of any organization, yet we see evidence indicating that this foundation was often misplaced. For example, at Lehman Brothers, CEO Fuld had nine members of the ten-person board who were retired and four were 75 years of age or older. Few had expertise in financial services.

Board directors are agents who are supposed to invest time, seek information and use expertise to ensure that shareholder interests are served (Shapiro, 1987). To warrant trust, boards of directors and shareholders' interests must be aligned. In practice, this is often not the case. Despite some use of board-nominating committees, in the USA most candidates are proposed by senior management of the company and corporate directors generally run for election unopposed and are not required to get a majority vote of shareholders to be elected (Bebchuk and Fried, 2004). It is clear that if someone was interested in becoming or remaining a director, the constituency whose interests they would appeal to would be management not shareholders. For most public boards, the invitation to join is influenced greatly by the CEO and he or she also influences which directors remain on the board. For example, Arthur Levitt, former Chairman of the SEC (Securities Exchange Commission), was invited to join the board of Apple but after some of his views concerning increasing shareholder influence were discovered, he was promptly uninvited from the board by Steve Jobs (Levitt and Dwyer, 2002).

Zingales (2009) argues that boards serving management at the expense of shareholders and not holding management accountable is the single biggest problem with trust in the financial system, enabling management fraud and mistakes to continue unfettered. The primary alignment of board members with management explains a great many decisions, which make little sense for investors but great sense for senior managers. For example, the board of the New York Stock Exchange approved a $140 million severance payment to its departing CEO, Dick Grasso. Board members who are not aligned with shareholders' interests or do not have the capacity or expertise to fulfill their responsibilities are misleading symbols of trust. Some have suggested the need for 'professional' board members who are truly independent and have the necessary time and expertise to adequately represent shareholders (Bebchuk and Weisbach, 2010).

Lack of benevolence
In the lead up to the GFC, there was a general lack of concern for stakeholders and many rules of fairness were violated. Within financial firms, decision-making was often driven by a single-minded focus on short-term stock price increase and its link to executive bonuses. This culture of pursuing stock price appreciation led executives to engage in risky earnings growth that betrayed the interests of employees, long-term investors and broader communities (Cohan, 2009; McDonald and Robinson, 2009; Lewis, 2010; Paulson Jr., 2010; Sorkin, 2010). Leaders gained millions in bonuses for generating earnings that would later turn into write-offs,

while shareholders and employees suffered loss of wealth, jobs or both. For example, CEOs Stan O'Neal of Merrill Lynch, Dick Fuld of Lehman Brothers and Jimmy Cayne of Bear Stearns, received well over $500 million in bonuses in total prior to the demise of their firms. These bonuses were based on earnings growth that would largely vanish due to subsequent write-downs of risky assets. The incentive structures approved by the boards of these companies benefited executives who received a portion of their compensation in cash but hurt long-term investors whose stocks turned out to be worth much less when the poor quality of the assets was uncovered. A lack of claw-back provisions in executive compensation, except in the case of fraud, left many investors with no recourse.

Consider in more detail the lack of benevolence to shareholders inherent in the compensation scheme at Lehman Brothers prior to its demise. The rule of thumb for Lehman traders was that if they made $20 million for the firm they could expect about a $1 million bonus. This could be paid roughly half in restricted stock and half in cash with no claw-back provision. The CEO Richard Fuld, who many blame for the disastrous management decisions that caused Lehman's bankruptcy, was awarded a $40 million dollar bonus the year before the company ceased to exist. While Fuld and the traders lost millions of dollars of stock compensation, they earned significant cash compensation, whereas stock investors and bondholders lost most of their principal invested.

In another demonstration of a lack of benevolence to clients and investors, mortgage brokers used 'no documentation' and 'predatory lending' techniques to sell loans to people who they knew would default, and then sold off those loans to clients knowing they would not collect (Hutton, 2009). These were known in the industry as NINJA (no income, no job, or assets) loans. Commission schedules were put in place that provided extra incentives to brokers to sell these higher-rate, riskier mortgages. One does not have to be a mortgage specialist or banker to know that lending significant amounts of money to people with no income, jobs or assets is unwise at best, and lacks any sense of due concern for the people taking out the loans, or the clients to whom the 'collateralized debt obligations' (CDOs) and mortgage-backed securities (MBSs) were sold.[2]

Lack of integrity
There are many clear cases of deception and fraud in the accounting practices used by the financial firms in the lead up to the GFC. For example, Citibank and others were using off-balance-sheet financing as Enron had done, and this made it hard for analysts to determine their true leverage ratios. They were also engaging in complex transactions to move risk and disguise the sliding value of assets (Stiglitz, 2008). Bear Sterns has

been described as a 'house of cards' (Cohan, 2009). Bear Stearns, Merrill Lynch and Lehman Brothers all made representations to employees and analysts that their firms were in excellent shape just prior to their demise (McDonald and Robinson, 2009; Paulson, 2010; Sorkin, 2010).

Misleading sales and marketing techniques that lacked full disclosure appeared to be widespread. For example, Goldman Sachs paid one of the largest fines in SEC history because it failed to disclose to investors purchasing the 'ABACUS' instruments that it was working with a hedge fund manager on the other side of the deal, who was selecting debt instruments that had obtained high safety ratings but that would most likely default; it was creating an instrument designed to fail. Some firms had less than transparent, and in some cases misleading, communication with their boards (Lehman with risk management and Merrill with payment of bonuses). Merrill Lynch and Bank of America were charged with fraud by the SEC because they failed to disclose to shareholders that they paid millions of dollars in bonuses to executives after the firm had received a multi-billion dollar bailout from taxpayers.

Ratings Agencies

Market perceptions of the risk of investing in CDOs, MBSs and associated products, were heavily influenced by the creditworthiness scores provided by ratings agencies such as Moody's, Standard and Poor's, and Fitches. Yet these agencies themselves were riven with incompetence and conflicts of interest.

Lack of ability, benevolence and integrity
Ratings agencies lacked people with the necessary skill and ability to evaluate some of the more exotic instruments being developed by the banks. The CDO products became so complex that many such credit ratings were little more than 'guesstimates' of the risk. Demonstrating a lack of integrity, the ratings agencies continued to rate these instruments and products without disclosing their lack of understanding. In email exchanges, ratings agency staff described giving misleading AAA ratings to financial products that they admitted to not fully understanding. Ratings agencies were paid for rating products by the institutions requesting them and earned consulting fees for advising these companies. Clearly they had a strong incentive to offer favorable ratings. In some cases people working at ratings agencies took higher-paid positions at companies for whom they were previously providing ratings. These incentive structures hurt investors. Self-interest, rather than a responsibility to provide accurate ratings and a concern for investors, appeared to be the guiding considera-

tion. These ratings agencies were unregulated by the government and not accountable to any other body.

Government and Regulatory Bodies

Lack of ability

The financial regulatory system in place today in the United States was largely designed in the 1930s in response to the financial crisis that led to the Great Depression. After the 1930s' market crash there were congressional hearings and reports of bank abuses, insider trading, corrupt business networks and favoritism. People had lost trust in the system and it imploded. A part of the system also exploded as a bomb went off at the offices of JP Morgan Bank, killing 30 people. In response, the SEC was created in 1934 to regulate the US financial sector. The problem is that this basic regulatory structure has not been fundamentally changed since it was created (Levitt testimony, 2009). The 2009 Financial Reform report by the Group of Thirty pointed out that our modern economy contains a myriad of entities that did not exist in the 1930s that now affect the financial markets (Reform, 2009). For example, the unregulated market for credit default swaps grew in the past ten years from $0 to $44 trillion, more than twice the size of the US stock market (Zingales, 2009). In testimony before Congress in 2009, former Chairman of the SEC, Arthur Levitt, suggested that the regulatory structure at the time of the GFC was under-resourced and over-matched in its capability to competently perform its function.

There are many agents whose behavior was largely unregulated leading up to the GFC, such as ratings agencies, mortgage brokers, hedge funds, sovereign wealth funds, private equity funds and commodities brokers. What makes this problematic for citizens and, therefore the government, is that major trust violations can materially affect the standard of living of millions of citizens. In the 1920s one in eight US households owned stock, today it is one in two. More importantly, there has been a significant move from retirements based on defined benefit plans to retired contribution plans (70 percent today). Retirement funds are a large portion of the US economy (60 percent of GDP). The fact that the reliability/performance of markets is directly linked to the retirement nest egg of millions of people with votes creates a strong force for politicization of the economy, which some have argued created the bubble and subsequent recession in 2009 (O'Brien, 2007).

Starting in the 1990s until 2007, there was a strong trend toward deregulation. Under the Clinton and Bush administrations, a number of rule changes were passed that reduced constraints and relaxed regulation of financial institutions, in favor of self-regulation. For example, as previously discussed, the government eliminated the Glass-Steagall Act in 1999, removing the long-standing separation between commercial banks and high-risk investment banks. The 2004 SEC decision to allow US investment banks to issue substantially more debt was seized upon to purchase more mortgage-backed securities. The expansion of less regulated markets was a deliberate move by industry groups and the government to create a two-tier system where there would be a 'somewhat regulated public market' and an 'unregulated private market' for more sophisticated investors. This addressed the fear that the costs imposed on companies by Sarbanes-Oxley or other regulations would lead to a flight of capital away from the United States. There was also a thought that the degree of regulation should be reduced if certain investors had the knowledge and resources to protect themselves rather than having regulators do so.

This unregulated private market led to a rapid growth in hedge funds, private equity ($5 billion raised in 1980 versus $250 billion in 2006) and an increase in capital raised through offerings to more sophisticated investors (more than 50 percent of capital raised in the USA in 2006; Zingales, 2009). The assumption behind the laissez-faire, hands-off approach was that 'reputational damage' would constrain fraud and deter improper behavior and that trust in the financial system could be maintained by active self-management of conflicts and the natural corrective mechanism of the free market (Greenspan, 2008). Arthur Levitt decried the fact that influential bankers and professional groups, who felt that the SEC was an annoyance, lobbied Congress to reduce regulation. Regulation became unpopular and deregulation became the order of the day. This lack of constraint and oversight directly contributed to the scale and scope of the financial crisis.

Failures among regulatory agencies included lax enforcement and a passive role on the part of the SEC in the USA and the Financial Services Authority (FSA) in the UK. In 2005, Chris Cox was offered the job of SEC Chairman by Vice President Dick Cheney, replacing William Donaldson. Donaldson stepped down after he frustrated fellow Republican commissioners by subjecting companies to multimillion-dollar fines and trying to impose new regulations on mutual funds and hedge funds. He also angered business groups, who complained to President Bush's administration after Donaldson tried to give shareholders more power to pick corporate directors. Under Cox, an 'anti-regulation' mentality was taken, enforcement penalties declined, as did agency morale based on reports of former staffers.

The central role that excessive deregulation played in facilitating the GFC is underscored by analysis suggesting that strong regulation played a primary role in the four big Australian retail banks retaining their AA credit ratings in the immediate aftermath of the GFC (four of only eight retail banks globally). Similarly, Canadian government regulation played a central role in keeping their banks in the AA list.

Lack of benevolence
The politicization of the economy also resulted in misdirected benevolence in the form of over-promotion of home ownership in the USA. After the September 11 terrorist attacks, the US government lowered interest rates, fueling a tremendous rise in household debt. The government pressured Fannie Mae and Freddie Mac to increase mortgages, as well as buy risky mortgages, in effect creating an incentive for self-interested mortgage brokers to originate more bad loans.

Escaping most people's attention concerning reform and regulation of the financial system is the conflict of interests among those governing the regulators, namely Congress. Congress has an oversight role with respect to the SEC, Fannie Mae, Freddie Mac and the Federal Reserve. As an example of the problem, Senator Chris Dodd chaired the Senate Banking Committee, which took as one of its mandates to clean up the financial regulatory system. In the 2008 election year cycle, Senator Dodd received almost $5 million in campaign contributions from the securities industry (see opensecrets.org). To be fair, the banking committee as a whole obtained approximately $13 million from the securities industry and this problem is endemic in Washington (Hamilton, 2004). While these lobbying practices are legal in the USA, the same practices would be considered bribery and unethical conduct in other Western democracies, such as the UK or Australia.

As Levitt (Levitt and Dwyer, 2002) argues, individual investors and voters have much less influence over policy and regulation than the business special interests groups (for example, the Securities Industry Association, the American Institute of Certified Public Accountants, US Chamber of Commerce and so on.). The securities industry alone gave $39 million dollars of soft money in the 2000 election cycle, making it the third largest contributor across all industries. Edelman (1985) explains that the tangible resources and intense commitment of special interest groups often outweigh the public quiescence and passivity, such that the public is satisfied with empty symbolic reassurances whereas the special interest groups command real benefits. So a Congressperson maximizes their chance of getting re-elected by helping well-financed special interest groups while maintaining a posture that he or she is protecting the interests of citizens. This explains a good deal of congressional behavior, including why more stringent safeguards for individual investors have not been made into law and why Congress has failed to end the cycle of legal corruption via campaign financing.

Summary

In sum, trust failed in the 2008 financial crisis because the foundation of the financial system was extremely fragile. The system was based on an intricate network of trust relationships: Home buyers trusted the knowledge and expertise of their mortgage brokers; banks trusted the mortgage brokers and the credit rating agencies on the viability of the loans and securities; investors, lenders and hedge funds trusted the banks and credit rating agencies on the predicted profitability and assessed risk levels of their products; bank shareholders trusted their leaders and their board to monitor institutional risks prudently; ordinary citizens with a pension trusted the pension fund managers as well as government regulators. Everyone trusted the market. The system relied upon reputational effects and indicators of trustworthiness that, in the final analysis, proved to be largely unwarranted.

As our analysis shows, all three dimensions of trustworthiness were comprehensively violated by multiple parties and at multiple levels. Significant conflicts of interest in the financial system undermined the system's trustworthiness. An examination of these conflicts leads to an inescapable conclusion that they exist because they benefit those with the most power and influence. Most often this is not the investor or the shareholder but another agent in the system, such as the government, industry groups, senior management, board members or ratings agencies. This perfect storm of violations led to a massive erosion of confidence in the financial system and loss of trust in firms and leaders. The 2011 Edelman Trust Barometer showed a 46 and 30 percentage point decline in trust in banks in the USA and UK respectively from 2008 to 2011.

These significant flaws and conflicts of interest in the system should have led knowledgeable market participants to choose suspicion over trust. However, as behavioral finance experts have indicated, the nature of financial markets involves not only assessing risk and return, but also the psychology of crowds that sometimes leads to market manias followed by panics and crashes. This brings us back to Luhmann (1988) and the interconnection between familiarity, trust and confidence. Market participants seemed not to calculate trustworthiness but rather adopted a familiar posture of assumed confidence, perhaps even unquestioned faith. This unwarranted confidence forced the entire system into a massive trust repair experiment.

REPAIRING AND BUILDING TRUST IN THE FINANCIAL SECTOR: A MULTI-LEVEL PERSPECTIVE

In the financial system there are a variety of stakeholders who consider different aspects of trustworthiness in a variety of agents and the level of trust required to exchange may vary depending on the trustor and trustee, and the level of vulnerability and risk involved. Hence, trust repair in the global financial system will require interventions at multiple levels with multiple agents, and will run the gambit from interpersonal trust (for example, between senior management and boards; between investors and financial advisors) to impersonal trust (for example, between firms and regulators).

Conceptually, trust repair after a violation aims to restore confident positive expectations, but must first overcome the negative expectations of the other party's trustworthiness caused by the betrayal (Kim et al., 2004). Dirks et al. (2009) identify that most research on trust repair adopts either an attribution or social equilibrium perspective. Repair from the 'attributional' perspective focuses on changing the victim's negative attributions and perceptions about whether a transgression occurred and whether it reflects on the enduring character of the transgressor. Tactics include apologies, explanations, denial and penance. It is largely a cognitive process focused on the individual behavior and characteristics of the transgressor. From the 'social equilibrium' perspective, transgressions lead to a disequilibrium in the relationship and social context. Repair involves restoring equilibrium in the relationship through social rituals that redistribute power, such as penance, punishment and apologies. Hence, the same repair tactics can operate through different causal mechanisms (attributional vs social equilibrium).

The literature on trust repair has largely focused at the interpersonal level, with most studies relying on experimental methods and scenarios focused on private dyadic relationships (Gillespie and Dietz, 2009). In contrast, the repair of trust in the financial system involves multiple actors operating at multiple levels, has systemic as well as individual and organizational causes and facilitating factors and has occurred in a very public manner. The literature on micro-level trust repair has its explanatory limits when applied to the problem of restoring trust at the institutional and systems level.

One way to conceptualize restoring trust in the global financial system is to view it as a problem of embedding trustworthiness into the entire system so that it reliably produces many more signals of trust than distrust. A strong institutional order makes it more likely that individuals' behavior will be consistent and predictable (Bachmann, 2001). While there is scant research on repairing system-level trust, the model of organizational level trust repair (OTR) offered by Gillespie and Dietz (2009) has been used to examine the repair strategies of agents at the various levels of the global financial system (for a comprehensive overview, see Gillespie et al., 2011). This framework adopts a 'structural' perspective (c.f., Dirks et al., 2009), arguing that after an organizational failure, trust repair requires 'distrust regulation' mechanisms, that is, implementing sufficient regulatory controls to discourage or prevent untrustworthy acts or future transgressions and encourage trustworthy acts by organizational agents. These mechanisms aim to prevent or constrain organizational actors and groups from behaving in ways that could lead to future violations, including the removal of incentives that may encourage untrustworthy behavior and imposing sanctions on miscreants (such as being fired, demoted, or losing privileges). Implementing these mechanisms typically requires reform of the organization's design (Nadler and Tushman, 1997) including structures, processes and systems (for example, incentive and promotion systems), cultural norms and values (for example, codes of conduct) and leadership and management practices. There is empirical support for the effectiveness of structural mechanisms for repairing trust (see Slovic, 1993; Nakayachi and Watabe, 2005).

In this section we focus on the role of control mechanisms (for example, regulation and enforcement) as a foundation for rebuilding institutional trust. In doing so, we connect with recent debates in the literature on the relationship between trust and controls. We argue that while a strong foundation of regulation is necessary, it is not a sufficient condition for trust repair in the financial system. Rather, to restore trust and protect against future trust failures, financial institutions need to also take active steps to embed trustworthiness into the foundation of the organization's strategy and design. We draw on sociological perspectives on institutional trust, as well as the OTR framework, to support these views.

The Role of Regulation and Control in Trust Repair

Most research regarding trust and control has focused at the interpersonal level (for an overview see Bijlsma-Frankema and Costa, 2005) or in the context of strategic alliances and inter-organizational relationships (Das and Teng, 1998, 2001; Bachmann, 2001). The role of control in the trust process is controversial, with some proposing that control undermines trust (for example, Ghoshal and Moran, 1996; Das and Teng, 1998), whilst others argue that it has a positive role (for example, Sitkin, 1995; Weibel, 2007). As Bachmann et al. (2001, p.v) note: 'while there are numerous examples in the literature where control chases out trust there are equally as many examples of trust and control being complementary, or going hand in hand'.

Das and Teng (1998) argue for a contingent relationship, where formal controls (such as behavior and output control) undermine trust because strict rules and objectives limit members' autonomy, whereas social (or cultural) control enhances trust by influencing behavior and mutual understanding through the establishment of shared goals and norms. However, recent empirical work suggests that both formal and normative controls can function to facilitate trust at the organizational level by reducing vulnerability and risk (Weibel et al., 2010). To date, the role of controls in the process of trust repair at the organizational or institutional level has received scant attention.

We propose that control is central to repairing stakeholders' trust in organizations and institutions. As we have outlined previously, in contrast to the interpersonal level, at the organizational level one trusts an impersonal organized system, and the collective actions of a range of interconnected organizational agents. Control mechanisms governing the system, such as regulations and rules, play a central role in ensuring that most of these agents operate in a predictable, reliable, fair and competent manner.

Indeed, financial regulation and governance concerns impersonal or system trust and thus involves strategies to constrain agents' behavior to reduce risks and uncertainty, acting as functional substitutes for interpersonal or relationship trust (Shapiro, 1987). Most investors will not know the CEO of the company they invest in or the members of the board of directors and therefore have no way of judging the motives of these people. The goal of financial regulation and governance is to engineer an impersonal system, which efficiently ensures that investors can confidently rely on those who employ their capital. An effective example of this is the capital requirement that life insurance companies are required to have to cover potential claims upon the death of the insured. State insurance commissioners monitor these reserves rather than leaving it up to the judgment of management of the insurance companies. Done correctly, regulation reduces the search and evaluation costs of those with capital while avoiding the cost and flight of capital that excessive bureaucracy and regulation would produce. Done poorly, regulation slows the velocity of capital flow, adds costs and lures people into an unwarranted confidence that they can rely on the system. A major challenge in rebuilding trust in the financial system is achieving a balanced and trustworthy level of regulation, and doing so with a number of actors and variety of transactions in a very complex system.

Consistent with this view of trust building through control, attempts to restore trust in the global financial system have focused on enhancing regulation and control (Gillespie et al., 2011). For example, governments across the globe have increased the capital reserves that banks must hold by law, new structures and agencies have been set up to police banks and financial services firms more strictly (for example, Consumer Protection Agency; Financial Oversight Council), and previously unregulated agents and products, such as ratings agencies and hedge funds are, or are about to be, regulated. Laws have been introduced to try to combat conflicts of interest in the financial sector. For example, firms selling securitized products now must retain a 5 percent interest and limits have been placed on proprietary trading. The G20 has endorsed principles to stop bonus schemes in banks from encouraging too much short-term risk-taking, such as deferral of part of a bonus, a claw-back mechanism, payment in the form of shares rather than cash, and avoiding multi-year guaranteed bonuses. Controls have also been introduced internally within financial firms. For example, most of the major financial firms have increased oversight and governance over compensation and adopted some form of deferral of compensation to tie executives and shareholders' interests more closely.

The Role of Enforced Sanctions in System Trust

Luhmann (1988) suggested that system trust requires a belief that mutual expectations will be met. Ensuring actual behavior meets expectations requires a need for swift and significant sanctions to be levied on actors who violate rules. This is the pointy end of the regulation stick. The severity of punishment is one of the most significant factors influencing ethical decision-making (Gurley, Wood and Nijhawan, 2007). These can include fines or loss of license or rights to participate in the system. There is extensive evidence that prior to the financial crisis, there were inadequate sanctions in the system to detect rule violations (Levitt, 2002; Zingales, 2009).

Furthermore, in order to be a deterrent, sanctions must be significant and expected if one commits fraud and they should penalize those in violation and not shareholders. While this seems obvious this is not always the case in the financial sector. The recent SEC case with Bank of America for failing to disclose material information about the Merrill Lynch deal is an example. The SEC and Bank of America settled the case with a fine that was small in relation to the violation. Also, the SEC did not locate who in the organization had violated disclosure rules and the fine was levied on the shareholders and not company executives. Federal Judge Rakoff did not approve the settlement, indicating that the victims (shareholders) were being victimized twice by the SEC settlement terms. The matter is still being litigated at the time of writing. As this example shows, in the financial sector, shareholders are sometimes victimized by fines, while board members and executives get a free pass, and fines may prove to be so small relative to potential earnings that they may not deter untrustworthy behavior.

To the degree that trust violations are not sanctioned, the threat of sanction loses credibility and its effect as a deterrent evaporates. The Galleon hedge fund arrests in late 2009 were a very public attempt to correct previously loose monitoring of insider trading behavior. Proper regulation requires some analysis of the magnitude of transgressions and allocating the necessary resources to uncover, investigate and prosecute fraud such that the error rate is acceptable. There is some evidence that publicized cases of fraud can *decrease* investor trust but that publicized cases of enforcement can have a *positive* impact on trust (Zingales, 2009). While public displays of enforcement by the Attorney General or the SEC might increase perceptions of politicizing, it also signals to those in the system that monitoring is alive and well and makes this deterrent more salient. This counteracts the social psychology of powerful norms, which leads some to convince themselves that if 'everyone is doing it', it is acceptable, even though illegal.

The Role of Regulation in Creating Predictability

It is well established that trust requires some ability to predict what trustees will do and that randomness inhibits trust formation (Hurley, 2012). This is particularly true concerning trust in the financial system because risk assessment is made more difficult when the rules and externalities affecting the system change for no apparent reason. When a clear set of values and principles underlies regulation and when regulatory behavior conforms to those principles, behavior in the system becomes more predictable. To the degree that the political forces at play agree on regulatory policy and have a transparent and reliable process to make any necessary shifts, it will increase trust in the system. On the other hand, if regulatory policy is shifted in a non-transparent and politically impulsive manner to serve whatever interests happen to be in power at the moment (as occurred in the USA prior to the GFC), it reduces the predictability of the system and hence trustworthiness. The politicization of financial regulation is of concern to trust building and repair not simply because of conflicts of interest, but also because it reduces the predictability of the system.

We see here how trust in the competence and coherence of government directly affects trust in the financial system and the economy at large. This interrelationship played out in the drama that unfolded when, in 2011, the United States saw its credit rating reduced as political parties failed to collaborate to raise the debt ceiling of the US Treasury. The stock market plunged and citizens watched their retirement investments shrink while politicians blamed each other. The financial system took yet another blow to its confidence.

Trust Repair Post-GFC: Unresolved Systemic Problems

Inevitably, restoring trust in a large system involves issues of inertia, entrenched bureaucracy and self-protective mechanisms that conspire to resist change (Nadler and Tushman, 1997; Burke, 2002). This is abundantly clear in the reform efforts to date in the financial system with several unpopular but critical reforms not yet implemented. Table 8.2 offers a list of trust repair interventions among various agents in the USA that are entirely or partially missing in the efforts to reform the financial system. These omissions in system-level trust repair are strategic and central to making the system more trustworthy. For example, if boards are not reformed and if money continues to corrupt government policy, there is every reason to believe that new crises will emerge. This repeats a pattern observed after the Enron debacle where Sarbanes-Oxley and other changes amounted to half measures that gave the appearance of trustworthiness but allowed dysfunctions to continue in the system, which later contributed to yet more betrayals during the GFC (for example, lack of real board reform and failure to curtail off-balance sheet financing).

We highlight here some of the major missing elements in creating a truly trustworthy financial system. At the company level many firms have not found a way to effectively implement internal monitoring and compliance with organizational systems that enhance trust (for example, through a combination of selection, training, leadership modeling and accountability systems). A case in point is UBS. It has made significant efforts at reform but still has a long way to go, as evidenced by the $2 billion rogue trader fraud in 2011. The culture on Wall Street is still largely a tournament for maximizing individual compensation, and at the senior manager level there are still many leaders that adopt a single-minded focus on short-term stock price, resulting in betrayals of the interests of other stakeholders (for example, employees, long-term investors). At the board level there is still little movement toward professional and independent boards, or holding boards more accountable for protecting the interests of all stakeholders in a fair and transparent manner.

With respect to the government and regulators, there is still no working understanding of what 'too big to fail' means. Money still has a major influence in political voice and resistance to new regulations runs strong

Table 8.2 Missing elements in trust repair

Agent	Ability	Benevolence	Integrity
Companies	Develop more effective processes for gauging the congruence between policies and practice (compliance and governance) Select and promote leaders in part based on demonstration of key elements of trustworthiness	Create a multi-stakeholder and fair process for strategic decisions	Develop cultures of candor, transparency and fairness
Senior managers	Develop tools and competence for a multi-stakeholder approach to leadership	Practice serving others over self Develop a stewardship orientation	Develop a practice for daily examination of integrity concerning values-based leadership
Boards	More independent, professional board members who devote more time to firm governance	Take CEO out of a central board recruitment role	Define and hold boards accountable for their fiduciary roles
Ratings agencies	Develop competency standards Decline rating instruments where firms lack competence	Realign incentives so users rather than issuers pay fees	Create mechanisms to eliminate 'ratings shopping'
Regulators	Devote more resources to monitoring Define all systemic risk factors and embed safeguards	Reduce the impact of political influence on regulation. Empower professional regulators who are impartial	
US government	Creation of effective regulatory agencies to cover systemic risk (e.g., commodities and mortgages)	Improve assessment of unintended effects of government policy (e.g., housing push)	Reduce influence of money and lobbying

197

among companies and certain political parties. It is not at all clear that all the protections added to the system will be implemented given the negotiations and political machinations at play. On 2 March 2010 Treasury Secretary Geithner published a *New York Times* opinion piece suggesting that the country had 'financial crisis amnesia' as attempts were being made to water down Dodd-Frank regulations.

In the OTR model, Gillespie and Dietz (2009) argue that organizational trust repair requires *successive systemic cycles of reforms*, interspersed with periodic *evaluation* to assess the effectiveness of reforms and identify further necessary reforms. This is necessary to achieve a sufficient level of *congruence* among the various organizational and system components to reinforce, rather than undermine, renewed trustworthiness. Applied to such a complex socio-technical system as the financial system, it is evident that it is nearly impossible to engineer all the required reforms in one process. Particularly when vested interests begin to attack reforms there is a real risk that key measures will be conveniently left out: power and politics are very much at the heart of the reality of repairing system trust. It is interesting to ask which agent will have the necessary independence and global systemic purview and authority to conduct an evaluation of reforms to the financial sector.

Our key point is that in any large multi-agent, multi-level system with entrenched interests among actors, trust repair must be framed as a long-term, social, technical and political process where success can only be declared after repeated evaluation and testing over a significant period of time. Rebuilding trust in the financial system requires reform to broader political and governance structures and processes: trust in one focal system (for example, investing in the global financial system) relies on confidence in the broader institutional systems that support and lay the foundation for the focal system (for example, legal, regulatory and political systems; see Luhmann, 1988). Post-GFC, governments, regulators and companies have proposed and adopted some changes and, to a large extent, trustworthiness resides in the details that are now being negotiated among the various interest groups largely behind the scenes.

Trust Repair Post-GFC: Opportunities for Financial Institutions

Another critical aspect of system-level trust repair is complementing system controls with trustworthiness demonstration at the organization and system level. We argue that regulation – while a necessary foundation to system-level trust repair – is not sufficient alone. Indeed, proactive attempts to repair trust have been shown to be more convincing than passive acceptance of externally enforced rules and regulations

(Tomlinson and Mayer, 2009). To rebuild a strong reputation of trustworthiness, financial institutions must also evaluate their own internal trust failures, and proactively put in place systemic reforms to embed trustworthiness into their organizational design (Gillespie and Dietz, 2009). This is important not only to rebuild external stakeholders' perceptions of the organization's trustworthiness, but also employees' trust. Without a strong foundation of internal trust, organizations will struggle to effectively reposition themselves and rebuild their reputation externally (Child and Rodrigues, 2004; Dietz and Gillespie, 2011, 2012).

The poor corporate governance and culture of excessive risk-taking driven by short-term incentive schemes that contributed to the trust failures are arguably best addressed at the organizational level. Child and Rodrigues (2004) argue that effective corporate governance requires management of a double agency relationship: between owners and corporate management on the one hand, and between corporate management and the firm's employees on the other. They argue that for senior management to be trusted by shareholders requires first that employees and middle managers trust senior management because internal trust is necessary to deliver competent, honest and fair organizational conduct. They further argue that internal trust can be enhanced and repaired through an inclusive approach to control and further that 'a good control system must operate with participation, transparency and evident fairness' (p. 149). Indeed, it is practically impossible for a CEO or senior managers to know all the details of what is going on within a large, complex firm, making it necessary for employees to have mechanisms to monitor each other, raise concerns, criticize and question upwards. Transparency in the form of open information sharing, monitoring and a culture that encourages employees to report concerns, reduces the likelihood of opportunism. Hence, not only does system-wide trust repair rest on control mechanisms, but controls also play a central role to trust repair within institutions.

Repairing organizational trust and redesigning organizations for trustworthiness is a complex and challenging task. For more extensive conceptual and practical guidance that draws on systems thinking and models of strategic organizational change and design (Burke and Litwin, 1992; Nadler and Tushman, 1997; Burke, 2002) we refer the reader to our recent work (Dietz and Gillespie, 2011, 2012; Gillespie and Dietz, 2009; Hurley, 2012). Our essential point here is that trust repair at the micro-organizational level, en masse, can contribute to trust repair at the macro-level of the financial system, as stakeholders' interaction with the system is significantly channeled through financial services firms (for example, one's bank, financial advisor, funds manager and so on). Organizations that take a proactive approach to diagnosing their own trust failures and implementing reforms to build and protect the trustworthiness of the organizational system are likely to enjoy the impressive benefits that research shows are associated with high trust organizations (Kramer, 1999; Dirks and Ferrin, 2002).

CONCLUSION

Trust failed in the 2008 financial crisis because its foundation was extremely fragile. There were significant flaws in the system that should have led knowledgeable market participants to choose suspicion over trust. Restoring trust will require not only strong regulation but also reform of broader political and legal institutional processes, as well as proactive steps by financial institutions to systematically embed trustworthiness into their organizational design. Without this broader set of interventions, reforms will likely center on symbolic actions that improve the appearance of trust but potentially increase the probability that the system will fail again and further erode trust (see Shapiro, 1987). A major obstacle in reform will be dealing with vested interests and conflicts in the system. It is unlikely that a system this complex and affecting so many people can be reformed in one grand set of regulatory changes. Given the difficulty of achieving congruence and repairing trust system-wide, successive cycles of evaluation followed by adjustments and further reforming interventions will be required (Gillespie and Dietz, 2009).

NOTES

1. For a review of the research on the foundational elements of trust and trustworthiness see Hurley (2012). For an examination of the applicability of ABI across cultures see Ferrin and Gillespie (2010).
2. MBSs and CDOs are financial products that combine prime mortgages with subprime mortgages (in other words, good with bad). These were sold to other investors and banks, and CDOs were insured, creating another lucrative and unregulated market in credit default swaps (CDSs).

REFERENCES

Bachmann, R. (2001), 'Trust, power and control in trans-organizational relations', *Organization Studies*, **22**(2), 337–65.
Bachmann, R., D. Knights and J. Sydow (2001), 'Trust and control in organizational relations', *Organization Studies*, **22**(2), v–vii.

Bebchuk, L. and J. Fried (2004), *Pay Without Performance: The Unfulfilled Promise of Executive Compensation*, Cambridge, MA: Harvard University Press.
Bebchuk, L.A. and M.S. Weisbach (2010), 'The state of corporate governance research', *Review of Financial Studies*, **23**(3), 939–61.
Bijlsma-Frankema, K.M. and A.C. Costa (2005), 'Understanding the trust–control nexus', *International Sociology*, **20**(3), 259–82.
Burke, W.W. (2002), *Organization Change: Theory and Practice*, London: Sage.
Burke, W.W. and G.H. Litwin (1992), 'A causal model of organizational performance and change', *Journal of Management*, **18**(3), 523–45.
Child, J. and S.B. Rodrigues (2004), 'Repairing the breach of trust in corporate governance', *Corporate Governance: An International Review*, **12**(2), 143–52.
Cohan, W. (2009), *House of Cards: A Tale of Hubris and Wretched Excess on Wall Street*, New York: Doubleday.
Colquitt, J.A., B.A. Scott and J.A. LePine (2007), 'Trust, trustworthiness, and trust propensity: a meta-analytic test of their unique relationships with risk taking and job performance', *Journal of Applied Psychology*, **92**(4), 909–27.
Das, T.K. and B-S. Teng (1998), 'Between trust and control: developing confidence in partner cooperation in alliances', *Academy of Management Review*, **23**(3), 491–512.
Das, T.K. and B-S. Teng (2001), 'Trust, control, and risk in strategic alliances: an integrated framework', *Organization Studies*, **22**(2), 251–83.
Deutsch, M. (1973), *The Resolution of Conflict: Constructive and Destructive Processes*, New Haven, CT: Yale University Press.
Dietz, G. and N. Gillespie (2011), *Building and Restoring Organisational Trust*, London: Institute of Business Ethics.
Dietz, G. and N. Gillespie (2012), *The Recovery of Trust: Case Studies of Organizational Failures and Successful Trust Repair*, London: The Institute of Business Ethics.
Dirks, K.T. and D.L. Ferrin (2002), 'Trust in leadership: meta-analytic findings and implications for research and practice', *Journal of Applied Psychology*, **87**(4), 611–28.
Dirks, K.T., R.J. Lewicki and A. Zaheer (2009), 'Repairing relationships within and between organizations: building a conceptual foundation', *Academy of Management Review*, **34**(1), 68–84.
Edelman, M. (1985), *The Symbolic Uses of Politics*, Champaign, IL: Illini Books.
Ferrin, D.L. and N. Gillespie (2010), 'Trust differences across national-societal cultures: much to do, or much ado about nothing?', in M.N. Saunders, D. Skinner, G. Dietz, N. Gillespie and R.J. Lewicki (eds), *Organizational Trust: A Cultural Perspective*, New York: Cambridge University Press.
Ghoshal, S. and P. Moran (1996), 'Bad for practice: a critique of the transaction cost theory', *Academy of Management Review*, **21**(1), 13–47.
Giddens, A. (1984), *The Constitution of Society*, Cambridge, UK: Polity.
Giddens, A. (1990), *The Consequences of Modernity*, Stanford, CA: Stanford University Press.
Gillespie, N. and G. Dietz (2009), 'Trust repair after an organizational-level failure', *Academy of Management Review*, **34**(1), 127–45.
Gillespie, N., R. Hurley, G. Dietz and R. Bachmann (2011), 'Trust repair in the context of the global financial crisis', in R.M. Kramer and T. Pittinsky, *Restoring Trust in Leaders and Organizations*, Oxford: Oxford University Press.
Greenspan, A. (2008), 'Testimony before the House Committee on Oversight and Government Reform', 23 October 2008.
Gurley, K., P. Wood and I. Nijhawan (2007), 'The effect of punishment on ethical behavior when personal gain is involved', *Journal of Legal, Ethical and Regulatory Issues*, **10**(1), 91–100.
Hamilton, L. (2004), *How Congress Works and Why You Should Care*, Bloomington, IN: Indiana University Press.
Hurley, R.F. (2006), 'The decision to trust', *Harvard Business Review*, **11**, 55–62.
Hurley, R. (2012), *The Decision to Trust: How Leaders Create High-trust Organizations*, Hoboken, NJ: John Wiley & Sons.

Hutton, W. (2009), 'The crash – how the banks went bust', Channel 4, *Dispatches*.
Katz, D. and R. Kahn (1966), *The Social Psychology of Organizations*, New York: Wiley.
Kim, P.H., D.L. Ferrin, C. Cooper and K.T. Dirks (2004), 'Removing the shadow of suspicion: the effects of apology versus denial for repairing competence- versus integrity-based trust violations', *Journal of Applied Psychology*, **89**(1), 104–18.
Kramer, R.M. (1999), 'Trust and distrust in organizations: emerging perspectives, enduring questions', *Annual Review of Psychology*, **50**(1), 569–98.
Lanchester, J. (2010), *Whoops! Why Everyone Owes Everyone and No One Can Pay*, New York: Allen Lane.
Levitt, A. (2002), *Take on the Street: What Wall Street and Corporate America Don't Want You to Know; What You Can Do to Fight Back*, New York: Random House.
Levitt, A. (2009), 'Hearing on enhancing investor protection and the regulation of securities markets, US Senate Committee on Banking, Housing, and Urban Affairs', 26 March 2009, accessed 3 May 2013 at http://banking.senate.gov/public/.
Levitt, A. and P. Dwyer (2002), *Take on the Street: What Wall Street and Corporate America Don't Want You to Know*, New York: Random House.
Lewis, M. (2010), *The Big Short: Inside the Doomsday Machine*, New York: Norton.
Luhmann, N. (1979), *Trust and Power*, New York: John Wiley.
Luhmann, N. (1988), 'Familiarity, confidence and trust: problems and alternatives', in D. Gambetta (ed.), *Trust: Making and Breaking Cooperative Relationships*, New York: Basil Blackwell, pp. 94–107.
Mayer, R.C., J.H. Davis and F.D. Schoorman (1995), 'An integrative model of organizational trust', *Academy of Management Review*, **20**(3), 709–34.
McDonald, L.G. and P. Robinson (2009), *A Colossal Failure of Common Sense: The Inside Story of the Collapse of Lehman Brothers*, New York: Crown Books.
Milgrom, P. and J. Roberts (1988), 'An economic approach to influence activities in organizations', *The American Journal of Sociology*, **94**(Supplement), 154–79.
Nadler, D.A. and M.L. Tushman (1997), *Competing by Design: The Power of Organizational Architecture*, New York: Oxford University Press.
Nakayachi, K. and M. Watabe (2005), 'Restoring trustworthiness after adverse events: the signaling effects of voluntary "hostage posting" on trust', *Organizational Behavior and Human Decision Processes*, **97**(1), 1–17.
O'Brien, J. (2007), *Redesigning Financial Regulation: The Politics of Enforcement*, Chichester: John Wiley.
Oxford Dictionary of English (2003), Oxford: Oxford University Press.
Paulson Jr., H.M (2010), *On the Brink: Inside the Race to Stop the Collapse of the Global Financial System*, New York: Business Plus.
Reform, W.G.o.F. (2009), *Financial Reform: A Framework for Financial Stability*, Washington DC: The Group of Thirty.
Rousseau, D.M., S.B. Sitkin, R.S. Burt and C. Camerer (1998), 'Not so different after all: a cross-discipline view of trust', *Academy of Management Review*, **23**(3), 393–404.
Schoorman, F.D., R.C. Mayer and J.H. Davis (2007), 'An integrative model of organizational trust: past, present and future', *Academy of Management Review*, **32**(2), 344–54.
Seidl, D. (2005), 'The basic concepts of Luhmann's theory of social systems', in D. Seidl (ed.), *Niklas Luhmann and Organization Studies*, Copenhagen: Copenhagen Business School Press.
Shapiro, D. (1987), 'The social control of impersonal trust', *American Journal of Sociology*, **93**(3), 623–58.
Sitkin, S.B. (1995), 'On the positive effect of legalization on trust', *Research on Negotiation in Organizations*, **5**(2), 185–217.
Slovic, P. (1993), 'Perceived risk, trust, and democracy', *Risk Analysis*, **13**(6), 675–82.
Sorkin, A.R. (2010), *Too Big to Fail: The Inside Story of How Wall Street and Washington Fought to Save the Financial System – and Themselves*, New York: Penguin Group.
Stiglitz, J. (2008), 'The fruit of hypocrisy; dishonesty in the finance sector dragged us here, and Washington looks ill-equipped to guide us out', 16 September 2008, *The Guardian*.

Tett, G. (2009), *Fool's Gold: How the Bold Dream of a Small Tribe at J.P. Morgan Was Corrupted by Wall Street Greed and Unleashed a Catastrophe*, New York: Free Press.
Tomlinson, E.C. and R.C. Mayer (2009), 'The role of causal attribution dimensions in trust repair', *Academy of Management Review*, **34**(1), 85–104.
Turbeville, W.C. (2010), 'Former Goldman VP: how the trader takeover of Wall Street created the obsession with short-term greed', 18 May 2010, *Business Insider*.
Weibel, A. (2007), 'Control and trustworthiness – shall the twain never meet?', *Group and Organization Management*, **32**(4), 500–517.
Weibel, A., R. Searle, D. Den Hartog, N. Gillespie, F. Six, T. Hatzakis and D. Skinner (2010), 'Control as a driver of trust in the organization', *Social Sciences Research Network*, accessed 3 May 2013 at http://www.researchgate.net/publication/228197932_Control_as_a_Driver_of_Trust_in_the_Organization.
Zingales, L. (2009), 'The future of securities regulation', *Journal of Accounting Research*, **47**(2), 391–425.
Zucker, L.G. (1986), 'Production of trust: institutional sources of economic structure, 1840–1920', in B.M. Staw and L.L. Cummings (eds), *Research in Organizational Behavior*, Greenwich, CT: JAI, pp. 53–111.

9. Public trust in the institution of business
Jared D. Harris, Adrian A.C. Keevil and Andrew C. Wicks

INTRODUCTION

The worst financial crisis in the past 75 years has raised vexing questions about the limits of markets, and particularly about the pathway to a prosperous future for the global economy. It has also brought to the forefront what appears to be a crisis in the public's confidence in the institution of business. Coming out of the global financial crisis, trust in the institution of business is currently scored at a historic low (Jacobe, 2011). Business leaders called for rebuilding public trust in business and capitalism as a top priority, even before the advent of the 2008 financial crisis (BRICE, 2004). Underlying the comments of these leaders is an appreciation that public trust is essential to the smooth functioning of markets, to limiting regulation, to fostering innovation and to supporting business and business-related activities. However, the score itself provides limited information, and raises a series of questions relevant for both scholars and managers. What constitutes a 'low' (or a 'high') level of public trust? What are the costs (real or perceived) of low levels of public trust, whether to individual businesses or to society or other stakeholders? Why is public trust at the level it currently is and what, if anything, can be done about it? Public trust is a topic that is of critical importance and that deserves greater attention from scholars.

While researchers have spent considerable energy on understanding trust within and between people and within and between specific organizations, this concept of 'public trust' is less well understood, and presents some unique complexities (Harris and Wicks, 2010; Cook and Schilke, 2010). Several researchers have commented on public trust and its potential impact on organizations (for example, Tyler and Kramer, 1996; Lane and Bachman, 1998; Cook and Schilke, 2010; Harris and Wicks, 2010) and there is growing interest in the area. Despite its importance, we really know very little about the public's trust in business as an institution (Harris and Wicks, 2010). In fact, there is very little known about the measure generally used to track the public's trust in major institutions.

One explanation for why public trust in business remains somewhat underexplored by researchers is because it falls in between various areas of research – generalized trust (sociology/political science) on the one hand, and organizational trust (organizational studies/management) on the other. Sociology and political science tend to be mainly interested in trust within social systems (Cook and Schilke, 2010). This literature is generally concerned with understanding mutual trust between and among citizens, rather than individuals' trust in institutions (for example, Arrow, 1974; Fukuyama, 1995; Sztompka, 1999; Putnam, 2000; Hardin, 2002; Kramer and Cook, 2004; Cook, 2005; Stickel et al., 2009). In contrast, organizational and management scholars tend to be interested in understanding inter-organizational and intra-organizational trust, its effects on organizational outcomes, and its relational origins (for reviews see Zaheer and Harris, 2006 and Schoorman et al., 2007). In Chapter 10 of this volume, Nickerson, Gubler and Dirks make a similar observation about trust in economics. While economic theory recognizes the importance of trust in economic exchange, scholars have not studied the role of trust in economic organization. The authors draw numerous connections between trust and the economic theory of the firm, arguing that trust becomes more important as firm governance structures move from market to hierarchy.

This chapter is focused on building our understanding of individual trust in the institution of business. While we pay particular attention to management and organizational research, we attempt to represent a broad range of perspectives on this emerging topic of research – both in terms of theory and methods. In this chapter we identify an approach to public trust based on combining insights from research on both generalized trust and organizational trust. We then discuss both established approaches and new approaches that seem promising for future research in this area.

DEFINING TRUST

In academic research, trust has been measured as an attitude, an intention, a behavior and a dispositional orientation. But definitions tend to convene on the notion that trust in some way represents an actor's (trustor) expectations about another actor or object/institution/organization (trustee), that one believes in and is willing to depend on another party (Schoorman et al., 2007). Extant research on trust has identified dispositional, situational and relational factors as antecedents of trust (Gargiulo and Ertug, 2006). In this chapter we are interested in individuals' trust in the institution of business, or *all* businesses, rather than a specific business.

Two definitions of trust have tended to be used interchangeably in the management and organizational literature, despite subtle differences

(Colquitt and Rodell, 2011). However, our interest in the institutional level leads us to prefer one approach. The most commonly used trust definition in organizational scholarship is attributed to Rousseau and her colleagues (1998), who define trust as a willingness to be vulnerable based on the positive expectations of the intentions or behavior of others. An alternative is attributed to Mayer and colleagues (1995), who define trust as the willingness to be vulnerable to the actions of a trustee on the basis of the expectation that the trustee will perform a particular action, irrespective of any monitoring or controls. While both recognize that trust is based in the willingness to be vulnerable, Rousseau and colleagues see trust based only on positive expectations, whereas Mayer and colleagues also note the role for monitoring and controls (Colquitt and Rodell, 2011).

Mayer and colleagues' definition for research on trust in business is particularly salient to trust in business as an institution because it encompasses monitoring and reliability, which are levers that governments tend to use to increase the public's trust in business. For example, the US Consumer Financial Protection Bureau was recently tasked with monitoring financial services firms on behalf of consumers, and created in response to a recent crisis of trust in the financial services sector connected to the recession. Further back, the Security and Exchange Commission (SEC) was created in 1933 in the aftermath of the stock market crash to monitor business on behalf of investors with the hope of restoring trust in the markets and, therefore, encouraging investment and promoting a healthier overall economy.

Assuming that the 'willingness' to be vulnerable infers a conscious decision, this definition raises two issues. First, it implies that individuals are aware that they have some risk exposure to the institution of business (as opposed to the specific businesses they deal with regularly). Second, it implies that people allow themselves to be vulnerable to business *willingly*.

IS WHAT WE CALL 'TRUST' ACTUALLY TRUST?

Despite the alarm of regulators and pundits about declining trust in business, it is not clear what this decline actually *means*. While we can observe a decline in the measure of trust in business, the measure used to track 'trust' is generally the single-item confidence measure, which was originally penned for the General Social Survey (GSS) over 40 years ago. The measure reads, 'How much confidence do you have in [business and industry]?' and responses are captured using Likert-type scales, generally with three to five response levels. While this is a fair question, there are

Table 9.1 Results from an open-ended question asking people what they mean by the word 'confidence'

Key Word or Concept	Proportion of Responses in Each Category
Trust	34.5
Capability	15.9
Believe in	12.4
Faith	10.0
Miscellaneous	5.4
Honesty	4.3
Common good	3.7
Dependability	3.4
Approval	3.0
Incorrect response	3.0
Sure	2.2
Don't know, nothing	2.2
	100.0

Note: N = 830 responses from 738 cases.

Sources: Data are from 1978 NORC General Social Survey. Reproduced from Smith et al. (1980).

myriad possibilities for what 'confidence' might mean to respondents in this context.

Despite the importance placed on the confidence measure, we are aware of only one study, Smith et al. (1980), which specifically examines the meaning of the word 'confidence' in the GSS measure. In a post-interview debrief, a randomly selected representative subsample of 1978 GSS respondents were asked two open-ended questions. These were, 'When we ask about "confidence" in these questions, what does that mean to you?', and, 'Is there a word that would be more clear than "confidence" but would describe the same idea?' Ninety-five percent of respondents provided definitions; and the overall favorite definition was that confidence in the people running institutions meant trusting them (Smith, Taylor and Mathiowetz, 1980). Results of the survey are represented in Table 9.1.

In addition to the statistics represented above, roughly 12.5 percent of respondents gave multiple responses, and 'trust' was the most common response that accompanied other responses (Smith et al., 1980). When asked to provide a suitable replacement for 'confidence', 58 percent replied that there was no substitute. Those who preferred alternatives tended to give the same list they had mentioned previously, with 20 percent naming 'trust' (48 percent), 4 percent 'faith', 3.5 percent 'believing in', 3 percent 'dependability', 3 percent 'honesty', 2 percent 'capability', 1 percent 'respect', 1 percent 'approval' and 5 percent of responses were coded miscellaneous/incorrect. All categories overlapped, except for 'common good' and 'personal approval', suggesting these are distinct from each other. Smith et al. (1980) organized the responses into four thematic categories: trust (34.5 percent); faith/belief (22.4 percent); capability/dependability/sure (21.5 percent); and common good/honesty/approval (11 percent).

On the surface, it appears that these results indicate that the meaning of the 'confidence' items is highly consistent with the dimensions of trustworthiness specified in organizational scholarship (for example, Mayer et al., 1995; Rousseau et al., 1998; Schoorman et al., 2007). That is, confidence is a psychological state that can be measured attitudinally (for example, Rousseau et al., 1998) based on an assessment of the characteristics (for example, ability, integrity and benevolence) of a focal object (for example, Mayer et al., 1995; Schoorman, et al., 2007). It is not clear that this measure represents 'trust' as a willingness to be vulnerable. Given the importance placed on inferences drawn from this measure and the shift in results over time, more work is warranted to understand related meanings.

Regardless of its meaning, a single item measure offers limited and potentially misleading information for scholars seeking to research how to repair trust in business (and other major institutions, for that matter). Researchers who study trust repair following its violation (for example, Kim et al., 2004, 2006; Pfarrer et al., 2008; Dirks et al., 2009) are careful to point out that different causes of trust violation require different facets of trustworthiness to repair. The single item measure fails to offer any means of understanding the nature of a trust violation, and it makes it impossible to track if the trustworthiness facet related to it is improving. For example, if trustworthiness is based on features related to ethics and competence, what might the creation of the Consumer Financial Protection Bureau (CFPB) in the USA do for assessments of the trustworthiness of the financial system? Might it alleviate concerns related to the function of the banking system? Might its creation also reinforce the idea that financial services companies are unethical? If we rely on single-item confidence measures, increases in competence-based trustworthiness facets might be under-reported due to declines in ethical-based trustworthiness. Clearly, a measure that captures this complexity would be useful. In the following sections we offer suggestions for what such a measure might capture.

A SIMPLIFIED VIEW OF INSTITUTIONS

How should we think about institutions? Clearly they are not all the same. Some are merely longstanding social traditions, like the institution of marriage. Some institutions can have a specific meaning, often referring to specific functional areas in society, such as the public transit system or the electrical grid or professional baseball. Although institutions certainly have much to do with myth and ceremony (for example, Durkheim, 1965), they are also much more than just myth and ceremony. North (1981, pp. 201–2) defines institutions as 'a set of rules, compliance procedures and moral and ethical behavioral norms designed to constrain the behavior of individuals in the interests of maximizing the wealth or utility of principals'. When political scientists talk about various institutions (for example, Braithwaite, 1998; Kim, 2005; Levi and Stoker, 2000; Warren, 1999) they generally refer specifically to those institutions that have some sort of explicit function in society. These are often referred to as 'major' institutions (for example, the National Opinion Research Center, or NORC). For example, the General Social Survey in the USA classifies the following as major institutions: the military; government; organized religion; education; and business. While the institution of business is generally considered a 'major' institution in society, it has some differences from other major institutions.

When thinking about institutions, organizational and management scholars tend to draw from theories in sociology (Bachmann and Inkpen, 2011). There are multiple camps within sociology that differ around what institutions are, and what role they play in society. These views tend to follow structural, functional, cultural, or symbolic interactionist perspectives, and tend to fundamentally disagree on the epistemological and ontological issues around how scholars should think about institutions. For example, Anthony Giddens (1984) takes a relatively functional view of institutions, arguing that institutions are structural arrangements of rules of behavior to which individual and collective action is oriented. Harold Blumer (1969) takes a symbolic interactionist perspective, arguing that institutions are simply symbolic statements that coordinate social behaviors. Thus, from Giddens's (1984) perspective, institutions are objectively 'real' things that are experienced jointly by a society; from Blumer's (1969) perspective, institutions exist solely in the minds of people and can only be jointly experienced through social interaction within a society. To be clear, each of these perspectives has merit. However, they are alone incomplete. If we take a philosophical approach informed by pragmatism (for example, Wicks and Freeman, 1998), we can say that functional, cultural and symbolic features – at least to some degree – jointly describe the institution of business. Too much emphasis on the ontological separations between academic subfields can impede scholars from thinking about things in more constructive and useful ways.

As a practical matter, institutions are often simply large organizations. Governments, for example, have identifiable leaders, a set of employees and a set of responsibilities to stakeholders that the organization is oriented towards (for example, Barnard, 1938). That said, the institution of business is not an organization, at least not in descriptive terms. It is not consciously coordinated; there is no identifiable leader; it is not a discrete entity, and so on. However, the way people *perceive* business, we would argue, is similar to how they think of other major institutions. While the institution of business is not an observable entity, and it does not move in an *intentionally* coordinated fashion, it does often move in a somewhat coordinated way, and it is – at least through the actions of specific businesses – observable (DiMaggio and Powell, 1983; Zucker, 1987). Business has a broadly understood responsibility in society – at a minimum, to create value for its key stakeholders (for example, Friedman, 1970; Freeman, 1984; Freeman et al., 2010). While there is no 'leader' that directs the affairs of the entire institution of business, who can be held to account when the institution fails to deliver on expectations, most people can conceive of what type of person that leader might be (for example, Bachmann and Inkpen, 2011). If we think about the institution of business as an organization, we can apply exchange models of attitude formation, like relational-based theories of trust, in addition to models of generalized trust.

TRUST IN BUSINESS: GENERALIZED TRUST, DISPOSITIONAL TRUST AND RELATIONAL TRUST

We tend to trust the businesses we deal with locally, but tend not to be willing to extend that trust to the institution of business (Cook and Schilke, 2010). We tend to trust our local politicians, but not politicians in general (Parker and Parker, 1993; Cook, 2001) and we tend to trust our own doctors, but not the health care system in general. People readily give their credit cards to online retailers they have never used before, suggesting they have faith in some regulatory body that makes transacting with a stranger over the internet a safe activity. But when you *ask* them if they trust institutions, and particularly economic ones, they often say no.

Every transaction with a business contains elements of vulnerability. By purchasing packaged food at a grocery store, I am consciously deciding to purchase food and accept some risk that the food could be spoiled, or poisonous, rather than grow my own food to reduce or eliminate the risk. However, this risk is seldom consciously acknowledged by individuals when they hand money to the grocery store cashier. Why? Because they have a general sense that business is trustworthy. People will opt to buy one manufacturer's products and not another's based on the trust they have in that manufacturer (for example, Tylenol). Few people actually opt out of interacting with business – no matter how low levels of trust are in business as an institution.

Trust can be the result of calculation of risk, or based on an automatic response (Cook, 2001). Calculative trust in some object tends to be informed through prior experiences that a trustor has with it (Mayer et al., 1995). Automatic forms of trust tend to be described in two ways – dispositional (for example, a feature of a person's personality), and generalized (for example, a feature of generalized culture or external environment). Dispositional trust tends to describe a person's natural proclivity towards trusting other people (Rotter, 1967; Gurtman, 1992; Bianchi and Brockner, 2012). To differentiate dispositional trust from generalized trust, dispositional trust levels tend to vary by person, but tend to be relatively stable with an individual over time. Generalized trust, however, tends to be widely distributed across groups of people, and is not stable over time.

This suggests that trust in business is based both on relational factors (prior experiences) and some form of generalized trust (either through widespread cultural practices or institutional protection). Scholars tend to treat relational forms of trust and generalized forms of trust separately. However, consistent with our view of institutions, it is logical to think that both relational and generalized forms of trust would be relevant to explaining actual behaviors. Relational, generalized and dispositional paths to trust are likely to play a role in the formation of trust in business as an institution. But it is currently unknown *how* they will be relevant and under what conditions. We explore relational trust and generalized trust in more detail in the next two sections.

Relational Trust

The relational view of trust formation, derived primarily from exchange theory (for example, Cook and Emerson, 1978), claims that individuals form trustworthiness attitudes based on transactions with the object in question (Mayer, Davis and Shoorman, 1995; Cook and Schilke, 2010). This form of trust has received considerable theoretical and empirical support (for example, Zand, 1972; Cook and Emerson, 1978; Mayer et al.,

1995; Robinson, 1996; Tyler et al., 1996; Brockner et al., 1997; Mayer and Davis, 1999; Schoorman et al., 2007; Cook et al., 2009). While the models differ, they are functionally similar. For example, Mayer et al.'s (1995) organizational trust model claims that the willingness to be vulnerable is a decision based on an assessment of *trustworthiness* (a trustor's assessment of a trustee based on relevant criteria). McAllister (1995) argues that that trust is based on cognitive (for example, what is the risk of trusting this object?) and affective (for example, do I like this object?) assessments. Scholars have argued that integrity and benevolence are synonymous in certain contexts, such as with trust repair (for example, Kim et al., 2004). Others refer to *competence* and *benevolence* (for example, Bromiley and Cummings; 1995; Zaheer et al., 1998; Bromiley and Harris, 2006; Harris and Wicks, 2010). In practice, the differences between these various terms and conceptions of trustworthiness are minor, and all have received considerable empirical support (Schoorman et al., 2007). For consistency with our view of trust, we will begin with Mayer and colleagues' trustworthiness construct, which consists of three facets: *ability* (is the object skilled at the relevant task?); *benevolence* (will the object take my interests into consideration?); and *integrity* (does this object seem to display acceptable values?) (ibid.).

People can't transact directly with the institution of business as a whole, nor would they realistically consider business in general to be 'committed' to them in future exchanges (for example, Cook et al., 2009). It is likely that people's transactions with representative agents of business, or business entities, serve to partially inform trustworthiness assessments of business as an institution. But it is also likely that the prior exchanges might not be as strongly associated with trustworthiness assessments as they would be in interpersonal or even organizational trust, where the trustee is less amorphous. Therefore, relational models are incomplete when we apply them at the institutional level (Cook, 2005). Theories of generalized trust can fill this void.

Generalized Trust

Generalized trust can refer to the quality of institutional protections that facilitate trust, or to the shared norms and familiarity rooted in tightly knit social networks (for example, Arrow, 1974; Granovetter, 1985; McKnight et al., 1998; Uzzi, 1999; Cook et al., 2009; Harrison et al., 2009; Kaina, 2011). Individuals tend to conform to the rules and belief systems prevailing in a given environment (Meyer and Rowan, 1977; DiMaggio and Powell, 1983; Suchman, 1995; Deephouse, 1996; Dacin, 1997). For example, Gambetta (2000) showed how trust can be conferred and inferred through a complex, specific and universally understood language of signaling in the setting of organized crime. Similarly, Meyerson et al. (1991) observed that a well-established selection process can produce a quickly emergent trust amongst people on film sets who may begin their interaction as strangers. Additionally, some recent research has shown that in situations of high institutional risk and uncertainty, networks of trust emerge to facilitate social exchange, as has been the case in Russia's transition from communism to capitalism (Cook, 2005). In these cases, strong cultural norms and tight networks facilitated exchange between strangers.

The key influences of generalized trust are the institutions that facilitate it (McEvily et al., 2006). The overall strength of their influence rests in their ability to steer behaviors and cover all contingencies (Kaina, 2011). Viktoria Kaina (2011, p.284) argues that, 'Institutions both enable and motivate people to cooperate with anonymous others, and that repeated successful cooperation will bring about trust in strangers. This is based on two factors: (1) institutions' standing and stability; and (2) institutions' efficacy'. Clearly, therefore, when understanding generalized trust in business, it is also important to consider generalized trust in the institutions that facilitate trust in business (for example, legal and regulatory entities, as well as social custom).

What happens when the underlying institutions themselves lack robustness (c.f., Mair and Marti, 2009)? For example, does increased governmental regulation cause individuals to desire less monitoring because they feel protected? Or might government regulation increase the perceived need to monitor because the mere existence of regulation suggests that business is fundamentally untrustworthy? ('If banks weren't crooked, why would we need a protection agency?'). Given the low levels of trust in most governments, these questions warrant more study.

The influence of other institutions on the institution of business is an interesting topic with many open questions. For example, some major institutions function both to shape generalized trust and to influence relational trust. The media shapes generalized trust through an editorial perspective (Giddens, 1984), and accounts about business in the news media shape the way that business is perceived by the public (Gauntlett, 2008). To the extent that the media shapes general perceptions it will also shape generalized trust (Schein, 1996), and influence how individuals respond to the environment. But the media also provides people with a sort of proxy interaction, in that it allows them to passively observe other people interacting with businesses. It therefore will provide individuals with data from which to assess the trustworthiness of all businesses (Schoorman et al., 2007). These two features will likely interact in interesting ways. As individuals aggregate their respective experiences of trust in particular businesses, the influence of exogenous narratives about business through the media will likely influence their attitudes, both directly and indirectly (Harris and Wicks, 2010). A negative overarching narrative about business could have a diminishing effect on a person's trust in business, even if his or her individual experiences have been positive.

If trust in business is based on generalized and relational factors, which type of trust matters more in terms of shaping behaviors? If so, is this relationship categorical or context-dependent? Some factors that could influence this may be related to an individual's experience with business. A person who has experienced repeated exchanges with an object will be more likely to rely on those exchanges for his or her assessment (Cook and Emerson, 1978; Butler, 1983; Dasgupta, 1988; Davis et al., 1989; Meyer et al., 1992). The degree to which a person would consider herself embedded in business culture might predict her assessment of the trustworthiness of business (for example, Jost et al., 2004; Tajfel and Turner, 2004). For instance, a university professor might tend to trust business less than an executive at a large company. Further investigating such questions is an important avenue for future research.

A MULTIPLEX VIEW OF THE PUBLIC

While much research in arenas of public opinion treats 'the public' as a monolithic entity, a stakeholder perspective challenges the validity of this conception. A recent empirical study by Pirson and Malhotra (2011) shows that stakeholder group influences how stakeholders trust a specific firm. They found that six facets of trustworthiness (benevolence, integrity, managerial competence, technical competence, transparency and identification) vary systematically as one moves across different stakeholder roles. One way to think about 'the public' is in terms of an aggregation of stakeholder groups (for example, employees, customers, investors and community members).

Whereas we tend to have consistent relationships to other major institutions (we are civilians in relation to the military and voters in relationship to government), all of us are simultaneously customers, employees, community members, investors in relation to business. With few exceptions (for example, Easley and Lenox, 2006; Goodstein and Wicks, 2007), the literature on stakeholders has proceeded with the assumption that the firm is at the 'center', focusing on the way in which firms interact with, or respond to, their stakeholders. However, extending recent work that explores the differential values of various stakeholder groups (for example, Harris and Wicks, 2010; Pirson and Malhotra, 2011), we suggest that research in this area should explore a deeper understanding of how a stakeholder role impacts a person's conception of (and attitudes towards) the institution of business. If stakeholder groups differ in terms of what they expect from specific businesses, shouldn't stakeholder groups also differ in what they value from all businesses – or business in general? If so, what are the conditions under which stakeholders will differ, and how might they differ?

Not only are there many different stakeholder roles one can occupy in relation to the institution of business but also the kind of trust that may be most important can vary across roles. Scholars maintain these differences are tied in part to the fact that each role carries a different set of expectations and responsibilities (for example, Harris and Wicks, 2010; Pirson and Malhotra, 2011). Thus, a critical challenge for future research may be not only understanding stakeholder roles and the particular opportunities and challenges they present, but also finding ways to highlight and shape stakeholder mindset (in other words, which 'role' is most salient to a stakeholder at a given time) when assessing the trustworthiness of business. It is likely that a person's stakeholder role mindset will interact with other influences we have identified so far. For example, from the perspective of an employee a news story about a company that is cutting costs and cutting staff is likely to reduce that person's trust in business (given the priority of job security for an employee). However, from the perspective of an investor, it may be that the very same story would increase that person's trust in business (given their interest in profits and financial returns). This area presents a set of important open questions for future research. What do different types of stakeholders pay attention to, and why? How do these different types of stakeholders approach the firms they associate with, and how does their relevant role (for example, employee, customer) influence their approach? How does one's stakeholder role impact the decision to trust a particular firm? How does it impact one's trust in business in general? These questions represent a series of additional avenues for future research in public trust.

STUDY DESIGN AND MEASUREMENT

The proliferation of operational definitions has left some rather large holes in our understanding of public trust (Bachmann and Zaheer, 2006), and particularly how public trust in institutions is formed (Cook and Schilke, 2010). However, because trust is a thoroughly researched concept, and many theories of trust are well-formed and mature, we can test extant theories of trust formation from social and organizational fields using quantitative methods (Edmondson and McManus, 2007).

Trust in business is based on both objective (for example, Giddens) *and* subjective (for example, Blumer) factors. When researching what drives trust in institutions, scholars should pay attention not only to the 'observable' or 'structural' factors (such as policies, regulation and oversight), but also to the less 'observable' factors (such as culture and individual attitudes). Measuring either one without the other is likely to yield an incomplete picture of what is driving behavior. For our purposes, sociologist Sharon Hays (1994) presents a particularly useful perspective that reconciles dichotomous views of institutions. Drawing from Giddens (1984), Bourdieu (1984), Foucault and Hurley (1978), Foucault and Gordon (1980), Mannheim (1971, 1985) and Geertz (1973), she concludes that institutions consist of two central and interconnected elements: systems of social relations and systems of meaning. Systems of social relations are 'real' in the sense that their form is observable from the outside looking in, and their effects can be quantified and reasonably determined. The laws under which businesses operate can be considered 'systems of social relations' because they prescribe how business is conducted and lay out the rules of the game. These are objective and observable through an examination of relevant legal code. Systems of meaning exist in people's minds and may or may not conform to what we could describe as 'objective' reality. These are not observable without getting inside individuals' minds – for example, through self-report questionnaires or participant observation. To study the public's trust in business, we need to consider both the subjective and objective features associated with it. Therefore, when scholars are measuring individual trust in business, we would recommend both a generalized measure (in other words, the confidence item) and a measure from organizational trust, such as the Mayer and Davis (1999) trust inventory, revised for the institutional level of analysis. For example, when we think about the *ability* of business, predictability (Zaheer et al., 1998) and displaying logical behavior patterns (Child and Möllering, 2003) are likely to be relevant features that are not captured in Mayer and Davis's (1999) inventory. Further exploration of this kind of extension, and devising theory and methods to support it, are ripe opportunities for scholars.

The vast majority of research in trust relies on self-report methods. In the laboratory and under controlled environments, this is not a problem for internal validity. However, self-report measures can be notoriously bad at predicting behaviors (Nisbett and Wilson, 1977), and thus can be a source of threat to external validity. It is likely that some factors associated with trust in institutions (as compared to more concrete objects) that will influence their behaviors are either difficult to assess by respondents or informed by cognitive processes that operate unconsciously. Therefore we advocate the use of behavioral measures as a vital source of information to enhance the quality of research in this domain.

There are many options available to researchers, and we will highlight two that we think are very promising. Most rely on the use of real money and involve situations in which a participant is at risk of being taken advantage of by another participant (or confederate). The Investment Game (also called the Trust Game) is the most common situation used to study behavioral trust (for example, Glaeser et al., 2002). The general form is as follows: there are two players, the sender and the receiver. At the beginning of the game the sender has $X. The sender decides how much of the money he would like to invest (the sender will keep the money that he does not invest). The receiver gets 3X the amount that the sender invests, and then decides how much money to return to the sender (and how much to keep for herself). This game tends to be most effective in a laboratory setting. McEvily and colleagues (2008) created a version that can be used in field and quasi-experimental settings. Their measure captures the extent to which individuals purchase insurance when they are dependent on the trustworthiness of strangers.

Ideally, researchers will employ both self-report and behavioral measures when possible. But there are other means of measuring the implied cognitive processes that separate self-report results from behavioral results. The most reliable method of which we are aware is the Implicit Association Test (IAT) (Nosek et al., 2007; Schnabel et al., 2008; Greenwald et al., 2009). In the IAT, subjects are asked to pair stimulus categories (for example, 'self' and 'other' in a measure of self-concept), to external concepts that represent semantically polar descriptors like 'fun' and 'boring', or 'bad' and 'good' as quickly as possible. The speed at which a person is required to respond in order to complete the task successfully requires that he or she cannot engage the conscious mind (Nosek et al., 2007). The latency between matching assignments indicates an implicit preference for one pairing (for example, business and bad) over another (for example, business and good).

CONCLUSION

One way to think about this relational/generalized distinction is through Giddens's (1990) discussion on abstract properties of institutions and access points to institutions. In his view, the ways in which people behave vis-à-vis institutions is based on an overarching shared view of the institution (its abstract properties), and their direct experiences with it (through access points). In the case of business, the shared view is likely derived through a variety of factors – including governmental regulation and oversight, entrenched cultural practices and mass communication vehicles that have an editorial point of view, such as the mass media. The access points that most people experience are through their transactions with individual businesses as customers, employees, investors, community members, and so on. It is therefore important to consider experiences (which influence relational trust) and externalities (which influence generalized trust) as a means of explaining the public's trust in business – both to understand more fully what the aggregate measure means and what might be done to alter it.

Arrow (1974) argued that institutions resolve issues of distributive fairness that are not resolvable between citizens. In a market economy, one of the government's principal roles is to make secondary institutions (such as business) seem trustworthy by implementing regulatory reassurances. But, as he points out, institutional safeguards have to be carefully balanced. Eventually if all we rely upon is institutional trust, relational trust will erode. When cognitive assurances are amplified, the corollary effect is that people tend to assume that a focal object is less trustworthy (Meyer et al., 1995).

Arrow's insights have implications for repairing the public's trust in business, particularly at a time when we are trying to recover from the 2008 financial crisis. Trust repair between an organization and its stakeholders occurs through two routes – improving the relational experiences (for example, Bies, 1987; Carter and Dukerich, 1998) (which falls on the shoulders of individual businesses) and implementing institutional reforms to regulate distrust (for example, Sitkin and Roth, 1993; Lewicki and Bunker, 1996) (which falls on the shoulders of institutional factors like government and the media). Unfortunately these forces are not coordinated, nor are we always able to determine how effective each is in isolation – let alone how they might interact in a given context. We also know that institutional forms of support for trust (for example, legislative solutions such as the Sarbanes-Oxley Act or the creation of the US Consumer Financial Protection Bureau) are expensive and have major limitations (for example, focusing on problems from the crisis that just occurred rather than anticipating and preventing kinds of problems that are likely to cause the next crisis). They also tend to erode relational trust (which may also be critical to restore), and may only make marginal improvements in the overall level of trust in business. As Nicole Gillespie and Robert Hurley argue in Chapter 8 of this volume, economic incentives might skew these relationships. The financial incentives in the system encouraged a willful blind trust in situations where there should have been some healthy suspicion. These complications limit our ability to make a normative recommendation for *how* to restore widespread trust in the institution of business.

Given the critical importance of a healthy economy to our overall social welfare, and the implications (financial, personal and political) of how we address the topic of public trust in business, the time is ripe for us to make public trust in business a subject of sustained scholarly attention. This chapter provides scholars and managers some guidance for *where* to look and *what* to look for to better understand the dynamics around public trust in business – including how might we understand it and go about trying to improve it (c.f., Poppo, Chapter 6 this volume). In this chapter we highlight the complex nature of trust in business and provide a framework with which researchers can use to understand and investigate it. To summarize the work of George Herbert Mead, in unstructured settings the introduction of symbolic statements can order perception so that the symbolic presentation is perceived as real (Cuzzort and King, 1989, p. 130). Ultimately, attitudes towards an institution are based on a collective set of beliefs about its role in society, and perceptions about how observed events match or do not match with expectations. Given that the institution of business is unstructured by design, it presents numerous challenges to our existing models of trust, and therefore opportunities for future research that could yield contributions of value both to theory and society.

REFERENCES

Arrow, K.J. (1974), *The Limits of Organization*, New York: W.W. Norton & Company.
Bachmann, R. and A.C. Inkpen (2011), 'Understanding institutional-based trust building processes in inter-organizational relationships', *Organization Studies*, **32**(2), 281–301.
Bachmann, R. and A. Zaheer (2006), 'Introduction', in R. Bachmann and A. Zaheer, *Handbook of Trust Research*, Cheltenham, UK and Northampton, MA, USA: Edward Elgar, pp. 1–12.
Barnard, C. (1938), *The Functions of the Executive*, Cambridge, MA: Harvard University Press.
Bianchi, E.C. and J. Brockner (2012), 'In the eyes of the beholder?: the role of dispositional trust in judgments of procedural and interactional fairness', *Organizational Behavior and Human Decision Processes*, **118**(1), 46–59.
Bies, R.J. (1987), 'Beyond "voice": the influence of decision-maker justification and sincerity on procedural fairness judgments', *Representative Research in Social Psychology*, **17**(1), 3–14.
Blumer, H. (1969), *Symbolic Interactionism: Perspective and Method*, Berkeley, CA: University of California Press.
Bourdieu, P. (1984), *Distinction*, Cambridge, MA: Harvard Business Press.
Braithwaite J. (1998), 'Institutionalizing distrust, enculturating trust', in M. Levi and V. Braithwaite (eds), *Trust and Governance*, New York: Russell Sage Foundation, pp. 343–75.
BRICE (2004), *Mapping the Terrain Issues that Connect Business and Ethics*, Charlottesville, VA: Business Roundtable Institute for Corporate Ethics.

Brockner, J., P.A. Siegel, J.P. Daly, T. Tyler and C. Martin (1997), 'When trust matters: the moderating effect of outcome favorability', *Administrative Science Quarterly*, **42**(3), 558–83.
Bromiley, P. and L.L. Cummings (1995), 'Transaction costs in organizations with trust', in R. Bies, B. Sheppard and R. Lewicki (eds), *Research on Negotiation in Organizations*, Vol. 5, Greenwich, CT: JAI Press, pp. 219–47.
Bromiley, P. and J. Harris (2006), 'Trust, transaction cost economics, and mechanisms', in R. Bachmann and A. Zaheer (eds), *The Handbook of Trust Research*, Cheltenham, UK and Northampton, MA, USA: Edward Elgar, pp. 124–43.
Butler, J.K. (1983), 'Reciprocity of trust between professionals and their secretaries', *Psychological Reports*, **53**(2), 411–16.
Carter, S. and J. Dukerich (1998), 'Corporate responses to changes in reputation', *Corporate Reputation Review*, **1**(3), 250–70.
Child, J. and G. Möllering (2003), 'Contextual confidence and active trust development in the Chinese business environment', *Organization Science*, **14**(1), 69–80.
Cialdini, R.B. (1993), *Influence – The Psychology of Persuasion*, New York: Auflage.
Colquitt, J.A. and J.B. Rodell (2011), 'Justice, trust, and trustworthiness: a longitudinal analysis integrating three theoretical perspectives', *Academy of Management Journal*, **54**(6), 1183–206.
Cook, K.S. (2001), 'Trust in society', in Karen S. Cook (ed.), *Trust in Society*, New York: Russell Sage Foundation, pp. xi–xxviii.
Cook, K.S. (2005), 'Networks, norms, and trust: the social psychology of social capital', *Social Psychology Quarterly*, **68**(1), 4–14.
Cook, K.S. and R.M. Emerson (1978), 'Power, equity and commitment in exchange networks', *American Sociological Review*, **43**(5), 721–39.
Cook, K.S. and O. Schilke (2010), 'The role of public, relational and organizational trust in economic affairs', *Corporate Reputation Review*, **13**(2), 98–109.
Cook, K.S., M. Levi and R. Hardin (eds) (2009), *Who Can We Trust?: How Groups, Networks, and Institutions Make Trust Possible*, New York: Russell Sage Foundation Publications.
Cuzzort, R.P. and E.W. King (eds) (1989), *Twentieth Century Social Thought*, Chicago: Holt, Rinehart and Winston.
Dacin, M.T. (1997), 'Isomorphism in context: the power and prescription of institutional norms', *Academy of Management Journal*, **40**(1), 46–81.
Dasgupta, P. (1988), 'Trust as a commodity', in D. Gambetta (ed.), *Trust: Making and Breaking Cooperative Relations*, Cambridge, MA: Blackwell, pp. 49–72.
Davis, J., L. Helms and A. Henkin (1989), 'Strategic conventions in organizational decision making: applications from game theory', *International Review of Modern Sociology*, **19**(1), 71–85.
Deephouse, D.L. (1996), 'Does isomorphism legitimate?', *Academy of Management Journal*, **39**(4), 1024–39.
DiMaggio, P.J. and W.W. Powell (1983), 'The iron cage revisited: institutional isomorphism and collective rationality in organizational fields', *American Sociological Review*, **48**(2), 147–60.
Dirks, K.T., R.J. Lewicki and A. Zaheer (2009), 'Repairing relationships within and between organizations: building a conceptual foundation', *Academy of Management Review*, **34**(1), 68–84.
Durkheim, E. (1965), *The Elementary Forms of Religious Life*, Old Tappan, NJ: Free Press.
Edmondson, A.C. and S.E. McManus (2007), 'Methodological fit in management field research', *Academy of Management Review*, **32**(4), 1155–79.
Easley, C. and M.J. Lenox (2006), 'Firm responses to secondary stakeholder action', *Strategic Management Journal*, **27**(8), 765–81.
Foucault, M. and C. Gordon (1980), *Power/Knowledge*, New York: Pantheon Books.
Foucault, M. and R. Hurley (1978), *The History of Sexuality. Vol. 1: An Introduction*, London: Penguin.

Freeman, R.E. (1984), *Strategic Management: A Stakeholder Approach*, Boston: Pitman.
Freeman, R.E., J.S. Harrison, A.C. Wicks, B.L. Parmar and S. de Colle (2010), *Stakeholder Theory: The State of the Art*, Cambridge, UK: Cambridge University Press.
Friedman, M. (1970), 'The social responsibility of business is to increase its profits', *New York Times Magazine*, **32**(13), 122–6.
Fukuyama, F. (1995), *Trust: The Social Virtues and the Creation of Prosperity*, New York: Free Press.
Gambetta, D. (2000), 'Can we trust?', in D. Gambetta (ed.), *Trust: Making and Breaking Cooperative Relations*, Oxford: Basil Blackwell, pp. 213–37.
Gargiulo, M. and G. Ertug (2006), 'The dark side of trust', in R. Bachmann and A. Zaheer (eds), *Handbook of Trust Research*, Cheltenham, UK and Northampton, MA, USA: Edward Elgar, pp. 165–86.
Gauntlett, D. (2008), *Media, Gender and Identity: An Introduction*, New York: Psychology Press.
Geertz, C. (1973), *The Interpretations of Cultures*, New York: Basic Books.
Giddens, A. (1984), *The Constitution of Society: Outline of the Theory of Structuration*, Cambridge, UK: Polity.
Giddens, A. (1990), *The Consequences of Modernity*, Palo Alto, CA: Stanford University Press.
Glaeser, E.L., D. Laibson and B. Sacerdote (2002), 'An economic approach to social capital', *The Economic Journal*, **112**(11), 437–58.
Goodstein, J.D. and A.C. Wicks (2007), 'Corporate and stakeholder responsibility: making business ethics a two-way conversation', *Business Ethics Quarterly*, **17**(3), 375–98.
Granovetter, M. (1985), 'Economic action and social structure: the problem of embeddedness', *American Journal of Sociology*, **91**(3), 481–510.
Greenwald, A.G., T.A. Poehlman, E. Uhlmann and M.R. Banaji (2009), 'Understanding and using the Implicit Association Test III: Meta-analysis of predictive validity', *Journal of Personality and Social Psychology*, **97**(1), 17–41.
Gurtman, M.B. (1992), 'Construct validity of interpersonal personality measures: the interpersonal circumplex as a nomological net', *Journal of Personality and Social Psychology*, **63**(1), 105–18.
Hardin, R. (2002), *Trust and Trustworthiness*, New York: Russell Sage Foundation Publications.
Harris, J.D. and A.C. Wicks (2010), '"Public trust" and trust in particular firm–stakeholder interactions', *Corporate Reputation Review*, **13**(2), 142–54.
Harrison, J.S., D.A. Bosse and R.A. Phillips (2009), 'Managing for stakeholders, stakeholder utility functions, and competitive advantage', *Strategic Management Journal*, **31**(1), 58–74.
Hays, S. (1994), 'Structure, agency and the sticky problem of culture', *Sociological Theory*, **12**(1), 57–72.
Jacobe, D. (2011), 'Americans trust governors, business leaders most on economy', *Gallup*, accessed 3 October 2011 at http://www.gallup.com/poll/147095/Americans-Trust-Governors-Business-Leaders-Economy.aspx.
Jost, J.T., M.R. Banaji and B.A. Nosek (2004), 'A decade of system justification theory: accumulated evidence of conscious and unconscious bolstering of the status quo', *Political Psychology*, **25**(6), 881–919.
Kaina, V. (2011), 'Why do we trust strangers? Revising the institutional approach to generalized trust creation', *West European Politics*, **34**(2), 282–95.
Kim, J-Y. (2005), '"Bowling together" isn't a cure-all: the relationship between social capital and political trust in South Korea', *International Political Science Review*, **26**(2), 193–213.
Kim, P.H., K.T. Dirks, C.D. Cooper and D.L. Ferrin (2006), 'When more blame is better than less: the implications of internal vs. external attributions for the repair of trust after a competence- vs. integrity-based trust violation', *Organizational Behavior and Human Decision Processes*, **99**(1), 49–65.
Kim, P.H., D.L. Ferrin, C.D. Cooper and K.T. Dirks (2004), 'Removing the shadow of

suspicion: the effects of apology vs. denial for repairing competence- vs. integrity-based trust violations', *Journal of Applied Psychology*, **89**(1), 104–18.

Kramer, R.M. and K.S. Cook (2004), 'Introduction', in R.M. Kramer and K.S. Cook (eds), *Trust and Distrust in Organizations: Dilemmas and Approaches*, New York: Russell Sage Foundation Publications.

Lane, C. and R. Bachmann (1998), *Trust Within and Between Organizations: Conceptual Issues and Empirical Applications*, New York: Oxford University Press.

Levi, M. and L. Stoker (2000), 'Political trust and trustworthiness', *Annual Review of Political Science*, **3**(1), 475–507.

Lewicki, R.J. and B.B. Bunker (1996), 'Developing and maintaining trust in work relationships', in R. Kramer and T.R. Tyler (eds), *Trust in Organizations: Frontiers of Theory and Research*, Thousand Oaks, CA: Sage, pp. 114–140.

Mair, J. and I. Marti (2009), 'Entrepreneurship in and around institutional voids: a case study from Bangladesh', *Journal of Business Venturing*, **24**(5), 419–35.

Mannheim, K. (1971), *From Karl Mannheim*, Oxford: Oxford University Press.

Mannheim, K. (1985), *Ideology and Utopia*, San Diego: Harcourt Brace Jovanovich.

Mayer, R.C. and J.H. Davis (1999), 'The effect of the performance appraisal system on trust for management: a field quasi-experiment', *Journal of Applied Psychology*, **84**(1), 123–36.

Mayer, R.C., J.H. Davis and F.D. Schoorman (1995), 'An integrative model of organizational trust', *Academy of Management Review*, **20**(3), 709–34.

McAllister, D.J. (1995), 'Affect and cognition-based trust as foundations for interpersonal cooperation in organizations', *Academy of Management Journal*, **38**(1), 24–59.

McEvily, B., J.R. Radzevick and R.A. Weber (2008), 'Whom do you mistrust and how much does it cost? An experiment on the measure of trust', *Games and Economic Behavior*, **74**(1) 285–98.

McEvily, B., R. Weber, C. Bicchieri and V. Ho (2006), 'Can groups be trusted? An experimental study of trust in collective entities', in R. Bachmann and A. Zaheer (eds), *Handbook of Trust Research*, Cheltenham, UK and Northampton, MA, USA: Edward Elgar, pp. 52–68.

McKnight, D.H., L.L. Cummings and N.L. Chervany (1998), 'Initial trust formation in new organizational relationships', *Academy of Management Review*, **23**(3), 473–90.

Meyer, J.W. and B. Rowan (1977), 'Institutionalized organizations: formal structure as myth and ceremony', *American Journal of Sociology*, **83**(2), 340–63.

Meyer, M., P. Milgrom and J. Roberts (1992), 'Organizational prospects, influence costs, and ownership changes', *Journal of Economics & Management Strategy*, **1**(1), 9–35.

Meyerson, D., K.E. Weick and R.M. Kramer (1996), 'Swift trust and temporary groups', in R.M. Kramer and T.R. Tyler (eds), *Trust in Organizations: Frontiers of Theory and Research*, Thousand Oaks, CA: Sage, pp. 166–95.

Nisbett, R. and T. Wilson (1977), 'Telling more than we can know: verbal reports on mental processes', *Psychological Review*, **84**(3), 231–59.

North, D.C. (1981), *Structure and Change in Economic History*, New York: Norton.

Nosek, B.A., F.L. Smyth, J.J. Hansen, T. Devos, N.M. Lindner, K.A. Ranganath, C.T. Smith, K.R. Olson, D. Chugh and A.G. Greenwald (2007), 'Pervasiveness and correlates of implicit attitudes and stereotypes', *European Review of Social Psychology*, **18**(1), 36–88.

Parker, S.L. and G.R. Parker (1993), 'Why do we trust our congressman?', *The Journal of Politics*, **55**(2), 442–53.

Pfarrer, M.D., K.A. DeCelles, K.G. Smith and M.S. Taylor (2008), 'After the fall: reintegrating the corrupt organization', *Academy of Management Review*, **33**(3), 730–49.

Pirson, M. and D. Malhotra (2011), 'Foundations of organizational trust: what matters to different stakeholders', *Organization Science*, **22**(4), 1087–104.

Putnam, R.D. (2000), *Bowling Alone: The Collapse and Revival of American Community*, New York: Simon and Schuster.

Robinson, S.L. (1996), 'Trust and breach of the psychological contract', *Administrative Science Quarterly*, **41**(4), 574–99.

Rotter, J.B. (1967), 'A new scale for the measurement of interpersonal trust', *Journal of Personality*, **35**(4), 651–65.
Rousseau, D.M., S.B. Sitkin, R.S. Burt and C. Camerer (1998), 'Not so different after all: a cross-discipline view of trust', *Academy of Management Review*, **23**(3), 393–404.
Schein, E.H. (1996), 'Culture: the missing concept in organization studies', *Administrative Science Quarterly*, **41**(2), 229–40.
Schnabel, K., J.B. Asendorpf and A.G. Greenwald (2008), 'Using implicit association tests for the assessment of implicit personality self-concept', in G.J. Boyle, G. Mathews and D. Saklofske (eds), *Sage Handbook of Personality Theory and Assessment*, Thousand Oaks, CA: Sage, pp. 508–28.
Schoorman, F.D., R.C. Mayer and J.H. Davis (2007), 'An integrative model of organizational trust: past, present, and future', *Academy of Management Review*, **32**(2), 344–54.
Sitkin, S.B., and N.L. Roth (1993), 'Explaining the limited effectiveness of legalistic remedies for trust/distrust', *Organization Science*, **4**, 367–92.
Smith, T.W., D.G. Taylor and N.A. Mathiowetz (1980), 'Public opinion and public regard for the federal government', in C. Weiss and A. Barton (eds), *Making Bureaucracies Work*, Beverly Hills, CA: Sage, pp. 37–63.
Stickel, D., R.C. Mayer and S.B. Sitkin (2009), 'Understanding social capital: in whom do we trust?', in V. Bartkus and J.H. Davis (eds), *Social Capital: Multi-disciplinary Perspectives*, Cheltenham, UK and Northampton, MA, USA: Edward Elgar Publishing, pp. 302–16.
Suchman, M.C. (1995), 'Managing legitimacy: strategic and institutional approaches', *Academy of Management Review*, **20**(3), 571–610.
Sztompka, P. (1999), *Trust: A Sociological Theory*, Cambridge, UK: Cambridge University Press.
Tajfel, H. and J. Turner (2004), 'The social identity theory of intergroup behavior', in J. Sidanius and J. Jost (eds), *Political Psychology: Key Readings*, New York: Psychology Press, pp. 276–93.
Tyler, T.R. and R.M. Kramer (1996), 'Whither trust?', in R.M. Kramer and T.R. Tyler (eds), *Trust in Organizations: Frontiers of Theory and Research*, Thousand Oaks, CA: Sage, pp. 1–14.
Tyler, T., P. Degoey and H. Smith (1996), 'Understanding why the justice of group procedures matters: a test of the psychological dynamics of the group-value model', *Journal of Personality and Social Psychology*, **70**(5), 913–30.
Uzzi, B. (1999), 'Embeddedness in the making of financial capital: how social relations and networks benefit firms seeking financing', *American Sociological Review*, **64**(4), 481–505.
Warren, M.E. (1999), *Democracy and Trust*, Cambridge, UK: Cambridge University Press.
Wicks, A.C. and R.E. Freeman (1998), 'Organization studies and the new pragmatism: positivism, anti-positivism, and the search for ethics', *Organization Science*, **24**(2), 123–40.
Zaheer, A. and J.D. Harris (2006), 'Interorganizational trust', in O. Shenkar and J.J. Reuer (eds), *Handbook of Strategic Alliances*, Thousand Oaks, CA: Sage, pp. 169–97.
Zaheer, A., B. McEvily and V. Perrone (1998), 'Does trust matter? Exploring the effects of interorganizational and interpersonal trust on performance', *Organization Science*, **9**(2), 141–59.
Zand, D.E. (1972), 'Trust and managerial problem solving', *Administrative Science Quarterly*, **17**(2), 229–39.
Zucker, L.G. (1987), 'Institutional theories of organization', *Annual Review of Sociology*, **13**, 443–64.

PART V

THEORETICAL ADVANCES

10. Trust and the economic theory of the firm
Jackson Nickerson, Timothy Gubler and Kurt T. Dirks

INTRODUCTION

During the past two decades the literatures on strategic management and organizational theory have exploded with papers studying the impact of trust on exchange relationships, be they dyadic or within a network.[1] Scholars have investigated how trust can be built (Gulati, 1995; Nooteboom, 1996; Zaheer et al., 1998; Lorenz, 1999; Lewicki et al., 2006), how it is maintained and used (Barney and Hansen, 1994; Nooteboom et al., 1997; Zaheer et al., 1998; Dirks et al., 2009; Gillespie and Dietz, 2009), the ways in which trust is damaged (Robinson, 1996; Zaheer et al., 1998), and the implications on the relationship when it is lost (Bies and Tripp, 1996; Dirks and Ferrin, 2001). Most of the research adopts units of analysis that reflect inter-personal relationships. For example, scholars in organizational behavior mostly explore how trust operates within groups or between superiors and subordinates (Dirks and Ferrin, 2001; Ferrin et al., 2006). Some scholars have explored the role of trust in the structuring and performance of inter-organizational exchanges (Chiles and McMackin, 1996; Nooteboom, 1996; Nooteboom et al., 1997; Gulati and Nickerson, 2008), including the role of inter-personal trust in inter-organizational trust (for example, Zaheer et al., 1998). Other scholars have investigated the extent to which pre-existing trust influences the choice of a firm's decision to make, buy, or ally, and the extent to which a particular governance choice encourages the emergence of trust during the exchange relationship (Williamson, 1996; Malhotra and Murnighan, 2002; Ferrin and Dirks, 2003; Gulati and Nickerson, 2008).

While much progress has been made in understanding the role of trust in exchange relationships, an area of unrealized potential involves the role of trust in the economic theory of the firm.[2] The economic theory of the firm is a central tent pole for strategic management and organization theory. It attempts to understand the purpose of the firm, why and where its boundaries are formed, how it selects its members, how it organizes and shapes the behavior of its members, and how all of these decisions translate into organizational performance outcomes (Williamson, 1975, 1985; Klein et al., 1978). The discriminating alignment hypothesis that informs much of the economic theory of the firm holds that exchanges, which differ in their characteristics, are aligned with governance structures (for example, market, hybrid, or hierarchy), which differ in their costs and competencies, in a discriminating way (Williamson, 1991). While scholars have shown that trust can act as a shift parameter and raise the switchover level from market to hybrid to hierarchy by reducing exchange hazards (Chiles and McMackin, 1996; Gulati and Nickerson, 2008), less is known about how the structural competencies inherent in the differing governance structures impact the organization's ability to build and maintain trust with exchange partners. This relationship is a hitherto underexplored yet key element to the economic theory of the firm.

In this chapter we seek to explore the extent to which the institutional archetypes of markets, hybrids and hierarchies vary in their capacity to support the building and maintenance of trust. Previous work relating trust to governance choice has focused on the benefits of trust in exchanges including lower transaction costs, increased knowledge sharing and increased coordination (Zaheer et al., 1998; Dyer and Chu, 2003) and how trust subsequently can influence governance choice (Chiles and McMackin, 1996; Gulati and Nickerson, 2008). Other work has also highlighted how trust can lead to exchanges built more on relationships or social structure (Uzzi, 1997; Dyer and Singh, 1998). Relatively few studies have looked, however, at how the inherent structural characteristics of each governance mode endogenously impact, both positively and negatively, the building of trust and its maintenance. We assert that a complete theory of the firm needs to understand this key relationship and provide insight into how it influences firm performance.

A vast amount of research highlights how markets, hybrids and hierarchies differ in the structure and relative strength of their incentives, administrative controls and conflict resolution methods including access to external contract law. Moreover, much theory has been proposed as to how these characteristics differentially affect the behavior and outcomes of exchanges (Williamson, 1975, 1985, 1991; Klein et al., 1978; Grossman and Hart, 1986; Hart and Moore, 1990). We suggest that this analysis is particularly well suited as a starting point in understanding how trust is differentially affected in each governance form by the structure and strength of each of these factors.

Our chapter reviews the literature on trust in the context of the economic theory of the firm. We provide a definition of trust and outline three mechanisms through which trust can be built. We then briefly review key fundamentals to the economic theory of the firm from the transaction cost economics perspective and review the literature that connects this theory to the building and use of trust in organizations. Lastly, we review the recent literature on the maintenance of trust, for which repairing trust is the central issue, and outline three processes of trust repair, highlighting aspects of repair that can be influenced by governance structure. We conclude that the role of trust in the economic theory of the firm remains preliminary, partial and piecemeal and overlooks our key question of how differing governance alternatives endogenously affect the building and maintenance of trust in exchange relationships.

With this background in hand, we launch an exploration of how the inherent differences in governance alternatives can influence each build and repair mechanism. We find that trust is endogenously impacted both positively and negatively in different ways by markets, hybrids and hierarchies and that this difference can yield varying performance outcomes. Furthermore, we find that managers have a key role to play in which the role and its potential implications depends on the managerial resources available given the governance mode. That said our exploration is not a theory-building exercise. Instead, our intent is to understand the potential for developing theory and to identify key elements of a possible theory to incorporate trust more fully into the economic theory of the firm. If successful, we anticipate future research will develop the theory not only with respect to the economic theory of the firm but also with respect to how leaders can better manage the building and maintenance – including the repair – of trust.

We finish our exploration by emphasizing three apparent paradoxes regarding trust and the choice of governance. While the paradoxes provide counterpoints to our exploration of trust in the context of the economic theory of the firm, our review suggests a potential path to resolve them. Managers, we argue, potentially play a pivotal role and are commonly overlooked in the economic theory of the firm. Incorporating the managerial role and notions of adept versus inept decisions and behaviors into the theory may help to resolve the paradoxes. We then conclude.

LITERATURE REVIEW

While many definitions of trust exist, we adopt a multidisciplinary definition that describes interactions both within and between firms as put forth by Rousseau et al. (1998). Trust is defined as a 'psychological state comprising the intention to accept vulnerability based upon positive expectations of the intentions or behavior of another' (ibid., p. 395).[3] It is important to highlight that trust is based on expectations about the future intentions or behavior of an exchange partner. These expectations have two main foundations: trust stemming from the relationship between exchange partners, either dyadic or in larger groups, and trust stemming from the exchange structure or some other outside party. While both are important and related, we largely focus on trust that is built and maintained by the exchange structure itself with support from management. That said, we do highlight the linkage between the two – how exchange structures can influence the building and maintaining of trust between exchange partners.[4]

Extant literature emphasizes three main ways through which trust is built both at the micro and macro levels. The first is through direct interaction between parties. Interaction allows each party to cultivate a relationship built on experience. Thus, exchange partners observe each other's behavior and draw inferences upon which expectations of future behavior and trustworthiness are built (Lorenz, 1999). Expectation building can occur between individuals (Ferrin et al., 2006), between individuals and an organization (Robinson, 1996), or between organizations (Gulati, 1995; Zaheer et al., 1998; Lorenz, 1999). Uncertainty is reduced over time as parties continue to interact and become more familiar with each other (Gulati, 1995). Thus, expectation building is a dynamic learning process wherein organizations are constantly updating perceptions of their counterparts and determining whether or not they can increase their level of trust.

The second way trust is built relies on the existence of a social structure in which exchange dyads are embedded. Social structure can transmit information about pre-existing trustworthiness and allows for reputation effects (Uzzi, 1997; Ferrin et al., 2006). Reputation effects increase incentive for trustworthy behavior to occur because otherwise a loss of reputation could expand beyond the focal relationship. Parties make inferences about trustworthiness both from the direct information they receive as well as from indirect information supplied by the social structure. Some mechanisms that lead to the creation of social structure are interorganizational asset connectedness, partner scarcity, resource indivisibility and co-evolution of capabilities, and a socially complex and difficult to imitate institutional environment (in other words, country-specific environment) (Dyer and Singh, 1998).

The last way trust is built is through formal structural factors. Formal structures provide differential incentives, administrative controls, conflict resolution methods and access to contract law that can influence trust positively or negatively. While formal governance structures have been shown to decrease exchange hazards (Klein et al., 1978; Williamson, 1985) and promote cooperation (Bromiley and Cummings, 1995; Zaheer et al.,

1998), they may also inhibit the building of trust between exchange partners directly through the problem of attribution. Attribution occurs when exchange partners attribute good behavior to structure instead of the other party, which results in little residual trust when the formal structure is removed (Malhotra and Murnighan, 2002; Ferrin and Dirks, 2003). It is precisely in formal governance structures, however, that trust is assumed to be of most benefit to the firm in reducing transaction costs and promoting cooperation. We therefore believe that integrating trust into the economic theory of the firm is needed to expose new insights into the extent to which each alternative structure supports and discourages the building and maintenance of trust.

The theory of the firm seeks ultimately to explain the organization of firms in a world in which potentially costly vulnerability creates exchange hazards. These hazards stem from the fact that agents are self-interested, sometimes with guile, and can act opportunistically, especially as their circumstances change (Klein et al., 1978; Williamson, 1979). Coase asserts that formal organizations arise precisely for this reason – to provide a mechanism for minimizing transaction hazards when the cost of transacting through a market is high (1937). Hazards to exchange largely result from the combination of three factors: asset specificity, frequency and uncertainty (Williamson, 1985). The discriminating alignment hypothesis that informs much of the economic theory of the firm holds that exchanges, which differ in their characteristics, can be aligned with governance structures, which differ in their costs and competencies, in a discriminating way (Williamson, 1991). To emerge and thrive, a governance structure must address the problems of adapting, coordinating and safeguarding exchanges more efficiently than alternative governance structures (ibid.).

Previous work has shown that trust and formal governance structures can function as partial substitutes. Many studies show that relational exchanges based on trust can substitute for complex contracts or vertical integration (for example, Granovetter, 1985; Bradach and Eccles, 1989; Gulati, 1995; Uzzi, 1997; Bernheim and Whinston, 1998; Dyer and Singh, 1998; Adler, 2001). Substitution comes from that fact that trust can allow for higher levels of cooperation (Barney and Hansen, 1994; Bromiley and Cummings, 1995; Zaheer et al., 1998; Dyer and Chu, 2003) and function as a more effective and less costly self-enforcement mechanism than some formal governance structures (Hill, 1990; Chiles and McMackin 1996; Uzzi, 1997; Gulati and Nickerson, 2008). These findings follow Arrow's (1974) observation that 'trust is an important lubricant of the social system' that adds efficiency to many economic exchanges. While the lubricant does not eliminate all frictions and replace governance structures in their entirety, trust can either act as a 'shift parameter' that lowers the cost of each governance mode (Chiles and McMackin 1996; Gulati and Nickerson, 2008), or can lead to a relational governance structure that uses trust and other informal safeguards to facilitate efficient exchange (for example, Uzzi, 1997; Dyer and Singh, 1998). In either case, governance is less costly and more efficient because of trust. The obverse and less common view, which is that structure (or trust in structure) can at times partially substitute for trust that occurs directly between exchange partners, is where this chapter seeks to make a contribution.

Trust and formal governance structures can also function as complements. Following North's assertion that 'formal rules can complement and increase the effectiveness of informal constraints' (1990, p. 46), scholars have found that higher levels of relational governance (via trust) are often coupled with customized complex contracts (for example, Poppo and Zenger, 2002) and that formal structure can enhance the level of trust among collaborators (Lorenz, 1999; Coletti et al., 2005). Some scholars have even argued that formal governance is essential for trust to be beneficial to exchange performance (Lazzarini et al., 2004). One key way trust can function as a complement is by allowing firms to both avoid conflict and to resolve it more quickly when it arises (for example, Uzzi, 1997; Dyer and Singh, 1998; Gulati and Nickerson, 2008). Gulati and Nickerson (2008) find that trust enhances exchange performance across all governance modes, the benefits being greatest for markets, followed by hybrids and then hierarchies.

While there is evidence that formal structure and trust can be either substitutes or complements for each other, it remains ambiguous how formal structures influence the building of trust. For instance, work on relational governance and social structures explores how frequent interactions between dependent exchange partners in a formal governance structure can lead to a separate governance mechanism that uses trust and other informal safeguards to facilitate efficient exchange. Increasing trust allows cooperation between a pair or network of firms and allows them to jointly own and utilize critical resources that span firm boundaries and that may be embedded in interfirm routines and processes (Uzzi, 1997; Dyer and Singh, 1998). Gulati (1995) observed such a pattern in alliances, finding that many alliances begin with the use of formal governance mechanisms and then progressively move towards more informal ones, mainly as a result of increased trust. Recent work has also argued, however, that formal governance structures are unable to build and support high levels of trust because of either a problem of attribution (Malhotra and Murnighan, 2002) or from formal structures 'crowding out' intrinsic motivation (such as trust) with external interventions (for example, Titmuss, 1970; Frey and Oberholzer-Gee, 1997; Uzzi, 1997). Some scholars have even argued that formal contracts can potentially encourage opportunistic behavior and undermine trust by signaling distrust to exchange partners (Macaulay, 1963; Ghoshal and Moran, 1996). These competing theories highlight the need for increased attention to how formal structure influences the building of trust.

While the building of trust has received much attention by researchers, only recently has increasing focus been placed on how trust is maintained and repaired between organizations. Exchange relationships can begin with a high level of trust (Kim et al., 2004). Trivially, trust is maintained as each party performs in a way that will not damage positive expectations. Trust, however, can be damaged. Damage through incidents that violate expectations causes positive expectations to be replaced by negative ones, motivating firms to restrict exposing to future vulnerability (Robinson, 1996; Lewicki et al., 1998). Breach of trust in these settings can result in reduced willingness for workers to share information and cooperate (Dirks and Ferrin, 2001) and may even result in acts of retaliation (Bies and Tripp, 1996). Trust can take months or years to build, while a single incident may violate expectations and severely damage trust. Furthermore, while research suggests that trust can be repaired (Dirks et al., 2009), how conflict and negative events are resolved are crucial to the future health of the relationship (Driver et al., 2003).

The current trust repair literature[5] emphasizes three main goals: trust repair, restoring positive exchange and reducing negative affect (Dirks et al., 2009). Three processes allow for the accomplishment of these goals: an attributional process, a social equilibrium process and a structural process (ibid.).[6] The attributional process builds on attribution theory (Heider, 1958) and emphasizes that to repair trust the offended party must perceive that the transgression does not reflect the true nature of the violator, or that the true nature of the violator has changed (Dirks et al., 2009). While time and continued expectation building through exchange with 'good' behavior serves to slowly restore positive expectations, believable apologies and accounts (Kim et al., 2004, 2006; Tomlinson and Mayer, 2009) and credible substantive actions to demonstrate trustworthiness (Gillespie and Dietz, 2009), such as voluntarily introducing monitoring systems and sanctions (Nakayachi and Watabe, 2005), can change perceptions, thereby repairing trust more rapidly in these instances. Managers also may play a key role by influencing perceptions and assigning blame.

The social equilibrium process refers to repairing the social and interpersonal aspects of the relationship by resolving a disequilibrium that results when transgressions impact the social order of the relationship (Goffman, 1967) and impact the social norms (in other words, resolving disputes in good faith, norms of reciprocity, fairness and so on) that once provided an economically beneficial self-enforcement mechanism to govern the exchange (Granovetter, 1985; Uzzi, 1997). Goffman argues that relationship repair does not occur in a vacuum. Transgressions call into question the prevailing norms that once governed the relationship and consequently result in reduced willingness for exchange partners to interact in the future. Ren and Gray (2009) posit that effective repair must reaffirm the norms governing interaction at two levels: the individual level and the dyadic level. Repair at the individual level removes negative emotions associated with the transgression and replaces them with a feeling of satisfaction with the restorative actions taken. Repair at the dyadic level entails restoring the social order by recommitting to the norms that govern the relationship and expressing a desire for continued interaction. Repair hinges on the reestablishment of social order by restoring the standing of the parties as well as the norms that govern them through various restorative actions (Goffman, 1967; Ren and Gray, 2009). Such actions may include penance, punishment and apologies (Bottom et al., 2002; Reb et al., 2006; Ren and Gray, 2009). Restorative actions allow exchange partners to 'settle the accounts' and to reestablish positive expectations through continued interaction.

The third process used in trust repair is structural in nature. Structural processes involve changing the context within which relationships are situated and consist of changing the structure, incentives and systems to shape behavior in such a way as to discourage future transgressions and restore positive expectations (Sitkin and Roth, 1993; Dirks et al., 2009). Changes to incentives may include adopting lower-powered incentives that dull the connection between pay and performance, or through crafting incentives that encourage cooperation such as compensating or promoting based on group performance. The introduction of financial penalties for the observation of particular behaviors also changes incentives. An example of changing the structure is through managers changing job descriptions to influence the role actors play in the exchange. While repair through formal structures has been shown by some scholars to inhibit trust repair by placing a barrier between parties that results in increased distance, formality and rules (for example, Granovetter, 1985; Zucker, 1986; Shapiro, 1987), other scholars have argued that structural remedies can be effective in repairing trust when violations are specific to a particular task or context (Sitkin and Roth, 1993). We argue that more attention is needed in order to better understand how structural factors and third parties such as managers influence the maintenance and repair of organizational trust.

Upon reviewing the literature it is apparent to us that the extant literature provides at best a fragmented and partial theory of trust and the economic theory of the firm. While there is a broad literature focusing on how trust impacts governance, the benefits to trust in exchanges, and the mechanisms that build and maintain trust in general, less is known about how the internal workings of governance structures impact the building and maintaining of trust – or how trust is endogenously impacted by governance structures. Furthermore, existing studies present at best mixed results. In the sections that follow we outline some fundamental elements that provide the groundwork for the further integration of trust and the economic theory of the firm.

THE NEED FOR TRUST IN THE ECONOMIC THEORY OF THE FIRM

We follow the standard assumption of Transaction Cost Economics (TCE) and assume that agents may act opportunistically and are boundedly rational. Increased incentive and opportunity, which implies probability of opportunistic behavior, follows mainly from three attributes of exchanges: asset specificity, uncertainty and frequency. Of the three, asset specificity, measured in terms of the difference in an asset's current value compared to value in its next best use, is the most impactful (Williamson, 1985). Asset specificity arises when exchanges require significant relation-specific investments in physical and/or human capital. Asset-specific investments transform the exchange from one in which relationship is irrelevant to one wherein maintenance of the relation is of paramount importance (Williamson, 1991). Continued exchange and preventing hold up is essential to capture the value created by these specialized investments (Klein et al., 1978).

The second factor, increases in uncertainty, in conjunction with asset specificity, results in a more complex contracting environment and leads to a heightened threat of opportunism through the need to adjust contracts ex post in response to unforeseeable changes. Third, recurrent transactions, especially in conjunction with asset specificity and uncertainty, not only affords the opportunity for cost-saving benefits through relation-specific investments and cooperation but also places pressure on an exchange through increasing the amount of contact, coordination and adaptation required to continue the exchange relationship (Williamson, 1991). We assume frequency and repeated ties as being driven primarily by asset specificity and its resulting co-dependency. Thus, for the purpose of pushing the theory forward we assume, all else being equal, that the higher levels of co-dependency, which leads to the choice of hybrids over markets and hierarchy over hybrids also leads to increased needs for coordination and necessitates increased contact, which results in increased frequency and in the number of repeated ties.

Firms can reduce exchange hazards in two ways. The first and perhaps more costly alternative is through adoption of a formal governance structure. For instance, the likelihood of opportunistic behavior can decrease as a firm increases administrative controls, utilizes low-powered incentives, offers career paths and adopts specialized monitoring by vertically integrating the exchange. The second way is through basing the exchange on a relationship of trust. Trust can respond positively to these hazards by allowing for more efficient ex post contracting (Gulati, 1995; Uzzi, 1997; Poppo and Zenger, 2002), increased cooperation (Bromiley and Cummings, 1995; Zaheer et al., 1998), and for the use of less costly governance structures to govern these idiosyncratic exchange relationships (Bradach and Eccles, 1989; Gulati, 1995; Chiles and McMackin, 1996; Gulati and Nickerson, 2008). Were relationship-based trust perfect there would be no threat of opportunism and each of these exchange hazards would be insignificant. However, as risk of opportunism is assumed present, trust based on relationships can at best substitute for formal structure, with potential cost-saving benefits. The key theoretical question then is to what extent formal structures influence, positively or negatively, the building and maintenance of trust.

GOVERNANCE STRUCTURES AND SUPPORT OF TRUST

Our exploration in this section seeks to understand the potential for developing theory and to identify key elements of a possible theory to incorporate trust more fully into the economic theory of the firm. The following analysis proposes that the alternative governance structures of markets, hybrids and hierarchies display different *capacities* for building and maintaining trust (see Table 10.1). Moreover, these capacities are not 'automatically' exercised by structural choice alone. Instead, we argue that utilizing at least some of these capacities requires managerial intervention, which is feasible and more efficacious in some organizational alternatives than others. Adept managers can help build and maintain trust while inept managers can inhibit its development and undermine it. It is critical to note that even though more formal organizational forms enjoy more mechanisms to build trust and processes to repair trust, these advantages may not automatically lead to increased trust between exchange partners when compared to less formal organizational forms that enjoy lower levels of asset specificity. For instance, even though hierarchies have access to

Table 10.1 *Governance structures of markets, hybrids and hierarchies displaying different capacities for building and maintaining trust*

	Governance Structure		
	Markets	Hybrids	Hierarchies
Build Direct interaction	Expectations build with experience: • Usually infrequent exchanges Individuals: • Few expectations • Difficult measurement • Few signals of commitment Trust between individuals	Expectations build with experience: • Usually more frequent than markets Contract: • Defines expectations • Defines measurements • Signals commitment between organizations Trust between individual and organizations	Expectations build with experience: • Usually more frequent than hybrids Managers: • Shape expectations • Engage in measurement • Shape commitment Trust between individuals in organization
Embedded in a social structure	Initial condition: • No embeddedness Embeddedness: • Develops slowly over time • Low need for adaptation • Individuals in a community Reputation not economically substantial: • Weak ties in community • Not much to lose at stake	Initial condition: • Embeddedness within each organization Embeddedness: • Develops faster than in markets • Moderate need for adaptation • Emerges between individuals and organizations Reputation economically substantial: • Moderate levels of co-specialization • Strong and weak ties	Initial condition: • Embeddedness in an organization Embeddedness: • Develops faster than in hybrids • High need for adaptation • Emerges within the organization Reputation economically substantial: • High level of co-specialization • Strong ties

Table 10.1 (continued)

	Governance Structure		
	Markets	Hybrids	Hierarchies
Build			
Structural factors	High-powered incentives	Intermediate-powered incentives	Low-powered incentive
	Structure based on classical contracting (court system):	Structure based on excuse doctrine:	Structure based on forbearance:
	• Protects against illegal activity	• Relieves parties from strict outside enforcement	• Disputes resolved internally
	• Low-cost switching of exchange partners	• Cooperate and adjust contract with court as a last appeal	• Access to fiat
	Contract:	Contracts:	• Courts do not intervene
	• Simple	• Contracting as a framework for exchange and allows for adaptability	Managers:
	Monitoring:	• Courts as last resort, uncertainty in decision	• Identify where trust is needed and adapt incentives and exchange structure to support it
	• Monitors of output	Monitoring advantages compared to markets	Monitoring advantages compared to hybrids
	Weak employee career concerns	Career concerns within each organization	Stronger employee career concerns than hybrids
Maintain			
Attributional process	Good behavior slowly rebuilds trust:	Good balance rebuilds trust quicker than in markets:	Good behavior rebuilds trust quicker than in hybrids:
	• Usually infrequent exchanges	• Usually more frequent than markets	• Usually more frequent than hybrids
	• Slow and imperfect process	Contracts:	Managers:
	Individuals:	• Contract provides framework	• Managerial oversight
	• Weak credibility for apologies	• More credibility for apologies and accounts	Managers:
	Replace exchange partner		• Most credibility for apologies and accounts

Social equilibrium process	Very weak from little embeddedness: • Few social norms Individuals: • Punish via exit • Restorative actions have very little economic value • Weak apologies and accounts	• Shift attribution • Binds offender to substantive actions Terminate or punish offending employees	Stronger than markets from increased embeddedness: • More social norms Contracts: • Punish via contract • Terminate employees • Binds offender to restorative actions • More credible apologies and accounts	• Shape attribution • Bind offender to substantive actions • Shape measurement Terminate, punish, move offending employees Change job description Stronger than hybrids from increased embeddedness: • Most social norms Managers: • Punish via authority • Terminate or move employees • Bind offender to restorative actions • Change job descriptions • Offer or encourage apologies to offended parties
Structural process	Classical contracting (court system): • Outside enforcement only Simple contracts: • Unable to change exchange structure, terms or incentives		Excuse doctrine: • Outside enforcement available • Can resolve disputes internally Contracts: • Renegotiate or rewrite contract to change structure, terms or incentives	Forbearance: • No outside enforcement • Disputes must be resolved internally Managers: • Change structure, terms or incentives through fiat

increased mechanisms and processes to support the building and maintenance of trust compared to hybrids, the overall level of trust in hybrids could be higher. Thus, support of trust should not be confused with the resulting outcome or level of trust.

We focus our analysis in two ways. First we outline the key differences between governance alternatives based on three attributes: internal incentives intensity, administrative controls and conflict resolution mechanisms. When formality of the governance structure increases, internal incentive intensity decreases and the influence of administrative controls and access to internal conflict resolution increases. Moreover, changes in governance structure dictate the contract law and social structure that supports the exchange. For instance, markets are characterized by classical contract law and little social structure. It organizes and governs exchanges under the bounds set by the law. Hierarchies, on the other hand, rely on forbearance, social norms and the adeptness of managers to govern exchanges. Differences in contract law and social structure also impact the employee relationships and allow managers different tools to influence the exchange relationship. For example, hierarchies allow managers to move employees or reassign them to different jobs in order to influence the exchange relationship. Market exchanges enjoy no such option. Understanding these differences in governance alternatives and managerial oversight provides a basis for understanding exchange relationships in each structure and, consequently, each structure's ability to support trust.

The second way we focus our analysis is through assessing how the attributes of governance structures affect the three mechanisms for building trust and the three processes of trust repair previously outlined in the literature review. Trust is built through direct interaction, interaction within a social structure, and through formal structural factors. Trust is maintained and potentially repaired through an attributional process, a process that restores social equilibrium, and through a structural process. The inherent attributes of governance structures impact each of these building and repair mechanisms in different ways. For instance, because of the lack of internal conflict resolution methods and administrative controls in markets, trust repair relies mainly on appeal to the law. Legal recourse, however, provides little benefit to trust repair as it does not resolve the attribution problem, restore social equilibrium, or place structural safeguards in place to reduce future opportunism. Hierarchies, on the other hand, have access to administrative controls and conflict resolution mechanisms that allow managers to influence and even manipulate social mechanisms in order to restore trust. For example, managers may take the blame for an action between parties that damages trust (an attributional repair process) thereby restoring positive expectations between the two partners. The following analysis seeks to better understand the linkage between these governance attributes and the mechanisms that build and maintain trust.

MARKETS' ABILITY TO BUILD AND MAINTAIN TRUST

Markets have little need for trust and have few mechanisms to support its building and maintenance. Low asset specificity, near perfect information, standardized goods, strong property rights and the functioning of an efficient price mechanism allows exchanges where, 'Faceless buyers and sellers ... meet in the marketplace for an instant to exchange standardized goods at equilibrium prices' (Ben-Porath, 1980, p. 4). The strength of markets lies in its ability to execute routine tasks efficiently (Ghoshal and Moran, 1996). Moreover, minimal needs for co-specialization allow dealings to take place at an 'arm's-length', and thus relationships beyond the focal exchange are rare (Williamson, 1979). Exchange efficiency is found through agents acting in self-interested ways largely without regard to the welfare of others (Smith, 1776). Furthermore, the presence of many outside options coupled with high-powered incentives leads to relatively little cooperation or coordination. Administrative controls in market structures are weak, supplanted instead by binding legal rules that rely mainly on government or the court system to enforce and only guard against explicit illegal behavior. Conflict resolution is similarly solved externally through classical contract law (legal recourse), or through replacing the exchange relationship altogether.

While pure markets that satisfy all these conditions are rare, this polar case provides the base from which to understand the relative strengths and weaknesses of markets in comparison to hybrids and hierarchies. Pure markets that satisfy these conditions have little need for trust and similarly possess few mechanisms to build and maintain it. As pure markets break down, for instance from the introduction of asset specificity or mutual dependence, the need for trust increases, creating additional pressure for organizations to adopt a more formal organizational structure.

Markets and Building Trust

To better understand the extent to which trust can be built in markets, we review the three principal mechanisms through which trust is built: direct interaction, embeddedness and structural supports.

242 *Handbook of advances in trust research*

Direct interaction
Market structures largely rely on the mechanism of direct interaction to build trust between individuals. Exchange partners are chosen based on price and initial positive expectations. Expectation building then occurs as partners interact and update their expectations based on behavior. Future interaction and the building of future trust depend on trust built through previous experience. Expectation building through experience alone can be a slow process because market exchanges are usually less repetitive and are often infrequent. It is also an imperfect process, compounded by the fact that expectations, aside from those explicitly illegal, are often either unclear or not formally stated and shared. Consequently, exchange partners may find evaluating their performance, relative to expectations, difficult because few expectations may exist. While market exchanges carry relatively few expectations (Williamson, 1979; Ben-Porath, 1980), they also do not inherently possess many signals of commitment, which contributes to slow and imperfect expectation building.

Embeddedness
Embeddedness in a social structure facilitates little building of trust in markets. Weak ties between individuals in a community develop slowly when interactions are not frequent. If the initial condition in the community is the absence of embeddedness, then building trust through an interaction mechanism can be slow and results in little trust (Williamson, 1985; Good, 1988; Gulati, 1995). Investments in co-specialized assets generate a type of embeddedness as the exchange partners come to rely on one another. Yet, as the need for co-specialization and consequently the possibility of loss of economic value is low in market settings, exchange partners have little need to depend on embeddedness for reputation, which can be shared throughout an embedded community. Instead partners expect 'sharp in by clear agreement [and] sharp out by clear performance' (MacNeil, 1974). Low co-specialization also results in little need for adaptation and consequently less benefit to embedded relationships.[7]

Structural supports
Structural supports in markets also only weakly support the building of trust. Market exchanges rely on high-powered incentives, which directly allow actors to increase their individual return through an increase of effort (Williamson, 1985). Such incentives, coupled with the low cost of switching exchange partners, means few opportunities to be opportunistic, decreased motivation to cooperate, and weak employee career concerns (Williamson 1985, 1991). The structure of markets is based on classical contracting, or the court system. While the law protects against

illegal activity, it leaves other aspects of the exchange, such as incentive intensity, untouched. Thus, the law is limited in mitigating 'legal' opportunism. Lastly, supports for monitoring effort and factor inputs are weak in markets; monitoring typically is restricted to output. Overall, the structural factors of markets fail to decrease opportunism and engender cooperation. They do little to structurally support the building of trust.

Markets and Maintaining Trust

Like the building of trust, market structures have few mechanisms to maintain and repair trust. Trust is maintained in markets as partners choose to act in non-opportunistic ways, especially when their exchange partner is vulnerable. In markets such behaviors include performing in a reliable, predictable and fair way (Zaheer et al., 1998) within the bounds of the law. While research has shown that these exchanges can begin with a fairly high level of pre-existing trust, any breach of expectations can have a large negative impact on trust. We next review the extent to which markets support the three main processes for trust repair: the attributional, social equilibrium and structural repair processes.

Attributional repair process
Markets provide some support for the attributional repair process, but it is slow and imperfect. Trust is naturally repaired if exchange partners continue to interact and the offending party proves that their nature has changed. However, as market exchanges are usually infrequent and expectations are not well defined, reparation through ongoing interaction can be a slow and imperfect process. Markets also allow for apologies and accounts to be given such that the offending party offers an explanation regarding their actions and asks forgiveness. However, given the low level of co-specialization in markets, many partners may find it easier to replace the offending exchange partner altogether instead of providing the opportunity to repair trust.

Social equilibrium repair process
The social equilibrium process of trust repair is similarly limited in markets because of the low level of embeddedness. Markets initially possess few social norms and legal recourse is unable to reestablish or recommit exchange partners to social norms should they be broken. While markets allow for restorative actions such as apologies and punishment, there is little incentive to recommit to norms as little economic value can be created because of low levels of co-specialization. Restoring the social equilibrium may simply be more costly than switching exchange partners.

Structural repair process

Markets provide little support for trust repair through the structural repair process. Markets rely on classical contracting (classical legal recourse) to resolve disputes. Outside enforcement via the courts is rigid, the terms precise and decisions legally binding. Even when contracts are incomplete the courts lack flexibility in how they respond to conflict in the exchange. The lack of internal conflict resolution mechanisms prohibits markets from changing the exchange structure, terms, or incentives in order to restore positive expectations. Instead exchange partners must either rely on legal recourse or choose to replace the exchange partner altogether.

In summary, markets possess few mechanisms that support the building and maintenance of trust. Furthermore, the mechanisms that markets do possess are limited in their speed of building and maintaining trust. Individuals similarly have little ability to influence the building and maintenance of trust in market structures.

HYBRIDS' ABILITY TO BUILD AND MAINTAIN TRUST

Hybrids, in contrast to markets, have greater need for trust and have more mechanisms to support its building and maintenance. The greater need for trust stems from the desire to support adaptation in the presence of co-specialized investments between exchange partners. Asset specificity, uncertainty and frequency in the presence of asset specificity lead to economic exchange hazards, which are mitigated through complex contracting and benefited by trust and cooperation.

Complex contracts may take the form of alliances, joint ventures, franchising, or simply through a well-specified long-term exchange contract. Hybrid forms of governance are characterized by moderate incentive intensity, administrative controls specified in the contract, internal conflict resolution mechanisms specific in the contract, and the use of contract law even though the complexity of hybrid contracts leaves gaps in their completeness, which opens disputes to uncertain legal interpretations (Williamson, 1991). With this definitional background in place, we turn our attention to assessing hybrid governance structures for their ability to build and maintain trust.

Hybrids and Building Trust

Hybrids support the building of trust between organizations as well as individuals through direct interaction, embeddedness in a social structure, and through increased structural supports that are not found in markets. Furthermore, they allow for greater and faster building of trust compared to markets.

Direct interaction
Like markets, expectations are built through exchange experience. Hybrids, however, offer several additional mechanisms for forming expectations that are unavailable in markets. First, exchanges mediated by a contract are usually more frequent than those found in markets because of co-specialization and the increase of repeated network ties, allowing for more positive experience to be built in a given timeframe (Gulati, 1995). All else being equal, trust can build at greater speed in hybrids. Second, contracts define expectations explicitly and thus offer a measuring stick for actors with which to evaluate their behavior. Evaluation enables adjustments to be made that can strengthen positive expectations of trust, which allows partners to contract more efficiently (Mayer and Argyres, 2004) and build trust more quickly as they continue to interact. Third, the act of contracting signals an exchange partner's commitment to working things out in a relationship (Poppo and Zenger, 2002), which further shapes expectations. In combination, the aforementioned mechanisms available in hybrids offer superior support and speed for building expectations of trust compared to markets.

Embeddedness
Hybrids facilitate the building of trust through embeddedness in social structures in a more significant way than do markets. Where the initial condition in markets lacked embeddedness, the initial condition in hybrids entails two or more organizations, with already established deep and broad intra-organizational networks, becoming connected through individuals directly participating in the hybrid relationship. Pre-existing network connections allow reputations from both organizations to be quickly communicated through the newly connected networks (for example, Macaulay, 1963).

Co-specialization, which is the underpinning of hybrids, affects the initial condition of embeddedness within each organization. Trading partners in hybrids often make joint idiosyncratic investments that embed them in a relationship as such investments introduce switching costs and thereby limit alternative exchange partners. The resulting bilateral dependence calls for more flexibility in adapting to and resolving disputes when unforeseen situations arise. Embeddedness facilitates adaptation through reciprocal favors and adherence to social norms without having to appeal to the economic structure alone (Uzzi, 1997). Reputation also becomes increasingly important to both organizations and individuals as negative behavior can impact exchanges beyond the focal one. When an organization does not behave according to the contract, for instance, negative expectations can be passed on to all other potential trading partners, possibly resulting in loss of future exchange. Similarly, individuals that damage a trusting relation and are terminated in one firm may find decreased future employment opportunities because of their negative reputation within the network (for example, Macaulay, 1963).[8]

Structural supports
Hybrids contain additional structural factors compared to markets that support the building of trust. Hybrids sacrifice some internal incentive intensity compared to markets in return for administrative controls and internal conflict resolution mechanisms. Lower incentive intensity decreases the payoff an individual receives from their own effort and can motivate increased cooperation and stronger career concerns (Williamson, 1991). The structure of hybrids relies on contracts built on the excuse doctrine (ibid.). While courts serve as the final appeal, Macaulay observed that 'businessmen often prefer to rely on "a man's word" in a brief letter, a handshake, or "common honesty and decency" – even where the transaction involves exposure to serious risks' (1963, p. 58). Excuse doctrine relieves parties from strict outside enforcement and provides cooperation by allowing exchange partners to adjust the structure and terms of the contract internally. Successful internal cooperation can even lead to heavy reliance on trust and result in more open-ended contracts that are socially, but not legally, binding (Jones et al., 1997). Hybrids also provide monitoring advantages compared to markets because they provide agreed upon focal points in contract evaluation and can facilitate specialized monitoring and increased information-sharing (Dyer and Singh, 1998). Thus, it becomes easier for an exchange partner to observe behavior and form well-informed expectations about future reliability. If exchange partners behave according to expectations, monitoring will increase trust by conveying positive information. Conversely, monitoring can act as a catalyst for contracts to be adjusted to support the building of trust should negative information be received. Overall, hybrids contain many additional structural factors compared to markets that support the building of trust.

Hybrids and Maintaining Trust

Hybrids offer support for maintaining trust in ways unavailable in markets. Indeed, unlike markets, hybrid structures support all three processes of trust repair. Below we explore attributional repair, social equilibrium repair and structural repair processes available in hybrids for maintaining trust.

Attributional repair process
Hybrids provide more support and speed than markets for trust repair through attributional repair processes. Similar to markets, trust can be repaired in hybrids as exchange partners continue to interact and prove their change of nature. Yet hybrids offer an advantage over markets as exchanges and interactions are usually more frequent, providing potential for greater repair speed. Moreover, contracts define expectations and provide a framework upon which partners may focus and model their behavior, which facilitates demonstrably correcting the behavior that initially damaged the relationship.

While hybrids support trust repair through apologies and accounts similar to markets, contracting also provides two major benefits to the attributional repair process not found in markets. First, hybrids can shift attribution from the organization to employees. Over time and through contracting, individual expectations move beyond individual actors and form about the behavior of a partner organization. When such expectations form, organizations have the opportunity to maintain and even build trust by attributing any breach of trust to an individual's motivation and behavior. Such attribution can be made credible by punishing – if not terminating – the offending employee. Second, contracts provide a credible method for offending partners to bind themselves to substantive actions to demonstrate trustworthiness. For instance, violators may voluntarily propose to implement a new monitoring system or to impose sanctions (Nakayachi and Watabe, 2005). Such actions, which may be directly written into the contract and are thus more credible than in markets, can repair damaged perceptions by showing that the nature of the exchange partner has changed.

Social equilibrium repair process
Unlike markets, social equilibrium processes of trust repair are supported in hybrids because they involve higher levels of co-specialization and increased embeddedness in the exchange relationship. Co-specialization results in increased dependence on self-enforcing agreements (based on social norms) as self-enforcing agreements allow for greater value creation initiatives. For example, even when contracts are incomplete, dependent exchange partners may be willing to make relation-specific investments because of credible assurances, based on social norms, that they will be compensated for their investment (Dyer and Singh, 1998). When trust is damaged, exchange partners may be unwilling to make

such investments as the norms that previously governed the exchange are called into question. Hybrids provide two mechanisms to 'settle the accounts' to repair social equilibrium. The first is through punishment via the contract. Offending parties may voluntarily submit to sanctions or less favorable contract terms as a means of proving their penance and resolving negative emotions in the offended partner. Second, the offending party may provide explanations and apologize for their actions while expressing their recommitment to the norms that previously governed the relationship. Higher levels of co-specialization in hybrids allow more credibility in such claims as each partner has a vested interest in the relationship continuing.

Structural repair process
Hybrids provide more support than markets for trust repair through structural repair processes. Hybrids rely on a neoclassical contracting regime – excuse doctrine – which relieves parties from strict enforcement and provides a more flexible contracting mechanism (Williamson, 1991). While outside enforcement is still available through legal recourse, excuse doctrine allows disputes to be resolved internally. Contracts allow partners to change the context within which the exchange is situated, through actions such as renegotiation and rewriting the contract, to change the terms and incentives in order to restore positive expectations and discourage future transgressions. For instance, exchange partners may choose to implement equity alliances and either form a new independent jointly-owned entity or take a minority equity stake in the other exchange partners' firm (Pisano, 1989). While contracting for such alliances may take longer and require higher cost compared to non-equity alliances, they can mitigate opportunistic behavior (Williamson, 1979) and potentially change the context of the exchange to allow for trust repair.

In summary, hybrids possess more mechanisms than markets to support the building and maintaining of trust. Furthermore, the mechanisms in hybrids allow for greater building and maintaining speed compared to markets. While hybrids have access to additional mechanisms, the use of such mechanisms depends on adept management of the contract by exchange partners.

HIERARCHIES' ABILITY TO BUILD AND MAINTAIN TRUST

Hierarchies have a high need for trust and support the most mechanisms for its building and maintenance. Hierarchical governance is characterized by weak incentive intensity, strong internal administrative controls, strong internal conflict resolution mechanisms and weak contract law (Williamson, 1991). While greater asset specificity and frequency increase exchange hazards beyond that experienced in hybrid structures, hierarchies also enjoy monitoring advantages as exchanges take place within the structure of the firm. When exchange hazards are significant, managers may craft well-specified complex contracts to govern the exchange. Under high levels of uncertainty, however, it quickly becomes too costly to contract for all unforeseeable circumstances. In these situations, firms can find efficiency through vertically integrating (Klein et al., 1978; Williamson, 1979). Integration allows for cooperation, coordination and flexibility. Low-powered incentives can encourage employee coordination and high-powered administrative controls allow managers to influence, manage and even manipulate exchange relationships. Access to fiat and internal conflict resolution mechanisms come at a loss of external contract law. Thus, exchanges rely solely on internal mechanisms and the firm becomes its own court of ultimate appeal (Williamson, 1991). Trust is essential for efficient exchanges in hierarchies, largely as a result of the highly dependent nature of the exchange as well as the lack of outside options.

While integration can decrease exchange hazards under high levels of asset specificity it is important to note that it is not unusual for integrated exchange partners, such as business units, to experience low levels of trust. Integrated exchange partners often face differing incentives and consequently vie for political power or an additional share of limited resources. Moreover, problems of asymmetric information may lead to inefficiencies as one exchange partner seeks to 'game the system' for their own personal benefit (for example, Pierce, 2012). These issues are particularly significant as the time horizon shortens. However, the added tools available for trust building and maintenance in hierarchies allow the exchange relationship to be organized and managed in order to minimize such difficulties in the long run. This highlights both an important managerial role as well as the importance of adept management in hierarchies.

Hierarchies and Building Trust

Hierarchies support the building of trust between individuals in an organization through direct interaction, embeddedness in a social structure and through increased structural supports not found in hybrids. Furthermore, when managed correctly, these mechanisms allow for greater building speed compared to hybrids.

250 *Handbook of advances in trust research*

Direct interaction
Because of heightened levels of asset specificity and co-dependency, direct interaction between parties in hierarchies is usually more frequent than in hybrids, allowing for more experience in a given timeframe and thus greater speed in building trust through interaction. In addition, hierarchies differ from hybrids by enabling managers to influence and shape the exchange relationship in important ways. First, managers shape expectations between exchange partners. This includes both defining expectations as well as tempering unrealistic expectations. Second, managers engage in measurement. Engaging in measurement allows managers to interpret actions taken by each exchange partner and influence the expectation building process. For example, if party A does not behave according to expectations, party B may form negative expectations about party A. Managers, however, can convince party B that party A was not behaving opportunistically but in effect doing the best it could given the situation. Thus, party B may instead form positive expectations and trust can continue to be built. Lastly, managers can shape commitment between exchange partners. For instance, managers may require exchange partners to signal commitment to each other by either incurring some sunk cost (in other words, making a relation-specific investment) or being subject to some punishment if they fail to cooperate. Managers also may choose to reward exchange partners based on how the exchange performs. These actions can influence the amount of commitment in exchange relationships. Overall, hierarchies support expectation building, when managed adeptly, through direct interaction that are better than hybrids and allow for greater building speed.

Embeddedness
Hierarchies facilitate the building of trust through embeddedness in a social structure in a more significant way than hybrids. More frequent exchanges and a tighter integrated community built on cooperation and coordination allow strong ties to be developed faster between partners than in hybrids. Highly recurrent exchanges also support additional norms such as norms of reciprocity and the keeping of social accounts. Similar to hybrids, the initial condition in hierarchies is embedded, resulting from the high need for co-specialization. Even more co-specialization in hierarchies, however, leads to higher switching costs and fewer alternative exchange partners compared to hybrids. Heightened dependence results in more need for flexibility in adapting exchanges and resolving disputes when unforeseen situations arise. Embeddedness in hierarchies provides structure to handle such exchanges by forming a single large community with a culture based on norms of cooperation and adaptation. Moreover, reputation is more

important in hierarchies than hybrids as negative behavior can impact reputation within the entire community. Strong ties and a small community provide information about the trustworthiness of parties that is easily transferred within the firm. The added embeddedness in hierarchies and the stronger reputation effects support more trust building and greater building speed than hybrids.

Structural supports
Hierarchies contain additional formal structural factors compared to hybrids that further support the building of trust. Hierarchies rely on low-powered incentives compared to hybrids and heightened administrative controls. Decreased incentive intensity means that employees are unable to immediately directly impact their compensation through their own efforts. Instead they have heightened motivation to cooperate and stronger career concerns. The structure of hierarchies is based on forbearance (Williamson, 1991). Forbearance is a stronger internal contract law than hybrids' excuse doctrine and requires disputes to be resolved internally. While the employee relation may still have some access to legal recourse, exchanges between parties within a firm fall under the jurisdiction of management and have no access to legal recourse. Thus, exchanges are ultimately overseen by managers who have access to fiat. These managers identify where trust is needed and adapt the incentives, particularly career paths, and exchange structure to support it. For instance, managers may choose, up to a point, to encourage competition or reward exchange partners for cooperation. Making adjustments in hierarchies is less costly than hybrids because they do not require costly negotiation and recontracting. Lastly, hierarchies have monitoring advantages compared to hybrids. Transparency between exchange partners is greater as they both reside in the same firm. Furthermore, exchanges are overseen by managers who have direct access to information about each exchange partner's situation. Increased monitoring provides added motivation for exchange partners to cooperate. It also allows managers to quickly identify and modify exchanges in order to support the building of trust. Overall, hierarchies contain many additional structural factors compared to hybrids that support the building of trust.

Hierarchies and Maintaining Trust

Hierarchies support a higher level of trust maintenance compared to hybrids when managed effectively. As managers set expectations and policies, engage in measurement and shape commitment, trust can be effectively maintained. When damaged, trust repair can be difficult in hierarchies as repair involves restoring trust in the system, which entails recalibrating the system.[9] Moreover, the compositional dimension of integration and the knowledge flows within the firm often necessitate repairing trust among many individuals (Dirks et al., 2009; Gillespie and Dietz, 2009). Hierarchies, however, possess access to a greater range of options in repairing trust because of high-powered administrative controls.

Attributional repair process
Hierarchies provide more support and greater speed than hybrids for trust repair through the attributional process. Similar to markets and hybrids, trust can be repaired in hierarchies as exchange partners continue to interact with good behavior. Hierarchies provide additional advantages as exchanges and interactions are usually more frequent than in hybrids. Moreover, managerial oversight and increased information sharing from co-specialization allow for expectations to be defined and communicated clearly. Thus, exchange partners are better able to efficiently identify and remedy behavior that damages positive expectations.

Access to managers (in other words, fiat) provides key benefits to attributional trust repair in hierarchies compared to hybrids. Similar to hybrids, exchange partners are able to offer apologies and accounts and terminate offending employees to restore credibility in exchanges. Different from hybrids, managers have access to three additional tools to repair trust. First, not only do hierarchies allow managers to terminate employees, but the employment relation also allows them to move employees to a different job or to change the job description altogether. Where in hybrids managers could only influence one side of the employment relation, hierarchies allow managers to influence both sides. Managers are therefore able to guide attribution by controlling who participates in the exchange relationship as well as the role they play. Second, managers may shape attribution between parties. For example, managers may choose to accept blame when trust is harmed, which, if effective, could restore the violator's credibility. Third, managers may shape measurement and influence the perceptions of exchange partners. Managers may use their authority and credibility to reliably blame some other source for lack of performance. Thus, instead of exchange partners blaming each other, managers can help attribute behavior to a third source.[10] Overall, the increased frequency of the exchange and the tools at the manager's disposal provide, if exercised, additional supports compared to hybrids for attributional trust repair.

Social equilibrium repair process
Social equilibrium processes of trust repair are supported more in hierarchies than hybrids because co-specialization and embeddedness of the

exchange relationship are greater than in hybrids. Hierarchies possess mechanisms through which managers can influence the social equilibrium repair process. First, managers can use administrative controls to punish offending parties. Punishment may include moving employees to new jobs or locations, changing employee job descriptions, or even termination. Such movements, in essence, introduce a new partner into the exchange, which can act to reset norms. Second, managers may use the powerful levers at their disposal to encourage offending parties to apologize and make reparations to compensate the offended party for their loss. Third, managers can encourage exchange partners to recommit to norms by communicating their expectations. Managers constantly send signals to employees about what behavior is expected and will be rewarded. These signals include whether or not untrustworthy or unethical behavior might be tolerated or even tacitly encouraged in the firm (Dickson et al., 2001). These restorative actions may recommit exchange partners to norms and allow for continued future exchange.

Structural repair process
Hierarchies provide more support for trust repair through the structural process than hybrids. Exchanges in hierarchies are built on forbearance, which removes outside enforcement of the exchange and requires that disputes must be solved internally using administrative controls (Williamson, 1991). Administrative controls allow managers some freedom in adjusting incentives, structure and terms of the exchange to motivate actors towards either competition or cooperation. For instance, managers may choose to encourage cooperation by promoting individuals who are team players or by compensating based on group performance. They can also introduce financial penalties for the observation of undesired opportunistic behavior. An example of changing the structure is through managers changing job descriptions to influence the role actors play in the exchange. Adept managers seek to influence structures and incentive systems to motivate efficient exchange, and skillfully identify how the terms, incentives and structure can be changed in order to repair trust and discourage future opportunistic behavior.

In summary, hierarchies possess more mechanisms that support the building and maintaining of trust than markets. Furthermore, the mechanisms in hierarchies allow for greater building and repair speed compared to hybrids. While hierarchies have access to additional mechanisms, managers are largely responsible for their efficient use. Simply put, adept managers can support high levels of trust; inept managers can destroy it.

PARADOXES AND THE IMPORTANCE OF MANAGERS FOR BUILDING AND MAINTAINING TRUST

While we argue that hybrids and hierarchies support mechanisms that can build and maintain higher levels of trust than markets, and are often chosen for their ability to do so, research has highlighted the potential for three paradoxes that argue for opposite outcomes – formal structure may inhibit the creation of relationship-based trust instead of building and maintaining it.

Three paradoxes may limit or reverse relationship-based trust through hybrids and hierarchy. The first paradox involves an attributional problem that occurs when exchange partners attribute 'good' behavior to the structure of the relationship instead of to the individual (Malhotra and Murnighan, 2002; Ferrin and Dirks, 2003). Attributing desirable behaviors and trust only to structure implies individual relationship-based trust would not exist should the structure be removed or changed.

The second paradox arises should formal governance structures 'crowd out' intrinsic motivations for trust with external structural interventions (Titmuss, 1970; Frey and Oberholzer-Gee, 1997; Uzzi, 1997). Should crowding out occur then exchange partners would have to move psychologically from an exchange based on intrinsic motivations to one that must rely on formal structure, which could lead exchange partners to behave in ways that may 'game the system'.

The third paradox suggests that in particular instances formal structure could potentially encourage opportunistic behavior and undermine trust should formal structure signal distrust to exchange partners (Macaulay, 1963; Ghoshal and Moran, 1996). Partners consequently may assume that the reason they are interacting through a formal governance structure is because their exchange partner is inherently untrustworthy. These paradoxes all predict that formal governance structures may undermine and eliminate relationship-based trust.

Resolving the paradoxes with respect to our exploration is beyond the scope of this chapter. Nonetheless, both our exploration and the paradoxes point us in a similar direction: that managers play a central role at least in hybrids and hierarchy in building and maintaining trust. Managers not only shape contracts and organizational structure, they also hold conversations and communicate with exchange partners and employees; play an important role in setting expectations, encouraging and managing embeddedness and establishing the formal structure of and running of governance structures; and play a central role in attributional, social equilibrium and structural repair processes. In other words, managers and their behavior are a necessary part of understanding the building and maintenance of trust and may provide an explanation for when the paradoxes arise. Formal structure may undermine and preclude certain types of trust if the actions of managers do not display complementarity. Put simply, inept management can destroy trust even in the best of formal governance structures. If so, then future research on the described paradoxes needs to adopt a more nuanced view of trust building and maintaining, one that involves both the structural dimensions of governance and those who manage exchanges and people.

CONCLUSION

In this chapter we explored the extent to which the institutional archetypes of markets, hybrids and hierarchies vary in their capacity to support the building and maintenance of trust. While a broad literature focuses on how trust impacts governance, the benefits to trust in exchanges and the mechanisms that build and maintain trust in general, less is known about how the internal workings of governance structures impact the building and maintaining of trust – or how trust is endogenously impacted by governance structures. We propose that integrating trust into the economic theory of the firm can provide insights into the relationship between trust, governance structures and exchange performance. This chapter seeks to provide a foundation and lay out essential elements whereupon future theory may be built to integrate trust more fully into the economic theory of the firm.

Our exploration identifies inherent differences in governance structures that influence each building mechanism and repair process. Furthermore, we find that the speed of building and repair is impacted differently by governance structure. Overall, we find that market structures provide little support for building and maintaining trust. In comparison, hybrid structures provide a variety of supports for building and maintaining trust. And, hierarchies offer an even greater variety of supports. While hybrids and hierarchies have access to a greater array of supports to affect trust, we find that the efficacy and use of these mechanisms is dependent upon managers. Moreover, while adept managers can support high levels of trust, inept managers can destroy it. In the initial governance decision such considerations are important. When high levels of trust are needed or desired between exchange partners it may be beneficial for a firm to align its governance structure accordingly in order to take advantage of managerial or structural resources used to build and maintain trust.

We propose that future efforts should build on our exploration to develop theory that provides testable implications and integrates trust into the theory of the firm. Such a theory should explain how trust is endogenously impacted by each governance structure and the resulting implications this may have on firm performance. Moreover, a complete theory must address the role of managers in the building and maintenance – including the repair – of trust. We assert that a fruitful area of future research concerns explication of exactly what managers can do (and not do) to build and maintain trust within and between organizations. A further understanding of the managerial role may provide insight into the resolution of the three paradoxes outlined earlier and lead to a more robust theory of the firm.

In conclusion, we emphasize that to resolve the difficult questions put forth in this chapter and to develop a complete theory of trust and the economic theory of the firm necessarily requires an interdisciplinary approach. Yet as trust impacts and can provide benefits to the firm and its employees at all levels of analysis, we propose that developing a more complete theory of trust in the context of the economic theory of the firm is a useful and necessary undertaking.

NOTES

1. A recent search in *Strategic Management Journal* and *Organization Science* revealed 1933 total articles written on the topic of trust, 1482 of these articles published in the last 20 years.
2. Williamson states that 'trust is important and businessmen rely on it much more extensively than is commonly realized' (Williamson, 1975, p. 108). However, Williamson does not integrate trust into the Transaction Cost Economics (TCE) model and argues that trust is not needed to explain economic organizations, instead relying on risk and calculative economic reasoning (Williamson, 1993, p. 486). Moreover, Williamson argues that trust should be reserved almost exclusively for personal relationships (1993, p. 483). In this chapter we develop a compatible but different perspective compared to Williamson that takes into account the intertemporal management of trust and expectations. Our theory identifies important ex post features of governance forms for building and managing trust and hence expectations. We argue that these ex post features should be considered and folded back into ex ante governance choice considerations because they affect the level of trust actually achieved, which in turn shapes ex post risk in a path dependent way. By doing so, we acknowledge, like Williamson, that a calculative ex ante approach for assessing expectations and risk is warranted but that actual creation and management of trust can vary over a considerable range. Ex post management of trust shapes the level of risk as the exchange unfolds. In essence, we believe that this chapter unpacks governance features not articulated in Williamson's initial ex ante calculus of governance choice.
3. Another oft-used definition of trust is the expectation that one organization will not act opportunistically against another, especially when the latter is vulnerable (Bradach and Eccles, 1989). These definitions highlight that trust often goes beyond calculative self-interest even to the point where exchange partners are 'willing to forego

guarantees based on coercion or self-interest' (Williamson, 1993; Nooteboom 1996; Nooteboom et al., 1997, p. 313). While our definition of trust acknowledges that it is based on an expectation of behavior and that past behavior provides important information, we largely remain agnostic about the cognitive processes by which the expectation is formed. Consequently, and largely because of space limitations, we will not specifically highlight or contrast the impact of differing types of trust such as institution-based or generalized trust (for example, Zucker, 1986; Burchell and Wilkinson, 1997; Child and Möllering, 2003). This is not to say that trust functions the same in each governance form or that trust is built and maintained in identical ways across forms. On the contrary, we believe that the differing organizational forms vary in their capacity to access tools to build and maintain trust. Our main objective in this chapter is to highlight some of these tools while leaving the work of linking types of trust to future theoretical work. By not restricting our analysis we expand the consideration set, realizing that economic actors or institutions may be able to shape expectations.

4. It is important to emphasize that trust should not be confounded with compliance. In our definition we allow the possibility for trust between exchange partners to be influenced by some outside third party, such as a manager, arbitrators, or the law. This broadening emphasizes that trust between exchange partners can be augmented, and in some cases substituted, by trust in third parties. While it may be the case that the type, overall level and potential level of trust may be different in these cases, access to third parties provides an important mechanism that influences trust creation and maintenance. For instance, a manager between two hostile divisions may play the role as a third party of ensuring that each party lives up to its end of the bargain. While these two divisions may have minimal trust between the two of them without the manager, the addition of the manager, and the trust each has in the manager, allows them to function as if they had a high level of trust between themselves in isolation.

5. For a review of the trust repair literature see Dirks et al. (2009).

6. These three processes are expected to be differentially related to the goals of repairing trust, restoring positive exchange and reducing negative affect. The attributional process is most strongly associated with trust repair, although the other processes may also have an effect.

7. While embeddedness may develop slowly over time in markets, especially as co-specialization and frequency increase, our focus is primarily on markets' initial condition of little embeddedness.

8. Macaulay gives an example of how this may occur. He notes that salesmen 'often know purchasing agents well. The same two individuals may have dealt with each other from five to 25 years. Each has something to give the other. Salesmen have gossip about competitors, shortages and price increases to give purchasing agents who treat them well' (1963, p. 63). On the other hand, when sellers do not satisfy their customers they 'become the subject of discussion in the gossip exchanged by purchasing agents and salesmen, at meetings of purchasing agents' associations and trade associations or even at country clubs or social gatherings' (p. 64).

9. Gillespie and Dietz (2009) put forth four primary internal components that define the organizational system: leadership and management practice, culture and climate, strategy, and structure, policies and processes.

10. It is important to note that many of these tools at the manager's disposal may be limited by information flows within the firm. The social structure may allow actors to receive information before managers are able to mediate it. Thus, adept managers must move quickly and decisively to repair through attribution before the problem spreads too widely.

REFERENCES

Adler, Paul S. (2001), 'Market, hierarchy, and trust: the knowledge economy and the future of capitalism', *Organization Science*, **12**(2), 215–34.
Arrow, K. (1974), *The Limits of Organization*, New York: John Wiley and Sons.
Barney, J.B. and M.H. Hansen (1994), 'Trustworthiness as a form of competitive advantage', *Strategic Management Journal*, **15**(8), 175–90.
Ben-Porath, Yoram (1980), 'The f-connection: families, friends, and firms and the organization of exchange', *Population and Development Review*, **6**(1), 1–30.
Bernheim, B. Douglas and Michael D. Whinston (1998), 'Incomplete contracts and strategic ambiguity', *The American Economic Review*, **88**(4), 902–32.
Bies, Robert J. and T.M. Tripp (1996), 'Beyond distrust: "getting even" and the need for revenge', in R.M. Kramer and T.R. Tyler, *Trust in Organizations: Frontiers of Theory and Research*, pp. 246–60.
Bottom, William P., Kevin Gibson, Steven E. Daniels and J. Keith Murnighan (2002), 'When talk is not cheap: substantive penance and expressions of intent in rebuilding cooperation', *Organization Science*, **13**(5), 497–513.
Bradach, Jeffrey L. and Robert G. Eccles (1989), 'Price, authority, and trust: from ideal types to plural forms', in *Annual Review of Sociology*, Vol. 15, pp. 97–118.
Bromiley, P. and L. Cummings (1995), 'Transaction costs in organizations with trust', in R.J. Bies, R.J. Lewicki and B.H. Sheppard (eds), *Research on Negotiation in Organizations*, Vol. 5, pp. 219–47.
Burchell, Brendan and Frank Wilkinson (1997), 'Trust, business relationships and the contractual environment', *Cambridge Journal of Economics*, **21**(2), 217–37.
Child, John and Guido Möllering (2003), 'Contextual confidence and active trust development in the Chinese business environment', *Organization Science*, **14**(1), 69–80.
Chiles, Todd H. and John F. McMackin (1996), 'Integrating variable risk preferences, trust, and transaction cost economics', *The Academy of Management Review*, **21**(1), 73–99.
Coase, R.H. (1937), 'The nature of the firm', *Economica*, **4**(16), 386–405.
Coletti, Angela L., Karen L. Sedatole and Kristy L. Towry (2005), 'The effect of control systems on trust and cooperation in collaborative environments', *The Accounting Review*, **80**(2), 477–500.
Dickson, Marcus W., D. Brent Smith, Michael W. Grojean and Mark Ehrhart (2001), 'An organizational climate regarding ethics: the outcome of leader values and the practices that reflect them', *The Leadership Quarterly*, **12**(2), 197–217.
Dirks, Kurt T. and Donald L. Ferrin (2001), 'The role of trust in organizational settings', *Organization Science*, **12**(4), 450–67.
Dirks, Kurt T., Roy J. Lewicki and Akbar Zaheer (2009), 'Repairing relationships within and between organizations: building a conceptual foundation', *Academy of Management Review*, **34**(1), 68–84.
Driver, J., A. Tabares, A. Shapiro, E.Y. Nahm and J.M. Gottman (2003), 'Interactional patterns in marital success and failure: Gottman laboratory studies', in F. Walsh (ed.), *Normal Family Processes: Growing Diversity and Complexity*, 3rd edition, pp. 493–513.
Dyer, Jeffrey H. and Wujin Chu (2003), 'The role of trustworthiness in reducing transaction costs and improving performance: empirical evidence from the United States, Japan, and Korea', *Organization Science*, **14**(1), 57–68.
Dyer, Jeffrey H. and Harbir Singh (1998), 'The relational view: cooperative strategy and sources of inter-organizational competitive advantage', *The Academy of Management Review*, **23**(4), 660–79.
Ferrin, Donald L. and Kurt T. Dirks (2003), 'The use of rewards to increase and decrease trust: mediating processes and differential effects', *Organization Science*, **14**(1), 18–31.
Ferrin, Donald L., Kurt T. Dirks and Pri P. Shah (2006), 'Direct and indirect effects of third-party relationships on inter-personal trust', *Journal of Applied Psychology*, **91**(4), 870–83.
Frey, Bruno S. and Felix Oberholzer-Gee (1997), 'The cost of price incentives: an empirical analysis of motivation crowding out', *The American Economic Review*, **87**(4), 746–55.

Ghoshal, Sumantra and Peter Moran (1996), 'Bad for practice: a critique of the transaction cost theory', *Academy of Management Review*, **21**(1), 13–47.
Gillespie, Nicole and Graham Dietz (2009), 'Trust repair after an organization-level failure', *Academy of Management Review*, **34**(1), 127–45.
Goffman, E. (1967), *Interaction Ritual: Essays in Face-to-face Behavior*, Chicago: Aldine Pub. Co.
Good, D. (1988), 'Individuals, inter-personal relations, and trust', in D. Gambetta (ed.), *Trust: Making and Breaking Cooperative Relations*, Cambridge, MA: Basil Blackwell, pp. 31–48.
Granovetter, Mark (1985), 'Economic action and social structure: the problem of embeddedness', *The American Journal of Sociology*, **91**(3), 481–510.
Grossman, Sanford J. and Oliver D. Hart (1986), 'The costs and benefits of ownership: a theory of vertical and lateral integration', *The Journal of Political Economy*, **94**(4), 691–719.
Gulati, Ranjay (1995), 'Does familiarity breed trust? The implications of repeated ties for contractual choice in alliances', *The Academy of Management Journal*, **38**(1), 85–112.
Gulati, Ranjay and Jack A. Nickerson (2008), 'Inter-organizational trust, governance choice, and exchange performance', *Organization Science*, **19**(5), 688–708.
Hart, Oliver D. and John Moore (1990), 'Property rights and the nature of the firm', *The Journal of Political Economy*, **98**(6), 1119–58.
Heider, Fritz (1958), *The Psychology of Inter-personal Relations*, New York: Wiley.
Hill, Charles W.L. (1990), 'Cooperation, opportunism, and the invisible hand: implications for transaction cost theory', *Academy of Management Review*, **15**(3), 500–513.
Jones, Candace, William S. Hesterly and Stephen P. Borgatti (1997), 'A general theory of network governance: exchange conditions and social mechanisms', *The Academy of Management Review*, **22**(4), 911–45.
Kim, Peter H., Kurt T. Dirks, Cecily D. Cooper and Donald L. Ferrin (2006), 'When more blame is better than less: the implications of internal vs. external attributions for the repair of trust after a competence- vs. integrity-based trust violation', *Organizational Behavior and Human Decision Processes*, **99**(1), 49–65.
Kim, Peter H., Donald L. Ferrin, Cecily D. Cooper and Kurt T. Dirks (2004), 'Removing the shadow of suspicion: the effects of apology vs. denial for repairing ability- vs. integrity-based trust violations', *Journal of Applied Psychology*, **89**(1), 104–18.
Klein, Benjamin, Robert G. Crawford and Armen A. Alchian (1978), 'Vertical integration, appropriable rents, and the competitive contracting process', *Journal of Law and Economics*, **21**(2), 297–326.
Lazzarini, Sergio G., Gary J. Miller and Todd R. Zenger (2004), 'Order with some law: complementarity versus substitution of formal and informal arrangements', *Journal of Law, Economics, and Organization*, **20**(2), 261–98.
Lewicki, Roy J., Daniel J. McAllister and Robert J. Bies (1998), 'Trust and distrust: new relationships and realities', *Academy of Management Review*, **23**(3), 438–58.
Lewicki, Roy J., Edward C. Tomlinson and Nicole Gillespie (2006), 'Models of inter-personal trust development: theoretical approaches, empirical evidence, and future directions', *Journal of Management*, **32**(6), 991–1022.
Lorenz, E. (1999) 'Trust, contract and economic cooperation', *Cambridge Journal of Economics*, **23**(3), 301–15.
Macaulay, Stewart (1963), 'Non-contractual relations in business: a preliminary study', *American Sociological Review*, **28**(1), 55–67.
MacNeil, Ian R. (1974), 'The many futures of contract.' *Southern California Law Review*, **47**, 691–94.
Malhotra, Deepak and J. Keith Murnighan (2002), 'The effects of contracts on inter-personal trust', *Administrative Science Quarterly*, **47**(3), 534–59.
Mayer, Kyle J. and Nicholas S. Argyres (2004), 'Learning to contract: evidence from the personal computer industry', *Organization Science*, **15**(4), 394–410.
Nakayachi, Kazuya and Motoki Watabe (2005), 'Restoring trustworthiness after adverse

events: the signaling effects of voluntary "hostage posting" on trust', *Organizational Behavior and Human Decision Processes*, **97**(1), 1–17.

Nooteboom, Bart (1996), 'Trust, opportunism and governance: a process and control model', *Organization Studies*, **17**(6), 985–1010.

Nooteboom, Bart, Hans Berger and Niels G. Noorderhaven (1997), 'Effects of trust and governance on relational risk', *The Academy of Management Journal*, **40**(2), 308–38.

North, Douglass C. (1990), 'A transaction cost theory of politics', *Journal of Theoretical Politics*, **2**(4), 355–67.

Pierce, Lamar (2012), 'Organizational structure and the limits of knowledge sharing: incentive conflict and agency in car leasing', *Management Science*, accessed 6 May 2013 at http://papers.ssrn.com/sol3/papers.cfm?abstract_id=1572062.

Pisano, Gary P. (1989), 'Using equity participation to support exchange: evidence from the biotechnology industry', *Journal of Law, Economics, & Organization*, **5**(1), 109–26.

Poppo, Laura and Todd Zenger (2002), 'Do formal contracts and relational governance function as substitutes or complements?', *Strategic Management Journal*, **23**(8), 707–25.

Reb, Jochen, Barry M. Goldman, Laura J. Kray and Russell Cropanzano (2006), 'Different wrongs, different remedies? Reactions to organizational remedies after procedural and interactional injustice', *Personnel Psychology*, **59**(1), 31–64.

Ren, Hong and Barbara Gray (2009), 'Repairing relationship conflict: how violation types and culture influence the effectiveness of restoration rituals', *Academy of Management Review*, **34**(1), 105–26.

Robinson, Sandra L. (1996), 'Trust and breach of the psychological contract', *Administrative Science Quarterly*, **41**(4), 574–99.

Rousseau, D.M., B. Sim, R. Sitkin, S. Burt and C. Camerer (1998), 'Not so different after all: a cross-discipline view of trust', *Academy of Management Review*, **23**(3), 393–404.

Shapiro, Susan P. (1987), 'The social control of impersonal trust', *American Journal of Sociology*, **93**(3), 623–58.

Sitkin, Sim B. and Nancy L. Roth (1993), 'Explaining the limited effectiveness of legalistic "remedies" for trust/distrust', *Organization Science*, **4**(3), 367–92.

Smith, Adam (1776), *An Inquiry into the Nature and Causes of the Wealth of Nations: 1776*, London: W. Strahan and T. Cadell.

Titmuss, Richard M. (1970), *The Gift Relationship*, London: Allen and Unwin.

Tomlinson, Edward and Roger C. Mayer (2009), 'The role of causal attribution dimensions in trust repair', *Academy of Management Review ARCHIVE*, **34**(1), 85–104.

Uzzi, Brian (1997), 'Social structure and competition in interfirm networks: the paradox of embeddedness', *Administrative Science Quarterly*, **42**(1), 35–67.

Williamson, Oliver E. (1975), *Markets and Hierarchies: Analysis and Antitrust Implications: A Study in the Economics of Internal Organization*, New York: Free Press.

Williamson, Oliver E. (1979), 'Transaction-cost economics: the governance of contractual relations', *Journal of Law and Economics*, **22**(2), 233–61.

Williamson, Oliver E. (1985), *The Economic Institutions of Capitalism*, New York: The Free Press.

Williamson, Oliver E. (1991), 'Comparative economic organization: the analysis of discrete structural alternatives', *Administrative Science Quarterly*, **36**(2), 269–96.

Williamson, Oliver E. (1993), 'Calculativeness, trust, and economic organization', *Journal of Law and Economics*, **36**(1), 453–86.

Williamson, Oliver E. (1996), *The Mechanisms of Governance*, New York: Oxford University Press.

Zaheer, Akbar, Bill McEvily and Vincenzo Perrone (1998), 'Does trust matter? Exploring the effects of inter-organizational and inter-personal trust on performance', *Organization Science*, **9**(2), 141–59.

Zucker, Lynne G. (1986), 'Production of trust: institutional sources of economic structure, 1840–1920', *Research in Organizational Behavior*, **8**(1), 53–111.

11. How is trust institutionalized? Understanding collective and long-term trust orientations*
Frens Kroeger

INTRODUCTION

The idea that trust can be institutionalized obviously resonates with trust researchers. It is invoked frequently and across a wide range of different subfields of trust research. This seems unsurprising considering the promise this notion holds. If we achieve a deeper understanding of an institutionalization of trust, this opens a range of relevant and exciting questions up to analysis. Can trust be more than just a dyadic relationship? Can it be impersonalized to a meaningful degree, that is, can it become partially (sic!) independent of the individual participants to the relationship? Can it, for instance, become an attribute of an organization or a system instead? If so, how does it travel across analytical levels? And, last but not least, does institutionalization mean that trust can be made to last? That is, can it endure over long periods of time, displaying relative stability due to its institutionalized status, maybe even beyond the life span of interpersonal trust?

Analysing the institutionalization of trust thus promises to help unravel questions surrounding two important issues: on the one hand, that of trust orientations that last over long periods of time, for example, in long-standing inter-organizational relations such as joint ventures, sometimes over generations of organizational actors (Janowicz-Panjaitan and Noorderhaven, 2009). On the other hand, that of collective trust orientations – be it those of employees towards their employing organization (Searle et al., 2011), of one organizational subgroup towards another (Ferrin et al., 2007), or those of the members of one organization towards another (Zaheer et al., 1998). The latter notion in particular has provided trust research with important impulses, and has been cited in numerous empirical studies; the present contribution holds that it also deserves further attention in conceptual terms. It is only through studying the institutionalization dynamics of trust that we can truly begin to understand how far and in what ways these long-term and collective trust orientations are more than the simple addition of individual trust orientations (Currall and Inkpen, 2002).

Considering these potential analytical benefits, the frequent references to an institutionalization of trust do indeed seem unsurprising. It is surprising, on the other hand, that nearly invariably they occur merely in passing, typically with no more than a single sentence (for example, Creed and Miles, 1996, p. 35n; Kramer, 1999, p. 581; Collins, 2005, p. 184), or a few at most (Doney and Cannon, 1997, p. 46), but without any further explanation of the concept. In some contributions this is the case even though institutionalization is emphasized as a central idea (Fox, 1974; Dodgson, 1993; Weingast, 1994; on Zucker, 1986, see below). Thus, the institutionalization of trust has never been studied in a sustained manner with any analytical rigour. Virtually the only exception to this are Sydow's (1998, 2006) insightful, but short observations from a structuration perspective. Zaheer et al. (1998, p. 144) and Gulati and Sytch (2008, p. 171) reflect on how institutionalization may mediate between trust on the interpersonal and inter-organizational levels. Their explanations, too, are highly instructive, but they remain restricted to one and two paragraphs, respectively, and what is more, they form a rare exception. In much of the literature, an institutionalization of trust is implied in the form of collective or long-term trust orientations, but is not explicitly spelled out or analysed (Zaheer and Harris, 2006).

The present contribution undertakes to fill this important gap, and to provide a conceptual model for studying how trust is institutionalized, and how this institutionalized form can persist and change over time. In the following I will outline the process of institutionalization, the structure of institutionalized trust and how it affects subsequent trusting conduct, the reproduction of institutionalized trust both in relative stability and change over time, and the fundamental consequences that follow for our understanding of long-term and collective trust orientations. The final section will reflect on these and further contributions of the analysis presented. But first, the broader theoretical framework adopted here to understand the institutionalization of trust needs to be outlined.

THE INSTITUTIONALIZATION CYCLE OF TRUST

The central theoretical foundation of this analysis will be the classic constructionist theory of Berger and Luckmann (1967). This is not to deny the analytical benefits of a range of theoretical approaches, particularly structuration theory (Giddens, 1984; see Sydow 1998, 2006), elements of which will be integrated into the present framework. But Berger and Luckmann's account of institutionalization seems ideally suited to studying the phenomenon at hand (particularly on an organizational level; see

Granovetter, 1992). This is not only due to its excellent epistemological fit with the broadly neo-institutionalist outlook adopted here (see Hall and Taylor, 1996), including the recognition of the symbolic dimension of social action both as internalized beliefs and external frameworks (Scott, 2008). More generally, in substantive terms this approach allows us to understand trust as an intersubjective phenomenon, and to continuously trace the constitutive links between individual and shared realities of trust actively constructed and reconstructed by the participants, and the processes by which they build trust on the basis of shared meanings (also see Möllering, 2006a, Ch. 3).

Beyond the initial institutionalization processes, Berger and Luckmann's theory is ideally suited to studying the (re)production of institutionalized trust. The latter clearly constitutes 'a phenomenon both of institutional change and of transformations of consciousness', and as Berger himself notes, 'it is precisely this duality that the paradigm was meant to deal with' (1992, p. 2). Their account thus seems an apt choice for studying the institutionalization of trust.

What, then, do I mean by this phrase? There are a few contributions that appear to address the institutionalization of trust in more depth, but what these contributions typically address is an institutionalization not of trust, but only of favourable *preconditions* for it (most prominently Zucker, 1986, which focuses on a higher degree of homogeneity among the populace, mechanistically equating it with higher trust). The present approach enables us to go beyond such accounts by considering trust *itself* as being institutionalized.

We can conceive of trust as institutionalized in roles and routines for trusting (alternatively, also see Giddens's concept of rules, 1984). These arise from trusting interaction, elements of which are externalized and objectified (more details on this process below). With this, they gain the 'life of their own' typical of institutions. That is, the actors encounter them essentially as external facts (Zucker, 1991) that influence subsequent trusting conduct.

At the same time, for institutionalized trust to persist it needs to be continuously 'brought to life' in interaction (Berger and Luckmann, 1967. p. 93). In doing so, the actors employ the institutionalized patterns subjectively and creatively. Establishing and maintaining trust is not just a matter of *whether* actors follow institutionalized roles and routines, but *how* they do so. Trusting behaviour has a strong performative side (Beckert, 2005). It is crucial that institutionalized trust not be reified, or misunderstood as set in stone and enacted by mere 'institutional dopes' (Hirsch, 1997). Rather, we need to be aware of the character of institutionalization as a continuous process (also see Möllering, Chapter 12 this

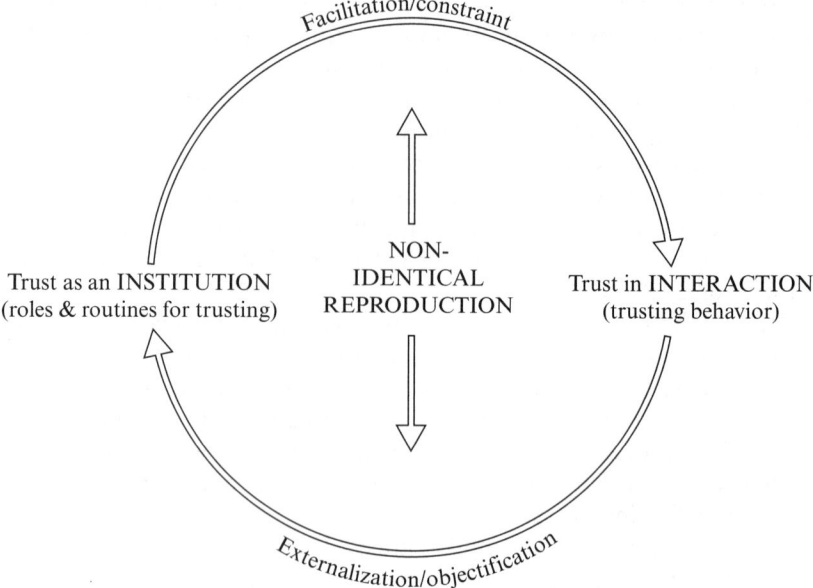

Figure 11.1   The institutionalization cycle of trust

volume), and of the fundamental and transformative role that individual agency plays in it. This concern will pervade the entire chapter.

Trusting interaction, then, contributes to but does not fully determine the (re)production of institutionalized forms of trust, and the latter in their turn contribute to but do not fully determine the (re)production of trusting interaction. In this, the freedom of actors within institutional boundaries, which are at the same time constraining and enabling, allows for highly variable degrees of identity/non-identity of reproduction. Institutionalized roles and routines for trusting can remain relatively stable over time, or change according to the way they are employed in interaction.

We can visualize these processes as a cycle of institutionalization (see Figure 11.1).

Following this cycle provides us with a concise guideline for the questions that will now need to be addressed in order to gain a fuller understanding of the institutionalization of trust. First, what are the elements of trusting interaction that subsequently go on to be institutionalized, and how does this institutionalization occur? Second, how can we envisage the resulting institution, and how does it affect further trusting interaction? And third – following Stinchcombe's (1968) insight that 'initial' institutionalization is distinct from subsequent reproduction – how is institutionalized trust reproduced over time, especially over long periods of time? These questions – concerning interaction and institutional production, structure, reproduction and transmission, respectively – will be addressed in consecutive sections before concluding with a summary of analytical insights afforded by this approach.

FROM INTERACTION TO INSTITUTION

Interaction: Trust Building as Symbolic Action

First, what elements of trusting conduct are institutionalized? In short, the answer given here concerns ways of signalling trust and trustworthiness. We may conceive of trust building as a form of 'symbolic exchange' (Haas and Deseran, 1981; also see Blau, 1964; Singelmann, 1972). That is, the actors engage in action that is apt to signal their trust and/or trustworthiness to each other. Action is then interpreted as indicative of the other's motives, character and relationship orientation as each actor watches for behavioural clues to the other's goodwill (Weber et al., 2005; Six et al., 2010).

The signalling intention need not always be in the foreground of acting. Most economic actions have dual value: functional as well as symbolic (Ravasi and Rindova, 2008). While serving instrumental purposes, they simultaneously provide signals that tell the participants about and/or adjust their relationship (Six, 2007). But equally, at least a subordinate aim of behaviour will often be to demonstrate (facets of) trust and trustworthiness, and trustors will be actively looking for such signals (Currall and Epstein, 2003). Symbolic exchange is thus clearly a manifestation of 'active trust' (Giddens, 1994; Möllering, 2006a).

Obviously, goodwill needs to be conveyed to the partner; factual trustworthiness may be of little consequence if it is not successfully communicated (Hardy et al., 1998). But why through symbolic action rather than explicit and unambiguous communication? On the one hand, direct and explicit communication has clear disadvantages. Stating one's own trustworthiness is a comparatively 'cheap' signal, as it is easy to imitate (Bacharach and Gambetta, 2001) unless supported by consequential action. Simple and explicit protestations of trustworthiness often even have the opposite effect (see Kawin, cited in Meyerson et al., 1996). Explicit verbal explanations are more helpful when trust has broken down and there is a need for the disambiguation of previous actions (Bacharach and Gambetta, 2001; Gillespie and Dietz, 2009).

On the other, the relatively less direct symbolic exchange offers distinct advantages. All symbols are by nature imprecise. This is not, however, always strictly a disadvantage (also see Six and Sorge, 2008). Following Cohen (1985), I want to argue that the imprecision of symbols is also the source of their greatest strength. Symbols do not simply stand for something else – if that was their sole function they would be redundant. Instead, they allow the participant actors to provide part of a symbol's meaning themselves – both in formulating and in interpreting it. Thus, precise meanings may differ across individual actors. 'But their *range* of meanings can be glossed over in a commonly accepted symbol' (Cohen, 1985, p. 15; original emphasis).

This enables the actors to signal their trust and trustworthiness to each other without the necessity of precise convergence of meanings or values (as has sometimes been surmised; for example, Schweer, 2003). Instead, the symbol can be embedded in the actors' differing cognitive and normative frames. Thus, symbols enable the actors to 'reintroduce the unfamiliar into the familiar'; their very form facilitates the building of trust (Luhmann, 1988, p. 95; Möllering, 2006b, pp. 367–9). Thus, in trust building, too, Cohen's dictum applies: 'Symbols are effective because they are imprecise' (1985, p. 21).

The behaviours that can be used as positive trust signals extend from the smallest of gestures (Goffman, 1967), like remembering somebody's birthday, to flexible renegotiations of business terms when unforeseen contingencies occur (thus spanning a range from a few seconds' talk to a value of hundreds of thousands of pounds involved).[1] As a general rule, the more potent trust symbols are those involving higher risks to the trustee (signalling stronger commitment; Bottom et al., 2002) and those that would be more difficult or costly to fake for a factually untrustworthy actor (Bacharach and Gambetta, 2001; on investment in relationship-specific assets see, for example, Zaheer and Venkatraman, 1995).

The range of the trust signals employed results partly from the context in which trust building takes place. As Goffman reminds us, actors devising symbolic action tend to use the 'depictive materials at hand' in a given situation or context (1983, p. 11). Accordingly, over time symbolic exchange is likely to engender a specialized, individualized repertoire of mutually comprehensible symbolic actions that arise from the context and interaction history of a specific relationship, and that the actors can use to continuously reassure each other of their trust and trustworthiness (also see Swidler, 1986; Mizrachi et al., 2007).

An empirical study (see endnote 1 below) revealed a variety of patterns that were intersubjectively understood as signals of trust and trustworthiness by respondents. A particularly interesting example among these, since it appears a purely instrumental category at first glance, is the handling of payment modalities. While timely payment was considered an important symbolic act to reassure the other party of one's trustworthiness, advance payment was intersubjectively interpreted as a signal of trust especially in relationships where no formal contractual obligations existed. (Also note how this coincides with Luhmann's, 1979 notion of trust itself as an 'advance'.) The pattern was derived from the specific context of the relationship and often adapted according to increasing knowledge about the other party's circumstances (for example, their cash flow).

While this pattern is comparatively easy to institutionalize, by making advance payment informal policy under definable circumstances with specific partners, we need a broader understanding of how ways of signalling trust and trustworthiness can become intersubjective realities.

Institutional Production: Creating Roles and Routines of Trust

Hence, now that we know what elements of trusting conduct go on to be institutionalized, we need to ask: what are the processes of this ('initial') institutionalization? Berger and Luckmann's (1967) account succeeds in describing these processes more lucidly than virtually any other. Their account of institutionalization can be condensed into one core statement: 'Institutionalization occurs whenever there is a reciprocal typification of habitualized actions by types of actors. Put differently, any such typification is an institution' (ibid., p. 72).

Thus, in a first step, ways of signalling trust and trustworthiness are 'habitualized'. All human behaviour in recurring social situations has a tendency towards habitualization – particularly in situations of recurring collective problems and resulting interlocking conduct of individuals, as are typical of organizational life. It promises psychological exoneration by narrowing down choices. This repetition itself lays the basis for 'typification'. 'Any action that is repeated frequently becomes cast into a pattern, which can then be reproduced with an economy of effort and which, *ipso facto*, is apprehended by its performer *as* that pattern' (ibid., p. 70–71; original emphasis).

Trust can only become truly intersubjective, however, when the typifications become reciprocal. If the actors involved are aware that the typifications are shared between them, the assumption of mutual awareness forms the basis for coordinated habitual conduct. The negotiation of institutional reality inherent in this process is captured well by Weick. Adapting a statement of his, we can say that the institution:

> is not [only] defined by what I do but by what I presume others know, believe, and mean when they do what they do. I act as if I know what they are doing, and I continually test this understanding by acting 'in kind'. Most of the time

I'm successful, but that is for them to judge, as well as me. They judge the appropriateness of my actions just as I specify and sanction the appropriateness of their actions. (Weick, 1985, pp. 387–8)

(Also note how well this account ties in with the description of trust building as 'symbolic exchange' above.)

Importantly, the typification of actions also leads to a typification of *actors*. With the recognition of specific interaction patterns comes a degree of awareness of the parts the actors play in it. 'The institution posits that actions of type X will be performed by actors of type X' (Berger and Luckmann, 1967, p. 72). Only that in the present case the institution is not 'hunting' and does not posit that its performer is a 'hunter' (as in Berger and Luckmann's ethnological example, 1967, p. 84). Instead, one of the actors, for instance, may be the 'trusting buyer', whose newly typified conduct encompasses offering further business without insisting on the contractual specification of quality and delivery time (and maybe paying an advance when, for some reason, a stronger token of trust is required). Meanwhile the other acts as the 'trusted supplier', whose new role includes delivering the expected quality at the expected time in the absence of monitoring or threat of sanctions (and possibly also delivering more than is asked for or sooner than agreed).

Rights, duties and other expectations of this sort ('must', 'must not', and 'may' rules; Clemens and Cook, 1999) can form part of an actor typification in great number and detail, depending on the history of the specific relationship. This is the process from which *roles* for trustors and trustees arise. It demonstrates that the institution creates the actor as much as the actor creates the institution.

FROM INSTITUTION TO INTERACTION

Institutional 'Structure': Trust Templates and their Embedding

How, then, can we envisage the resulting 'structure' of institutionalized trust? Since the literature on institutional structures and mechanisms is complex and rather diffuse in nature (Hall and Taylor, 1996; Campbell, 2004), a suitable understanding of institutional structure needs to be distilled from it. For this purpose, the constructionist framework presented is enriched with elements of structuration theory (Giddens, 1984).

Following Barley and Tolbert's (1997) conceptualization, we may assume that the typifications of trusting behaviour whose emergence was traced in the previous sections subsequently function as 'trust templates'.

How is trust institutionalized? 269

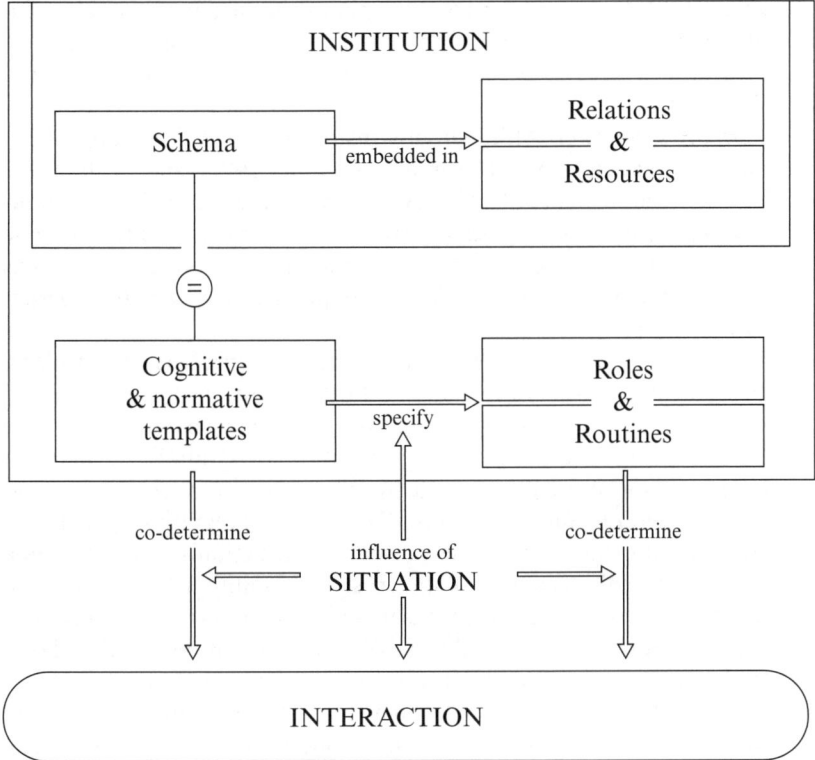

Figure 11.2 The structure of institutionalized trust

They are specified in *roles* and *routines* for trusting. (in other words, as described above, the institution typifies both actions and actors). The institutional templates and their specifications are the central means of channelling expectations and interactions. Both the specification of roles and routines and their effects on interaction are moderated by situational influences (Figure 11.2).

The structure of institutionalized trust takes more concrete shape when we consider three institutional dimensions:

1. *Cognitive vs normative.* The institutionalized trust templates are both cognitive and normative in nature (rather than either/or; see, for example, Scott and Christensen, 1995). Cognitive trust templates channel interpretations of the meaning of both one's own and others' trust-relevant actions through 'predefinitions' and legitimating 'pre-interpretations' (and by defining what is 'thinkable' in the first place;

Zucker, 1991). Normative trust templates channel quasi-moral evaluations of these actions through predefinitions and preinterpretations of what is desirable (Berger and Luckmann, 1967; also see Sitkin and Roth, 1993).

2. *Formal vs informal.* Although any institution comprises both formal and informal elements (Thelen and Steinmo, 1992), and the boundaries between them are often fuzzy, it is evident that trust is institutionalized predominantly on an informal plane. Its maintenance over time is largely implicit and tacit in nature. Importantly, however, this does not render it any less 'real' or less consequential (also see Granovetter, 1985).

3. *Symbolic vs material.* That this is the case becomes particularly clear from a consideration of the third dimension: institutionalized trust is not *solely* symbolic in nature, but has a material side, too. Counteracting the undue dichotomization of symbolic vs material aspects found in much of the institutional literature (Friedland and Alford, 1991) forms a central motivation for integrating elements of structuration theory into the present constructionist understanding of institutional structure. While trust is certainly a largely 'virtual' institution, that is, it exists primarily in interaction and in the memory traces of human actors (Giddens, 1984, p. 17), this perspective shows trust typifications or templates to be only a part of the whole institution (albeit a central one). They form the institution's 'schema' (Sewell, 1992), that is, its ideational 'content' (Campbell, 2004). The schema is embedded into networks of relationships and resource configurations (Clemens and Cook, 1999; also see Giddens's [1984] original formulation as 'rules and resources'). Thus, symbolic action employed to build and maintain trust takes place on the background of interpersonal relationships and typically makes use of material resources employed for symbolic purposes. Vice versa, both the shape of interpersonal relations and aspects of resource allocation in organizations are influenced by the presence/absence and degree of trust, as 'we organize our material world in accordance with our mental categories' (Scott, 2008, p. 127; also see Schein, 1991).

Institutional Impact on Interaction: The Process of Symbolic Mediation

Once institutionalized trust has achieved this degree of crystallization, how, then, does it influence further trusting interaction? The general answer to this question is, of course, well known: institutions both constrain and enable action (Giddens, 1984). *How* they do so is a question rarely asked beyond highly specific and limited empirical contexts. For present purposes, however, it is useful to sketch the outlines of those mechanisms that translate institutionalized trust back into symbolic action.

The institutionally available trust templates (see above) provide what might be called 'reading guides' and 'writing guides' for symbolic action. That is, they give actors a guideline for understanding, interpreting and evaluating specific actions as symbolic of trust and trustworthiness, as well as for constructing their own trusting and trustworthy conduct. Thus, we may conceive of institutionalized trust as 'symbolically mediated'. This process can be portrayed by adapting a graph from Barley and Tolbert (1997), effectively unrolling the institutionalization cycle into a rhythmic sequence. This model chimes with the present framework as Barley and Tolbert, too, combine Berger and Luckmann's constructionist theory with structurationist ideas.

Following their conception, we may consider an additional conceptual level between institution and interaction. However, where Barley and Tolbert (1997) see 'scripts' as mediating between the two levels, here *symbols* are viewed as the pivots between institutionalized trust and trusting conduct (Figure 11.3).

Thus, actors can use the more generic institutionalized templates and 'encode' them in a specific symbolic action to signal trust and trustworthiness. It is this symbol that is enacted and interpreted both by the observing partner and by the actor herself as she self-reflexively evaluates her symbolic efforts. The – potentially varying – enactment can then feed back into the symbol itself. This will extend or alter the repertoire of actions subsumed under it (Feldman and Pentland, 2003) and enter into the institutional templates if the modified patterns are externalized and objectified.

This conception of symbolically mediated reproduction allows for

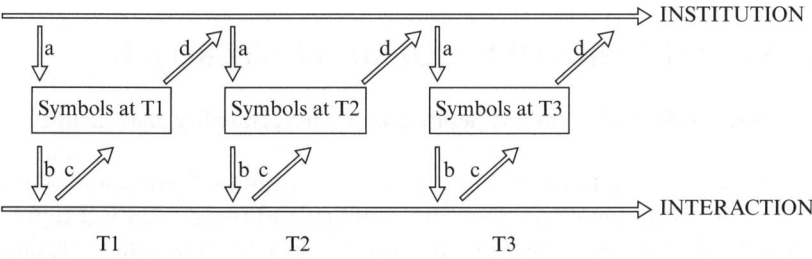

Notes: a = encode, b = interpret and enact, c = replicate or revise, d = externalize and objectify

Figure 11.3   The symbolic mediation of institutionalized trust (adapted from Barley & Tolbert 1997)

a closer look at the mechanisms involved in both (near-)identical and non-identical reproduction. For this, consider again Cohen's (1985) insight, emphasized above, that symbols are imprecise by their very nature and allow actors to supply part of their meaning.

For what the institution supplies are not ready-made trust symbols. As Luhmann (1979) reminds us, the mere repetition of given patterns does not constitute a potent signal of trust; trust needs to be perceived as personalized by the actors. Thus, the institutionalized templates provide (1) symbolic *cores*, and (2) a 'writing guide' for symbolic action that suggests how to structure more specific and personalized meanings around those cores. The combination of a commonly recognizable core and individually devised meaning encapsulated in each symbol allows the actors to compose symbolic expressions of trust and/or trustworthiness that are simultaneously commonly legible and individually credible. Thus, the templates 'do not tell us *what* to mean, but they give us the capacity to make meaning' (Cohen, 1985, p. 16; original emphasis).

The subsequent interpretation of the symbol by the beholder introduces further potential for variation. Whatever the signaller's intention in constructing the symbol, it is its interpretation by the receiver that determines their reaction (Homans, 1961).

One of the chief benefits of this perspective is that it draws our attention to the multiple interpretative processes that are involved in enacting trust templates and making these enactments part of the institution's history. Thus, it recognizes both the great scope for variation within the enactment and institutionalization of trust symbols and the common thread that makes them commonly legible. That is, this perspective is able to accommodate both structure and agency, both stability and change. We will consider each in turn.

INSTITUTIONAL DEVELOPMENT OVER TIME

Institutional Reproduction: Structure and Agency, Stability and Change

First, how does relative stability arise in institutionalized trust? What effects of institutional templates are conducive to (near-)identical reproduction, that is, to preserving particular ways of organizing trusting conduct? We may assume that this is rarely achieved by direct social control. The persistence of specific patterns of trust can be manipulated by the intentional use of power if it is politically desired (Hardy et al., 1998). However, trust can only be maintained if the use of power is seen to be legitimate (Bachmann, 2001). Coercive measures seem generally better suited to pursuing a disruption rather than the perpetuation of particular ways of trusting. Accordingly, we should turn our attention more towards the cognitive and normative rather than coercive pillars of institutions (to use the taxonomy of Scott, 2008).

Normative templates, in the eyes of actors, give a kind of 'moral authority' (Parsons, 1990; Selznick, 1957) to some ways of trust building but not to others, while cognitive templates define what, under given circumstances, is meaningful or even thinkable. The latter type of influence is particularly powerful. Symbols are at their most effective where their influence is tacit (Cohen, 1976). Their taken-for-grantedness removes them from direct scrutiny, and instead invests them with 'the undisputed authority of habit, normality, and common sense' (Schütz, 1967; Swidler, 1986, p. 281). The institutional templates enter into the practical knowledge of actors and form part of an institutionally or organizationally bounded rationality (Simon, 1945; Barley and Tolbert, 1997). These tacit frames form conceptual constraints that:

> enter into the full range of information-processing activities, from determining what information will receive attention, how it will be encoded, how it will be retained, retrieved, and organized into memory, to how it will be interpreted, thus affecting evaluations, judgments, predictions, and inferences. (Scott, 2008, p. 57; also see Scott and Christensen, 1995)

Thus, while the templates do not prescribe conduct in detail, they can act as cognitive and normative 'locks' on interaction (Campbell, 2004). They do so not by force, but simply by providing 'publicly available meanings [which] facilitate certain patterns of action, making them readily available, while discouraging others' (Swidler, 1986, p. 283). That is, institutionalized trust provides a 'symbolic repertoire' that actors can use to construct their actions (Mizrachi et al., 2007).

The elements in this repertoire range from simple, relatively generic gestures to long and complex interlinked action sequences like organizational routines (Feldman and Pentland, 2003). They can be used as building blocks in individually devised and improvised interaction (Swidler, 1986, 2001; also see Bourdieu, 1977, 1984). This shows how the predefinitions and preinterpretations provided by the institutionalized templates *constrain* actors' conduct, but also serve to *enable* trusting interaction.

Institutional repertoires are also translated into those of individual actors. Within their role sets and institutionally bounded rationality, they develop individual 'decision styles' and other sets of skills and habits that are equally individually distinctive and typical of the institution or organization (Scharpf, 1989; Swidler, 2001).

The tacit influences described are conducive to the (near-)identical reproduction of existing templates, when actors use elements of the symbolic repertoire, enact them relatively unreflexively and without significant variation, and contribute to the confirmation of existing institutional patterns without notable changes.

Such an analysis of relative stability over time forms an important element of the novel perspective on trust advocated here. But we should not fall victim to an oft-criticized lapse of institutional theory, viz, ignoring or underestimating the fundamental significance of agency. Much of the institutional literature has portrayed institutions as stable and persistent unless or until exogenous shocks necessitate change (Streeck and Thelen, 2005). Attention to endogenously triggered change may thus be an important response to the 'inertial impasse', which has been criticized as characteristic of much of the new institutionalism (Hay and Wincott, 1998; also see Suddaby et al., 2010). What is more, institutional theorists are increasingly emphasizing the purposive nature even of (near-)identical reproduction of institutional patterns (Lawrence and Suddaby, 2006). Therefore, it is essential to infuse the analysis of institutionalized trust with a greater understanding of the role of agency.

We may take our leads from the analysis by Emirbayer and Mische (1998), who succeed in disaggregating it into three temporal orientations by means of which actors relate to, engage with, and ultimately change, institutional structures. These are: the 'iterational' dimension of agency, which selectively extrapolates elements of past experiences to form a basis for concrete trust decisions; the 'projective' dimension, which relates to the predicted future behaviour of the trustee, especially in regard to the question of honouring or disappointing trust; and the 'practical-evaluative' dimension, which seeks to marry up the idealized contents or 'models' of the institutionalized trust templates with the requirements and limitations of the present context.

These three agentic components represent different ways of relating to institutionalized trust templates. They are, of course, only analytically separable, and in social reality are closely intertwined. Importantly, they not only occur simultaneously but also shape one another. The actors seek to integrate the three temporal orientations not only into a chronological, but also into a logical sequence. As Mead reminds us, 'the past . . . is as hypothetical as the future' (1932, p.12) – both are constructed by reflexive actors. Accordingly, a partner's previous acts can acquire an entirely new meaning in the light of a reinterpretation of their future intentions based on their present behaviour. If an actor's present behaviour calls into question their future trustworthiness, past acts that seemed to be based on goodwill may suddenly come to appear pure calculation in retrospect. Trust, in both its institutional and interactional forms, refers to the future, builds on the past and is continuously reproduced in the present. But at the same time these three orientations form one overarching, integrative narrative in which present, future and past of a trust relation are continuously reconstructed by the actor. This supports Poppo et al.'s (2007) finding that trust builds on an amalgam of the 'shadow of the past' and the 'shadow of the future'.

For present purposes, it is notable that in all three dimensions of agency as well as their overarching narrative, the potential for change in interaction and institution is located in the relationship between actor and institutional context. That is, the transformative potential of agency resides in different ways of relating to the institutionalized trust templates (Emirbayer and Mische, 1998).

On the one hand, all of these different ways are the result of creativity and imagination. Whether in hypothesizing possible futures, weighing up present practicalities, or (re)constructing the meaning of the past, it is the human capacity for 'imaginative distancing' that introduces new perspectives and possibilities into the otherwise uniform institutional context (also see Schütz, 1962, and Mead's 'deliberative attitude', 1932).

On the other hand, agency should not therefore be portrayed as the 'opposite' of structure (Reed, 1997). It does not generate action out of thin air, but generally refers to existing institutional structures. '[J]ust as consciousness is always consciousness *of* something . . ., so too is agency always agency *toward* something' (Emirbayer and Mische, 1998, p.973; original emphasis). The institutionalized trust templates, themselves the result of historical processes, are thus highly consequential for any interaction linked to them. But at the same time this interaction is the result of 'the interpretive processes whereby choices are imagined, evaluated, and contingently reconstructed by actors in ongoing dialogue with unfolding situations' (ibid., p.966). Change in the institutionalized trust templates is dependent, subsequently, on whether the new interactional patterns based on novel ways of relating to them are externalized and objectified. We cannot, therefore, understand the reproduction of long-standing or collective trust orientations over time without careful attention to the interplay of *both* institutional 'structure' and individual agency.

Institutional Transmission and Translation: Trust and Socialization

The above consideration of structure and agency is not only an important element in a conceptual guideline to analysing trust and its institutionalization. It is also crucial for an explanation of how institutionalized trust develops the 'life of its own' typical of institutions, that is, how it can acquire its collective and long-term character. But our understanding of this is only complete once we consider the transmission of institutionalized trust patterns between individual actors.

Indeed, as Berger and Luckmann emphasize, institutionalization itself is only complete once the objectified patterns are passed on to third actors. This occurs in the process of 'socialization' (1967, Ch. III). Socialization has been shown to be connected to (inter-)organizational trust both theoretically and empirically (Farris et al., 1973; Das and Teng, 2001; Six and Sorge, 2008). Importantly, this concerns not only the formal but also the informal dimension of the actor's new context (Louis, 1980; Fine and Holyfield, 1996). A new actor entering the scene is introduced to the typifications created by the original participants to the trust relationship. In this process, the patterns are typically communicated *as fact* ('this is how these things are done'; also see Zucker, 1991). That is, the new actor encounters the roles and routines for trusting as a pre-existent 'facticity outside of himself'. At the same time, the fact that the original creators of the patterns witness this process produces a 'mirror effect' through which institutional reality 'thickens' and 'hardens' for them too (Berger and Luckmann, 1967, p. 76). The transmission of the institutionalized patterns in socialization thus completes the process of objectification for everyone involved.

At the same time, note that communication 'as fact' does not necessarily result in identical transmission, but will typically have a significant element of translation that adapts the institutionalized trust patterns to new contexts and backgrounds (Campbell, 2004, Ch. 3). This also applies to their aforementioned translation into the repertoires of individual actors, who are likely to interpret and employ them in differing ways as a result of different biographical experiences of trust (Hardin, 1993). But as noted, the structuring of individualized meanings around common 'cores' in symbolic mediation means that the resulting symbols of trust can be simultaneously individually distinctive and organizationally typical (or, rather, typical of the organizational team or subgroup to whom the institutionalized trust patterns are relevant).

In organizational reality, the institutionalized trust patterns are typically diffused within teams or other often more informal organizational subgroups. They can also be passed on across organizational generations. This may occur directly, where a transitional phase allows a newcomer to be introduced to their formal and informal roles by their predecessor in a sufficiently long handover period, for example, through 'shadowing'. Perhaps most commonly, the two patterns are combined, as the new role incumbent is socialized into their formal and informal roles by remaining team or group members who are familiar with the relevant formal and informal roles. That is, it is indeed only in socialization that the institutionalization of trust perfects itself. Here, the institutionalized trust patterns become a *collective* characteristic of the organizational team or subgroup. Subsequently, their cross-generational transmission allows them to become *long term* in nature – in particular, more long term than trust, which is a property merely of a dyadic relationship.

This is of central importance to the present argument. If patterns of trust can be objectified and transmitted across generations of organizational actors, then the core of an (inter-)organizational trust relationship can be maintained even beyond the point at which the original creators of the trust relation have moved on and left the organization (that is, in Figure 11.3, the actors at times T1, T2 and T3 need not be the same individuals). Counter to the assumption, implicit in much research and practice, that trust disappears when a participant leaves the relationship, this perspective posits that trust (that is, ways of signalling, building, using trust) can become an attribute not just of individuals, but of groups, teams and organizations themselves (Kroeger, 2012a).

A striking example from the aforementioned empirical study revealed an inter-organizational trust relationship between one of the major UK publishing houses and their chief printing partners, which, according to a respondent, had developed over 'sixty, seventy years'. This trajectory was confirmed by several employees or previous employees of the two companies, who traced it back to an 'intuitive time' of trust building between the two businesses' chief executives in the postwar decades, and found that since then, the trust relation had somehow become part of the 'DNA' of the two organizations and their relationship.

While more detailed research would be necessary to trace specific symbolic continuities over the years, this example illustrates well the continuity of a trust relationship over a period of time of such length that all members of both organizations are likely to have been replaced since its beginning. Here, it would seem we are within our rights to infer that an institutionalization of trust has enabled trust to become a collective and, consequently, a long-term orientation.

CONCLUSION

What, then, to take away from this contribution? First and foremost, a simple insight, yet one not previously conceptualized in any depth: trust can be institutionalized. Let us briefly summarize the analysis of this process presented here. Trust is built and maintained centrally through symbolic action. These patterns of signalling trust and trustworthiness can be institutionalized through processes of habitualization and typification. The typifications, embedded in networks of relationships and resource configurations, serve as templates for subsequent trusting interaction. Actors can use the templates as symbolic 'cores' and enrich them with individualized and contextualized meanings. The reproduction of institutionalized trust thus relies on a particular combination of institutional structure and individual agency fit to create trust symbols that are at the same time interpersonally credible and collectively legible, distinctive to the individual and typical of the group of actors they relate to. Because in institutionalization the patterns of signalling trust become, in principle, transmittable across groups and generations of organizational actors, the resulting symbolic repertoire of trust can become partially (sic!) independent of the individuals enacting the relation at a given point in time.

With this, the analysis fulfils what it initially set out to do: it provides a step-by-step investigation tracing the genesis of collective and long-term trust orientations. Consider especially that it has shown that trust between organizations or groups can exhibit a significant degree of continuity even beyond the point where the original participants to the trust relationship have left. This trust is both collective, as it goes beyond the original dyadic trust relation, and long term in nature, as it may continue over subsequent generations of newly arriving organizational actors. (More precisely, it can be long term *because* it is collective in nature, as in its reproduction trust oscillates across analytical levels, as depicted in Figure 11.3. This process is described in more detail in Kroeger, 2012a.) Here, both long-term and collective trust orientations clearly appear as *institutionalized* trust orientations (with individual variations in the translation of these collective orientations into interpersonal ones).

This perspective is fit to inform a range of empirical investigations of how specific ways of building (and using) trust can arise in concrete organizations or groups within them, and how they can come to be regarded as typical of the organizational 'way of life' both by its members and by outside observers. Essentially, thus, this perspective provides us with an analytical handle on the emergence, persistence and change of 'trust cultures'. These may be those of organizations as a whole, or of (potentially conflicting) groups within them (Kroeger, 2012b).

In practical terms, some have noted that the idea of institutionalizing trust may hold the promise of making trust more stable and enduring (Dasgupta, 1988; Schweer, 2003). Acknowledging the potential for an institutionalization of trust can help demonstrate that under specific circumstances trust may be less idiosyncratic, less ephemeral and less arduous to build up than it has hitherto seemed (see Gambetta, 1988). Certainly, the possibility of such long-term and collective trust orientations may play a constitutive role in any kind of 'trust-sensitive management' within and between organizations (Sydow, 2006).

Conceptually, too, the analysis presented has some important ramifications. I would like to stress three interrelated points in particular. First, it invests effort in systematically analysing the relationship of (individual) agency and (social) structure in trust building, as called for emphatically by a number of trust researchers (Bachmann, 1998; Sydow, 1998, 2006; Möllering, 2006b). This helps avoid, on the one hand, 'undersocialized' or pure micro-level accounts in which trust appears as little more than a personal attribute, the result of individual predispositions or idiosyncratic life experiences (Rotter, 1971; Hardin, 1993). And on the other, it also avoids 'oversocialized' or pure macro-level accounts in which we look at trust from so far away that we cannot make out the dynamics of individual trust relations and can only equate institutional-structural preconditions with trust levels (see again Zucker, 1986; also see Lane, 1998).

Second and relatedly, the present approach answers calls by an increasing number of trust researchers to pay more, and more systematic, attention to dynamics of trust on and across multiple analytical levels (Lewis and Weigert, 1985; Fang et al., 2008). Especially conceptual research in this area is still nascent at best; few studies address trust on more than one analytical level (Janowicz and Noorderhaven, 2006). This is the case even for fields such as the study of inter-organizational trust, where multi- and cross-level dynamics form a constitutive element (Gulati and Sytch, 2008). Thus, the analysis of multi- and cross-level dynamics of trust has been identified by some scholars as one of the most pressing challenges facing current trust research (Zaheer et al., 1998; Schoorman et al., 2007). The institutionalization perspective presented offers a systematic approach to analysing both the development of trust on, and its movement across the individual micro- and the group or organizational meso-level.

Third, in doing so the analysis presented is fit to elucidate the role that the *organization*, as an entity in its own right, plays in (inter-)organizational trust building – an aspect that to date has remained curiously obscure in organizational trust research (Currall and Inkpen, 2002; Six and Sorge, 2008). Especially in its identification of organizational-level continuities of trust over time, it goes beyond existing research by demonstrating that in trust building, too, the organizational and group levels unfold dynamics irreducible to the trusting orientations of individuals (also see Rousseau and House, 1994).

Many potential extensions of this theoretical approach are conceivable. For instance, it would seem a particularly promising undertaking to extend this analysis to include symbolic expressions of power, entwined with those of trust, in order to capture the institutionalization and reproduction of the two most significant channels of control within and between organizations (Bachmann, 2001). For the time being, however, there would seem to be grounds for confidence that the framework presented represents a worthwhile and fruitful contribution to trust research.

NOTES

*   I would like to thank Christel Lane, Reinhard Bachmann and Guido Möllering for their helpful comments.
1.   All examples used in this contribution are taken from an empirical study of trust building in the UK book publishing industry. It consists of 21 semi-structured interviews, 90 minutes on average in length, with executives at some of the major UK publishing houses, as well as some of their most significant external partners. The study is not described here in any more depth since the data will serve as a source of illustrative examples only. Its methodology is laid out in more detail in Kroeger (2012a).

REFERENCES

Bacharach, M. and D. Gambetta (2001), 'Trust in signs', in K.S. Cook (ed.), *Trust in Society*, New York: Russell Sage, pp. 148–84.
Bachmann, R. (1998), 'Conclusion: trust – conceptual aspects of a complex phenomenon', in C. Lane and R. Bachmann (eds), *Trust Within and Between Organizations: Conceptual Issues and Empirical Applications*, Oxford: OUP, pp. 298–322.
Bachmann, R. (2001), 'Trust, power and control in trans-organizational relations', *Organization Studies*, **22**(2), 337–65.
Barley, S.R. and P.S. Tolbert (1997), 'Institutionalization and structuration: studying the links between action and institution', *Organization Studies*, **18**(1), 93–117.
Beckert, J. (2005), 'Trust and the performative construction of markets', MPIfG Discussion Paper No. 05/8, Cologne: Max Planck Institute for the Study of Societies.
Berger, P.L. (1992), 'Reflections on the twenty-fifth anniversary of *The Social Construction of Reality*', *Perspectives*, **15**(2), 1–4.
Berger, P.L. and T. Luckmann (1967), *The Social Construction of Reality: A Treatise in the Sociology of Knowledge*, London: Allen Lane.
Blau, P.M. (1964), *Exchange and Power in Social Life*, London: Wiley.
Bottom, W.P., K. Gibson, S.E. Daniels and J.K. Murnighan (2002), 'When talk is not cheap: substantive penance and expressions of intent in rebuilding cooperation', *Organization Science*, **13**(5), 497–513.
Bourdieu, P. (1977), *Outline of a Theory of Practice*, Cambridge, UK: CUP.
Bourdieu, P. (1984), *Distinction: A Social Critique of the Judgement of Taste*, London: Routledge.
Campbell, J.L. (2004), *Institutional Change and Globalization*, Princeton, NJ: Princeton University Press.
Clemens, E.S. and J.M. Cook (1999), 'Politics and institutionalism: explaining durability and change', *Annual Review of Sociology*, **25**(1), 441–66.
Cohen, A.P. (1976), *Two-Dimensional Man*, Berkeley, CA: University of California Press.
Cohen, A.P. (1985), *The Symbolic Construction of Community*, Chichester: Horwood.
Collins, G. (2005), 'Trust in post-bureaucratic organizations', in J. Finch and M. Orillard (eds), *Complexity and the Economy*, Cheltenham, UK and Northampton, MA, USA: Edward Elgar, pp. 172–90.

Creed, W.E.D. and R.E. Miles (1996), 'Trust in organizations: a conceptual framework linking organizational forms, managerial philosophies, and the opportunity costs of controls', in R.M. Kramer and T.R. Tyler (eds), *Trust in Organizations: Frontiers of Theory and Research*, London: Sage, pp. 16–38.
Currall, S.C. and J. Epstein (2003), 'The fragility of organizational trust: lessons from the rise and fall of Enron', *Organizational Dynamics*, **32**(2), 193–206.
Currall, S.C. and A.C. Inkpen (2002), 'A multilevel approach to trust in joint ventures', *Journal of International Business Studies*, **33**(3), 479–95.
Das, T.K. and B.S. Teng (2001), 'Trust, control, and risk in strategic alliances: an integrated framework', *Organization Studies*, **22**(2), 251–83.
Dasgupta, P. (1988), 'Trust as a commodity', in D. Gambetta (ed.), *Trust: Making and Breaking Cooperative Relations*, New York: Blackwell, pp. 49–72.
Dodgson, M. (1993), 'Learning, trust, and technological collaboration', *Human Relations*, **46**(1), 77–95.
Doney, P.M. and J.P. Cannon (1997), 'An examination of the nature of trust in buyer–seller relationships', *Journal of Marketing*, **61**(2), 35–51.
Emirbayer, M. and A. Mische (1998), 'What is agency?', *American Journal of Sociology*, **103**(4), 962–1023.
Fang, E., R.W. Palmatier, L.K. Scheer and N. Li (2008), 'Trust at different organizational levels', *Journal of Marketing*, **72**(2), 80–98.
Farris, G.F., E.E. Senner and A.D. Butterfield (1973), 'Trust, culture, and organizational behavior', *Industrial Relations*, **12**(2), 144–57.
Feldman, M.S. and B.T. Pentland (2003), 'Reconceptualizing routines as a source of flexibility and change', *Administrative Science Quarterly*, **48**(1), 94–118.
Ferrin, D.L., M.C. Bligh and J.C. Kohles (2007), 'Can I trust you to trust me? A theory of trust, monitoring, and cooperation in interpersonal and intergroup relationships', *Group and Organization Management*, **32**(4), 465–99.
Fine, G. and L. Holyfield (1996), 'Secrecy, trust and dangerous leisure: generating group cohesion in voluntary organizations', *Social Psychology Quarterly*, **59**(1), 22–38.
Fox, A. (1974), *Beyond Contract: Work, Power and Trust Relations*, London: Faber and Faber.
Friedland, R. and R.R. Alford (1991), 'Bringing society back in: symbols, practices, and institutional contradictions', in W.W. Powell and P.J. DiMaggio (eds), *The New Institutionalism in Organizational Analysis*, Chicago: University of Chicago Press, pp. 232–63.
Gambetta, D. (1988), 'Can we trust trust?', in D. Gambetta (ed.), *Trust: Making and Breaking Cooperative Relations*, Oxford: Blackwell, pp. 213–37.
Giddens, A. (1984), *The Constitution of Society*, Cambridge, UK: Polity.
Giddens, A. (1994), 'Risk, trust, reflexivity', in U. Beck, A. Giddens and S. Lash (eds), *Reflexive Modernization*, Cambridge, UK: Polity Press, pp. 184–97.
Gillespie, N.A. and G. Dietz (2009), 'Trust repair after an organization-level failure', *Academy of Management Review*, **34**(1), 127–45.
Goffman, E. (1967), *Interaction Ritual*, New York: Pantheon.
Goffman, E. (1983), 'The interaction order', *American Sociological Review*, **48**(1), 1–17.
Granovetter, M. (1985), 'Economic action and social structure: the problem of embeddedness', *American Journal of Sociology*, **91**(3), 481–510.
Granovetter, M. (1992), 'Economic institutions as social constructions: a framework for analysis', *Acta Sociologica*, **35**(1), 3–11.
Gulati, R. and M. Sytch (2008), 'Does familarity breed trust? Revisiting the antecedents of trust', *Managerial and Decision Economics*, **29**(2–3), 165–90.
Haas, D.F. and F.A. Deseran (1981), 'Trust and symbolic exchange', *Social Psychology Quarterly*, **44**(1), 3–13.
Hall, P.A. and R.C.R. Taylor (1996), 'Political science and the three new institutionalisms', *Political Studies*, **44**(5), 936–57.
Hardin, R. (1993), 'The street-level epistemology of trust', *Politics and Society*, **21**(4), 505–29.
Hardy, C., N. Phillips and T. Lawrence (1998), 'Distinguishing trust and power in

interorganizational relations: forms and façades of trust', in C. Lane and R. Bachmann (eds), *Trust Within and Between Organizations: Conceptual Issues and Empirical Applications*, Oxford: OUP, pp. 64–87.

Hay, C. and D. Wincott (1998), 'Structure, agency and historical institutionalism', *Political Studies*, **46**(5), 951–7.

Hirsch, P.M. (1997), 'Sociology without social structure: neoinstitutional theory meets brave new world', *American Journal of Sociology*, **102**(6), 1702–23.

Homans, G.C. (1961), 'Social behavior as exchange', *American Journal of Sociology*, **63**(6), 597–606.

Janowicz, M. and N. Noorderhaven (2006), 'Levels of inter-organizational trust: conceptualization and measurement', in R. Bachmann and A. Zaheer (eds), *Handbook of Trust Research*, Cheltenham, UK and Northampton, MA, USA: Edward Elgar, pp. 264–79.

Janowicz-Panjaitan, M. and N. Noorderhaven (2009), 'Trust, calculation and inter-organizational learning of tacit knowledge: an organizational roles perspective', *Organization Studies*, **30**(10), 1021–44.

Kramer, R.M. (1999), 'Trust and distrust in organizations: emerging perspectives, enduring questions', *Annual Review of Psychology*, **50**(1), 569–98.

Kroeger, F. (2012a), 'Trusting organizations: the institutionalization of trust in interorganizational relationships', *Organization*, **19**(6), 743–63.

Kroeger, F. (2012b), 'Organizational trust cultures: emergence, persistence and change', paper prepared for the 28th EGOS Colloquium, Helsinki.

Lane, C. (1998), 'Introduction: theories and issues in the study of trust', in C. Lane and R. Bachmann (eds), *Trust Within and Between Organizations: Conceptual Issues and Empirical Applications*, Oxford: OUP, pp. 1–30.

Lawrence, T. and R. Suddaby (2006), 'Institutions and institutional work', in S. Clegg, C. Hardy, T. Lawrence and W.R. Nord (eds), *Handbook of Organization Studies*, London: Sage, pp. 215–54.

Lewis, J.D. and A. Weigert (1985), 'Trust as a social reality', *Social Forces*, **63**(4), 967–85.

Louis, M.R. (1980), 'Surprise and sense making: what newcomers experience in entering unfamiliar organizational settings', *Administrative Science Quarterly*, **25**(2), 226–51.

Luhmann, N. (1979), *Trust and Power*, Chichester: Wiley.

Luhmann, N. (1988), 'Familiarity, confidence, trust: problems and alternatives', in D. Gambetta (ed.), *Trust: Making and Breaking Cooperative Relations*, Oxford: Blackwell, pp. 94–107.

Mead, G.H. (1932), *The Philosophy of the Present*, Chicago: University of Chicago Press.

Meyerson, D., K.E. Weick and R.M. Kramer (1996), 'Swift trust and contemporary groups', in R.M. Kramer and T.R. Tyler (eds), *Trust in Organizations: Frontiers of Theory and Research*, London: Sage, pp. 166–95.

Mizrachi, N., I. Dori and R.R. Anspach (2007), 'Repertoires of trust: the practice of trust in a multinational organization amid political conflict', *American Sociological Review*, **72**(1), 143–65.

Möllering, G. (2006a), *Trust: Reason, Routine, Reflexivity*, Amsterdam: Elsevier.

Möllering, G. (2006b), 'Trust, institutions, agency: towards a neoinstitutional theory of trust', in R. Bachmann and A. Zaheer (eds), *Handbook of Trust Research*, Cheltenham, UK and Northampton, MA, USA: Edward Elgar, pp. 355–76.

Parsons, T. (1990), 'Prolegomena to a theory of social institutions', *American Sociological Review*, **55**(3), 319–39.

Poppo, L., K.Z. Zhou and S. Ryu (2007), 'Alternative origins to interorganizational trust: an interdependence perspective on the shadow of the past and the shadow of the future', *Organization Science*, **19**(1), 39–55.

Ravasi, D. and V. Rindova (2008), 'Symbolic value creation', in D. Barry and H. Hansen (eds), *Handbook of New Approaches in Management and Organization*, London: Sage, pp. 270–87.

Reed, M.I. (1997), 'In praise of duality and dualism: rethinking agency and structure in organizational analysis', *Organization Studies*, **18**(1), 21–42.

Rotter, J.B. (1971), 'Generalized expectancies for interpersonal trust', *American Psychologist*, **26**(5), 443–52.
Rousseau, D.M. and R.J. House (1994), 'Meso organizational behavior: avoiding three fundamental biases', in Cary L. Cooper and Denise M. Rousseau (ed.), *Trends in Organizational Behavior*, Vol. 1, pp. 13–30.
Scharpf, F. (1989), 'Decision rules, decision styles and policy choices', *Journal of Theoretical Politics*, **1**(2), 149–76.
Schein, E.H. (1991), 'The role of the founder in the creation of organizational culture', in P.J Frost, L.F. Moore, M.R. Louis, C.C. Lundberg and J. Martin (eds), *Reframing Organizational Culture*, London: Sage, pp. 14–25.
Schoorman, F.D., R.C. Mayer and J.H. Davis (2007), 'An integrative model of organizational trust: past, present, and future', *Academy of Management Review*, **32**(2), 344–54.
Schütz, A. (1962), 'On multiple realities', in *Collected Papers I: The Problem of Social Reality*, The Hague: Martinus Nijhoff, pp. 207–59.
Schütz, A. (1967), *The Phenomenology of the Social World*, Evanston, IL: Northwestern University Press.
Schweer, M.K.W. (2003), 'Vertrauen als Organizationsprinzip: Vertrauensförderung im Spannungsfeld personalen und systemischen Vertrauens', *Erwägen Wissen Ethik*, **14**, 323–32.
Scott, W.R. (2008), *Institutions and Organizations: Ideas and Interests*, London: Sage.
Scott, W.R. and S. Christensen (1995), 'Conclusion: crafting a wider lens', in W.R. Scott and S. Christensen (eds), *The Institutional Construction of Organizations: International and Longitudinal Studies*, London: Sage, pp. 302–13.
Searle, R., D.N. Den Hartog, A. Weibel, N. Gillespie, F. Six, T. Hatzakis and D. Skinner (2011), 'Trust in the employer: the role of high-involvement work practices and procedural justice in European organizations', *International Journal of Human Resource Management*, **22**(5), 1069–92.
Selznick, P. (1957), *Leadership in Administration: A Sociological Interpretation*, New York: Harper and Row.
Sewell, W.H. (1992), 'A theory of structure: duality, agency, and transformation', *American Journal of Sociology*, **98**(1), 1–29.
Simon, H.A. (1945), *Administrative Behavior*, New York: Macmillan.
Singelmann, P. (1972), 'Exchange as symbolic interaction: convergences between two theoretical perspectives', *American Sociological Review*, **37**(4), 414–24.
Sitkin, S.B. and N.L. Roth (1993), 'Explaining the limited effectiveness of legalistic "remedies" for trust/distrust', *Organization Science*, **4**(3), 367–92.
Six, F. (2007), 'Building interpersonal trust within organizations: a relational signalling perspective', *Journal of Management and Governance*, **11**(3), 285–309.
Six, F. and A. Sorge (2008), 'Creating a high-trust organization: an exploration into organizational policies that stimulate interpersonal trust building', *Journal of Management Studies*, **45**(5), 857–84.
Six, F., B. Nooteboom and A. Hoogendoorn (2010), 'Actions that build interpersonal trust: a relational signalling perspective', *Review of Social Economy*, **68**(3), 285–315.
Stinchcombe, A.L. (1968), *Constructing Social Theories*, Chicago: University of Chicago Press.
Streeck, W. and K.A. Thelen (2005), 'Introduction', in W. Streeck and K.A. Thelen (eds), *Beyond Continuity: Institutional Change in Advanced Political Economies*, Oxford: OUP, pp. 1–39.
Suddaby, R., K.D. Elsbach, R. Greenwood, J.W. Meyer and T. Zilber (2010), 'Organizations and their institutional environments – bringing meaning, values and culture back in: introduction to the Special Research Forum', *Academy of Management Journal*, **53**(6), 1234–40.
Swidler, A. (1986), 'Culture in action: symbols and strategies', *American Sociological Review*, **51**(2), 273–86.
Swidler, A. (2001), *Talk of Love: How Culture Matters*, Chicago: University of Chicago Press.

Sydow, J. (1998), 'Understanding the constitution of interorganizational trust', in C. Lane and R. Bachmann (eds), *Trust Within and Between Organizations: Conceptual Issues and Empirical Applications*, Oxford: OUP, pp. 31–63.

Sydow, J. (2006), 'How can systems trust systems? A structuration perspective on trust-building in inter-organizational relations', in R. Bachmann and A. Zaheer (eds), *Handbook of Trust Research*, Cheltenham, UK and Northampton, MA, USA: Edward Elgar, pp. 377–96.

Thelen, K. and S. Steinmo (1992), 'Historical institutionalism in comparative politics', in S. Steinmo, K. Thelen and F. Longstreth (eds), *Structuring Politics: Historical Institutionalism in Comparative Analysis*, Cambridge, UK: CUP, pp. 1–32.

Weber, J.M., D. Malhotra and J.K. Murnighan (2005), 'Normal acts of irrational trust: motivated attributions and the trust development process', in B. Staw and R. Kramer (eds), *Research in Organizational Behavior*, Vol. 26, pp. 75–101.

Weick, K.E. (1985), 'The significance of corporate culture', in P.J. Frost, L.F. Moore, M.R. Louis, C.C. Lundberg and J. Martin (eds), *Organizational Culture*, London: Sage, pp. 381–9.

Weingast, B. (1994), 'Institutionalizing trust: the political and economic roots of ethnic and regional conflict', paper prepared for the conference 'What is Institutionalism Now?', Maryland.

Zaheer, A. and J. Harris (2006), 'Interorganizational trust', in O. Shenkar and J. Reuer (eds), *Handbook of Strategic Alliances*, London: Sage, pp. 169–98.

Zaheer, A. and N. Venkatraman (1995), 'Relational governance as an interorganizational strategy: an empirical test of the role of trust in economic exchange', *Strategic Management Journal*, **16**(5), 373–92.

Zaheer, A., B. McEvily and V. Perrone (1998), 'Does trust matter? Exploring the effects of interorganizational and interpersonal trust on performance', *Organization Science*, **9**(2), 141–59.

Zucker, L.G. (1986), 'Production of trust: institutional sources of economic structure, 1840–1920', *Research in Organizational Behavior*, **8**(1), 53–111.

Zucker, L.G. (1991), 'The role of institutionalization in cultural persistence', in W.W. Powell and P.J. DiMaggio (eds), *The New Institutionalism in Organizational Analysis*, Chicago: University of Chicago Press. pp. 83–107.

12. Process views of trusting and crises*
Guido Möllering

INTRODUCTION

For decades, surveys have been used to measure the level of trust people have in other people generally as well as in various institutions, organizations, or groups and to show changes in trust over time (see, for example, Barber, 1983; Putnam, 1995; Glaeser et al., 2000; Uslaner, 2002; Delhey and Newton, 2005). However, because of the nature of the questions asked, the survey results mostly cannot *explain* the levels and changes observed. The focus tends to be descriptively on 'how much' (or even just, 'how many') people trust – and hardly on 'how' people work on trust continuously. This is deeply problematic especially when survey reports call implicitly for means to produce or restore higher levels of trust, meaning that they call for solutions to a problem they cannot really pin down. At the least, this would require a simultaneous measurement of (changes in) the antecedents of (changes in) trust. More rigorously, people's trust should be conceptualized and operationalized as a continuous process of forming and reforming the attitudes that static surveys have measured so far and, crucially, as part of larger social processes. However, it is much easier to advocate a process perspective of trust in general than to devise a specific process framework for empirical research. This is because 'process' has many meanings ranging from pragmatic to paradigmatic persuasions when it comes to defining and applying the term in research (for an overview in organization studies, see Hernes, 2008).

This chapter wants to reinforce the call for process approaches in trust research (Nooteboom, 2002, pp. 84–101; Möllering, 2006, pp. 77–103). Key contributions such as those by Blau (1964), Zand (1972), Luhmann (1979), Sabel (1993), Ring and Van de Ven (1994) and Nooteboom (1996) have established the fact that trust is a result as well as a condition of social interaction processes. Lewicki and Bunker (1996) showed how the quality of trust changes over time as actors interact and gain knowledge about each other in their relationships. We can go further and study trust not only as part of a process but as a process in itself (see Khodyakov, 2007). This deviates from the notion of 'trust' as a choice at a particular point in time as well as from the notion of 'trust' as an attitude or even predisposition that is fairly stable over time.

A shared starting point for highlighting the process character of trust could be to speak of 'trusting', not 'trust' (see Wright and Ehnert, 2010, p. 116). 'Trusting' expresses that the object of study is not just a measurable outcome (in other words, attitude or behaviour) but the particular ways such outcomes are produced and used (see Zucker, 1986, who writes on the 'production of trust'). 'Trusting' acknowledges that the 'product' of trust is always unfinished and needs to be worked upon continuously (note also how Vlaar, Chapter 4 this volume, analyses contracting and not just contracts). For example, if 'trust' implies a 'willingness of a party to be vulnerable' (Mayer et al., 1995, p. 712), 'trusting' encompasses how people generate, maintain, apply and possibly lose such willingness. Another example, my own preoccupation with suspension (or the leap of faith, see Möllering, 2001) is only a peripheral concern for those interested in 'trust', but essential for 'trusting', because suspension tries to clarify *how* people trust: 'the *process* that enables actors to deal with irreducible uncertainty and vulnerability' (Möllering, 2006, p. 110; emphasis added).

Moreover, recent work on trust repair still focuses in many ways on the more or less desirable outcome of 'trust', but it also goes a long way in recognizing that (re-)building trust is contingent upon the circumstances and history of specific social relationships so that there are different ways of 'trusting' in the sense of developing positive expectations in the face of uncertainty (Kim et al., 2004; Dirks et al., 2009; Gillespie and Dietz, 2009; Kramer and Lewicki, 2010). Clearly, this line of thinking can be applied not only to cases of trust repair in existing relationships but also to processes of trust development in new relationships (for example, McKnight et al., 1998) and over time (for example, Lewicki and Bunker, 1996; Lewicki et al., 2006). The crucial point here is to recognize more than just the mere shift in the bases of trust, for example, from calculus to knowledge to identification (according to Lewicki and Bunker, 1996) at different stages of the relationship. These shifts imply important changes in the way trustors (can) use the bases for their trust and, hence, they are changes in the quality of trusting. In Lewicki and Bunker's (1996) model trust bases build up on top of each other and are combined in trust, but when we focus on 'trusting' we see that the logic of calculation is not easily reconciled with the notion of identification to the point that the former has to stay very much in the background in close relationships. Certain checks may be appropriate in a new relationship but not in an established one: 'Once mutual trust has been safely established, it would be blatantly tactless – if not quite a disastrous lapse – if one of the participants wanted to return to the learning stage and to use the cautious strategies which were sensible at that early juncture' (Luhmann, 1979, pp. 44–5). Trusting is not only influenced by the stage of a relationship but also by the context of the relationship (for example, business or friendship) and by the cultural context that influences the appropriateness of using one trust basis or the other (Wright and Ehnert, 2010).

The conceptual shift from 'trust' to 'trusting' seems subtle but it is significant. Process views of 'trusting' emphasize that trust is always 'in process' and is even a process in itself (see below). For illustration, consider the difference between 'life/death' and 'living', in analogy to 'trust/distrust' and 'trusting'. We may be interested in determining whether an organism is dead or alive but it is a different question to ask how the organism manages to keep on living. Process views of trusting are interested in the latter kind of question. This chapter attempts to give an overview of approaches that appear useful in this vein. They hold the potential to study 'trusting' and not just 'trust'.

However, even if we can agree on 'trusting' as our main object of research, particularly in relation to crises that make trusting more difficult or that have arisen because trusting has become difficult, we may not agree on a single avenue for doing process research on trusting. For instance, Dibben (2000) adopted and developed a remarkable Whiteheadian approach to study trust as process, but there are other process views as well. In this chapter I offer a framework for categorizing process views of trusting, without suggesting that one is principally superior to the others. They are all needed to build knowledge about trusting. It will be evident, though, that some are just loosely committed to the notion of 'process' while others refer more rigorously to the ontological and epistemological assumptions of a particular process theory (see, for example, Bakken and Hernes, 2006 on 'strong' and 'weak' process views of organizing). Hence my contribution will be a framework for positioning process studies of trusting and for facilitating exchange and inspiration between different process views. The value of integration will be illustrated by discussing how different views of trusting, together, enable a more holistic understanding of crises. The next part of this chapter is devoted to conceptual development, followed by a discussion of my framework's methodological and practical implications, and finally some preliminary conclusions.

CONCEPTUAL DEVELOPMENT

Mental and Social Processes of Trusting

A first important analytical distinction needs to be introduced as to whether the process of trusting is understood mainly as a mental process or as a social process. For a full understanding of trusting, mental and social processes need to be reconnected eventually, but research differs across disciplines according to whether mental or social processes are focused on. On the one hand, when mental processes of trusting are emphasized, investigators are interested in how trusting produces and maintains a certain state of mind cognitively and affectively at specific points in time, for example, decisions, or over longer periods of time, for example, attitudes (for example, Rotter, 1967; Deutsch, 1973; Coleman, 1990; Hardin, 1993; McAllister, 1995). The common question is how individual actors develop and hold positive expectations in the face of uncertainty and vulnerability toward others. The idea of process can be applied here, for example, in the sense that antecedents will not automatically result in trust but need to be interpreted, combined, reconciled, or suspended by trustors (for example, Möllering, 2001) as well as in the sense of the mental dynamics of trusting such as confirmatory bias or framing that make the temporary, unfinished outcome of 'trust' an idiosyncratic accomplishment (for example, Good, 1988; Jones, 1996).

On the other hand, though not in opposition to mental processes of trusting, researchers study social processes of trusting, which means that they investigate, for example, interactions between trustors and trustees, the development of relationships between actors, the continuous impact of social context on trusting, and also the mechanisms that give rise to desirable (or perhaps undesirable) social effects of trust (for example, Blau, 1964; Zand, 1972; Giddens, 1994; Ring and Van de Ven, 1994; McKnight et al., 1998; Bacharach and Gambetta, 2001; Beckert, 2005; Serva et al., 2005; Sydow, 2006; Tsui-Auch and Möllering, 2010; Wright and Ehnert, 2010; Bachmann and Inkpen, 2011; Kroeger, 2012). Trusting as a social process entails behaviours such as signalling, negotiating, sense-making, contracting, cooperating, reciprocating, investing, imitating, or complying. Such behaviours, however, do not merely reflect mental states of the actors. For one, they may *alter* their mental states and, overall, they (re)produce the relevant social system's structures and resources (for example, Sydow, 1998; Wright and Ehnert, 2010). Trusting, then, is a process occurring in any social system, but in various ways so that systems can be described and differentiated by how 'trusting' happens in them as well as how much 'trust' between actors they contain and how this 'trust' is structured. In this light, the question is not so much if the system 'itself' can be trusted (Luhmann, 1979; Giddens, 1990) but if the system supports the social process of trusting (Zucker, 1986; Bachmann and Inkpen, 2011).

Regarding the question of how to conceptualize trust in organizations and institutions (as objects of trust), the distinction between mental and social processes of trusting can be useful in the following ways: first, organizations and institutions can be assessed as to whether they are perceived to support social processes of trusting that are related to individual actors' mental processes of trusting. Zucker (1986) calls this 'institutional-based trust', Sydow (1998) highlights structuration-theoretical rules and resources for trust, and I point to phenomenological, ethnomethodological and neoinstitutional concepts that emphasize the underlying routines of trusting (Möllering, 2006, pp. 51–75). This will probably cover most aspects of contemporary discussions about trust in organizations and institutions (see also Bachmann and Inkpen, 2011). Second, whether organizations and institutions possess actor-like qualities thus becomes a very different question that revolves around attributions of agency (in other words, decision-making, formulation of expectations, or implementation of policies) at levels above and beyond human individuals (for example, Luhmann, 1979; Giddens, 1990; Meyer and Jepperson, 2000; see also Zaheer et al., 1998). Such quasi-actors would also be engaged in 'mental' and social processes of trusting, enacted through routines and by their members. Yet the more interesting point seems to be the first one: how organizations and institutions provide resources and structures to the social process of trusting (Bachmann and Inkpen, 2011). For example, Perrone et al. (2003) find that trust between inter-organizational boundary spanners as individuals depends on the organizational empowerment or constraint they experience. However, substantial organizational and institutional change, failure, or demise might also be the result as much as the cause of people stopping to rely on particular social structures that used to channel their social processes of trusting. Hence, it is by looking at changes in the social processes of trusting that we can explain changes in 'trust' – toward more or less abstract and generic actors. Often, in one crisis or another, it will make more sense to say that a system no longer supports the processes of trusting than to say people have lost trust in the system – a point I shall return to toward the end of this chapter.

Five Process Views of Trusting: A Framework

Alongside the distinction between mental and social processes of trusting, which may be seen as different though interconnected levels at which trusting takes place, I will now introduce five process views that highlight different mechanisms in trusting. These mechanisms may be at work at mental and social levels as well as across levels. They are labelled process views of trusting as (1) continuing, (2) processing, (3) learning, (4) becoming and (5) constituting. To some extent, they build onto each other and develop from relatively moderate to more pronounced notions of process.

1 Trusting as continuing

The emphasis on 'trusting', instead of 'trust', can mean, first of all, the mere acknowledgement that trust is not momentary and static but continuous and dynamic in the most fundamental sense: it has a temporal dimension. Accordingly, researchers develop an interest in changes of trust over time and typical cycles (or life cycles) of trust (Lewicki and Bunker, 1996; Lewicki et al., 2006). This kind of longitudinal perspective (Polyhart and Vandenberg, 2010) is very common in work on generalized trust and social capital (for example, Paxton, 1999). While such work often discusses alleged declines in trust, stable trust levels are just as remarkable as rising or volatile ones if, in a process view, we take to heart that trusting expresses the fact that trust needs to be continuously (re)produced. Generally, any trustful state of mind is preliminary and unfinished; it has to been seen in relation to prior states of mind and likely future states of mind. However, this kind of process view is primarily descriptive and still focuses on the notion of 'trust' as an outcome, an entity, though it could be the starting point for explaining how trust changes over time, using the notion of 'trusting' to connect different states of trust at different points in time or around critical events and to consider the relative importance of past, present and future in different instances (see Khodyakov, 2007 and Wright and Ehnert, 2010, who suggest useful links to Emirbayer and Mische's, 1998 temporal conceptualization of agency). Several authors have studied trust levels before and after major interventions – for example, Sitkin and Stickel (1996) for a quality management programme and Walgenbach (2001) for ISO certification. Clearly, in a process view such work should focus on how the practical implementation of an intervention changes the way people trust – their 'trusting' – but most longitudinal studies of trust still analyse mainly the trust level at different points in time, not the process.

2 Trusting as processing

Many studies of trust, especially those focusing on mental processes but also those on social processes, can be reframed as studies of how trustors and trustees generate and 'process' (in other words, handle) information in order to produce the outcome of trust (of some quantity/quality or another). This is not a proper process view yet but could be developed in this direction. Most prominently, Mayer et al.'s (1995) framework builds on the idea that indicators of trustworthiness are somehow perceived and, presumably, processed by actors to determine their level of trust and subsequent willingness to take risks. Rational choice models of trust as a bet, since Coleman (1990) at the latest, specify a simple algorithm for trust that processes information about expected losses, gains and probabilities. Hardin (1993) speaks of 'instinctive Bayesianism' and Kramer (1996) sees an 'intuitive auditor at work'. This is further elaborated on the basis of signalling theory (for example, Dasgupta, 1988; Bacharach and Gambetta, 2001). A number of formal models of trust have been suggested (for example, Bhattacharya et al., 1998) and researchers have been preoccupied with 'optimal' trust (Wicks et al., 1999). Actors' limitations in calculating trust have been noted early on, even from within the rational choice camp (for example, Elster, 1984, 1989), but the idea that trust involves information processing is solidly established. It is even still prominent in Khodyakov's (2007, p. 126) 'definition of trust as a process', which describes trust as 'constant imaginative anticipation' that is 'based on' four factors, echoing the logic of a black-boxed input–output relationship despite the sophisticated concept of agency Khodyakov adopts from Emirbayer and Mische (1998).

As has been hinted at in the introduction, a process view of trusting as processing requires a closer look at how information becomes a preliminary state of trust. For one, different categories of trustworthiness cues may become more or less important over time as relationships develop (Aubert and Kelsey, 2003; Schoorman et al., 2007). More importantly, we are reminded that perceived trustworthiness is not to be equated with trust; that perceptions of trustworthiness are subjective; that interests and pay-off structures are not always conclusive; that people misjudge and miscalculate; and that trust is characterized by insufficient information and emotionally enabled leaps of faith (Möllering, 2006). All of this makes the process of 'trusting' the decisive link between the various antecedents of trust that have been identified and the state of trust as an outcome. Information processing that is relevant for trust does not happen solely within individual minds of course, but also in all kinds of social processes of communicating and sense-making (for example, Adobor, 2005; Wright and Ehnert, 2010) and is shaped by organizational and institutional contexts as well as social networks (for example, Child and Möllering, 2003; Brownlie and Howson, 2005; Barrera and van de Bunt, 2009; Bachmann and Inkpen, 2011).

3 Trusting as learning

From Bayesian updating and auditing discussed in rational choice explanations of trust (for example, Hardin, 1993), to Zucker's (1986) category of 'process-based trust', Luhmann's (1979) 'principle of gradualness', and the trust development model by Lewicki and Bunker (1996) among others, trust has been explained in terms of a learning process (for example, Barrera and van de Bunt, 2009). Sabel's (1993) idea of 'studied trust' largely means 'learned trust', too. Needless to say, seminal work such as Erikson (1965) and countless studies building on it argue that trust, or rather 'trusting', is (ideally) learned in childhood and to some extent also in later phases of personal development. Some parts of the literature already express clearly how it is not just the quantity but also the quality of trust that changes as a result of learning, for example from initial calculus-based trust all the way to identification-based trust (Lewicki and Bunker, 1996), or from fragile to resilient trust (Ring, 1997; see also Lewicki and Polin, Chapter 2 this volume, and Nooteboom, Chapter 5 this volume). In a more pronounced process perspective, though, different modes and degrees of trust are not merely the outcome of learning but part of it. Hence studies of 'trusting', instead of 'trust', will focus on how trusting enables learning and vice versa (see Coopey, 1998; Chakravarthy and Cho, 2004) and how trust processes draw on familiarity in order to facilitate familiarization (for example, Möllering, 2006). Inkpen and Currall (2004) develop some propositions along similar lines and suggest the dynamic co-evolution of trust, control and learning in joint venture relationships. As experiences feed back into such processes (Zand, 1972), the dynamics of trusting are clearly more than quantitative patterns in the amount of 'trust' over time and more than the result of individuals' subjective biases. The mental and social processes of trusting produce *trust histories* shared by actors within their relevant communities.

It has been an interesting but unduly peripheral question in trust research to what extent the learning process of trust can be started without a trust basis but with the aim to develop trust. In other words, will actors engage in interaction in order to gain experience with others, thus 'testing' if trust might be developed? What would be the status of this kind of 'trusting as testing'? Recall Axelrod's (1984) findings for a 'nice' tit-for-tat strategy that always starts with cooperation on the first move, or Luhmann's (1979) idea of trust as a risky, supererogatory investment. I was also struck by Hardin's (1993) concept of 'as-if trust', which means cooperative behaviour that is not based on calculation yet but feigns trust willingly in order to trigger the information that might allow the development of a proper basis for trust (see also Sztompka, 1999, p. 109). Earlier, Hardin (1991) suggested that actors can wilfully ignore the game-theoretical backward induction problem (for example, Hollis, 1998, pp. 54–60) in order to test the interaction partner's willingness to reciprocate. This 'testing' involves a willingness to be vulnerable, as is typical for trust according to widely accepted definitions, but lacks the element of positive expectations in the face of uncertainty, which is another important element of trust definitions. So is this 'testing' already 'trusting'? Consider Meyerson et al.'s (1996) well-known description of swift trust in temporary groups: while it is observed that 'people have to wade in on trust' (p. 170), which sounds a bit like Hardin's as-if trust, they insist that swift trust is 'not a sort of pseudo-trust or "trustoid" behaviour' (p. 192) but, presumably, proper trust at an early stage (see also Möllering, 2006, pp. 106–9, 112). It will be a matter of further research to determine the point at which 'testing' turns into 'trusting' but the learning perspective of trusting is already instructive because it highlights how, as actors learn, trust develops in quality as well as in strength, and how growing trust facilitates further learning (Coopey, 1998). This adds depth to Zand's (1972) widely recognized spiral reinforcement model (based on Gibb, 1964) as well as Gulati's (1995) findings on repeated ties at the inter-organizational level (see also Serva et al., 2005). The trust histories driven by such spiral forces are not detached from the actors, of course. Trusting as learning potentially also changes the trustors and trustees themselves. This leads on to the next perspective.

4 Trusting as becoming

Not histories, but actors' identities are at the centre of this process view of trusting. 'Identity-based trust' has been highlighted as a particularly interesting form of trust in organizations, for example by Kramer (2001). Yet again, we need to move away from the idea that 'trust' is a kind of end-state shaped by the identity (and social identification) of the actors involved, toward a process view that presents 'trusting' as part of the actors' continuous becoming. Put somewhat melodramatically, people are who they are because of whom they trust and who trusts them, and so the continuous need to work on trust makes 'trusting' a developmental project of the self that is never finished (Giddens, 1991, 1994; see also Rose, 1989). Wright and Ehnert (2010, p. 115) highlight how trust 'produces knowledge, social identities and relationships between people through its becoming'. This contrasts with classic work that focused on predisposition to trust as largely a matter of innate personality (Wrightsman, 1966; Rotter, 1967). The process view accepts and actually reinforces the idea that trusting is highly idiosyncratic and dependent on the individual actor, not just the circumstances, but it goes against the idea of predisposition because changes in trust should be examined as to their corresponding changes in identity and identification as well as taking them as evidence of more or less iterative, evaluative, or projective agency (Emirbayer and Mische, 1998).

Looking, first, from the side of the trustor the process of trusting 'presumes the opening out of the individual to the other' (Giddens, 1990, p. 121). It has to be noted that the vulnerability that is so readily included in trust definitions goes beyond material losses and includes emotional losses and potential damage to the trustor's self-esteem and self-image, which is evident from literature on trust and deception (for example,

Möllering, 2009a). In the same way, positive trust experiences generally enhance the trustor's mental well-being. From the side of the trustee, we can observe the need for Goffmanian self-presentation as well as signalling of intentions (see Luhmann, 1979; Beckert, 2005). This is not merely a mechanical matter of signalling or concealing one's 'objective' trustworthiness (or lack thereof) as described by Bacharach and Gambetta (2001), but a matter of identity construction. Luhmann (1979, p. 62) states: 'Whoever wants to win trust must take part in social life and be in a position to build the expectations of others into his own self-presentation'. And Giddens (1991, p. 96) emphasizes: '[T]he trust of the other has to be won'. Thus, trustee and trustor keep on constructing their identities together in the process of trusting (see also Li, Chapter 7 this volume, on adaptive learning; see Wright and Ehnert, 2010, on trusting as social construction). These identities may have a fictional quality to start with (see Hardin, 1993; Adobor, 2005; Beckert, 2005; Möllering, 2006, 2009a) but turn 'real' when trusting enables the actors to become who they aspire to be by granting and honouring trust. Clearly, trusting as becoming needs to be seen as an ongoing process, too. If trust 'has to be energetically treated and sustained' (Giddens, 1994, p. 187) and 'worked upon' (Giddens, 1990, p. 121), then it is trustors and trustees who perform this active work on 'trust-in-the-making' (Möllering, 2006, p. 102) and who reflexively work on themselves all the time.

A prominent study on the relationship between trust and identity has been reported by Maguire et al. (2001). They analysed the relationships between pharmaceutical companies and HIV/AIDS community organizations in Canada. Through the discursive construction of new categories of identity and changes in existing ones the parties involved were able to develop identification-based trust (Lewicki and Bunker, 1996), even though the initial setting was highly antagonistic. In the process, over many years, actors redefined themselves eventually into a positive identity of 'advocates collaborating with compassionate and consultative partners' (Maguire et al., 2001, pp. 295–9; see also Möllering, 2006, p. 113). An additional dimension comes into play when we recognize that trusting involves not only personal identities but also collective identities and, not least, the shift from an individualistic to a collective identity can often explain why trusting succeeds in some contexts but not in others (see Kramer et al., 1996). Trusting signals and confirms an actor's willingness to belong to a collective. It does not merely use in-group forces of identification as a basis for positive expectations. It also helps to maintain those very forces, as they are never completely unproblematic and identity-based trust can be fragile (see Kramer, 2001). Thus, ideally, trusting builds on and sustains personal and collective identities.

Process views of trusting and crises 295

This line of thinking is still very much concerned with individuals and with the collective identity of multiple individuals but it can be extended to organizations and institutions, if we want to assume that they can been analysed as actors that have identities. For example, a firm's identity develops over time at least partly in relation to whom it trusts and who it is trusted by (for example, customers and suppliers) and in relation to how it regulates its various trust relationships formally and informally (see also Poppo, Chapter 6 this volume). This is why it is important to discuss trusting in the context of organizational values and cultures (see Saunders et al., 2010) instead of treating trust and trustworthiness merely as organizational resources. The crucial point, however, is that the notion of trusting highlights how an actor's identity and trust are not just connected but entangled in process. At the organizational level, the notion of 'becoming' has been advanced prominently by Tsoukas and Chia (2002). It is very fruitful for analysing how organizations-as-actors are in flux, evidenced in part by their 'trusting' over time, while it also points reflexively to the significance of organizations-as-structures that are constituted continuously: this suggests yet another process view of trusting.

5 Trusting as constituting

This last process view of trust presented here builds on the idea of social constitution as laid out, for example, in structuration theory (developed by Giddens, 1979, 1984). Compared to the previous view of trusting as becoming, the emphasis of trusting as constituting is on social structures rather than actors though the whole point is that structuration encompasses agency. While Giddens has written on trust (notably in Giddens, 1990) he hardly applied structuration theory explicitly to trust in any depth, but some research has already used his theory fruitfully for analysing trust (especially Sydow, 1998; Sydow and Windeler, 2003). Incidentally, structuration theory holds considerable potential for conceptualizing organizational and institutional trust (Möllering, 2009b). The most important point for the process view developed here will be the emphasis on trusting as 'practice', which also distinguishes this approach from the previous one that focused on the actors' 'identity'. To emphasize practice means to view trusting not simply as dependent on social context (for example, organizational or institutional) but as also (re)producing the rules and resources in which it is embedded. If social systems are in an ongoing, multi-level process of constitution, just like individual actors are continuously developing their identity (see above, but in a different sense here), then 'trusting' is to be studied as one practice in this larger, reflexive process of social constitution (see also Wright and Ehnert, 2010). When reported levels of 'trust' change, this may be simply an indicator of far broader changes, for better or worse. We can only know if this is the case, if we study processes of trusting instead of just the outcome of 'trust' at a given point in time.

Although I would partly criticize Sztompka's (1999) conceptualization of trust, he has produced a remarkable account of the relationship between trust and large-scale social change in East-Central Europe. His theory of social becoming (Sztompka, 1991) serves as an ideal backdrop for this and takes us from *individual* identity and becoming (see above) to *societal* becoming and constitution. Sztompka (1999) manages to look behind the Eurobarometer time series data on trust in institutions and shows the cultural changes that influenced not just 'how much' but also 'how' people trusted in a country like Poland. It is well known that personal networks became an even more important basis for trust among people in the collapsing Soviet structures (see Rose-Ackerman, 2001). However, personal trust declined in importance when some level of stability was achieved (for example, Chepurenko and Malieva, 2005) and a different mode of trust production became feasible: Zucker's (1986) institutional-based trust (see also Möllering and Stache, 2010). The picture is incomplete, though, if we only look at the institutional context's influences on trust and do not recognize that practices of trusting are part of this context and, structurationally speaking, part of its ongoing (re)production (see Mizrachi et al., 2007; Kroeger, Chapter 11 this volume).

Comparative empirical studies, notably the Cambridge Contracting Study (for example, Deakin et al., 1997; see also Möllering, 2006, pp. 146–50) show not only different levels of trust between firms across Germany, Italy and the UK but also important differences in the meaning of trust, the signalling of trustworthiness, and the decision to trust (Lane and Bachmann, 1996; Burchell and Wilkinson, 1997). Hence, 'trusting' as a practice varies across countries, cultures, and also, for example, across industries. This implies that *how* people trust is a noteworthy element in how social systems are constituted, how they work and develop. At the same time, when people start to trust differently, they start to change the system that has been the reference point for their trust (see Weibel and Six, Chapter 3 this volume, on how cooperation affects 'trust climate'). By trusting, actors influence and change their contexts (Wright and Ehnert, 2010, p. 117). The effect from the interpersonal level to the system level and vice versa will not be immediate, though, and the multi-level perspective of trusting as constituting is also a longitudinal perspective, stretching perhaps many decades (for example, 80 years in Zucker, 1986). Then again, in highly volatile contexts, characterized for example by political conflict, practices of trusting can alternate relatively fast (Mizrachi et al., 2007).

The purpose of sketching these five process views of trust is, first and foremost, to enable researchers who think that they have applied a process view, or who intend to do so, to position themselves within the range of views outlined here. The framework is provisional and the views may not be exhaustive nor are they in any way mutually exclusive. They also contain one unifying idea about 'trusting': to view 'trust' as continuous and preliminary and to study how it is achieved dynamically (Wright and Ehnert, 2010). For illustration, this goes beyond comparative but static accounts of cultural differences in trust development (as put forward, for example, by Doney et al., 1998; see also Saunders et al., 2010) and requires researchers' conceptual openness and focus on creative interaction, especially in cross-cultural contexts (Möllering, 2011). All process views move away from the search for solid trust bases that enable trustful expectations toward an analysis of trusting as continuously (re)making the paths, information, experiences, identities and structures that the willingness to be vulnerable in the face of uncertainty is entangled with. The implications of the process views will be discussed briefly below, including methodological aspects and a process-based interpretation of trust and crises.

DISCUSSION

This chapter will inspire trust researchers to advance this field of study by developing process views of trusting further, based on a common framework of reference. The modest contribution at this stage is mainly a tool for locating the points of departure, the destinations and the key assumptions of different research projects that want to study trust as process. The tool itself is preliminary. Yet it does suggest a number of significant implications. One important area for developing trust research is its methodological basis (Lyon et al., 2012). Another key area is to enhance the contribution trust research can make to explaining and improving current empirical issues, such as economic and financial crises and how they may be dealt with (see Gillespie et al., 2012 on this topic, who also call for more process-based trust research). In this section I will discuss both areas and show briefly how they are related to the process views of trusting outlined above as well as to each other.

Methodological Implications of Different Process Views

The different process views of trusting sketched above tend to correspond with some methods more than with others. For example: (1) trusting as continuing could imply in the first instance that longitudinal and time series studies offer considerable advantages over merely cross-sectional data, even though the measurements may not be very different and, crucially, not very process-oriented yet (Polyhart and Vandenberg, 2010). Hence, often the first step will be to have several points of measurement (for example, Robinson, 1996; Newell and Swan, 2000; Aubert and Kelsey, 2003; Serva et al., 2005; Barrera and van de Bunt, 2009), but more important than the number of measurement points is the ability to assess at a particular point in time *how* people trust and how any *changes* from the past into the present and the future are interpreted (Alvesson and Sköldberg, 2000; see Möllering, 2006, pp. 152–3). (2) The study of trusting as processing could move from questionnaires about perceived trustworthiness and experiments in which the information given as input to participants is varied by the experimenter to much more qualitative and interpretative methods that generate, for example, narratives about how people deal with inconclusive or overwhelming information (for example, Brownlie and Howson, 2005). A narrative approach is essential from the point of view of trusting as a process of social construction (Wright and Ehnert, 2010). The shift from pre-defined survey or experiment to open-ended narrative is not just a shift in method but also a conceptual acknowledgement of empirical variety in the processing that trust entails (Klein Woolthuis et al., 2005). (3) Trusting as learning requires, for example, methods that can detect when the quality of trust changes and that can connect earlier episodes of trusting to later ones (for example, discourse analysis, Maguire et al., 2001; critical incident technique, Münscher and Kühlmann, 2012). (4) Trusting as becoming is closely related to research on identity and calls for qualitative-interpretative methods though the main point to be operationalized may be the assessment of how much trusting is not just about making decisions vis-à-vis specific others but about maintaining, for example, one's self-image (for example, Frederiksen, 2012). (5) Trusting as constituting challenges researchers to apply, for example, the apparatus of institutional analysis not just to the question of trust in institutions (Barber, 1983) or institution-based trust (Zucker, 1986), but to trusting as an institution (or: 'trust' as an institutionalized practice; see Kroeger, 2012, and Kroeger, Chapter 11 this volume), which ethnomethodological views of trust used to highlight (Garfinkel, 1963; Henslin, 1968; see also Maguire et al., 2001; Möllering, 2006) and that also matches a conception of trust as based in morality (Hosmer, 1995; Uslaner, 2002) if trusting is understood as a continuous effort in assessing if and when moral standards will be upheld (Khodyakov, 2007). As Sydow (1998) demonstrates, trust research can also apply directly some structuration theoretical frameworks such as the dimensions of the duality of structure (Giddens, 1984, p. 29).

Overall, 'trusting' can be studied with many different methods, because of the many facets to the core question of *how* people achieve, or fail to achieve, 'trust' over time. These facets are expressed in the five process views of trusting outlined above.

Process Views of Trust Issues Within Crises

The general approach presented here has the potential to strengthen the practical relevance of trust research. I focus here on how process views might enhance our understanding of trust's role in crises (see also Gillespie and Hurley, Chapter 8 this volume). First, and most broadly, any loss of trust during a crisis, making it also a 'crisis of trust', calls for a deeper analysis of changes in trusting: how did people produce trust before and why are they no longer able to do it to the same extent as before? Second, this question has several possible answers due to the different facets of trusting that the five process views highlight. Thus, it will not do to simply infer, for example, that a crisis has caused a decline in trust, or vice versa. It will be necessary to include an analysis of how trusting has changed, in which respects it has become difficult. Third, the five process views outlined above suggest different ways of conducting such an analysis. The most basic requirement would be to obtain longitudinal data on 'trust' levels, which may already put any recent decline or low level into perspective.

More pronounced process analyses could show, for example, if the issue is mainly one of information processing, identity or system effectiveness. When trust levels fall, for example, during the restructuring of an organization or during the fiscal troubles of Euro member states, trust on the part of employees and citizens respectively may go down, because: (1) they feel they lack information, which makes trusting as processing difficult; (2) they are no longer sure about their own identity and they experience a problematic phase of trusting as becoming; or (3) they perceive the system that used to support their trusting is no longer effective and falls apart. Recall Webb (1996, p. 290) who pointed out that what 'defines the presence or absence of a crisis' is less the threat itself than the resource adequacy of those facing the threat. In other words, low trust in critical situations need not be a verdict on the trustworthiness of individual, organizational or institutional trustees, but may often reflect issues of information and identification on the trustors' part in the process of trusting. This is even more likely when it is difficult to name the 'guilty' trustees who may claim to be just an innocent part of an unaccountable 'system'. There is an important difference between 'withdrawal of trust' as one interpretation and 'difficulties in trusting' as another explanation. A crisis situation makes people more cautious; they look for new ways of trusting; and, yes, they may also come to trust various actors less than before the crisis, or even more if the crisis was handled well. Any crisis should be analysed as to which facet of trusting it affects and is affected by.

Moreover, we can also learn by analogy, for example from research on trust and deception (see Möllering, 2009a) how trust is in fact quite robust due to confirmatory bias (Good, 1988) and may thus delay the discovery of problems and misbehaviour, for example due to accusatory reluctance (for example, O'Sullivan, 2009). Research on deception also shows that victims of betrayal frequently question their own competence and judgement, which makes them feel less confident in trusting others in general, instead of focusing the blame on the perpetrator. Again, a lack of trust could be the result of a lack of readiness to engage in processes of trusting, above and beyond a lack of perceived trustworthiness. This is in line with Barbalet's (2009) characterization of trust and the central role he attributes to emotion and self-confidence. Trusting is about the trustor as much as about the trustee.

PRELIMINARY CONCLUSIONS

In various parts of the trust research community, a process approach has been advocated but not very often applied explicitly. There is a broad range of options for a 'process view', as this chapter demonstrates, and they all promise important insights. Integration is possible if the core question remains one about 'trusting' as the process of *how* people develop the preliminary outcome of 'trust'. Paraphrasing Bakken and Hernes (2006), 'trusting' is both a noun and a verb; hence we need to study both the activities and the effects of trusting (and give not only Weick but also Whitehead his due). Wright and Ehnert (2010, p. 116) claim that '"trust" the verb has been superseded by "trust" the noun' and, overcompensating a bit, they advocate focusing on 'trust as a verb'. My chapter supports their emphasis on 'trusting' but there is value in maintaining the marvellous ambiguity of trust as noun and verb, too. Other process-like phenomena, such as crises, are entangled with trusting. Since any crisis, by definition, denotes a decisive phase within a process, accounts of trust in crisis should be process-oriented, too. As this chapter has shown, different ways of studying trust as process reveal different aspects of trusting and, consequently, different interpretations of critical situations, highlighting different issues and potential solutions.

NOTE

* Key ideas for this chapter were presented and discussed constructively at an Academy of Management PDW (Möllering, 2009b) and in a keynote lecture at the second seminar of the Nordic Research Network on Trust Within and Between Organizations, University of Roskilde, 23 November 2011 (http://trust.ruc.dk). A previous version of the chapter was also presented at the EGOS Colloquium in Helsinki, 5–7 July 2012 (www.organisationaltrust.org). I thank Reinhard Bachmann, Morten Frederiksen and Frens Kroeger for very helpful comments on an earlier draft.

REFERENCES

Adobor, H. (2005), 'Trust as sensemaking: the microdynamics of trust in interfirm alliances', *Journal of Business Research*, **58**(3), 330–37.
Alvesson, M. and K. Sköldberg (2000), *Reflexive Methodology*, London: Sage.
Aubert, B.A. and B.L. Kelsey (2003), 'Further understanding of trust and performance in virtual teams', *Small Group Research*, **34**(5), 575–618.
Axelrod, R. (1984), *The Evolution of Cooperation*, New York: Basic Books.
Bacharach, M. and D. Gambetta (2001), 'Trust in signs', in K.S. Cook (ed.), *Trust in Society*, New York: Russell Sage Foundation, pp. 148–84.
Bachmann, R. and A.C. Inkpen (2011), 'Understanding institutional-based trust building processes in inter-organizational relationships', *Organization Studies*, **32**(2), 281–301.
Bakken, T. and T. Hernes (2006), 'Organizing is both a verb and a noun: Weick meets Whitehead', *Organization Studies*, **27**(11), 1599–616.
Barbalet, J. (2009), 'A characterization of trust, and its consequences', *Theory and Society*, **38**(4), 367–82.
Barber, B. (1983), *The Logic and Limits of Trust*, New Brunswick: Rutgers University Press.
Barrera, D. and G.G. van de Bunt (2009), 'Learning to trust: networks effects through time', *European Sociological Review*, **25**(6), 709–21.
Beckert, J. (2005), 'Trust and the performative construction of markets', MPIfG Discussion Paper No. 05/8, Cologne: Max Planck Institute for the Study of Societies.
Bhattacharya, R., T.M. Devinney and M.M. Pillutla (1998), 'A formal model of trust based on outcomes', *Academy of Management Review*, **23**(3), 459–72.
Blau, P. (1964), *Exchange and Power in Social Life*, London: John Wiley.
Brownlie, J. and A. Howson (2005), 'Leaps of faith and MMR: an empirical study of trust', *Sociology*, **39**(2), 221–39.
Burchell, B. and F. Wilkinson (1997), 'Trust, business relationships and the contractual environment', *Cambridge Journal of Economics*, **21**(2), 217–37.
Chakravarthy, B. and H.J. Cho (2004), 'Managing trust and learning: an exploratory study', *International Journal of Management and Decision Making*, **5**(4), 333–47.
Chepurenko, A. and E. Malieva (2005), 'Trust-milieus of Russian SMEs: cross-regional comparisons', in H.-H. Höhmann and F. Welter (eds), *Trust and Entrepreneurship: A West–East Perspective*, Cheltenham, UK and Northampton, MA, USA: Edward Elgar, pp. 136–55.
Child, J. and G. Möllering (2003), 'Contextual confidence and active trust development in the Chinese business environment', *Organization Science*, **14**(1), 69–80.
Coleman, J.S. (1990), *Foundations of Social Theory*, Cambridge, MA: Harvard University Press.
Coopey, J. (1998), 'Learning to trust and trusting to learn: a role for radical theatre', *Management Learning*, **29**(3), 365–82.
Dasgupta, P. (1988), 'Trust as a commodity', in D. Gambetta (ed.), *Trust: Making and Breaking Co-operative Relations*, Oxford: Basil Blackwell, pp. 49–72.

Deakin, S., C. Lane and F. Wilkinson (1997), 'Contract law, trust relations, and incentives for co-operation: a comparative study', in S. Deakin and J. Michie (eds), *Contracts, Cooperation and Competition: Studies in Economics, Management and Law*, Oxford: Oxford University Press, pp. 105–39.

Delhey, J. and K. Newton (2005), 'Predicting cross-national levels of social trust: global pattern or Nordic exceptionalism?', *European Sociological Review*, **21**(4), 311–27.

Deutsch, M. (1973), *The Resolution of Conflict*, New Haven, CT: Yale University Press.

Dibben, M.R. (2000), *Exploring Interpersonal Trust in the Entrepreneurial Venture*, Basingstoke: Macmillan.

Dirks, K.T., R.J. Lewicki and A. Zaheer (2009), 'Repairing relationships within and between organizations: building a conceptual framework', *Academy of Management Review*, **34**(1), 68–84.

Doney, P.M., J. P. Cannon and M.R. Mullen (1998), 'Understanding the influence of national culture on the development of trust', *Academy of Management Review*, **23**(3), 601–20.

Elster, J. (1984), *Ulysses and the Sirens: Studies in Rationality and Irrationality*, Cambridge, UK: Cambridge University Press.

Elster, J. (1989), *Solomonic Judgements: Studies in the Limitations of Rationality*, Cambridge, UK: Cambridge University Press.

Emirbayer, M. and A. Mische (1998), 'What is agency?', *American Journal of Sociology*, **103**(4), 962–1023.

Erikson, E.H. (1965), *Childhood and Society*, Harmondsworth: Penguin.

Frederiksen, M. (2012), 'Suspending the unknown: the foundations, limits, and variability of intersubjective trust', PhD thesis, Copenhagen: Department of Sociology, University of Copenhagen.

Garfinkel, H. (1963), 'A conception of, and experiments with, "trust" as a condition of stable concerted actions', in O.J. Harvey (ed.), *Motivation and Social Interaction*, New York: The Ronald Press Company, pp. 187–238.

Gibb, J.R. (1964), 'Climate for trust formation', in L.P. Bradford, J.R. Gibb and D. Benne (eds), *T-Group Theory and Laboratory Method*, New York: John Wiley, pp. 279–301.

Giddens, A. (1979), *Central Problems in Social Theory: Action, Structure and Contradiction in Social Analysis*, London: Macmillan.

Giddens, A. (1984), *The Constitution of Society*, Berkeley, CA: University of California Press.

Giddens, A. (1990), *The Consequences of Modernity*, Stanford, CA: Stanford University Press.

Giddens, A. (1991), *Modernity and Self-identity*, Cambridge, UK: Polity Press.

Giddens, A. (1994), 'Risk, trust, reflexivity', in U. Beck, A. Giddens and S. Lash (eds), *Reflexive Modernization*, Cambridge, UK: Polity Press, pp. 184–97.

Gillespie, N. and G. Dietz (2009), 'Trust repair after an organizational-level failure', *Academy of Management Review*, **34**(1), 127–45.

Gillespie, N., R. Hurley, G. Dietz and R. Bachmann (2012), 'Restoring institutional trust after the global financial crisis: a systemic approach', in R.M. Kramer and T.L. Pittinsky (eds), *Restoring Trust in Organizations and Leaders: Enduring Challenges and Emerging Answers*, Oxford: Oxford University Press, pp. 185–215.

Glaeser, E.L., D.I. Laibson, J.A. Schenkman and C.L. Soutter (2000), 'Measuring trust', *Quarterly Journal of Economics*, **115**(3), 811–46.

Good, D. (1988), 'Individuals, interpersonal relations and trust', in D. Gambetta (ed.), *Trust: Making and Breaking Co-operative Relations*, Oxford: Basil Blackwell, pp. 31–48.

Gulati, R. (1995), 'Does familiarity breed trust? The implications of repeated ties for contractual choice in alliances', *Academy of Management Journal*, **38**(1), 85–112.

Hardin, R. (1991), 'Trusting persons, trusting institutions', in R.J. Zeckhauser (ed.), *Strategy and Choice*, Cambridge, MA: MIT Press, pp. 185–209.

Hardin, R. (1993), 'The street-level epistemology of trust', *Politics and Society*, **21**(4), 505–29.

Henslin, J.M. (1968), 'Trust and the cab driver', in M. Truzzi (ed.), *Sociology and Everyday Life*, Englewood Cliffs, NJ: Prentice Hall, pp. 138–58.

Hernes, T. (2008), *Understanding Organization as Process: Theory for a Tangled World*, London: Routledge.
Hollis, M. (1998), *Trust Within Reason*, Cambridge, UK: Cambridge University Press.
Hosmer, L.T. (1995), 'Trust: the connecting link between organizational theory and philosophical ethics', *Academy of Management Review*, **20**(3), 379–403.
Inkpen, A.C. and S.C. Currall (2004), 'The coevolution of trust, control, and learning in joint ventures', *Organization Science*, **15**(5), 586–99.
Jones, K. (1996), 'Trust as an affective attitude', *Ethics*, **107**(1), 4–25.
Khodyakov, D.M. (2007), 'Trust as a process: a three-dimensional approach', *Sociology*, **41**(1), 115–32.
Kim, P.H., D.L. Ferrin, C.D. Cooper and K.T. Dirks (2004), 'Removing the shadow of suspicion: the effects of apology versus denial for repairing competence- versus integrity-based trust violations', *Journal of Applied Psychology*, **89**(1), 104–18.
Klein Woolthuis, R., B. Hillebrand and B. Nooteboom (2005), 'Trust, contract and relationship development', *Organization Studies*, **26**(6), 813–40.
Kramer, R.M. (1996), 'Divergent realities and convergent disappointments in the hierarchic relation: trust and the intuitive auditor at work', in R.M. Kramer and T.R. Tyler (eds), *Trust in Organizations*, Thousand Oaks, CA: Sage, 216–45.
Kramer, R.M. (2001), 'Identity and trust in organizations: one anatomy of a productive but problematic relationship', in M.A. Hogg and D.J. Terry (eds), *Social Identity Processes in Organizational Contexts*, Philadelphia: Psychology Press, pp.167–80.
Kramer, R.M. and R.J. Lewicki (2010), 'Repairing and enhancing trust: approaches to reducing organizational trust deficits', in J.P. Walsh and A.P. Brief (eds), *The Academy of Management Annals*, Vol. 4, pp.245–77.
Kramer, R.M., M.B. Brewer and B.A. Hanna (1996), 'Collective trust and collective action: the decision to trust as a social decision', in R.M. Kramer and T.R. Tyler (eds), *Trust in Organizations*, Thousand Oaks, CA: Sage, pp.357–89.
Kroeger, F. (2012), 'Trusting organizations: the institutionalization of trust in interorganizational relationships', *Organization*, **19**(6), 743–63.
Lane, C. and R. Bachmann (1996), 'The social constitution of trust: supplier relations in Britain and Germany', *Organization Studies*, **17**(3), 365–95.
Lewicki, R.J. and B.B. Bunker (1996), 'Developing and maintaining trust in work relationships', in R.M. Kramer and T.R. Tyler (eds), *Trust in Organizations*, Thousand Oaks, CA: Sage, pp.114–39.
Lewicki, R.J., E.C. Tomlinson and N. Gillespie (2006), 'Models of interpersonal trust development: theoretical approaches, empirical evidence, and future directions', *Journal of Management*, **32**(6), 991–1022.
Luhmann, N. (1979), *Trust and Power: Two Works by Niklas Luhmann*, Chichester: Wiley.
Lyon, F., G. Möllering and M.N.K. Saunders (eds) (2012), *Handbook of Research Methods on Trust*, Cheltenham, UK and Northampton, MA, USA: Edward Elgar.
Maguire, S.P., N. Phillips and C. Hardy (2001), 'When "silence = death", keep talking: trust, control and the discursive construction of identity in the Canadian HIV/AIDS treatment domain', *Organization Studies*, **22**(2), 285–310.
Mayer, R.C., J.H. Davis and F.D. Schoorman (1995), 'An integrative model of organizational trust', *Academy of Management Review*, **20**(3), 709–34.
McAllister, D.J. (1995), 'Affect- and cognition-based trust as foundations for interpersonal cooperation in organizations', *Academy of Management Journal*, **38**(1), 24–59.
McKnight, D.H., L.L. Cummings and N.L. Chervany (1998), 'Initial trust formation in new organizational relationships', *Academy of Management Review*, **23**(3), 473–90.
Meyer, J.W. and R.L. Jepperson (2000), 'The "actors" of modern society: the cultural construction of social agency', *Sociological Theory*, **18**(1), 100–120.
Meyerson, D., K.E. Weick and R.M. Kramer (1996), 'Swift trust and temporary groups', in R.M. Kramer and T.R. Tyler (eds), *Trust in Organizations*, Thousand Oaks, CA: Sage, pp.166–95.
Mizrachi, N., I. Drori and R.R. Anspach (2007), 'Repertoires of trust: the practice of trust

in a multinational organization amid political conflict', *American Sociological Review*, **72**(1), 143–65.
Möllering, G. (2001), 'The nature of trust: from Georg Simmel to a theory of expectation, interpretation and suspension', *Sociology*, **35**(2), 403–20.
Möllering, G. (2006), *Trust: Reason, Routine, Reflexivity*, Amsterdam: Elsevier.
Möllering, G. (2009a), 'Leaps and lapses of faith: exploring the relationship between trust and deception', in B. Harrington (ed.), *Deception: From Ancient Empires to Internet Dating*, Stanford, CA: Stanford University Press, pp. 137–53.
Möllering, G. (2009b), 'Neither person nor hierarchy? Trust(ing) in practice(s)', Academy of Management Meeting, Chicago, 7 August.
Möllering, G. (2011), 'Conceptual openness and actor focus in research on international business relationships', in S. Schmid (ed.), *Internationale Unternehmungen und das Management ausländischer Tochtergesellschaften*, Wiesbaden: Gabler, pp. 333–53.
Möllering, G. and F. Stache (2010), 'Trust development in German–Ukranian business relationships: dealing with cultural differences in an uncertain institutional context', in M.N.K. Saunders, D. Skinner, G. Dietz, N. Gillespie and R.J. Lewicki (eds), *Organizational Trust: A Cultural Perspective*, Cambridge, UK: Cambridge University Press, pp. 205–26.
Münscher, R. and T.M. Kühlmann (2012), 'Using critical incident technique in trust research', in F. Lyon, G. Möllering and M.N.K. Saunders (eds), *Handbook of Research Methods on Trust*, Cheltenham, UK and Northampton, MA, USA: Edward Elgar, pp. 161–72.
Newell, S. and J. Swan (2000), 'Trust and inter-organizational networking', *Human Relations*, **53**(10), 1287–328.
Nooteboom, B. (1996), 'Trust, opportunism and governance: a process and control model', *Organization Studies*, **17**(6), 985–1010.
Nooteboom, B. (2002), *Trust: Forms, Foundations, Functions, Failures and Figures*, Cheltenham, UK and Northampton, USA: Edward Elgar.
O'Sullivan, M. (2009), 'Why most people parse palters, fibs, lies, whoppers, and other deceptions poorly', in B. Harrington (ed.), *Deception: From Ancient Empires to Internet Dating*, Stanford, CA: Stanford University Press, pp. 74–91.
Paxton, P. (1999), 'Is social capital declining in the United States? A multiple indicator assessment', *American Journal of Sociology*, **105**(1), 88–127.
Perrone, V., A. Zaheer and B. McEvily (2003), 'Free to be trusted? Organizational constraints on trust in boundary spanners', *Organization Science*, **14**(4), 422–39.
Polyhart, R.E. and R.J. Vandenberg (2010), 'Longitudinal research: the theory, design, and analysis of change', *Journal of Management*, **36**(1), 94–120.
Putnam, R.D. (1995), 'Bowling alone: America's declining social capital', *Journal of Democracy*, **6**(1), 65–78.
Ring, P.S. (1997), 'Processes facilitating reliance on trust in inter-organizational networks', in M. Ebers (ed.), *The Formation of Inter-Organizational Networks*, Oxford: Oxford University Press, pp. 113–45.
Ring, P.S. and A.H. Van de Ven (1994), 'Developmental processes of cooperative interorganizational relationships', *Academy of Management Review*, **19**(1), 90–118.
Robinson, S.L. (1996), 'Trust and breach of the psychological contract', *Administrative Science Quarterly*, **41**(4), 574–99.
Rose, N. (1989), *Governing the Soul: The Shaping of the Private Self*, London: Routledge.
Rose-Ackerman, S. (2001), 'Trust and honesty in post-socialist societies', *Kyklos*, **54**(2/3), 415–43.
Rotter, J.B. (1967), 'A new scale for the measurement of interpersonal trust', *Journal of Personality*, **35**(4), 651–65.
Sabel, C.F. (1993), 'Studied trust: building new forms of cooperation in a volatile economy', in R. Swedberg (ed.), *Explorations in Economic Sociology*, New York: Russell Sage Foundation.
Saunders, M.N.K., D. Skinner, G. Dietz, N. Gillespie and R.J. Lewicki (eds) (2010),

Organizational Trust: A Cultural Perspective, Cambridge, UK: Cambridge University Press.

Schoorman, F.D., R.C. Mayer and J.H. Davis (2007), 'An integrative model of organizational trust: past, present and future', *Academy of Management Review*, **32**(2), 344–54.

Serva, M.A., M.A. Fuller and R.C. Mayer (2005), 'The reciprocal nature of trust: a longitudinal study of interacting teams', *Journal of Organizational Behavior*, **26**(6), 625–48.

Sitkin, S.B. and D. Stickel (1996), 'The road to hell: the dynamics of distrust in an era of quality', in R.M. Kramer and T.R. Tyler (eds), *Trust in Organizations*, Thousand Oaks, CA: Sage, pp. 196–215.

Sydow, J. (1998), 'Understanding the constitution of inter-organizational trust', in C. Lane and R. Bachmann (eds), *Trust Within and Between Organizations*, Oxford: Oxford University Press, pp. 31–63.

Sydow, J. (2006), 'How can systems trust systems? A structuration perspective on trust building in inter-organizational relations', in R. Bachmann and A. Zaheer (eds), *Handbook of Research on Trust*, Cheltenham, UK and Northampton, MA, USA: Edward Elgar, pp. 377–92.

Sydow, J. and A. Windeler (2003), 'Knowledge, trust, and control: managing tensions and contradictions in a regional network of service firms', *International Studies of Management and Organization*, **33**(2), 69–99.

Sztompka, P. (1991), *Society in Action: The Theory of Social Becoming*, Cambridge, UK: Polity Press.

Sztompka, P. (1999), *Trust: A Sociological Theory*, Cambridge, UK: Cambridge University Press.

Tsoukas, H. and R. Chia (2002), 'On organizational becoming: rethinking organizational change', *Organization Science*, **13**(5), 567–82.

Tsui-Auch, L.S. and G. Möllering (2010), Wary managers: unfavorable environments, perceived vulnerability, and the development of trust in foreign enterprises in China', *Journal of International Business Studies*, **41**(6), 1016–34.

Uslaner, E.M. (2002), *The Moral Foundations of Trust*, Cambridge, UK: Cambridge University Press.

Walgenbach, P. (2001), 'The production of distrust by means of producing trust', *Organization Studies*, **22**(4), 693–714.

Webb, E.J. (1996), 'Trust and crisis', in R.M. Kramer and T.R. Tyler (eds), *Trust in Organizations*, Thousand Oaks, CA: Sage, pp. 288–301.

Wicks, A.C., S.L. Berman and T.M. Jones (1999), 'The structure of optimal trust: moral and strategic implications', *Academy of Management Journal*, **24**(1), 99–116.

Wright, A. and I. Ehnert (2010), 'Making sense of trust across cultural contexts', in M.N.K. Saunders, D. Skinner, G. Dietz, N. Gillespie and R.J. Lewicki (eds), *Organizational Trust: A Cultural Perspective*, Cambridge, UK: Cambridge University Press, pp. 107–26.

Wrightsman, L.S. (1966), 'Personality and attitudinal correlates of trusting and trustworthy behaviours in a two-person game', *Journal of Personality and Social Psychology*, **4**(3), 328–32.

Zaheer, A., B. McEvily and V. Perrone (1998), 'Does trust matter? Exploring the effects of inter-organizational and interpersonal trust on performance', *Organization Science*, **9**(2), 141–59.

Zand, D.E. (1972), 'Trust and managerial problem solving', *Administrative Science Quarterly*, **17**(2), 229–39.

Zucker, L.G. (1986), 'Production of trust: institutional sources of economic structure, 1840–1920', in B.M. Staw and L.L. Cummings (eds), *Research in Organizational Behavior*, Vol. 8, Greenwich, CT: JAI Press, pp. 53–111.

Index

ability-based trust 35–6, 46, 178–9, 181–4, 186–9
Adair, W. 151
Adler, N. 146, 148, 151, 154–5
Adler, P. 61, 65, 231
Adobor, H. 291, 294
Akkermans, H. 98–9
Alderfer, C. 64
Alfes, K. 10
Alford, R. 270
Allen, T. 18, 21
Ambrose, M. 20
Andersen, P. 98–9
Anderson, E. 84, 133
Anton, R. 19
Appelbaum, E. 17
Argyres, N. 84, 89–90, 96–9, 245
Argyris, C. 61, 69
Ariño, A. 101, 128, 131, 134, 139, 141, 153
Armstrong-Stassen, M. 18
Arrighetti, A. 82, 84, 94
Arrow, K. 114, 205, 212, 218, 231–2
Artz, K. 126, 131
Aryee, S. 12–13
Asheim, B. 118
Ashleigh, M. 18
attributional process 231–3, 243, 247, 252, 254
Aubert, B. 291, 298
Axelrod, R. 129–30, 292

Bacharach, M. 265–6, 288, 291, 294
Bachmann, Reinhard 1–6, 59, 62, 88, 92, 98, 138–9, 148, 180, 192–3, 204, 209–10, 215, 272, 279–80, 288–9, 291, 296
Bakhtin, M. 99
Bakken, T. 287, 300
Ball, K. 11
Bandura, A. 63
Barbalet, J. 300
Barber, B. 13, 69, 285, 298

Barkema, H. 61
Barley, S. 268, 271, 273
Barney, J. 12–13, 62, 127, 136, 227, 231
Baron, J. 67
Barrera, G. 291, 298
Barry, B. 41
Batson, D. 41
Baumeister, R. 64
Bebchuk, L. 184
Becker, T. 13
Beckert, J. 263, 288, 294
Begley, T. 20
behaviour
 disposition to trust 68–70, 74
 opportunism *see* opportunism
 personal differences in styles and experiences 15–17, 68, 85–7, 89–91, 214, 273–4, 279
 psychological and behavioural traditions 128–32, 134
Bell, J. 127
Ben-Porath, Y. 241–2
benevolence-based trust 36–7, 46, 92–3, 96, 98, 137, 178–9, 184–90
Bennigson, C. 45–6
Bercovitz, J. 127, 130, 133, 135, 139
Berger, P. 262–3, 267–8, 270–71, 276
Bernheim, B. 231
Berry, J. 148, 153, 156, 166, 168
Bhattacharya, R. 291
Bianchi, E. 211
Bies, R. 12, 42–3, 66, 218, 227, 233
Bigley, G. 15
Bijlsma-Frankema, K. 58, 61, 63, 192
Billsberry, J. 14, 18, 21
Blader, S. 70
Blau, P. 134, 265, 285, 288
Blomqvist, K. 69
Blumer, H. 209, 216
Blunsdon, B. 13, 15–17
Boles, T. 42–3
Bond, M. 148–9
Boon, C. 18

307

Borys, B. 61, 65
Boselie, P. 17
Bottom, W. 47, 234, 266
Bourdieu, P. 216, 273
Bourgeois, L. 162
Boyle, E. 99
Bradach, J. 75, 128–9, 133, 231, 236, 256
Braithwaite, J. 209
Brewer, M. 57, 71, 73
Briner, R. 18
Brinsfield, C. 50
Brockner, J. 18, 211–2
Brodt, S. 18
Bromiley, P. 127, 137, 212, 230–31, 236
Brownlie, J. 291, 298
Brush, T. 126–7, 131, 139
Bryne, D. 150
Buckley, F. 18
Bunker, B. 2, 13, 34, 51, 72–3, 119, 134–6, 218, 285–6, 290–92, 294
Burchell, B. 257, 296
Burger, J. 146
Burke, W. 196, 199
Burt, R. 117
Butler, J. 38–9, 136, 214

calculus-based trust 34–5, 38, 135
Caldwell, R. 21
Campbell, J. 268, 270, 273, 276
Cannon, J. 262
Cantrell, R. 136
Carnevale, D. 10
Carnevale, P. 37, 42
Carson, S. 84, 126, 130
Carson, T. 42
Carter, S. 218
Chakravarthy, B. 292
Chen, M.-J. 150
Chepurenko, A. 296
Chia, R. 295
Child, J. 88, 199, 216, 257, 291
Chiles, T. 227–8, 231–2, 236
Cho, H. 292
Christensen, S. 269, 273
Chu, W. 126, 129, 228, 231
Chua, R. 153
Clemens, E. 268, 270
Clinton, M. 18
Coase, R. 231

Cohan, W. 184, 186
Cohen, A. 266, 272–3
Cohen-Charash, Y. 11
Coleman, J. 117, 288, 290
Coletti, A. 232
collective trust *see* institutionalization and collective and long-term trust orientations
Collins, G. 262
Colquitt, J. 2, 13–16, 20, 51, 68, 178, 206
competence-based trust 66–7, 92–3, 96–8, 136, 195–6
conflict resolution 97, 115–16, 233, 240, 249
Conger, J. 64–5
contracts and trust 82–105
   abstract contracts 93–4
   antecedents 85–8
   benevolence-based trust 92–3, 96, 98
   collaboration process 94–100
   competence-based trust 92–3, 96–8
   complementary effect 84
   conflict resolution 97
   conforming to contracts, ability to verify 90, 92–3
   cooperation, effects of previous 87–8, 92–3
   definition 83
   dissolution stage 96–7
   formation stage 94–6
   future research 101
   goodwill-based trust 83–4, 97
   hold-up situations 97
   individual differences in involvement and perceptions 89–91
   institutional and cultural contexts 88–9
   integrity-based trust 92–3, 96, 98
   inter-organizational relationships 98–9
   legal documents, negotiating and drafting 89–91
   management stage 96
   multi-dimensional and multi-functional dimensions, ignorance of 91–4
   opportunism and self-interest 83, 86, 94, 98

personal characteristics as antecedent 85–7
prevailing perspectives 83–5
renegotiation stage 96–7
risk factors 86–7, 89, 94–5
secrecy and lower-level employees 89–90
substitution effect 83–4
trust definition 83
trust, distrust and understanding, conflation amongst 97–100
trustworthiness evidence 95–6
control and trust and role of intrinsic motivation 57–81
   control and/or trust analysis 60–62
   control and distrust 60–61, 74
   cooperation and trust 70–73
   cost considerations 58
   disposition to trust 68–70, 74
   employee participation and autonomy 65
   feedback systems 66–7
   future research 74–5
   identification-based trust 73
   knowledge-based trust 72
   opportunism and self-interest 60
   organizational climate 57–8, 72–3
   performance appraisal system 66
   self-determination theory 62–4
   social dilemma problem, handling 57–8, 60–61, 68, 73
   sucker-effect 58
   voluntary cooperation 58, 61–2, 66, 70
   see also monitoring
control and trust and role of intrinsic motivation, hierarchical control
   and autonomy 64–6
   and competence 66–7
   and economic theory of the firm 240–41, 248–53
   effects of 57–61, 73–5
   supervisor's trust, effects of 67–70, 73
Conway, N. 16, 18–21
Cook, J. 268, 270
Cook, K. 88, 204–5, 210–15
cooperation effects 70–73, 87–8, 92–3, 134–5, 139, 231–2
Coopey, J. 292–3

Costa, A. 58, 63, 192
Costa, P. 15, 68
Crawshaw, J. 18
Creed, W. 262
Cronin, M. 101
Crooker, K. 16
Croson, R. 42
Cullen, J. 72
cultural factors
   inter-cultural trust *see* inter-cultural trust and trust-building
   negotiation processes 40, 50
Cummings, A. 67
Cummings, L. 19, 147, 212, 230–31, 236
Currall, S. 84, 130–32, 158, 261, 265, 279, 292

Dacin, M. 212
Das, T. 84, 128, 141, 192–3, 276
Dasgupta, P. 214, 278, 291
Davis, J. 9, 12–13, 17, 66, 212, 214, 216
Davis, T. 12
Dawes, R. 57–8, 71
De Charms, R. 63
De Cremer, D. 58, 70–71
De La Torre, J. 134, 141
Deakin, S. 296
Deci, E. 62–4, 70
DeConinck, J. 21
Deephouse, D. 212
Degoey, P. 57
Delery, J. 17
Delhey, J. 285
Den Hartog, D. 11, 13, 18
DeNisi, A. 66–7
Deseran, F. 265
Desmet, P. 48
deterrence-based trust 33–4
Deutsch, M. 34, 178, 288
Deutsch-Salamon, S. 19
Dibben, M. 287
Dickson, M. 253
Dietz, G. 10–11, 13, 49, 137, 179, 191–2, 198–200, 227, 233, 257, 265, 286
DiMaggio, P. 210, 212
Dionisi, A. 18
Dirks, Kurt T. 2, 10, 12, 44, 48, 50, 191–2, 200, 208, 227–60, 286

310   *Handbook of advances in trust research*

distrust, effects of
  and contracts 97–100
  and control 60–61, 74
  and innovation 112, 115, 119–20
  negotiation processes 30–31, 35
Dobbins, G. 17
Dodgson, M. 83, 262
Doney, P. 262, 297
Doz, Y. 98
Driver, J. 233
Druckman, D. 38
Dukerich, J. 218
Dwyer, P. 184, 189
Dyer, J. 84, 97, 126, 129, 228, 231–2, 246–7

Earley, P. 17
Easley, C. 214
Eberl, P. 68–9
Eccles, R. 75, 128–9, 133, 231, 236, 256
economic theory of the firm 227–60
  attribution problems and formal structures 231–3, 254
  breach of trust and vulnerability concerns 233
  co-specialization 245, 250, 252–3
  conflict resolution 233, 249
  cooperation and substitution 231–2
  crowding out concerns 254
  excuse doctrine and hybrids 246
  formal structural factors 230–36, 254
  future research 255–6
  governance structures 236–41, 246
  hierarchies' ability to build and maintain trust 248–53
  hybrids' ability to build and maintain trust 244–8
  inter-organizational trust 233
  literature review 229–35
  markets' ability to build and maintain trust 241–4
  monitoring systems 233, 236, 243, 246–7, 249, 251
  opportunism and exchange hazards 231–3, 235–6, 241–3, 248–9, 254
  reputation and trustworthiness 230, 245–6, 250–51
  social structure 230
  transaction frequency and opportunism 235–6
  trust definition 229–30
  trust and formal governance, complementary nature of 232
  trust, need for 235–6
  uncertainty increase and opportunism 235
economic theory of the firm, trust building
  direct interaction 230, 242, 245, 250
  embeddedness 242, 245–6, 250–53
  and expectation 242, 245, 252
  hierarchies 249–51
  hybrids 244–6
  macro and micro levels 230–33
  management role 254–5
  and markets 241–3
  and structural supports 242–3, 246
economic theory of the firm, trust repair 233–4, 240–41
  attributional process 243, 247, 252
  hierarchies 251–3
  hybrids 246–8
  incentive changes 234, 236, 242–3, 253
  social equilibrium process 233–4, 243, 247–8, 252–3
  structural changes 234–5
  structural repair process 243–4, 248, 253
Edelman, M. 189–90
Edmondson, A. 216
Ehnert, I. 286–8, 290–91, 293–5, 297–8, 300
Eisenberger, R. 22
Eisenhardt, K. 58, 60
Elster, J. 291
embeddedness, and trust building 242, 245–6, 250–53
Emerson, R. 211, 214
Emirbayer, M. 274–5, 290–91, 293
employees
  human resource management 12–16, 19–20, 22
  losses, global financial crisis effects 184–5, 194–5
  lower-level, and contract secrecy 89–90
  participation and autonomy 65

Enosh, G. 18
Epstein, J. 265
Ertug, G. 205

Faems, D. 90, 132
Falk, A. 59, 61, 69
Fang, E. 279
Farrell, J. 47
Farris, G. 276
feedback systems 37, 66–7
Fehr, E. 58, 70, 73
Feld, L. 65
Feldman, M. 271, 273
Ferrin, D. 2, 10, 12, 35–6, 47, 71–2, 82–3, 88, 146, 153, 200, 227, 230–31, 233, 254, 261
financial crisis *see* global financial crisis effects
Fine, G. 276
Fischbacher, U. 58, 73
Flaste, R. 62
Folger, R. 17, 137
Foss, N. 93, 101
Foucault, M. 216
Fox, A. 19, 262
Francis, J. 151, 161–2
Frantz, C. 45–6
Frederiksen, M. 298
Freeman, R. 209–10
Frey, B. 58, 61, 65–6, 232, 254
Fried, J. 184
Friedland, R. 270
Frost, J. 58, 71
Fukuyama, F. 1, 69, 205
Fulmer, I. 37, 42
Furlotti, M. 93
future research
  contracts and trust 101
  control and trust and role of intrinsic motivation 74–5
  economic theory of the firm 255–6
  human resource management (HRM) and trust 22
  institutionalization and collective and long-term trust orientations 277, 279–80
  inter-cultural trust and trust-building 169–70
  inter-organizational trust 128, 131, 137, 140–41

negotiation processes, role of trust in 45, 48–51
process views of trusting and crises 293, 297–300
public trust in institution of business 213–16, 219

Gachter, S. 73
Gagne, M. 62
Gambetta, D. 73, 129, 137–9, 212–13, 265–6, 278, 288, 291, 294
Ganesan, S. 130, 133
Garfinkel, H. 298
Gargiulo, M. 205
Gauntlett, D. 213
Gelfand, M. 146, 148
George, E. 62
Ghoshal, S. 61, 69, 71, 84, 132, 192, 241, 254
Gibb, J. 293
Gibson, K. 47
Giddens, A. 10–11, 179–80, 209, 213, 216–18, 262–3, 265, 268, 270, 288–9, 293–8
Gill, H. 15
Gillespie, Nicole 10, 13, 49, 137, 146, 153, 177–203, 227, 233, 257, 265, 286, 297
Gilsing, V. 118
Glaeser, E. 217, 285
global financial crisis effects 177–203
  ability-based trust 178–9, 181–4, 186–9
  benevolence-based trust 178–9, 184–90
  confidence-inducing system mechanisms 180–81, 193
  delayed response to crisis 183
  deregulation and self-regulation 187–9
  disclosure failures and marketing techniques 186
  financial institutions 181–6
  government and regulatory bodies 187–90
  integrity-based trust 178–9, 185–7
  loss of trust, understanding 181–90
  management board failures and accountability 183–4

312 *Handbook of advances in trust research*

organizational level trust repair (OTR) 192, 199–200
ratings agencies 186–7
risk management and capital allocation 181–3
securitization 185, 187–90, 195
shareholder and employee losses 184–5, 194–5
systems level trust, understanding 177–81
traders as aggressive risk-takers 183
trust definition 177–8
trustworthiness evaluation 178–9, 180, 191–2
see also process views of trusting and crises; public trust in institution of business
global financial crisis effects, trust, repairing and building 191–200
competence-based trust 195–6
internal monitoring and compliance 181, 190, 193, 195–6
organizational trust, internal 199
post-crisis opportunities for financial institutions 198–9
post-crisis systemic problems, unresolved 196–8
regulation and control 192–6, 199
system trust and enforced sanctions 194–5
systemic cycles of reforms, need for 198–9
'too big to fail', lack of understanding of 196–8
globalization effects, inter-cultural trust 158–9
Goffman, E. 233–4, 266
Good, D. 242, 288, 300
Goodstein, J. 214
goodwill-based trust 83–4, 97
Gordon, C. 216
Gould-Williams, J. 17
Gouldner, A. 70
Govier, T. 15, 69
Graebner, M. 42
Graham, J. 148, 151, 154–5
Granovetter, M. 117, 128, 134, 212, 231, 234, 263, 270
Gray, B. 88, 234
Greenspan, A. 188

Greenwald, A. 217
Gregersen, H. 19
Grossman, S. 228
Grover, S. 16
Grund, C. 59
Gubler, Timothy 227–60
Guest, D. 16, 18, 20–21
Gulati, R. 72, 82, 84, 101, 126, 134, 227–8, 230–32, 236, 242, 245, 262, 279, 293
Gunia, B. 35, 40
Gurley, K. 194
Gurtman, M. 211

Haas, D. 265
Hackman, J. 64
Hall, P. 263, 268
Hamilton, L. 189
Han, Y. 39
Hanke, R. 41–2
Hansen, M. 12–13, 62, 127, 136, 227, 231
Harbring, C. 59
Hardin, G. 57
Hardin, R. 60–61, 98–9, 205, 276, 279, 288, 291–4
Hardy, C. 265, 272
Harkins, S. 71
Harrington, S. 18, 21–2
Harris, Jared D. 126–7, 131, 138, 204–23, 262
Harrison, J. 99, 212
Hart, O. 228
Hashimoto, K. 148–9, 154
Haslam, S. 73
Hattie, J. 67
Hay, C. 274
Hays, S. 216
Heide, J. 130, 132–3
Heider, F. 233
Hennart, J. 127
Henslin, J. 298
Hernes, T. 285, 287, 300
hierarchical relationships, and economic theory of the firm 240–41, 248–53
see also control and trust and role of intrinsic motivation, hierarchical control
Higgins, R. 67

Hill, C. 135, 231
Hirsch, P. 263
Hirschman, A. 111
Hoetker, G. 139
Hofstede, G. 147
Hollis, M. 292
Holyfield, L. 276
Homans, G. 272
Hope-Hailey, V. 11, 19
Hosmer, L. 298
House, R. 279
Howson, A. 291, 298
Huber, G. 98
Huemer, L. 98
human resource management (HRM) and trust 9–29
  contract breach and performance 19
  definition 10–12
  dilemma game studies 16
  employees' attitudes to work 12–16, 19–20, 22
  employment cycle 12, 18, 21
  fairness perceptions 20
  future research 22
  high involvement work systems (HIWS) 17
  importance of 12–14, 16–19
  individual disposition to trust 15–17, 68
  information sharing and employee participation 17
  moral and ethical principles, links to 13–14
  organizational exit effects 18, 21
  organizational and interpersonal trust, relationship between 11, 13–16, 21–2
  performance appraisal, effects of 17
  personality factors 15–16
  policies and implementation 14–17, 19–22
  psychological contract 18–19
  risk factors 14, 21
  trust and justice researchers, divisions between 13–14
  trust repair 13, 16, 19
  untrustworthiness levels, dealing with 16, 21
Hurley, Robert 177–203, 216
Huselid, M. 17

Husted, B. 137
Hutton, W. 185

identity-based trust 34–5, 38, 73, 293–5, 298
Iles, P. 16
incentives, and economic theory of the firm 234, 236, 240, 242–3, 246, 253
information *see* knowledge
Inkpen, A. 2, 84, 88, 92, 130–32, 138–9, 158, 209–10, 261, 279, 288–9, 291–2
Innocenti, L. 10
innovation and trust 106–21
  and altruism 112–13, 119
  and collaboration 108–11
  conflict resolution, and third parties 115–16
  dependence levels 111
  development processes 119–20
  distrust, effects of 112, 115, 119–20
  exclusiveness demand 112
  flexibility, need for 119
  hostage use 107, 111, 116
  knowledge transfer 112–14, 116, 118
  networks 117–18
  opportunity and incentive control, distinction between 107
  radical and incremental innovation, distinction between 106–107
  relational governance 111–13
  reputation mechanism, importance of 112, 115–16
  risk factors 106–7, 118
  third party involvement 113–17
  and transaction cost economics 108, 111, 114
  trust building, third party as intermediary 115–17
  trust, increased need for 112–13
institutional role 2, 209–10, 213–14, 216, 218
  cultural contexts 88–9
  institution of business, public trust in *see* public trust in institution of business
  process views of trusting and crises 288–9, 291, 295–6
  trustworthiness, inter-organizational 138–9

institutionalization and collective
    and long-term trust orientations
    261–84
  agency, significance of 274–7, 279
  cognitive vs normative
    institutionalized trust 269–70,
    273–5
  creative use of 263–4
  decision styles 273–4, 279
  formal vs informal institutionalized
    trust 270
  future research 277, 279–80
  generational patterns of trust 277
  institution to interaction process
    268–72
  institutional development over time
    272–7
  institutional production, creating
    roles and routines of trust
    267–8
  institutional reproduction 272–5
  institutional structure and trust
    templates 268–71
  inter-organizational trust 277, 279
  interaction impact 265–7, 270–72,
    276
  payment modalities as symbolic acts
    266–7
  preconditions 263–4
  reciprocity 267–8
  reproduction 264–5, 274
  signalling methods 266–8
  socialization, and institutional
    transmission and translation
    275–7
  symbolic trust 265–7, 270–72, 276
  trust cycle 262–5
  trust repair 272–5
integrity-based trust 37, 46, 92–3, 96,
    98, 137, 178–9, 185–7
inter-cultural trust and trust-building
    146–73
  cultural stereotypes 155
  culture-specific/indigenous stage 153
  distinction-attraction puzzle and
    out-group favoritism 155, 161,
    170
  etic and emic forces, co-existence of
    152–5
  future research 169–70

  globalization effects 158–9
  inter-cultural interaction, cultural
    distance as imperative premise
    149–52
  inter-cultural interaction, cultural
    interface and adaptive learning
    151–2, 154–7, 159–62, 164–8
  national context, limiting effect of
    153, 170
  organizational level and inter-firm
    trust 157–62, 166, 170
  trust asymmetry and cultural
    distance 153–6, 159–60
  trust asymmetry and trust
    integration 156–7, 159–64
  trust-as-attitude/trust-as-choice
    distinction 161
  typologies, trust-building contexts
    162–5
  typologies, trust-building strategies
    164–8
  Yin–Yang balance 150, 153, 161, 170
inter-cultural trust and trust-building,
    inter-cultural and intra-cultural
    distinction 148–52, 158, 160–61
  cross-cultural code-switching
    process 151
  empirical study problems 149
  in-group and out-group favoritism
    150–51, 154–5, 158
  similarity–attraction paradigm
    150–51, 161, 170
  and social identity theory 150–51,
    161
inter-organizational trust 125–45
  behavioral traditions 129–32
  benevolence-based trust 137
  calculus-based trust 135
  company comparisons 125–6
  competence-based trust 136
  conflict resolution 97
  contracts 98–9
  control mechanisms, value of 131
  cooperation effects 134–5, 139
  decision rights 130
  definition 128–32
  economic theory of the firm 233
  future research 128, 131, 137, 140–41
  institutionalization and trust
    orientations 277, 279

integrity-based trust 137
inter-personal trust, difference from 128, 131, 137
knowledge-based trust 135–6
legal regulation effects 139
management role 129, 133
monitoring controls 128, 132, 138–9
opportunistic behavior and risk 133
origins of 133–40
prior experiences, learning from 133–5
psychological and behavioral traditions 128–32, 134
relational trust 133–6
simple vs contingent effects 131
single vs multiple respondents 131–2
temporal dynamics 133–7
transaction costs, minimizing 128, 131, 133, 139
trust types 132, 135–7
trustworthiness and cooperation, credible signals of 137–40
Irmer, C. 38
Isaksen, A. 118
Isen, I. 37

Jacobe, D. 104
Janowicz, M. 279
Janowicz-Panjaitan, M. 261
Janssens, M. 151–2, 156, 162
Jap, S. 84, 130
Jehn, K. 150
Jepperson, R. 289
John, G. 130, 133
Johnson, J. 146, 153–4, 156
Jones, C. 246
Jones, K. 288
Jones, S. 63
Jost, J. 214

Kahn, R. 179
Kaina, V. 212–13
Kanungo, R. 64–5
Katsikeas, C. 158
Katuščásk, P. 88
Katz, D. 179
Kee, H. 15, 68
Keevil, Adrian A. C. 204–23
Kelley, H. 32
Kelsey, B. 291, 298

Kennedy, A. 151–2, 156, 158
Khodyakov, D. 285, 290–91, 298
Kim, D. 88
Kim, J.-Y. 209
Kim, P. 46, 51, 137, 191, 208, 212, 233, 286
Klein, B. 97, 228, 230–31, 235, 249
Klein Woolthuis, R. 83–4, 107, 298
Klijn, E. 84, 88, 98
Kluger, A. 66–7
Knights, D. 84, 96
knowledge
  adaptive learning in acculturation pattern 151–2, 154–7, 159–62, 164–8
  information exchange 17, 30, 32, 38, 40, 42, 114, 291
  innovation and knowledge transfer 112–14, 116, 118
  knowledge-based trust 34–5, 38, 40, 72, 135–6
  trusting as learning 291–3, 298
Knox, R. 15, 68
Kollock, P. 57, 71
Komorita, S. 69
Konovsky, M. 12, 17
Korsgaard, M. 17
Kosfeld, M. 59, 61, 69
Kramer, R. 12–13, 15, 45, 50, 57–8, 71, 136, 138, 200, 204–5, 262, 286, 291, 293–4
Krishnan, R. 126, 129, 131
Kroeger, Frens 261–84, 288, 298
Kruglanski, A. 61
Kuhlmann, T. 146, 149, 151, 154–5, 298
Kumar, R. 98–9
Kurtzberg, T. 39
Kuwabara, K. 151
Kvaløy, O. 82–3

Lambe, J. 137
Lanchester, J. 183
Landa, M. 12
Lane, C. 148, 204, 279, 296
Larson, A. 134
Latham, G. 63
Latusek, D. 95
Lawler, E. 64, 137
Lawrence, T. 274

Lazzarini, S. 232
Leana, C. 65
Leary, M. 64
Lee, K. 146
Legge, K. 11
Lenox, M. 214
Leung, K. 146, 148
Leventhal, G. 20
Levi, M. 209
Levine, T. 37
Levitt, A. 184, 194, 289
Lewicki, Roy J. 2, 13, 29–54, 72–4, 84, 98–9, 119, 129, 134–6, 218, 227, 233, 285–6, 290–92, 294
Lewis, J. 279
Lewis, K. 98
Lewis, M. 150, 184
Li, J. 82, 84, 94, 126, 131
Li, Peter Ping 146–73
Li, Y. 158
Lind, E. 20, 65
Lindenberg, S. 74, 119
Lindkvist, L. 88
Litwin, G. 199
Liu, M. 40
Locke, E. 63
London, M. 67
long-term trust *see* institutionalization and collective and long-term trust orientations
Lorenz, E. 227, 230, 232
Louis, M. 276
Luckmann, T. 262–3, 267–8, 270–71, 276
Luhmann, N. 14, 179–80, 190, 194, 198, 266–7, 272, 285–6, 288–9, 291–2, 294
Lumineau, F. 97
Lyon, F. 297

McAllister, D. 13, 60, 86, 119, 212, 288
Macaulay, S. 84, 233, 245–6, 254
McCornack, S. 37
McCrae, R. 15, 68
McDonald, L. 183–4, 186
McEvily, B. 2, 213, 217
McGregor, D. 69
McKnight, D. 2, 88, 212, 286, 288
McMackin, J. 227–8, 231–2, 236
McManus, S. 216

MacNeil, I. 83, 130, 140, 242
Madhok, A. 140
Maguire, S. 294, 298
Mair, J. 213
Malecki, E. 118
Malekzadeh, A. 166
Malhotra, D. 35, 40, 84, 97, 136, 214–15, 227, 231–2, 254
Malieva, E. 296
management role 69, 96, 129, 133, 183–4, 254–5
Mannheim, K. 216
March, J. 106
Marti, I. 213
Masgoret, A. 151
Mather, K. 19
Mayer, K. 84, 89–90, 93, 96, 98–9, 245
Mayer, R. 2, 9, 11–13, 15, 17, 32, 35, 60, 65–6, 71, 83, 92, 137, 178, 199, 206, 208, 211–12, 216, 233, 286, 290
Mellewigt, T. 139
Messick, D. 71
Meyer, J. 62, 212, 214, 218, 289
Meyerson, D. 213, 265, 292–3
Miles, R. 262
Milgrom, P. 181
Millar, M. 45
Miller, G. 57
Mische, A. 274–5, 290–91, 293
Mishra, A. 18, 21, 65
Mishra, K. 18, 60
Missner, M. 41
Mizrachi, N. 266, 273, 296
Moag, J. 66
Möllering, Guido 59, 88, 95, 216, 257, 263, 265–6, 279, 285–305
monitoring controls
  economic theory of the firm 233, 236, 243, 246–7, 249, 251
  and global financial crisis 181, 190, 193, 195–6
  inter-organizational trust 128, 132, 138–9
  negotiation processes 30–31, 34, 40–41, 44, 48–9
  public trust in institution of business 206, 213
  see also control and trust and role of intrinsic motivation

Monlinsky, A. 151
Moore, J. 228
Moran, P. 61, 69, 84, 132, 192, 241, 254
Morrison, E. 19
motivation, intrinsic *see* control and trust and role of intrinsic motivation
Mueller, J. 14
Münscher, R. 298
Murnighan, J. 35, 84, 227, 231–2, 254

Nadler, D. 192, 196, 199
Nahapiet, J. 71
Nahavandi, A. 166
Nakayachi, K. 48, 192, 233, 247
Naquin, C. 39
negotiation processes, role of trust in 29–54
  ability-based trust 35–6, 46
  BATNAs (best alternatives to negotiated agreements) 50
  benevolence-based trust 36–7, 46
  broken trust 41–4, 48, 50
  calculus-based trust (CBT) 34–5, 38
  cues and signals, interpretation of 30
  cultural effects 40, 50
  current research 37–41
  deceptive tactics, net effects of 42–3
  definitions 31–5
  deterrence-based trust 33–4
  dilemma of honesty 30, 32–3, 41–3
  distributive negotiation process, anticipation of 50
  distrust, effects of 30–31, 35
  effective negotiation 29–31
  feedback, importance of 37
  future research 45, 48–51
  identification-based trust (IBT) 34–5, 38
  information exchange 30, 32, 38, 40, 42
  integrity-based trust 37, 46
  interdependence role 30, 32
  knowledge-based trust (KBT) 34–5, 38, 40, 72
  measurement and calibration over time 50–51
  monitoring controls 30–31, 34, 40–41, 44, 48–9

  negotiating skills 36
  negotiation medium, effects of 39
  question and answer (Q&A) tactics 40
  reciprocity calculation 39
  substantiation and offers (S&O) tactics 40
  transaction costs, minimizing 30
  trust as dependent and independent variable 38–40
  Trust Game 39
  trustor/trustee perspective differences 40–41
  trustworthiness 30, 35–7, 42, 46
  turning point in negotiation direction 38–9
  types of trust, distinguishing between 33–5
  understanding others' trust 40
  untrustworthy behaviour, effects of 39, 44
negotiation processes, role of trust in, trust repair 39–40, 43–9, 50–51
  economic damage, restoring 44
  hostage posting 48
  reciprocity aspect 43
  reparative compensation 44, 47–8
  structural solutions 44, 48–9
  verbal accounts 44–7
  violation categorization 41, 43–4
Netzer, R. 148, 154–7, 160
Newell, S. 149, 152, 156–7, 163, 298
Newton, K. 285
Nickerson, Jackson 126, 227–60
Nisbett, R. 216
Nishii, L. 20
Noorderhaven, N. 261, 279
Noordewier, T. 133
Nooteboom, Bart 84, 106–21, 227, 257, 285
North, D. 232
Nosek, B. 217

Oberholzer-Gee, F. 232, 254
O'Brien, J. 187
O'Connor, K. 42
Oetzel, J. 150
Oinas, P. 118
Oldham, G. 67
Olekalns, M. 38

Olsen, C. 134
Olsen, T. 82–3
opportunism
   and exchange hazards 231–3, 235–6, 241–3, 248–9, 254
   and incentive control, distinction between 107
   and risk 133
   and self-interest 60, 83, 86, 94, 98
Orbell, J. 58
organizations
   control and trust and role of intrinsic motivation 57–8, 72–3
   governance structures 236–41, 246
   hierarchical relationships *see* hierarchical relationships
   human resource management *see* human resource management (HRM) and trust
   inter-cultural trust and trust-building 157–62, 166, 170
   inter-organizational trust *see* inter-organizational trust
   process views of trusting and crises 288–9, 291, 295–6
   trust repair and global financial crisis 192, 199–200
Osadchiy, S. 94
Osterloh, M. 58, 66
O'Sullivan, M. 300
Oxley, J. 83

Pagden, A. 106
Parker, S. and G. 210
Parkhe, A. 84, 127, 130, 135
Parks, C. 16, 69
Parsons, T. 273
Paulson, G. 39
Paulson, H. 184, 186
Paxton, P. 290
Pearce, J. 15, 17, 19, 62
Pearson, C. 65
Pentland, B. 271, 273
Perrone, V. 20, 289
personality *see* behaviour
Pettijohn, C. 66
Petty, R. 71
Pfarrer, M. 208
Phelps, C. 19

Pierce, L. 249
Pillai, R. 12
Pillutla, M. 39
Pirson, M. 136, 214–15
Pisano, G. 248
Podsakoff, P. 12
Polin, Beth 29–54
Polyhart, R. 290, 298
Poppo, Laura 72, 82, 84, 125–45, 232, 236, 245, 275
Pornpitakpan, C. 146, 154
Powell, W. 158, 210, 212
Prichard, J. 18
process views of trusting and crises 285–305
   as-if trust 292–3
   crisis issues 299–300
   future research 293, 297–300
   identity-based trust 293–5, 298
   information as preliminary state of trust 291
   mental and social processes of trusting 287–9
   methodological implications 297–9
   organizational and institutional trust 288–9, 291, 295–6
   relationship stage, significance of 286–7
   social effects of trust 288–9, 293–7
   structuration theory 295–8
   trust histories, sharing of 292, 296
   trust repair 286
   trust testing 292–3
   trust to trusting shift 287
   trusting attitude 286
   trusting as constituting 295–6, 298
   trusting as continuing 290, 297–8
   trusting as learning 291–3, 298
   trusting as processing 290–91, 298
   trustworthiness perceptions 291, 298
   see also global financial crisis effects
public trust in institution of business 204–23
   business as systems of social relations 216
   dispositional and generalized trust, distinction between 211

future research 213–16, 219
generalized trust 211–14
Implicit Association Test (IAT) 217
individual experiences, influence of 214
institutions, concept of 209–10, 213–14, 216, 218
monitoring controls 206, 213
relational trust 211–13
risk assessment 211
self-report measurement, problems with 216–17
stakeholder perspective 214–15, 218
study design amd measurement 215–17
trust definition 205–6
Trust Game and behavioral trust 217
trust repair 206–8
trust types 210–14
trustworthiness assessment 212, 214
see also global financial crisis effects
Pugh, D. 12
Puranam, P. 101
Putnam, R. 205, 285

Rabin, M. 47
Ramaswami, S. 61
Rao, A. 148–9, 154
Ravasi, D. 265
Ravlin, E. 151, 155–7, 160–62
Rayner, C. 18, 22
Reb, J. 234
Redfield, R. 151
Reed, K. 13, 15–17
Reed, M. 275
regulation effects 89–91, 139, 192–6, 199
relational trust 133–6, 211–13, 286–7
Ren, H. 88, 234
reputation, importance of 112, 115–16, 230, 245–6, 250–51
Reuer, J. 139
Rhodes, S. 65
Rico, R. 101
Rindova, V. 265
Ring, P. 101, 127, 130, 134, 136, 140, 285, 288, 292

risk factors 86–7, 89, 94–5, 106–7, 118, 181–3, 211, 235
Robbins, T. 71
Roberts, J. 181
Robinson, P. 183–4, 186
Robinson, R. 41
Robinson, S. 11–12, 18–19, 212, 227, 230, 233, 298
Rodell, J. 14, 16, 20, 206
Rodrigues, S. 199
Rodriguez, C. 151, 153
Rose, N. 293
Rose-Ackerman, S. 296
Roth, A. 48
Roth, N. 61, 84, 98, 137–9, 218, 234, 270
Rotter, J. 15, 68–70, 211, 279, 288, 293
Rousseau, D. 2, 10–11, 18, 32, 34, 127–29, 178, 206, 208, 229, 279
Rowan, B. 212
Rupp, D. 22
Ryan, R. 62–4, 70

Sabel, C. 285, 291
Sako, M. 2
Sandberg, J. 100
Saunders, M. 18, 50, 295, 297
Scharpf, F. 273
Schein, E. 213, 270
Schilke, O. 204–5, 210–11, 215
Schminke, M. 20
Schnabel, K. 217
Schoorman, F. 13, 65, 178, 205, 208, 212–13, 279, 291
Schütz, A. 273, 275
Schweer, M. 266, 278
Schweitzer, M. 39, 42
Scott, W. 157, 263, 269–70, 273
Searle, Rosalind H. 9–28, 68, 261
Seidl, D. 180
Selznick, P. 273
Serva, M. 83–4, 288, 293
Sewell, W. 270
Shah, P. 18
Shane, S. 158
Shapiro, D. 33–4, 42–3, 178–81, 184, 193, 200
Shapiro, S. 14, 20, 117, 234
Shell, R. 36

Sheng, S. 133
Simmel, G. 117, 129
Simon, H. 57–8, 273
Singelmann, P. 265
Singh, H. 84, 228, 231–2, 246–7
Sitkin, S. 48, 60–62, 65–7, 84, 98, 137–9, 192, 218, 234, 270, 290
Six, Frédérique 2, 57–81, 119, 265–6, 279
Skinner, D. 10–12, 14, 16, 18
Slemrod, J. 88
Sliwka, D. 61
Slovic, P. 192
Smircich, L. 162
Smith, B. 71
Smith, P. 146
Smith, T. 207
Smith, W. 150
Smither, J. 67
social dilemma problem, handling 57–8, 60–61, 68, 73
social identity theory 150–51, 161
social structure 230, 233–4, 243, 247–8, 252–3
Sorge, A. 62, 266, 279
Sorkin, A. 184, 186
Spector, P. 11
Spender, J. 99
Spreitzer, G. 18, 21, 63, 65
Srinivasan, R. 127, 139
Stache, F. 296
Stack, L. 15, 70
Steers, R. 65
Steinmo, S. 270
Stevenson, M. 34
Stickel, D. 205, 290
Stiglitz, J. 181, 185
Stinchcombe, A. 264
Stoker, L. 209
Stolle, D. 69
Streeck, W. 274
Strickland, L. 61, 69
Strudler, A. 37
Stubbart, C. 162
Suchman, M. 62, 212
Suddaby, R. 274
Sullivan, J. 146, 148, 153–4
Sutter, M. 148, 154–5, 157, 160
Swan, J. 298
Swidler, A. 266, 273

Sydow, J. 115, 262, 279, 288–9, 295, 298
symbolic trust 265–7, 270–72, 276
system trust, global financial crisis effects 177–81, 194–5
Sytch, M. 134, 262, 279
Sztompka, P. 205, 292, 296
Szulanski, G. 131

Tajfel, H. 150, 214
Takahashi, C. 148, 154–5
Tallman, S. 140
Tan, H. and C. 11
Tannenbaum, A. 64–5
Taras, V. 146, 148
Targama, A. 100
Taylor, R. 263, 268
Tenbrunsel, A. 42
Teng, B. 84, 128, 141, 192–3, 276
Tett, G. 183
Thelen, K. 270, 274
Thomas, D. 151, 155–7, 160–62
Thomas, R. 45
Thompson, P. 21, 61
Tillmar, M. 88
Timperley, H. 67
Ting-Toomey, S. 150
Tinsley, C. 43
Titmuss, R. 232, 254
Tjosvold, D. 146, 148
Tolbert, P. 268, 271, 273
Tomlinson, E. 44–6, 199, 233
Torgler, B. 58
Tortoriello, M. 2
transaction costs 108, 111, 114
  minimizing 30, 128, 131, 133, 139
Tripp, T. 12, 227, 233
trust
  broken 41–4, 48, 50
  cycle 262–5
  definitions 1–2, 83, 177–8, 205–6, 229–30
  game 16, 39, 217
trust building
  cultural factors *see* inter-cultural trust and trust-building
  and economic theory of the firm *see* economic theory of the firm, trust building

financial crisis *see* global financial crisis effects, trust, repairing and building
third party as intermediary 115–17
trust repair
  and confidence measure 206–8
  economic theory of the firm *see* economic theory of the firm, trust repair
  financial crisis *see* global financial crisis effects, trust, repairing and building
  human resource management (HRM) 13, 16, 19, 21
  institutionalization and trust orientations 272–5
  negotiation processes *see* negotiation processes, role of trust in, trust repair
  process views of trusting and crises 286
trustworthiness
  assessment, and public trust in institution of business 212, 214
  and cooperation, credible signals of 137–40
  evidence, and contracts 95–6
  global financial crisis effects 178–80, 191–2
  negotiation processes 30, 35–7, 42, 46
  perceptions, process views of trusting and crises 291, 298
  and reputation 230, 245–6, 250–51
  untrustworthy behaviour 16, 21, 39, 44
Tsoukas, H. 295
Tsui, A. 10, 62
Tsui-Auch, L. 288
Tung, R. 170
Turbeville, W. 183
Turner, J. 214
Tushman, M. 192, 196, 199
Tyler, T. 12, 20, 57–8, 62, 65, 70, 204, 212
Tzafrir, S. 10, 12, 16, 18–19

USA
  Congress oversight role 189
  Glass-Steagall Act 183, 188

global financial crisis effects *see under* global financial crisis effects
Group of Thirty Financial Reform report 187
Sarbanes-Oxley Act 188, 196, 218
Uslaner, E. 285, 298
Uzzi, B. 136, 212, 228, 230–32, 234, 236, 245, 254

Van de Bunt, G. 291, 298
Van de Ven, A. 101, 130, 134, 136, 140, 285
Van de Walle, S. 74
Van Knippenberg, D. 70
Van Vugt, M. 57–8, 71
Vandenberg, R. 17, 290, 298
Venkatraman, N. 84, 266
Victor, B. 72
Vlaar, Paul W.L. 82–105
voluntary cooperation 58, 61–2, 66, 70

Walgenbach, P. 290
Wang, C. 40
Ward, C. 150–52, 156, 158, 161
Warhurst, C. 61
Warren, M. 209
Wasti, S. 153
Watabe, M. 48, 192, 233, 247
Wathne, K. 132
Watson, W. 152, 156
Webb, E. 299
Weber, J. 265
Weber, L. 84, 93
Weber, M. 61–2
Weibel, Antoinette 16, 57–82, 192
Weick, K. 99–100, 267–8, 300
Weigert, A. 279
Weingart, L. 101
Weingast, B. 262
Weisbach, M. 184
Weiss, H. 22
Weitz, B. 133
Whinston, M. 231
White, R. 63
Whitener, E. 10–11, 16, 20–22, 60
Whitley, R. 11
Whitney, J. 12
Wicks, Andrew C. 204–23, 291
Wilkinson, F. 257, 296

Williamson, O. 60, 83, 86, 98, 114, 127–8, 137, 139, 227–8, 230–31, 235, 241–2, 244, 246, 248–9, 251, 253, 256–7
Wilson, D. 151, 153
Wilson, T. 216
Wincott, D. 274
Windeler, A. 295
Witt, U. 101
Wright, A. 286–8, 290–91, 293–5, 297–8, 300
Wright, P. 20
Wrightsman, L. 293

Yakovleva, M. 16, 69
Yamagishi, T. 151, 154–5, 157, 160
Yoon, J. 137
Yuki, M. 153, 158

Zaheer, Akbar 1–6, 10, 83–4, 126–9, 131, 137–8, 146, 153, 158, 205, 212, 215–16, 227–8, 230–31, 236, 243, 261–2, 266, 279, 289
Zaheer, S. 146, 153
Zajac, E. 134
Zand, D. 84, 119, 211, 285, 288, 292–3
Zenger, T. 82, 84, 130–31, 133–4, 139, 232, 236, 245
Zhang, Z. 39
Zhao, H. 19
Zhou, K. 86, 138
Zingales, L. 183–4, 187, 194–5
Zolin, R. 152, 156, 157, 163
Zollo, M. 134
Zucker, L. 84, 138, 179–80, 210, 234, 257, 262–3, 270, 276, 279, 286, 288–9, 291, 296, 298